I0879558

# *The Woman I Am*

RELIGION AND AMERICAN CULTURE

*Series Editors*
John M. Giggie
Charles A. Israel

*Editorial Advisory Board*
Catherine A. Brekus
Paul Harvey
Sylvester A. Johnson
Joel W. Martin
Ronald L. Numbers
Beth Schweiger
Grant Wacker
Judith Weisenfeld

# The Woman I Am

## Southern Baptist Women's Writings, 1906–2006

Melody Maxwell

THE UNIVERSITY OF ALABAMA PRESS
*Tuscaloosa*

Copyright © 2014
The University of Alabama Press
Tuscaloosa, Alabama 35487-0380
All rights reserved
Manufactured in the United States of America

Typeface: Caslon

Cover photographs: Above, left to right, Our Mission Fields (July/August/September 1906), Royal Service (October 1914), Royal Service (March 1948), Royal Service (July 1948), Missions Mosaic (October 1995); below,Royal Service editorial staff, 1915. All photos used by permission of WMU Library and Archives, Woman's Missionary Union®, auxiliary to Southern Baptist Convention.

Cover design: Gary Gore

∞

The paper on which this book is printed meets the minimum requirements of American National Standard for Information Sciences—Permanence of Paper for Printed Library Materials, ANSI Z39.48-1984.

Library of Congress Cataloging-in-Publication Data

Maxwell, Melody, 1980–
The woman I am : southern Baptist women's writings, 1906–2006 / Melody Maxwell.
pages cm.
— (Religion and American culture)
Includes bibliographical references and index.
ISBN 978-0-8173-1832-1 (trade cloth : alk. paper) — ISBN 978-0-8173-8763-1 (e book) 1. Baptist women—United States—History—20th century. 2. Christian literature—Authorship. 3. Southern Baptist Convention—History. I. Title.
BX6462.3.M39 2014
286'.132082—dc23

2013049870

# Contents

# Acknowledgments

I am indebted to a large number of people for their assistance and support with this project. Most of all, I thank Ian Randall and Pamela Durso for their tireless guidance throughout multiple drafts of my manuscript spanning many months. Others who helped suggest and review revisions include Keith Jones, Karen Smith, and Anne Phillips. My gratitude also goes to the Woman's Missionary Union Library and Archives and its staff, Cindy Johnson and Dianne Baker, as well as graphic designer Bruce Watford, for their continued assistance. I am thankful to many other librarians who have helped me on a number of occasions at International Baptist Theological Seminary, Samford University Special Collection, Southern Baptist Historical Library and Archives, North Shelby Library, University of Alabama at Birmingham, and Duke University Archives. For the assistance of Dan Waterman, Jon Berry, Jennifer Backer, J. D. Wilson, and others at the University of Alabama Press throughout the publication process, I am likewise grateful. I appreciate Rachael Price's efforts in preparing the index for this book. Thanks also go to the editors of *Baptist History & Heritage* for allowing me to reprint here a revised version of an article I published in their journal in winter 2010. In addition, I appreciate tremendously the support of colleagues at International Baptist Theological Seminary, Woman's Missionary Union, East Texas Baptist University, and Howard Payne University, as well as many other friends and family members along the way—from those who provided time and funding for research to those who lent a sympathetic ear when it was most needed. Thanks be to God for providing me with a strong community of support.

# Abbreviations

| | |
|---|---|
| AAEO | Annie Armstrong Easter Offering |
| AAO | Annie Armstrong Offering |
| *AB* | *Alabama Baptist* |
| *BB* | *Baltimore Baptist* |
| *BHH* | *Baptist History & Heritage* |
| *BP* | *Baptist Press* |
| *BR* | *Biblical Recorder* |
| *BS* | *Baptist Standard* |
| BWA | Baptist World Alliance |
| *C* | *Contempo* |
| CBE | Christians for Biblical Equality |
| CBMW | Council on Biblical Manhood and Womanhood |
| CLC | Christian Life Commission |
| ERA | Equal Rights Amendment |
| FMB | Foreign Mission Board |
| *HH* | *Heathen Helper* |
| *HM* | *Home Missions* |
| HMB | Home Mission Board |
| LMCO | Lottie Moon Christmas Offering |
| *MM* | *Missions Mosaic* |
| *OMF* | *Our Mission Fields* |
| *R&E* | *Review & Expositor* |
| *RH* | *Religious Herald* |
| *RS* | *Royal Service* |
| SBC | Southern Baptist Convention |
| *SBCA* | *Southern Baptist Convention Annual* |

| | |
|---|---|
| SBHLA | Southern Baptist Historical Library and Archives, Nashville, TN |
| *SBJ* | *Southern Baptist Journal* |
| SBTS | Southern Baptist Theological Seminary |
| SSB | Sunday School Board |
| SWBTS | Southwestern Baptist Theological Seminary |
| WCTU | Woman's Christian Temperance Union |
| WMS | Woman's Missionary Society |
| WMU | Woman's Missionary Union |
| WMUA | Woman's Missionary Union Archives, Birmingham, AL |
| *WMUAR* | *WMU Annual Report* |
| WMUTS | WMU Training School |
| *WR* | *Western Recorder* |
| WUMS | Woman's Union Missionary Society |
| *YB* | *WMU Year Book* |

# 1
# Southern Baptist Women's Writings in Context

Wife. Mother. Children's worker. Teacher. Missionary. Deacon. Executive. Pastor. Which roles are acceptable for Southern Baptist women? It depends on whom you ask. Southern Baptist Addie Davis demonstrated her view by becoming an ordained minister; pastor's wife Joyce Rogers, by exhorting each woman to be "submissive to her husband [and] to the male leadership in the church."[1] Such divergent opinions about women's roles are evident in a survey of the nearly 170-year history of the Southern Baptist Convention (SBC). Over the decades, Southern Baptists have debated everything from the priority of homemaking to the appropriateness of female presidential candidates. Should a woman teach teenage boys and men? Is it biblical for women to serve in high-profile leadership positions? Can a female missionary preach a sermon if she encounters a crowd that hasn't heard about Jesus? Ask such questions at a Southern Baptist church even today, and you are likely to receive strong responses.

More often than not, Southern Baptists refer to the Bible as the authority that determines their beliefs on women's roles. The SBC's Baptist Faith and Message, after all, declares that the Bible is "the supreme standard by which all human conduct . . . should be tried."[2] But while the Bible's text has remained the same, typical Southern Baptist views on what is appropriate for women have changed significantly over a relatively short period of time. An 1883 article in the *Alabama Baptist*, for example, cautioned readers against letting a woman "ascend the platform and the pulpit." If this occurred, the writer warned, "not only will home run to waste and children to ruin, but she will lose her own delicacy, and loveliness, and feminineness."[3] In 1972, however—less than a century later—Southern Baptist editor Walker Knight echoed the sentiments of other denominational leaders in proposing that "this should be the year we elect a woman [as president of the SBC]; not in tokenism, but in recognition of her service and her role of equality."[4] But Knight's hope went unrealized. Instead, the SBC moved in a conservative direction, declaring in 2000 that "a wife is to submit herself graciously to the servant leadership of her husband even as the church willingly submits to the headship of Christ."[5] From an admonition about women's public speaking to an affirmation of their equality with men to a declaration of wives' submission—such words reveal the drastic shifts that occurred in Southern Baptist attitudes toward women over a little more than a century.

What accounts for these rapid changes of perspective, and what views did Southern Baptist women themselves hold during this time? This book seeks to answer these questions by examining the gender roles that Southern Baptist women promoted throughout the twentieth century in their writings—specifically, in the magazines of Woman's Missionary Union (WMU), the women's auxiliary to the SBC. These monthly magazines, with a peak circulation of nearly five hundred thousand, constitute the most significant collection of materials written by Southern Baptist women in the twentieth century. WMU editors and writers penned thousands of pages on topics loosely related to missions, including social ministry, race, and motherhood. Their words influenced what generations of Southern Baptist women thought about "the woman I am," as a series of magazine ads in the 1970s phrased it.[6] Analyzing historical WMU magazines reveals the fascinating ways that editors and writers throughout the century reshaped the roles they advanced for Southern Baptist women, influenced by changes in contemporary Southern Baptist life and broader American culture.

The chapters of this book trace the historical development of the roles that WMU women's magazines suggested for their readers, with an emphasis on missions, WMU's primary concern. From 1906 to 1918, these magazines portrayed women's role as engaging in and supporting the "uplift" of women and children in North America and overseas, replicating the emphases of the wider woman's missionary movement. Between 1919 and 1945, however, the magazines depicted women's task as supporting the SBC, reflecting the denominational identity developing among Southern Baptists and leading WMU members to a new role in the denomination. Informed by conservative American culture, from 1946 to 1967 WMU women's magazines limited their readers' role to cultivating a Christian influence, most notably in the home. In contrast, between 1968 to 1983 these magazines mirrored many of the activist, pro-women sentiments prevalent in American culture. Finally, from 1984 to 2006 the magazines emphasized concepts of spirituality popular among many American evangelical women, scarcely mentioning WMU's conflicts with conservative SBC leaders.

Examining these changing ideals provides insight into the relationship between gender roles and culture within the largest Protestant denomination in the United States. Southern Baptist women's experiences and ideas have traditionally been so underreported that historian Leon McBeth once declared, tongue in cheek, "If any of you men ever want to get away from women, here is one way you can do it: just get into the pages of Baptist history. Women will not bother you there."[7] In recent years scholars such as Elizabeth Flowers and Susan Shaw have worked to remedy this omission, joining historians of women in other American religious traditions in demonstrating that "women's history *is* American religious history."[8] As these historians recognize, considering Southern Baptist women's words and actions reshapes our knowledge of the past, often revealing significant cultural and social dynamics that studies of male-dominated denominational structures and theology overlook. Research about Southern Baptist women also augments the growing body of scholarship on American evangelicalism[9] and gender, demonstrating how members of what is perhaps the world's largest group of Protestant women negotiated their roles within their conservative context. Southern Baptist women's writings lend insight not only into the history of the SBC but also into the larger story of American religion and culture.

## Woman's Missionary Movement

In order to understand the significance of the roles that WMU magazines suggested for their readers in the twentieth century, one must first examine the nineteenth-century context from which the organization arose. Like other American women, Baptist women were not always actively engaged in formal leadership of their own organizations. Before the Civil War, the domestic roles deemed proper for American women—especially in the conservative South—allowed for only limited cultivation of female charitable work. Most women who wanted to influence the lives of the "heathen" were encouraged simply to "train your sons for Christ . . . for ministers or missionaries."[10] But during the war, many women assumed new responsibilities in maintaining their homes and communities in their husbands' absence. In the South, some women found themselves managing plantations or banding together to collect supplies for soldiers. Women in at least a few Baptist churches led Sunday School and prayer meetings because of the dearth of male leaders. Many women took on new duties within and beyond the home.

After the war ended, many women continued to assume roles that expanded their traditional sphere of influence. Survival required everyone's efforts in the South, a region scarred by fighting, devoid of its slave labor force and many of its leaders, and fraught with conflict over the federal government's policies of Reconstruction. Many Southern women worked to meet the new needs that arose around them. A falling birthrate and the development of a more industrialized, urban society also affected postwar women's roles, especially in the North. An increasing number of women were able to purchase clothing, canned food, and labor-saving devices to help with household chores. Instead of spending all day tending to their homes, children, and servants, some women—particularly those from wealthy, urban families—gradually found themselves with leisure time that they had not enjoyed in the past.

These changing conditions motivated American women to engage in benevolent activity beyond the home at a quickening pace. Growing numbers of women ventured outside their homes to spread their piety and maternal influence into their communities. First many increased their involvement in religious work, forming Ladies Aid Societies to help their churches and communities and then establishing missionary societies to promote foreign and home mission work. The Woman's Christian Temperance Union (WCTU), founded in 1874, also urged women to use their virtuous influence to improve the world around them. These organizations, safely within the culturally dictated bounds of women's traditional sphere, provided their members with experience in leading meetings, managing money, speaking publicly, and learning about the broader world. Although most women's motivation was to support charitable efforts, not to develop leadership skills, such societies enabled them to do both.

Because of the rural and conservative nature of their region, Southern women often lagged behind their Northern counterparts in forming such organizations and embracing new roles. Many Southern Baptists, for example, felt that the WCTU, with its "women lecturing mixed audiences" and increasing emphasis on suffrage, was too extreme.[11] But Southern women were nonetheless affected by the general climate of change in late nineteenth-century America. Like their Northern sisters, Southern women soon began to reappropriate traditional ideas of female piety to encompass not only the home but also the world. In this period, Northern and Southern women alike gradually adopted new roles through their charitable work at home and abroad.

Women's missionary societies were some of the most significant new organizations that flourished among Protestant women throughout the country during this time. While a few societies had been formed during the first half of the nineteenth century, the first organized effort of the woman's missionary movement began in New York in 1861. In that year Sarah Doremus, a Reformed woman frustrated with Protestant mission boards' hesitation to appoint unmarried women, founded the Woman's Union Missionary Society (WUMS). This interdenominational mission board, led by women, sent single women to the mission field, "untrammeled by the duties of wives and mothers . . . [to] Christianize exclusively heathen women for whom no other mode of elevation was practicable."[12] As female charitable work increased, women from many denominations soon began organizing their own mission societies. In 1868 the Woman's Board of Missions was founded as an auxiliary to the Congregational mission board to support all of the board's single female missionaries. Congregational women in Chicago formed a similar regional organization the same year. In 1869 Northern Methodist women created a denomination-wide Woman's Foreign Missionary Society; the following year, Northern Presbyterians in Philadelphia organized their own Woman's Foreign Missionary Society. Northern Baptist women were not far behind, establishing in 1871 both the Woman's Missionary Society and the Woman's Baptist Missionary Society of the North-West.[13] For the first time, in addition to supporting missions efforts led by men, women guided an entire segment of the missionary enterprise themselves.

By 1880 more than twenty women's missions organizations had been created.[14] Twenty years later, over forty such groups were active, involving millions of laywomen and supporting hundreds of female missionaries.[15] In nearly every denomination—even those in the conservative South—women formed their own organizations for the purpose of mission work. Less than fifty years after the woman's missionary movement began, missions leader Helen Barrett Montgomery remarked, "It is hard to realize that there ever was a time when there were none of the active and ubiquitous Women's Missionary Societies that seem so much a part of the structure of church life."[16] The woman's missionary movement captured the hearts of a generation of laywomen in what was the largest mass organization of American women to that time.[17]

What endeavors did these societies undertake to generate and maintain the interest of such a tremendous number of women? The movement's motto explained it: "woman's work for woman." Like WUMS, women's missions organizations supported female missionaries, often single women. Some of the societies—especially those in the South—served as auxiliaries to their denominational boards, helping fund and encourage the female missionaries that the boards appointed. Many others were completely independent, both selecting and sending female missionaries themselves. The majority of these women's missionary groups focused on foreign mission work, while a few included home missions as well. All advocated an increase in the number of female missionaries, especially unmarried women, whom they felt were not bound by domestic tasks. As a result of the efforts of such groups, women outnumbered men on many mission fields by the late nineteenth century.

Collecting donations to support these missionaries was a key role for women's missionary groups. As the women became aware of missions needs, they gave their pennies, nickels, dimes, and occasionally dollars to aid the missions cause. In many denominations, women organized groups of girls and boys to support missions as well. The sum of the women's and children's small contributions amounted to millions of dollars for missions each year. As they worked, the women carefully explained that their efforts did not take away from their "feminine loyalty"[18] to their denominational mission boards. Instead of campaigning for a more equal role for themselves in denominational affairs, which would have created considerable tension, the women assured male leaders of their organizations' ancillary position.

Not only did women's missionary societies raise money for missions efforts; they also distributed missions information among their members to help them understand and meet needs on the mission field. Many societies began publishing missions leaflets, tracts, and magazines soon after they were organized. Advances in printing and an increased rate of literacy among women enabled societies to create and distribute their own publications among thousands of women at a reasonable cost. Soon the woman's missionary movement developed what Montgomery called the "light infantry of missionary literature."[19] Dozens of magazines were created in rapid succession: the Congregationalist *Light and Life for Women* (1869), the Northern Methodist *Heathen Woman's Friend* (1869), the Presbyterian *Woman's Work for Woman* (1871), the Northern Baptist *Helping Hand* (1877), and the Southern Methodist *Woman's Missionary Advocate* (1880), among others.[20] These new missions publications roughly coincided with the advent of the "big six" magazines targeted more generally at middle-class white women: *Delineator* (1873), *McCall's* (1873), *Ladies' Home Journal* (1883), *Good Housekeeping* (1885), *Woman's Home Companion* (1896), and *Pictorial Review* (1899).[21] It is not surprising that female missions advocates used the same popular medium as other influencers of women did. However, woman's missionary movement editors did not simply provide homemaking advice or fashion news in their publications. Instead, these women shaped their magazines' message around what they considered to be a loftier missions purpose.

Most women's missionary publications were quite similar: "not too bookish and intellectual,"[22] they recounted missions information from a personalized, woman-to-woman perspective, often including stories and concrete information that editors hoped would help women visualize life for their compatriots on the mission field and pray for their ministries. Each lamented the plight of unevangelized "heathen" women, who often lived in conditions that American women found appalling. For example, a typical article in *Light and Life for Women* described the "Story of a Native Woman" who "had never seen schools or churches" but who soon became a Christian and learned to read as a result of missionary efforts.[23] Editors thus applauded not only the Christianization but also the Westernization of women around the world. Magazines of different organizations frequently quoted each other, furthering the exchange of missionary information and the feeling of "sisterhood" among women of many denominations.

Thousands of women subscribed to each magazine; *Heathen Woman's Friend*, for example, had a readership of nearly twenty-five thousand.[24] Studying the information in these publications—as well as reading mission study books and attending missions conferences—became a hallmark of woman's missionary society members. These women established their unique place in the late nineteenth-century Protestant world by becoming experts about and advocates for women's mission work with other women. Such an emphasis gradually broadened the influence of missionary society members, as missions leaders urged them to help women and children in ways that they believed only women could.

As women read reports from the growing number of missionaries serving overseas during this time, they noticed frequent descriptions of their "untaught, heathen sisters" who were "stretch[ing] out their hands . . . for the bread of life"[25]—women to whom male missionaries believed they could not directly minister because of cultural gender role divisions. This "sorrow of heathen womanhood"[26] compelled some American women to consider serving on the mission field themselves, whether they were married or single. Perhaps, they thought, work with foreign women would produce the large number of conversions that male missionaries hoped for but generally failed to realize. The women's mission work could be the "key . . . which shall fit in the lock that is barring out Christ from the homes of heathendom."[27] Millions of women thus became enthusiastic supporters of the woman's missionary movement and the unique role it provided for women.

The new ministry roles that emerged from the woman's missionary movement were influenced by the accepted model of womanhood that developed in the late nineteenth century. While a few missions advocates such as Montgomery called for gender equality, urging women to revolt against the "cribbed, cabined, and confined sphere to which the natural prejudices of a man-monopolized world has assigned them,"[28] the majority of late nineteenth-century female missionaries and mission supporters—especially those from the conservative South—worked within the "separate sphere" that society assigned to women during this period. They directed their ministry efforts almost exclusively toward women and children: "whatever [ministry] *woman only* can do."[29] By teaching girls, addressing women's issues, and showing "the heathens . . . the beauty of Christian homes," these women applied "the same modest, ladylike deportment they maintained in the homeland" to the world outside their home.[30] The women served as "mothers" of their communities in a way that was increasingly common in the late nineteenth century.

Adopting such roles—approved by men and women alike—allowed female missionaries to gain their supporters' trust and gradually to stretch the bounds of what was considered acceptable for their gender. Although these women would likely have been criticized for embarking upon professional careers in the United States at that time, they were applauded for their dedication to working overseas as teachers, medical workers, and evangelists to "those who had been left in the lowest degradation."[31] Millions of other American women who remained at home enthusiastically supported these women's ministries and developed new skills as they led missionary societies and participated in interdenominational women's missions events. A handbook for women's missionary societies even claimed, "There is no organization that offers a wider field for every talent, spiritual, literary, social, executive."[32] During this period, mission work became a fulfilling pursuit for thousands of American women.

## Southern Baptist Women in Missions

Southern Baptist women observed the beginnings of the woman's missionary movement with interest, but their early missions efforts were stymied by the conservative tendencies of Southern Baptist men. The SBC, organized in 1845 in part to allow slaveholders to serve as missionaries, demonstrated a strong affinity for all things Southern—including the region's conservative gender roles. Thus a number of the SBC's leaders opposed the formation of female organizations, especially on the national scale. Most Southern Baptists of the late nineteenth century were convinced that it was unbiblical for women to speak in "mixed public assemblies." Citing the "express prohibitions" of the Apostle Paul, as well as women's "lack of mental vigor,"[33] male SBC leaders such as seminary professor John Broadus pronounced that women should remain silent in church, deferring to the authority of their husbands. To do otherwise, according to their interpretation of the Bible, would be "changing Scripture teaching to fit the nineteenth century," as Kentucky pastor and editor T. T. Eaton put it.[34]

In addition, many Southern Baptist men were suspicious of any movement with Northern connections. Championing regional separatism, especially after the Civil War, these men eschewed any action they felt might lead women to "follow in the footsteps of our Northern sisters, in having separate, independent organizations," as Georgia women's leader Martha Wilson explained.[35] Most Southern Baptist women did not believe that Northern women's autonomous action and public speaking were appropriate—but they also felt compelled to participate in a unique form of mission support in the company of other women. As Reverend G. W. Hall asserted in the women's *Heathen Helper* newspaper, "While it is improper for [a] woman to enter the pulpit and become a public preacher of the Gospel, yet [it] is plain, from the teachings of the New Testament, that she has more to do than simply attend the meetings of the church and sit."[36] Southern Baptist women, though products of their Southern evangelical context, gradually took advantage of women's expanding roles in American culture and developed their own organizations to support mission work at home and overseas.

In 1868 these Southern Baptist women took their first tentative steps toward organized mission work. In that year Ann Baker Graves—mother of Southern Baptist missionary Rosewell Graves—convened a gathering of women who had accompanied their husbands to the SBC annual meeting in Baltimore. Breaking convention, Graves implored the women to organize societies in their churches to raise money for Chinese Bible women, who evangelized women they believed no male missionary could reach. Around three years later, Graves officially organized Woman's Mission to Woman, a society of Baptist women founded "'to give light' to the woman that sits in darkness because of Bible destitution."[37] Graves's concern for women in other countries apparently eclipsed her deference to male SBC leaders' views.

The impact of Woman's Mission to Woman stretched far beyond Baltimore. The organization's leaders sent mite boxes and letters to women's societies throughout the South, encouraging them in guilt-inducing language to "dispense with some luxury for your table, some costly adornment or tasteful garment for yourself or your children, that your sorrowing, burdened sisters of China and India, Burhmah [*sic*], Siam and Africa, may hear of Him who alone can make them free."[38] Soon the group even informed the SBC's Foreign Mission Board (FMB) that it reserved the right to control all the money it raised.[39] As Southern Baptist women engaged in "woman's work for woman" with others across the convention for the first time, they gained an influence greater than any local society could wield.

Soon FMB, led by its new corresponding secretary Henry Allen Tupper, heeded the women's concern for their "sisters" in non-Christian lands by sending its first single female missionaries since a short-lived attempt in 1849. Lula Whilden and Edmonia Moon departed for China, with many promises of Southern Baptist women's support, in 1872. Edmonia's sister Lottie, probably the most famous Southern Baptist missionary, set sail the following year. Most Southern Baptist women were thrilled at the news of "their" missionaries and quickly organized new missionary societies to gather money for the women's salaries and mission projects.

For their part, FMB leaders were pleased with the women's outpouring of missions enthusiasm and funding, although they realized that men's reactions would be mixed. An article in the Kentucky Baptist *Western Recorder* reflected the complex attitudes of even some men who supported these new missionaries: "We predict that, keeping within her proper sphere, woman will be a most valuable auxiliary in the work of spreading the gospel. Why shouldn't she? Didn't she have much to do in bringing the curse upon the race? And ought she not to do all she can to remove it?"[40] Such comments exemplified many Southern Baptist men's belief that women—tainted by Eve's original sin—should limit their influence to home, family, and work with other women. WMU leader Annie Armstrong later complained, "I have heard so much about the 'woman's sphere,' and her going beyond proper bounds, that I think I am beginning to feel on this point as the children do when they are told 'children should be seen and not heard.'"[41]

Reports of the women's efforts *were* heard in 1872, when "women's work" was mentioned at the SBC for the first time. Tupper encouraged the convention's male messengers to arouse "the sisterhood of our Southern Zion . . . to the grand mission of redeeming their sister-woman from the degrading and destroying thralldom of Paganism."[42] Another FMB leader moved that the SBC endorse such women's work, and debate ensued. Although the motion passed, it was obvious that women's missions efforts were a cause of contention among Southern Baptist men.

But as the men discussed women's acceptable roles, the women's missionary work moved forward. In 1874 FMB appointed central committees for women's work in each state, although some were squelched by opposition. Four years later, convention action approved these committees and created similar committees under the auspices of the denomination's Home Mission Board (HMB). Each committee was formed to help organize missionary societies and "by the circulation of periodicals and other means to cultivate the missionary spirit."[43] An 1878 FMB report reflected the boards' typical attitude toward these groups: "Many of our Christian sisters are working nobly with us, in connection with their respective churches and state organizations. The Board anticipate [*sic*] grand results from their pious and self-denying labors. More general and separate organization seems undesired, and undesirable, as not in harmony with the views and genius of the women of the South."[44] Male missions leaders lauded women's missions efforts at the local and state levels but dismissed as unladylike the idea of a convention-wide committee to coordinate women's work.

As local missionary societies and state central committees multiplied in the 1880s, the women's influence in the convention rapidly expanded. More than five hundred women's missionary societies were counted in 1882. Convention leaders praised these societies' combined annual gifts of more than $8,000, to which they attributed "the comparative [*sic*] easy financial condition of our Foreign Mission Board."[45] The following year, while their husbands attended the SBC, the women began holding their own missions meetings in nearby churches. Influenced by women's expanding roles in broader American culture, women's publications spoke enthusiastically of the "grand uprising of our Christian women" and the "power of organized effort."[46] The women began seriously discussing the possibility of forming a permanent convention-wide organization.

In response, the pages of state Baptist newspapers and the halls of convention venues were filled with arguments about how to "deal with this problem."[47] In addition to discussing what they considered women's proper roles according to Scripture, concerned men such as John Shaffer of Alabama warned others about women whom he feared would "rob the church of its dignity and honors, and transfer the work which God assigned to the church, to societies."[48] This position demonstrated the influence of Landmarkism, an ecclesiology popular among some Southern Baptists that emphasized the authority and exclusive validity of local Baptist congregations and disapproved of mission boards and societies. The local church, as even one woman argued, was "a missionary society for both sexes," and women would do well to avoid the contemporary "*mania* for forming new societies."[49]

But other Southern Baptist men and women, including leaders of the mission boards, urged the convention to consider the "ever-broadening streams of revenue"[50] and devotion that would result from a central women's organization. One Maryland writer cautioned, "They have started in this great work, and are going forward. There is no power under heaven that can stop them. We shall repent of our folly when it is too late, and like our Northern brethren, knock at their doors only to receive the answer that they can manage their own affairs themselves. Their work is the right arm of our strength. Let us not be guilty of the suicidal act of cutting it off."[51] Southern Baptist women were moving with increasing power toward organization for missions, such sympathizers pragmatically argued, and their efforts would support the convention, not harm it. After all, the women desired to work in cooperation with the mission boards; as a writer reassured North Carolina Baptists, "Anything else would be out of harmony with the clinging, tendril nature of the refined Southern woman."[52]

However, most Southern Baptist men believed that women's growing efforts for missions were not in keeping with the image of a Southern lady. Even Georgia central committee president Martha Wilson feared that a national women's organization would be "the first step to public speaking by ladies" and would lead to women's suffrage.[53] Denominational leaders were similarly alarmed at the 1885 SBC annual meeting, when two women arrived to serve as messengers. According to Alabama messenger J. J. D. Renfroe, the women's presence "threw us into a spasm";[54] strident debate ensued. Recognizing that their participation was viewed as a threat, the women ultimately withdrew their names from consideration. After a vote, the convention's constitution was reworded to specify that messengers must be "brethren," although women comprised approximately 60 percent of Southern Baptist church members at the time.[55] The same year, the supervision of each women's central committee was reassigned to "a brother of their own state"[56] instead of to the mission boards, which were generally more sympathetic to their work. Male leaders reacted in alarm to the women's expanding power.

## Woman's Missionary Union

By 1887 Southern Baptist women's interest in missions, and the strength of their growing numbers, overruled their deference to male leaders' concerns. As Fannie Heck later remarked, the women "rose above criticism and defied custom and convention to undertake the work they felt constrained to do."[57] Meeting in Louisville, Kentucky, in conjunction with the SBC, the women planned to organize on the national level the following year "to be more efficient in collecting money and disseminating information on mission subjects."[58] Their leaders asked each state to send three female delegates to the women's meeting in 1888 in Richmond, Virginia.

At the 1888 meeting, women from twelve states gathered at Richmond's Broad Street Methodist Church—near the Baptist church hosting the SBC meeting, as was the women's custom. A speaker urged the women to "put into action the convictions of so many hearts,"[59] and the majority was in favor of immediate organization. As Annie Armstrong explained, "Time is needed to perfect plans of work. . . . The States have virtually committed themselves to the movement."[60] But after discussion, the group decided not to take an official vote until after the men of the convention had met to consider the idea. They did, however, appoint a committee to plan for a new organization. Although several male messengers were adamantly opposed to the women's organization—one mocked the group as "a handful of women," not "the women of the churches"[61]—the women decided to continue with their plans. On May 14, 1888, the women voted to organize the Executive Committee of Woman's Mission Societies, Auxiliary to Southern Baptist Convention.[62] In 1890 the organization's name was officially changed to Woman's Missionary Union, Auxiliary to Southern Baptist Convention.

The women decided that the organization's headquarters would be in Baltimore; its purposes would be "to distribute missionary information and stimulate effort" and "to secure the earnest systematic co-operation of women and children in collecting and raising money for missions," while "disclaiming all intention of independent action."[63] Unlike Northern Baptist women, they would not send their own missionaries; as one of the "most closely auxiliary" women's organizations,[64] WMU would support the work of the existing SBC mission boards. As Lottie Moon, who advocated the creation of WMU, remarked, "What we want is not power. . . . Power of appointment and of disbursing funds should be left, as heretofore, in the hands of the Foreign Mission Board. . . . Organization in subordination to the Board is the imperative need."[65] Southern Baptist women assured male leaders that they desired to assist, not compete with, the men's missions efforts. In deference to denominational leaders, the women formed WMU as an auxiliary to the SBC and not as a separate agency. Ironically, however, the organization's status as an auxiliary, with its own grassroots leaders, later gave it more freedom to depart from the views of the convention's leadership.

By 1889, only one year after WMU's official founding, a remarkable 600,000 Southern Baptist women were involved in the organization. Women in Baptist churches across the South formed Women's Missionary Societies—open to all the women in a church—to collect money for foreign, home, and local mission projects, including a Christmas offering for missionaries in China.[66] In 1889 alone, the women raised over $72,000, all of which they sent to denominational leaders to expend.[67] They also packed and mailed boxes of supplies to the mission field and prayed regularly for missionaries. Similarly, women's groups met monthly and read literature produced by WMU to learn more about mission work. The WMU headquarters soon became a "veritable bee-hive of missionary activity."[68] A corresponding secretary, president, recording secretary, and treasurer were elected to lead the national organization. Initially all four officers were unpaid and able to survive off their families' wealth, using the whole of women's contributions for missions efforts. The corresponding secretary directed the work of the Baltimore office full-time; the president led annual meetings but did not usually live in Baltimore. State WMU organizations selected their own leaders as well.[69]

Before long, Southern Baptist men's concerns about women's increasingly public roles were eclipsed by the united and supportive efforts of women for missions. The 1889 *Southern Baptist Convention Annual* stated that women were "becoming one of the most fruitful sources of missionary influence and income."[70] The 1893 *Annual* reflected contemporary Southern gender norms as it commended the "modest, womanly, scriptural manner in which they [WMU members] have done their work, the sweet spirit in which they have heartily co-operated with the Board, but above all, the incense of fervent, humble, effective prayer which has gone up from so many loving hearts."[71] Later scholars would call WMU "the backbone of Southern Baptist missions," "the most unique female contribution to missions," and part of "the most significant contribution women have made to the Southern Baptist Convention."[72] Through WMU many female Southern Baptists created a new outlet for their piety that male denominational leaders gradually accepted, and they showed the men the power of their dedication to a common purpose.

The new roles that WMU provided for Southern Baptist women revealed women's growing influence in the late nineteenth century. In keeping with the broader woman's missionary movement, WMU gave women a way to expand their roles within their conservative Southern context. Although contemporary historians focus on the difficulties WMU frequently faced in navigating Southern Baptist separatism and conservatism, many WMU leaders of the time likely joined Fannie Heck in rejoicing at the way "the proper sphere and activity of women were revolutionized" at the organization's founding.[73] As Southern Baptist women worked determinedly for missions, they were doubtless pleased with the new roles that emerged as a result of their service. Without promoting views that Southern men found objectionable, WMU leaders reinterpreted traditional understandings of female piety to increase the influence of Southern Baptist women. Their ideas were expressed, in large part, through WMU magazines.

## WMU Magazines

Although they were forbidden from speaking to groups of men, nineteenth-century Southern Baptist women wielded a wider influence through the power of the pen. One woman who wrote pseudonymously as Mrs. Sarah Dobbins—perhaps out of fear of the repercussions of her words—nonetheless maintained in the Virginia Baptist newspaper, "We cannot speak in church, nor in many other places where our interests are discussed, but . . . I have never yet seen anything in Paul's writings against our speaking through the *Religious Herald*."[74] For this reason, female Southern Baptist leaders such as Annie Armstrong realized that printed materials were "essential to quicken zeal and arouse interest in missions."[75] They rapidly joined the publishing trend that was attracting the attention of many women's groups in the late nineteenth century.

Several Southern Baptist women began publishing missions information—typically for other women—even before WMU was officially organized. In 1882 Kentucky Baptist women mailed the first issue of the *Heathen Helper*, a monthly newspaper that encouraged women across the South "to go to foreign lands to tell our heathen sisters that there is life, light, liberty, peace and happiness in this life and the life to come, in the gospel of Jesus Christ."[76] The *Baptist Basket*, a similar publication, was created in Kentucky in 1888. In Baltimore Armstrong and other local leaders gathered several denominations' missions leaflets and wrote their own, housing the publications in the Maryland Baptist Mission Rooms beginning in 1887. Soon Southern Baptist women also began writing missions columns for state Baptist newspapers, Sunday School materials, Baptist Young People's Union publications, the *Foreign Mission Journal*, and *Our Home Field*. Male SBC editors gladly accepted these columns, which they probably felt would broaden their publications' readership while still keeping women within their accepted realm of influence among other women and children.

After WMU was organized, its leaders began to produce a "steadily growing" amount of missionary leaflets, prayer cards, tracts, and program helps that they hoped would "arouse a greater interest . . . and result in larger contributions."[77] These endeavors were financed in part by HMB and FMB, both of which helped fund WMU's budget—supplying the organization with its primary income in its earliest years and later contributing more token amounts. Such gifts revealed that the mission boards' leaders likely believed that WMU's expanding influence would benefit their efforts as well. By 1906 local Women's Missionary Societies were clamoring for additional missions information, and WMU's literature department began a magazine publishing enterprise that remained a significant aspect of the organization's work for years to come.

In July 1906, WMU published the first issue of *Our Mission Fields*, a thirty-six-page quarterly magazine. As the "official organ" of WMU, *Our Mission Fields* attempted to "reflect the Union's plans, purposes, and aims."[78] The magazine also mirrored the content of the publications of the broader woman's missionary movement. The majority of the space in *Our Mission Fields*, as in other women's missions magazines, was devoted to monthly programs of study about its denominational missionaries' work around the world, for use during Woman's Missionary Society (WMS) meetings. These programs usually included prayer, Bible study, music, and pages of in-depth missions information. While women's mission work was not the sole focus of each program, missions topics were considered from a female point of view. Demand for *Our Mission Fields* was so great that its subscription numbers nearly doubled in the first year, sometimes outpacing WMU leaders' print estimates.[79] Approximately fifteen thousand women subscribed by 1914.[80]

Requests for *Our Mission Fields* came from "as far north as Canada and as far west as Seattle,"[81] although it had been publicized only among Southern Baptist women. No known distribution lists for the magazine remain, but its primary subscribers were most likely the same Southern women whom records indicate received pamphlets and other literature from WMU. Living in the eleven states of the former Confederacy

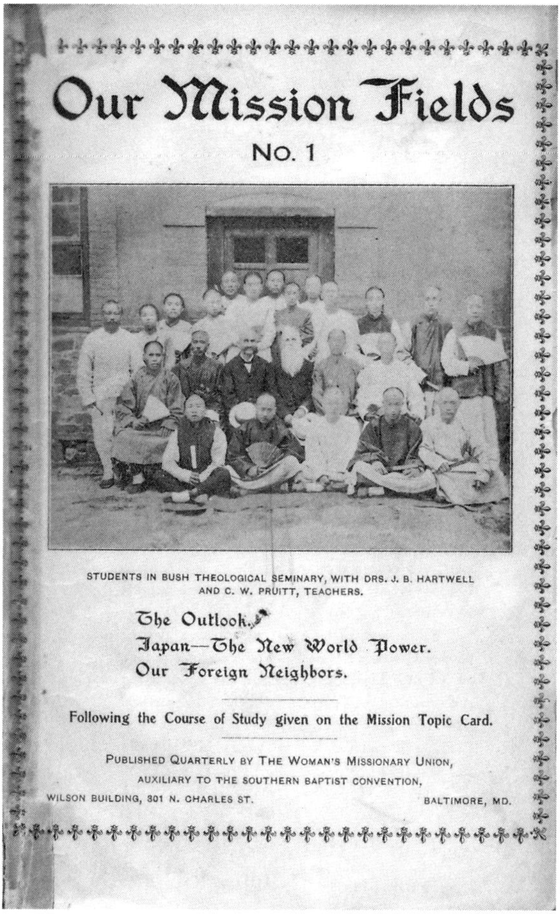

Our Mission Fields

No. 1

STUDENTS IN BUSH THEOLOGICAL SEMINARY, WITH DRS. J. B. HARTWELL AND C. W. PRUITT, TEACHERS.

The Outlook.

Japan—The New World Power.

Our Foreign Neighbors.

Following the Course of Study given on the Mission Topic Card.

PUBLISHED QUARTERLY BY THE WOMAN'S MISSIONARY UNION, AUXILIARY TO THE SOUTHERN BAPTIST CONVENTION,

WILSON BUILDING, 301 N. CHARLES ST. BALTIMORE, MD.

1. First issue of *Our Mission Fields*, July/August/September 1906. (Used by permission of WMUA.)

plus the border states of Oklahoma, Missouri, Kentucky, and Maryland, most Southern Baptist women probably spent much of their time caring for their homes, husbands, and multiple children. Some early WMU members, including most of the organization's founders, attended urban churches, whose middle- and upper-class members were often the first to adopt new emphases such as missionary societies. But an increasing number of WMU members, like the great majority of Southern Baptist women, lived in rural areas, where their families struggled to make a living primarily through farming. Like other Southern women in this period, few were educated beyond the secondary level; pressing family duties kept some from advancing even that far.

The editors of *Our Mission Fields* were among WMU's more privileged members. For the magazine's first two issues, no editors were listed, although popular WMU president Fannie Heck may have guided the new publication. Heck, daughter of a wealthy Southern businessman, edited the magazine from 1907 to 1911. From 1911 to 1912, the editor was Edith Crane, WMU corresponding secretary who attended Baltimore's Eutaw Place Baptist Church with Annie Armstrong. Claris Crane, Edith's sister and a graduate of Bryn Mawr College for women, served as editor of *Our Mission Fields* from 1912 to 1914. Writers of individual articles were seldom named. The magazine's design changed slightly over the years, and programs for young people were added, but its basic purpose remained the same.

In October 1914, *Our Mission Fields* was replaced by a thirty-two-page monthly magazine titled *Royal Service*, with an expanded table of contents: "mission programs for each grade of society . . . news from our home and foreign women missionaries, from the [WMU] Training School, the Margaret Home Fund [to support children of missionaries], Woman's Missionary Union Headquarters, an exchange of society methods, a department of Personal Service [social ministry], a department of Bible study and brief items of current events in the missionary world."[82] Thousands of Southern Baptist women quickly came to rely on *Royal Service* for the latest information about WMU and women's mission work. Approached by SBC leaders about merging the publication with the new *Home and Foreign Fields* in 1916, editors decided "after careful thought" to continue *Royal Service* as a stand-alone magazine for Baptist women.[83] Thus WMU leaders exercised the autonomy implicit in their auxiliary status, an action possible in part because of the financial strength of their magazine, which by this time was funded entirely from subscription revenue. For years, *Royal Service*'s monthly programs—designed "to plant precious seeds of information in the fertile soil of willing hearts"[84]—remained the most important part of the magazine, but supplementary features continued to be added.

Although the authors of individual articles were not always listed or were listed using their husbands' names, most issues of *Royal Service* included the name of one of the many editors who served during the magazine's long history. While early editors largely belonged to the white Southern elite, by mid-century these leaders were somewhat more representative of their growing middle-class constituency. Elia Nimmo, the daughter of a physician, edited the magazine from 1914 to 1920; Kathleen Mallory, WMU corresponding secretary and a member of a wealthy Alabama family, served as editor from 1920 to 1948. From 1948 to 1957, Juliette

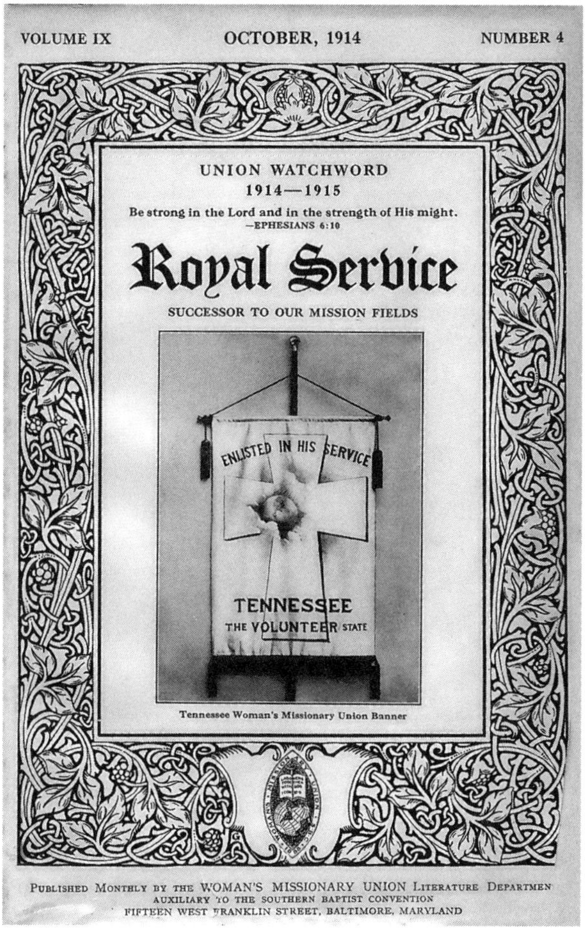


2. First issue of *Royal Service*, October 1914. (Used by permission of WMUA.)

Mather, WMU editorial secretary and graduate of the WMU Training School (WMUTS), edited *Royal Service.* Mather's former assistant and longtime WMU employee Ethalee Hamric was editor from 1957 to 1969.

Rosanne Osborne, who spent the rest of her career as an English professor at a Baptist college, edited the magazine from 1969 to 1973. Laurella Owens, veteran WMU editor and daughter of FMB missionaries to Palestine, assumed this responsibility from 1973 to 1977; Lane Powell, a graduate of New Orleans Baptist Theological Seminary, edited *Royal Service* from 1977 to 1978. From 1978 to 1981, ten-year WMU employee and former SBC Sunday School Board (SSB) editor Adrianne Bonham was the maga-

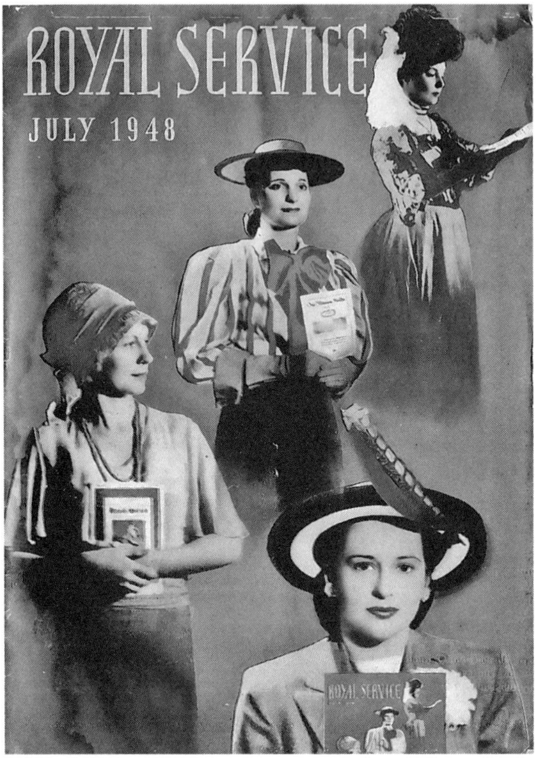


3. New design for *Royal Service*, July 1948. (Used by permission of WMUA.)

zine's editor. Anne Leavell Mann, a former Georgia WMU employee, served for a brief stint in 1982 and 1983; Betty Merrell, a former missionary to Vietnam, edited *Royal Service* from 1983 to 1985. Edna Ellison, a popular WMU speaker with a PhD in education, assumed the role of editor from 1986 to 1993. From 1993 to 1995, *Royal Service* had two editors, both Texans and graduates of Southwestern Baptist Theological Seminary (SWBTS): Cindy Dake and Laura Savage. All of these editors came to WMU with previous denominational experience, revealing the influence of broader Southern Baptist culture upon WMU and *Royal Service*. The number of subscribers to this magazine ranged from thirty thousand in 1916 to nearly five hundred thousand in the 1960s, when WMU enjoyed its peak enrollment.[85]

In an effort to attract younger women, in 1970 WMU introduced Baptist Young Women, an organization for women ages eighteen to twenty-nine (later ages eighteen to thirty-four). *Contempo*, a magazine for Baptist Young Women, joined *Royal Service*, which WMU began to promote for women thirty (later thirty-five) and older, who became members of Bap-

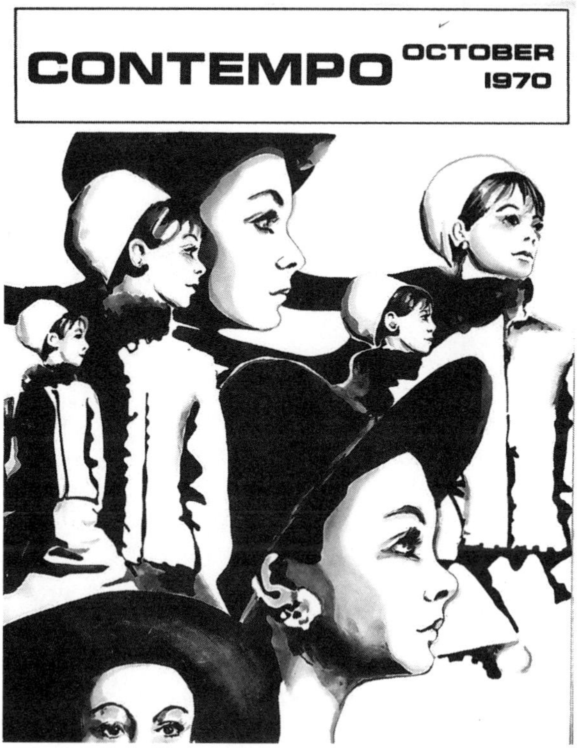


4. First issue of *Contempo*, October 1970. (Used by permission of WMUA.)

tist Women. *Contempo* was edited by Owens from 1970 to 1973; by Ellen Dossett, a former missionary and English teacher, from 1973 to 1974; and by Mary Ann Ward, a former FMB staff writer, from 1975 to 1987. Diana Woodcock, a former missionary to Macau, edited *Contempo* from 1988 to 1989. From 1990 to 1991, the magazine's editor was Eleanor Clay, a native of Trinidad and apparently the first editor who was not Caucasian. Dake served as editor from 1991 to 1993; Dake and Savage again shared this role from 1993 to 1995. Most of these editors were in their twenties and thirties. Probably because of their age and the age of their readers, these editors were slightly more inclined to address women's expanding vocational options than were their older colleagues. During these years, the number of subscribers to *Contempo* remained between forty and sixty thousand.[86] The magazine attracted a core of dedicated readers but was never as popular as *Royal Service*.

In 1995 *Royal Service* and *Contempo*—as well as Baptist Women and Baptist Young Women—were discontinued. In their place, WMU leaders created *Missions Mosaic*, a redesigned magazine for women of all ages whom WMU hoped to involve in its new Women on Mission organization. As in previous years, editors of *Missions Mosaic* had strong ties to WMU and the SBC and thus included magazine content that they hoped would attract all Southern Baptist women to WMU. These editors included Dake, who served from 1995 to 1997; and Becky Nelson, a pastor's wife and former WMU products editor, from 1997 to 1999. Joanne Parker, a graduate of Southern Baptist Theological Seminary (SBTS), edited *Missions Mosaic* from 2000 to 2005. The magazine's editor from 2005 to 2006 was Sue Sprenkle, a former missionary journalist in Africa. In 2006 Janet Erwin, a former missionary to Latvia and the Caribbean, assumed the role of editor.[87] As they had in earlier years, support staff in the WMU office also assisted with editorial functions related to the magazine. During this period, the number of subscribers to *Missions Mosaic* varied from 160,000 to 230,000.[88] While still possessing a substantial readership, the magazine no longer retained the pervasive influence among Southern Baptist women that it had enjoyed during the 1950s and 1960s.

Each WMU editor's work was carefully guided by the WMU Executive Committee. This committee, renamed Executive Board in 1954,[89] was led by WMU's elected president and composed of the organization's recording secretary, treasurer (until 1957), and vice presidents elected by WMU members in each state. The WMU corresponding secretary—later retitled executive secretary and then executive director—also influenced the Executive Board's decisions, although she did not have an official vote on the board after 1957.[90] No male SBC leaders served on this board or had the authority to appoint its members. The women thus enjoyed autonomy from the broader structures of their denomination.

Aware of the power of the printed word, this Executive Board asserted in the early years of WMU's publishing efforts that WMU magazines should "keep in closest touch with the work of the Union . . . following in general the determined lines of Union work in its various branches."[91] The board also established editorial policy throughout the twentieth century, in many years voting to approve the magazines' topics as well as editors of magazine sections. Over the years, the WMU Executive Board established various committees to plan and oversee these magazines, including a literature committee, which in early years was chaired by the corresponding secretary, and a committee on topics, which surveyed state WMU leaders about magazine emphases. Later the Executive Board created a board of editors, who were responsible for various magazine features; an editorial committee, chaired by the WMU president; and then

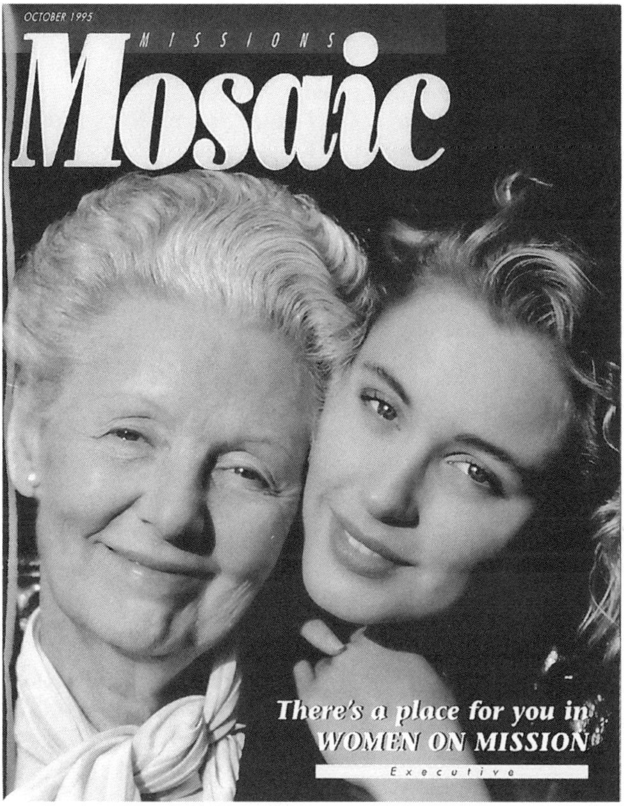


5. First issue of *Missions Mosaic*, October 1995. (Used by permission of WMUA.)

a committee on areas of study, which recommended monthly magazine topics. The Executive Board was concerned that WMU present a consistent perspective about the issues it addressed and consequently took seriously its responsibility to oversee WMU magazines.

By the 1970s, the WMU Executive Board guided a complex process of reviewing magazine topics more than a year before their publication. Curriculum work groups, chaired by state WMU leaders, presented annual Dated Plans (later called Dated Designs) to the Executive Board for review several weeks before board meetings. These plans outlined the general content of each magazine—especially the monthly program designed for use during Baptist Women meetings. At board meetings, small groups of state and national leaders evaluated each Dated Plan. The entire board approved the plans, often as amended by the review groups. Dozens of

WMU leaders demonstrated a vested interest in the content of *Royal Service* and *Contempo*, which they apparently viewed as a significant means of communicating WMU's purpose and message.

This review process became even more complicated in the 1980s and 1990s, as representatives of WMU, FMB, HMB, SSB, and the Brotherhood Commission met together on the Missions Education Curriculum Work Group in an attempt to coordinate broadly the regions or types of mission work they would emphasize, prior to any other ideation from WMU leaders. Although relationships among the leaders of these organizations were sometimes tenuous during these years, staff at the work group level continued their joint planning. By 2000, however, these entities—modified by the SBC's restructuring—no longer attempted to coordinate their themes. At this time, the WMU Executive Board asked the WMU president to appoint a committee to plan WMU's overarching emphasis, which helped guide the direction of the organization and its magazines for two years at a time. These magazines, which generated the majority of WMU's revenue, clearly continued to be of interest to the WMU Executive Board.

Throughout the century, then, although WMU's magazine review processes varied, their purpose was the same: to ensure that the content published in *Our Mission Fields*, *Royal Service*, *Contempo*, and *Missions Mosaic* represented the views of the WMU Executive Board, not just those of the magazines' editors. From a survey of these magazines, it appears that WMU leaders succeeded in this goal. Topics mentioned in each magazine generally corresponded with emphases included in WMU's annual *Year Book*. And although many WMU editors served for fewer than five years, the magazines' content changed very little as a result of personnel transitions. Most editors assumed this role from other positions within WMU or the SBC, not as outsiders bringing new views to the organization. For one-third of the century, the WMU corresponding secretary or president actually edited the organization's magazine herself. And for at least part of the century, WMU leaders reviewed each manuscript (as they do today) to ensure that it corresponded with the organization's plans. Thus WMU magazines to a large extent reflected WMU's goals and viewpoints, not just those of their writers and editors.

Although WMU produced numerous other publications between 1906 and 2006, including *Year Books*, children's magazines, and mission studies, the organization's magazines for women contained the most in-depth discussion about featured missions areas, organizational trends, and women's roles in missions and Baptist life. These magazines, guided by laywomen from throughout the SBC, both reflected and shaped the grassroots perspective that has characterized WMU throughout the years. While not all Southern Baptist women from 1906 to 2006 were members of WMU, WMU publications provide the most comprehensive information about women in Southern Baptist life during this period, especially in the early years of the twentieth century.

Mission work was a constant theme in WMU magazines throughout the century, but this book does not attempt to analyze in detail the missiological developments that occurred during this time among Southern Baptist women or SBC leaders. Thus many of the missions topics featured in WMU magazines are unremarkable for the purpose of this study. This book focuses especially on women's roles in missions—both at home and on the mission field—as described by WMU editors and writers. It also examines women's roles in church and society when the magazines addressed these subjects. Editors did not always consciously seek to emulate cultural emphases in their publications; however, the influence of broader culture on the magazines' content is unmistakable. From 1906 to 2006, WMU editors continually reshaped their ideal of Christian womanhood to correspond with gender constructs popular within American culture and Southern Baptist life.

# 2
# Woman's Work for Woman, 1906–1918

Broidery-Work

*Beneath the desert's rim went down the sun,*
*And from their tent-doors, all their service done,*
*Came forth the Hebrew women, one by one.*

*For Bezaleel, the master—who had rare*
*And curious skill, and gifts beyond compare,*
*Greater than old Mizraim's greatest were—*

*Had bidden them approach at his command,*
*As on a goat-skin spread upon the sand*
*He sat, and saw them group on every hand.*

*And soon, as came to pass, a silence fell,*
*He spake, and said, "Daughters of Israel,*
*I bring a word; I pray ye, hearken well."*

*"God's tabernacle, by his pattern made,*
*Shall fail of finish, though in order laid,*
*Unless ye women lift your hands to aid!"*

*A murmur ran the crouched assembly through,*
*As each her veil about her closer drew,*
"We are but women! What can women do!"

*And Bezaleel made answer: "Not a man*
*Of all our tribes, from Judah unto Dan,*
*Can do the thing that just ye women can!"*

*"The gold and broidered-work about the hem*
*Of the priest's robes—pomegranate knop and stem—*
*Man's clumsy fingers cannot compass them.*

*"The sanctuary curtains that must wreathen be,*
*And bossed with cherubim—the colors three,*
*Blue, purple, scarlet—who can twine but ye?*

*"Yours is the very skill for which I call;*
*So bring your cunning needlework, though small*
*Your gifts may seem; the Lord hath need of all!"*

*O Christian women! for the temples set*
*Throughout earth's desert lands, do you forget*
The sanctuary's curtains need your broidery yet?

—Margaret J. Preston
*Our Mission Fields*, October 1907, 33–34

WMU began publishing *Our Mission Fields* in July 1906, at the height of the woman's missionary movement. During this time, Progressive optimism and activism permeated many missions organizations, influencing missionary activities at home and abroad. Women's missions publications of many denominations emphasized the importance of the "uplift" of "heathen" women through the Westernization and Christianization of their societies. Writers for such publications stressed female missionaries' unique roles in ministering to women on foreign mission fields—usually through education, health care, and evangelism—under the rubric of "woman's work for woman." Likewise, articles portrayed missionaries in North America as improving conditions for impoverished women and children through social ministry. Writers also encouraged thousands of women at home to participate in similar ministries in their own communities, as well as to pray for, learn about, and give to support mission work.

*Our Mission Fields* and, beginning in 1914, its successor, *Royal Service*, clearly shared these emphases with the broader woman's missionary movement. These magazines urged women to expand their influence through work that was acceptable to and generally endorsed by male SBC leaders. Like other women's missions publications, WMU magazines challenged their readers to assume unique roles in "uplifting the heathen" overseas, showing social concern at home, and supporting mission work through prayer, study, and giving.

## Missions in the Progressive Era

The woman's missionary movement began in the late nineteenth century, during the "golden age" of Protestant missions in the United States. The rise of the Progressive movement in the country in the decades that followed at first only added to the general missionary zeal. Progressivism, a social and political reform movement, arose in response to problems brought by the industrialization and urbanization of many parts of the United States. Its adherents sought to improve conditions for urban workers, curb child labor, raise living standards for immigrants, and right a wide range of other social injustices. Progressive sentiment was strongest in the urban North, but the movement's influence was felt in the southern United States as well.

Even conservative Southern groups such as Southern Baptists—who eschewed many of the more radical tenets of Progressivism—were influenced by the general climate of reform during this period. Along with other Protestants and thus the majority of the U.S. population at the time, Southern Baptists interpreted the idea of progress on a global scale, especially with reference to the gospel. The late nineteenth-century vision of Manifest Destiny—the God-ordained westward expansion of the United States—led to a postmillennial sense of the providential rightness and inevitability of the spread of Western Christianity around the world. FMB leader T. P. Bell, for example, was convinced that "Christianity is everywhere aggressive; heathenism everywhere on the defensive, and in many cases demoralized and its leaders anticipating defeat."[1] Influenced by Bell and other denominational leaders, many Southern Baptists espoused similar views.

Because of their faith in Western Christianity, early twentieth-century Protestants deemphasized the missiology of Henry Venn, Rufus Anderson, and John Nevius, nineteenth-century missions leaders who had promoted a model of self-supporting indigenous churches. Instead, most Protestant missions leaders understood American culture and Christianity to be inseparable agents of modernization. While realizing that colonial exploitation was dubious at best, these leaders did not hesitate to propose as an alternative a "fine spiritual imperialism," as Baptist missions professor W. O. Carver put it.[2] The gospel, in their thinking, contained truths that would liberate members of all societies from superstitious and harmful premodern practices into a peaceful, forward-looking Christian civilization. In the words of faith mission leader Henry Frost, who was quoted in a 1915 issue of *Royal Service*, "It is always true that Christianity civilizes."[3] Although such sentiments may sound paternalistic to twenty-first-century interpreters, they were widespread and largely uncontroversial in American culture at the beginning of the twentieth century.

The woman's missionary movement interpreted this idea of liberation as an apologetic for mission work with women and children. If the gospel contained emancipating elements for men in a specific culture, the women reasoned, how much greater would be the liberation of the "oppressed" sex and their offspring? Unable to control broader denominational structures, these women used their own organizations within their accepted sphere of influence to meet what they felt were the pressing needs of women around the world. By 1906, the inaugural publication year of *Our Mission Fields*, the woman's missionary movement as well as the broader evangelical missions movement were arguably at their zenith. Four years later, WMU president Fannie Heck claimed, "In no year of the world's history has the word 'missions' been so often on the lips of so many people."[4] By the end of the first decade of the twentieth century, Progressive idealism coupled with evangelistic zeal allowed mission work to capture the attention of American women and men in a way that has never been repeated.

Two ecumenical missions conferences in 1910 reflected the strength of the missions movement at this time. The World Missionary Conference at Edinburgh is generally regarded as one of the most important missions events of the twentieth century. WMU leaders' views about this conference were typical of wider missions thinking. Edith Crane, WMU corresponding secretary and later editor of *Our Mission Fields*, declared, "The echoes of the World Conference of Foreign Missions . . . will long resound, and it is believed many great and significant movements will look back to this time as the date of their birth."[5] Like leaders of many denominations—but unlike many male Southern Baptists—WMU leaders such as Crane demonstrated an affinity with ecumenical missions efforts.

Less well-known but still significant in its impact was the Woman's Missionary Jubilee. Designed to commemorate the fiftieth anniversary of the founding of WUMS, the Jubilee featured a series of ecumenical women's missions rallies in dozens of cities across the United States. Although historian Patricia Hill suggests that women's involvement in missions was declining by this time, Jubilee participants numbered in the thousands.[6] Largely as a result of the Jubilee, more than one hundred thousand copies of the mission study book *Western Women in Eastern Lands* were purchased in its first year of publication.[7] The strength of the woman's missionary movement was obvious from the rapid sales of this volume, written by Helen Barrett Montgomery, the most influential leader of the movement.

Although—somewhat paradoxically—the social reform tendencies of Progressivism would lead to the end of what historian Kenneth Latourette called the "great century"[8] of Christian missions in the coming years, between 1906 and 1918 the activism, optimism, and imperialism of the Progressive Era intensified both women's and men's interest in missions. In spirit, and sometimes in collaborative efforts, Southern Baptists joined other denominations (and nondenominational groups) from across the country in the missions fervor of the day. Through WMU Southern Baptist women participated in missions endeavors similar to those of Methodist, Presbyterian, and Episcopal women, among others. Although their theological conservatism and strong regional identity set Southern Baptist women apart in some respects, WMU magazines of the time reveal that these Baptist women had much in common with others involved in the woman's missionary movement.

Those who are familiar with the somewhat separatist tendencies of the present-day SBC may be surprised by the extent to which WMU leaders considered themselves part of the wider woman's missionary movement and interacted with female missions advocates from many denominations. WMU leaders such as Heck frequently attended ecumenical missions conferences and strategized with other Protestant women's missions leaders. WMU representatives participated in the 1910 World Missionary Conference, 1910 Woman's Missionary Jubilee, 1911 Women's Committee of the Baptist World Alliance (BWA), 1915 Interdenominational Conference of Woman's Boards of Foreign Missions of the United States and Canada, and 1915 Woman's Congress of Missions, among other gatherings.[9] Heck encouraged Southern Baptist women to learn from leaders of other denominations: "I am profoundly thankful that we are not working at this task alone. The woman's missionary problem, solvable, but difficult, will find its answer only by the united wisdom of Christian women of every name. We do not hold the patent for all knowledge on all known missionary methods."[10]

Significantly, then, *Our Mission Fields* and *Royal Service* often included emphases similar to those of women's missions magazines of other denominations. WMU leaders, not content simply to tell the Southern Baptist mission story, helped women understand "how we are linked up with the big movements that are on foot [*sic*] in the world."[11] Numerous issues of these magazines quoted or recommended publications of other missions groups. The October 1911 issue of *Our Mission Fields*, for example, listed on its Magazine References page not only Southern Baptist publications but also the Episcopal *Spirit of Missions*, the Northern Baptist *Missionary Herald*, the interdenominational *Missionary Review of the World*, and the interdenominational *Everyland* for children.[12] Lucy Peabody, chairperson of the Central Committee on the United Study of Foreign Missions, graced the magazine's cover.[13] The relationship was mutual: Montgomery included a photo of Heck—along with those of other female missions leaders—in her book *Prayer and Missions*, which was published by the Central Committee.[14]

Like women of other denominations, WMU writers agreed with woman's missionary movement leaders such as Peabody and Montgomery about the importance of "woman's work for woman." Although Montgomery was a Northerner, women in missions organizations in both the North and the South consistently respected her missiology, if not always her feminist ideology. Many woman's missionary movement publications conspicuously failed to mention Montgomery's support for "the complete emancipation of women,"[15] as she put it in 1910, while assenting enthusiastically to her more frequent argument for female mission work. Discussions of "heathen" women among missions leaders such as Montgomery and Peabody stirred scores of American women to action.

These women endorsed Montgomery's assertion about the importance of female missionaries: "Men were shut out from ministry [to women in the 'Orient'] by the iron bars of custom. . . . The missionary wife at best could give only a fragment of her strength and time to the work; then why not send out women to minister to the uncounted millions of women in non-Christian lands?"[16] According to such a view, God could use female missionaries alone to reach out effectively to women overseas. Writers for *Our Mission Fields* and *Royal Service* frequently included heart-rending descriptions of "heathen" women in other countries, quickly followed by descriptions of female Southern Baptist missionaries' efforts on their behalf. Like others involved in the woman's missionary movement, these WMU leaders emphasized women's unique ministry to women and children.

## "Uplifting the Heathen" Overseas

Because the primary concern of the woman's missionary movement was work among women and children overseas, many of the organizations that arose from this movement sent or supported only foreign missionaries.[17] WMU supported both FMB and HMB, but between 1906 and 1918 editors devoted more pages of *Our Mission Fields* and *Royal Service* to international than to domestic mission work. The glamor of "exotic" locales no doubt contributed to this emphasis, as did wealthy WMU editors' perception of the neediness of women overseas. Under the guidance of editors Fannie Heck (1907–1911), Edith Crane (1911–1912), Claris Crane (1912–1914), and Elia Nimmo (1914–1920), WMU magazines detailed the condition of these "heathen" women at some length. Articles explained how female missionaries ministered to such women through education, health care, and direct evangelism.

*Our Mission Fields* and *Royal Service* included numerous descriptions of the plight of non-Christian women, using what Joan Brumberg calls the "formulaic vocabulary" of the woman's missionary movement—language full of references to the degradation of women in other cultures.[18] The magazines' studies of mission work in particular countries or regions regularly included elaborate accounts of the poor conditions for women in each place, written in the florid, maudlin style of the time. These descriptions varied little from country to country; non-Christian women worldwide were portrayed as oppressed and hopeless without Christ. WMU writers during this period unhesitatingly referred to them using phrases such as "custom-bound" women, "a multitude of helpless women," "densely ignorant and hard to reach . . . mentally and morally paralyzed," women living a "narrow secluded life," "poor, stupid, heathen women," and "willing slave[s] to . . . husband and children."[19] A 1918 *Royal Service* feature about China asserted that "the minds and hearts of the women are bound up tightly like their feet."[20] The same issue of the magazine included a graphic of a stone bulwark, with "the women" as the foundation beneath stones representing ignorance, superstition, idolatry, immorality, polygamy, widowhood, child marriage, and suicide. At the top of the fortress, the flag "heathenism" waved brazenly. The caption below the illustration challenged readers, "Will our faith bring down these walls?"[21]

This type of language, prejudiced as it may seem to present-day readers, was standard fare for women's missions publications. According to Julia Carrothers, a Presbyterian missionary to Japan, "Heathen women are under a curse" of "filth and vice."[22] D. B. Wells, a writer for *Woman's Work for Woman* magazine, similarly described her experience with a non-Christian woman: "Can one ever forget the first contact with real heathenism? Waking up one morning . . . in Old Mexico . . . I saw it . . . [an] old woman, with the dull, sullen, hopeless face, the unkept [*sic*] gray hair, the ragged dirty clothing, is fixed in my memory for the rest of this life at least."[23] The "heathen" woman's physical haggardness was regarded as an outward expression of the spiritual emptiness of life without Christ and as a motivation for Christian women to share the gospel—and American grooming habits—with others like her. To female missions advocates, Christianization and civilization were closely related; a culture that accepted the gospel would quickly realize numerous forms of social progress as well.

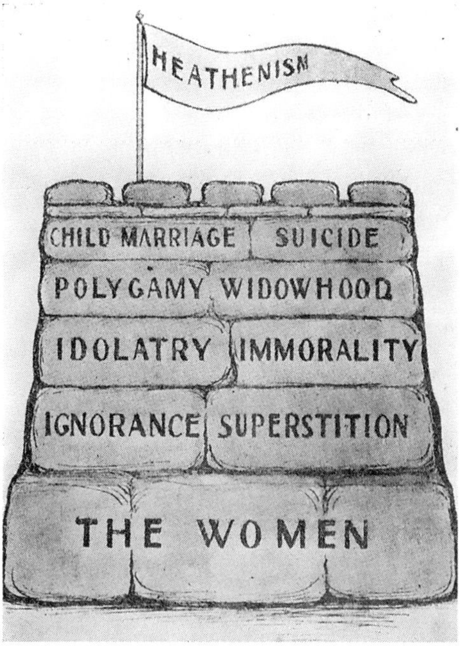


6. Illustration from October 1918 *Royal Service.* (Used by permission of WMUA.)

Female missionaries especially emphasized the need to improve social conditions for women overseas, perhaps because of a sense of sisterhood and their own past experiences of powerlessness among men. Throughout this period, *Our Mission Fields* and *Royal Service* consistently included reports about the transformation that took place in women's lives because of the gospel. A program on China, the largest Southern Baptist—and probably the largest Protestant—mission field at the time, asserted, "To sum up what Christianity has done for women in China, we may say it has opposed the casting away of female infants, it has sct its facc against foot-binding, it has made parents see it was their duty to educate their daughters, it has discountenanced infant betrothals and forced marriages, it has admitted women to the same church privileges as men, it has proclaimed that the same standard of purity is binding on men as on women, it has enjoined monogamy and given woman her rightful place in the family. It has been the greatest force for the elevation of woman."[24] Such fervent sentiments, written in this instance by WMU leader Laura Whitfield, mirror Montgomery's belief in the "emancipatory nature of the pure religion of Jesus."[25] In comparison to the "heathen" women with whom they worked, female missionaries—and their supporters—considered themselves privileged.

WMU editors, then, focused on bringing liberation to women overseas, not to themselves. Aware of the conflicting opinions about women's roles within the SBC and even among their own constituency, each of the magazines' editors during this period avoided taking a stance on contemporary debates regarding the rights of women. Editors made no mention of women's suffrage, a contested right urged by organizations such as the National Woman Suffrage Association and—beginning in 1917—the National Woman's Party. Editors also failed to mention the internal denominational debate over allowing women to serve as messengers to the SBC annual meeting, a multiyear struggle that culminated with a vote in the women's favor in 1918. Socialized as demure Southern ladies, WMU editors and editorial committee members were more hesitant than Northern women to advocate for parity in their own context. Even bold FMB missionary Lottie Moon opposed introducing "Northern ideals of womanhood" into Southern Baptist mission work.[26] More significantly, WMU editors recognized that women's role in the SBC was a controversial subject among their readers. As Gregory Vickers claims, the women's silence on this topic was "politic, not apathetic."[27] In order to move forward without opposition, these women embraced missions, not suffrage, as a cause in which all could find unity. As demands for female enfranchisement provoked dissension among Southerners and especially among Southern Baptists, WMU magazines simply "stuck to missions."[28]

Inevitably, though, WMU magazines' descriptions of "heathen" women —and subsequently Christianized "new women"—revealed the editors' ideal of Southern womanhood, transported into various cultural settings. A letter from Kate White, an FMB missionary in Brazil, bemoaned the "poor weak race with their empty lives—no homes (only houses)—no home ties! The women are not honored as wives and queens of the home, but are simply the woman in the house."[29] The expression of home life White observed in this context did not align with her understanding of a woman's proper role, and so she sought to "emancipate" the foreign women by inculcating to them her own value system. Similarly, a missionary writing to readers of *Our Mission Fields* demonstrated her own cultural ideals as she expressed delight at the change in a "dark home" when its matriarch became a Christian: "That neatly dressed, placid-faced woman sitting there has no palm oil on her hair. We listen as she spells out the words of her Sabbath-school lesson, and the little children playing on the floor are singing 'I am so glad that Jesus loves me.'"[30] Other missionaries described WMU groups formed by converted women on the mission field.

Clearly, Westernization was an expected—and celebrated—by-product of Christianity.

From today's vantage point, the weaknesses of a missions theory that borders on imperialism are obvious. However, this method proved quite attractive to women in the early twentieth century. By describing from their cultural perspective the spiritual and social needs of women and children in other countries, writers aroused the sympathy of like-minded American women toward missions. Readers became convinced that it was necessary for them to fill a unique ministry role with women and children overseas. According to North Carolina WMU leaders, "The condition of women in heathen lands is an irresistible appeal to Christian women."[31] Depictions of "enlightened" foreign women in WMU magazines—as well as other women's missionary publications—strengthened women's convictions of the importance of taking Christianity and "Christian culture" to transform lives in every land. Like other women's missionary magazines, *Our Mission Fields* and *Royal Service* included numerous descriptions of female missionaries doing just that.

Although "woman's work for woman" was not the sole focus of *Our Mission Fields* and *Royal Service*, the ministries of female missionaries were frequently highlighted in their pages. Writers described the work of both single and married women serving overseas, and the missionaries themselves often shared their stories with eager readers. Articles sometimes portrayed married female missionaries in stereotypical, androcentric terms: a "charming young wife," a "gentle but brave wife," a wife who "presides at the piano" while her husband preaches, and so forth; but they nevertheless emphasized that these women were missionaries in their own respect.[32] Thousands of Southern women likely thrilled to their stories.

Realistically, though, much of married women's time on the mission field was consumed with household duties. Even the few married women who attended WMUTS—which prepared women for mission service abroad or at home—were commended for completing their course "through struggle" while most of their time was dedicated to making a home for their husbands.[33] If finding extra time was hard for these women while they were still enjoying the familiar comforts of the United States, one can only imagine how much more difficult it was for them to set aside time from their family duties once they were overseas. Indeed, missionary Maude Burke Dozier confirmed the demands that a married woman faced on the mission field: "She is called upon to entertain more in the Orient than is usual in America. . . . She must mean more to the children than is necessary to the mothers in America. . . . Certainly a liberal share of her time must be given to the duties of her home."[34]

During the height of the woman's missionary movement, however, thousands of single women flocked to the mission field to join their married counterparts. As the February 1911 *Our Mission Fields* program noted, "One hundred years ago there were no female single missionaries on the [Southern Baptist] foreign field doing work among the women and the children. Today work of that character is carried on by at least five thousand female missionaries."[35] For the first time, large numbers of women, free from family constraints, engaged in ministries to women and children overseas. Because in most Protestant denominations these women could not be ordained or even attend seminary, they quickly developed new mission strategies that differed in many cases from men's mission work. Where men served as pastors, developing and maintaining institutional forms of the church, women worked within—and gradually enlarged—their prescribed sphere by caring for the human needs they saw around them.

Thus single female missionaries from many denominations rapidly developed extensive ministries in fields such as health care and education. For example, a Presbyterian missionary referred to as Miss Hunter cared for "poor suffers" of the plague in India; a Miss Bunch led the Methodist Girls' School in Malaysia.[36] Some male missionaries also served in these ministries, but the large numbers of women on the mission field helped elevate education and health care until they were at least as important as more direct evangelistic efforts such as preaching. According to one estimate, by 1911 only half of the American missionaries in China were engaged in direct evangelistic work—a significant change from previous years. Most of the rest were teachers.[37]

In keeping with this trend, WMU magazines—like other woman's missionary movement publications—most frequently depicted female missionaries' role as that of educator. Educational ministry assumed prime importance as female missionaries arrived in new areas and sought to influence the lives of women and children—usually girls. First missionaries typically established primary schools in rural villages. When girls completed these schools, high schools—often boarding schools—were begun. Eventually missionaries established a few women's colleges for exceptional graduates. (Male missionaries correspondingly began seminaries for men.) In some areas, female missionaries also created training schools to increase uneducated women's knowledge of the Bible and evangelistic work, including preparation for service as traveling "Bible women." In China, for example, by 1909 Southern Baptists counted a remarkable seventy-nine primary schools, twelve girls' high schools (and nine boys' high schools), one "high grade Baptist College," and four women's training schools.[38] This pattern of school establishment was typical among not only Southern Baptists but also missionaries of many other denominations.

Writers for *Our Mission Fields* and *Royal Service*—and other woman's missionary magazines—considered education to be an effective way to evangelize large numbers of girls on the foreign mission field. Pupils studied the Bible as well as traditional disciplines. A 1907 writer explained that at the Saltillo School for Girls, students received instruction in personal evangelism and handed out tracts door-to-door with the school's principal.[39] The following year, another writer described a typical village school in China: "Large parts of the Gospels are committed to memory, also the Lord's prayer and many hymns; so that a child who remains for several years is likely to have a good foundation of Bible truth beside considerable knowledge of the three thousand Chinese characters."[40] Similarly, missionary S. E. Jones of Mexico reported in 1909 that pupils at her school studied "Biblical truths in opposition to Catholicism, Mormonism, spiritualism and other false isms."[41] Typical of Progressive missions efforts, doctrines and methods of Western Protestantism were an important part of converts'—and potential converts'—training.

But these schools' curriculum was broader than just religious instruction, and missionaries were often successful in training girls in many parts of the world at higher levels than those they had previously been allowed to attain. Writers for *Our Mission Fields* and *Royal Service* often sought to demonstrate the value of educational missions efforts by describing the influence and Christian character of graduates of Baptist mission schools. Several girls who had attended the Madera Institute in Mexico returned to teach in primary schools established by the mission, while others "married pastors, and are letting their light shine in the home."[42] Graduates of the Girls' Boarding School in Canton, China, went out "to do Bible woman's work . . . and otherwise to teach by life and word what it means to be a Christian."[43] These women's stories convinced missions leaders that educational work was profitable and even essential for the propagation of the gospel, especially in places that might otherwise be hard to reach. Writers rejoiced in what they considered a meaningful missions role for women; as missionary teacher Julia McKenzie exclaimed, "So glorious is our work, I'd rather do it than to be the noblest of earth's crowned queens."[44]

In *Our Mission Fields* and *Royal Service*, as in other women's missionary magazines, letter after letter reported the results of female mission schools and advocated the necessity of educational work with women and girls. One writer claimed in 1908 that "the elementary school which has been found gathered at the knees of women missionaries from the days of Ann Judson to the present, is a mighty force 'for making Christ known to the world.'"[45] Thus the writer used the legacy of revered missionary Ann Judson to promote her contemporary emphasis. Again prioritizing educational ministry, another article declared the following year that "the door of the school room is today the open door to the life of China."[46] And in 1915 missionary Alice Duval asserted to *Royal Service* readers the importance of her efforts: "It is hardly necessary to explain why educational work is not only an advantage, but an absolute necessity for any denomination that would grow, either at home or abroad."[47] In Duval's thinking, the benefits of mission schools were so obvious that they needed no explanation.

A justification of educational work was provided, however, by Laura Whitfield in the December 1914 issue of *Royal Service*: "The character of the great, new China will be determined in no small measure by the women of the nation, and what these women will be depends very largely upon whether they receive education, and upon the type of that education. To give Christian training to many, and through them indirectly to many more of the young women who are to be the mothers and teachers of new China, is to invest life or money in a way that will yield the richest of returns."[48] Although this description was specific to China, writers made similar comments about the education of women and girls in many other countries where Southern Baptists sent missionaries. A 1909 program pleaded for the establishment of Southern Baptist girls' schools in Japan by quoting a Northern Baptist educational missionary in that country: "Sometimes when . . . I realize what it is going to mean in this country, if the future mothers are really strong Christian women, wielding a strong influence for Christ in their homes and through their children, I feel as nothing could be too much trouble to do for them."[49] Along with women of several denominations, WMU leaders espoused the idea that the education of girls was "the quickest method for elevating the home life of the East" and a way of "training the leaders of the future."[50] Within the home, editors believed, Christian women exercised significant authority. Hence education not only evangelized individual girls; it also eventually Christianized entire nations.

Thus WMU members happily pledged to support all the schools led by female FMB missionaries—likely the majority of Southern Baptist mission schools.[51] Nearly every issue of *Our Mission Fields* and later *Royal Ser-*

*vice* included some mention of mission schools and female missionaries' significant roles in their leadership. For example, the December 1917 issue of *Royal Service* included photographs of seven girls' schools in China on its back cover.[52] This emphasis on women's unique role in teaching women and girls was shared by the woman's missionary movement as a whole; education was probably the most common form of mission work for female missionaries in the Progressive Era. WMU's focus on educational ministry, then, was closely aligned with broader "woman's work for woman" thinking.

After education, health care was the mission strategy mentioned most frequently in *Our Mission Fields* and *Royal Service*, as well as in other publications of the woman's missionary movement. During this period, a number of Southern Baptist women served as nurses or physicians on the foreign mission field, often in mission hospitals. In Lai-Chow-Fu, China, for example, unmarried missionary nurse Cynthia Miller "ha[d] charge of the woman's department in the medical work."[53] Both single and married women found satisfaction in medical missions careers, although male physicians continued to dominate the field. References to missionaries such as "Mrs. Neal, our woman physician in Mexico"[54] not only demonstrated that female medical missionaries were in the minority, but also revealed the affinity women at home felt with "their" female physicians around the world.

According to *Our Mission Fields*, the foreign mission field presented an "unparalleled" need for female medical workers.[55] Medical missionaries were considered pioneers, able to enter areas where people were resistant to other forms of evangelistic work but in need of healing.[56] More importantly, writers expressed, female health care workers were able to reach the half of the population that might otherwise remain unreached. As with other "woman's work for woman" strategies, these workers' ministry was directed primarily toward women and children. Using the heart-rending characterizations of "heathen" women common in the woman's missionary movement, writers spoke of the great need for female physicians to care for the "secluded" women of Eastern lands. One 1913 program quoted M. R. Edwards, who explained: "There are tens of thousands of sick women who would rather die than have a male physician attend them in sickness. And because there are no women physicians in many large districts[,] they die."[57]

A 1908 writer, however, explained the necessity of female medical ministries in terms not of women's choice but of men's oppression of women—a view common within the woman's missionary movement. In many foreign lands, the writer lamented, women were "kept within four walls" and only "rarely . . . male physicians are permitted to relieve their sufferings."[58] Although this explanation and Edwards's sentiment differed in their logic, both assumed that without care from Western female medical workers, women in a number of countries would suffer greatly and perhaps die. This supposition about the superiority of Western women's medical efforts likely motivated many young women to consider a career in medical missions; as a 1910 program declared rather stereotypically, "Women have always rejoiced in the relief of suffering."[59]

And relieve suffering the women did, at least according to a 1908 writer who graphically described female medical missionaries' work with "the little slave girl, almost murdered, the childless wife whose husband is about to discard her, the thirteen year old daughter-in-law, whose mother-in-law has beaten her eye out, and the child whose poor little crushed feet, inflamed and suppurating with decaying bones, appeal to her from the cruel bandages."[60] Such descriptions reveal missionaries' belief that "heathen" customs were often emotionally and physically harmful, as well as the women's corresponding priority of providing Western medical care among women and children overseas. During 1907 alone, Jessie Pettigrew of north China reported a total of 6,842 patients at her mission's dispensary and 57 in the hospital.[61] And Edna Teal of Yangchow, China, explained in a 1916 letter, "If you will walk over to the hospital with me in a few minutes you will soon understand why I have not written as often as I would wish."[62] Other female medical missionaries, busy tending to the needs of the sick, probably found no time to submit letters to *Our Mission Fields* or *Royal Service.*

While many of these women chose to serve as medical missionaries primarily because of their compassion, some most likely also appreciated the professional opportunities such work provided. On the mission field, female physicians were more widely accepted than they were in America. One-third of the missionary physicians serving overseas in 1910 were women—a greater ratio of female to male physicians than existed in the United States nearly seventy years later.[63] Such women often had greater freedom and experienced less discrimination in their medical practices on the mission field than they did at home. Though serving as a female Southern Baptist missionary in the early twentieth century was not an experience that many today would describe as liberating, such service provided a comparative level of equality and autonomy that women—especially professional women—did not frequently experience in the United States at that time.

But the foremost motivation that WMU magazines ascribed to women's service as medical missionaries was to share the good news of Jesus Christ with non-Christian women. Female nurses and physicians consistently offered "healing for soul as well as body,"[64] hoping by their caring acts and evangelistic words to convert their patients to Christianity. They served not just out of sympathy or a desire for autonomy but also because of the conviction that only women could effectively minister to "heathen" women. Southern Baptist women were probably familiar with Helen Barrett Montgomery's claim that female church attendance increased in missions locations with women's hospitals.[65] They attempted, through their service, to enlarge that number even more. In devoting their attention to women's health care, Southern Baptist missionaries joined hundreds of other female workers from various denominations in hopes of healing and ultimately evangelizing women in many lands.

In addition to education and health care, direct evangelism was the final component of the tripartite strategy of the woman's missionary movement. Although women's evangelistic efforts were mentioned less frequently in *Our Mission Fields* and *Royal Service* than were medical ministry and educational work, multiple articles in these magazines did portray evangelism as a common task for female Southern Baptist missionaries. Most of these references depicted female missionaries talking with women and children in homes, sometimes accompanied by national "Bible women" they had trained. In 1906 a woman called simply "one of our missionaries" mentioned her attempt to witness when she paid a visit to a non-Christian woman in her home.[66] Ten years later, Henrietta North of China told women in America that she was "privileged to give the Gospel to many heathen women."[67] The same month, Maude Dozier of Japan expressed, "It is a great joy to have so many girls, young women and older women come to my home where I have the opportunity of showing them the way of life eternal."[68] Evangelism in these instances apparently did not involve large gatherings or formal preaching but instead included a natural extension of women's traditional role in the home. The female missionary broadened her sphere to incorporate the homes of the world.

But this expanded role included the same limitations as other forms of "woman's work for woman." Almost all references to direct evangelism in WMU magazines portrayed female missionaries as working within a "separate sphere" to evangelize only women and children. In the October 1907 issue of *Our Mission Fields*, a missionary, presumably male, was happy to tell readers that "Mrs. Pruitt has kept up a weekly prayer meeting in a village about a mile away." He then reported that "a great many women and children have heard the Gospel during the year."[69] In deference to Chinese culture—and in accord with the gender roles of the American South—female missionaries such as Pruitt apparently did not regularly share the gospel with groups of Chinese men. In at least one instance, however, a female Southern Baptist missionary was credited with helping begin a church. A report in *Our Mission Fields* on mission work in Cuba, edited by Heck, claimed that "through the agency chiefly of Miss [Jennie] Edwards . . . and her orphanage, a church had been established." The writer went on to explain, though, that Edwards asked FMB to "supply a missionary pastor," and a young male theological student was appointed to the position.[70] It is not surprising that pastoring a congregation was seen as an exclusively male role at this time.

Certainly it is possible—perhaps probable—that Southern Baptist women took at least a few more liberties on the mission field than did their compatriots back home. For example, on one occasion revered Southern Baptist missionary Lottie Moon confessed that she talked with a mixed audience: "I hope you won't think me desperately unfeminine, but I spoke to them all, men, women, and children. . . . I should not have dared to remain silent with so many souls before me sunk in heathen darkness."[71] However, no articles in *Our Mission Fields* or *Royal Service* mentioned female missionaries' teaching or preaching to men. The evangelistic roles that these magazines portrayed for missionary women conformed to the model of ministry with women and children prevalent in the woman's missionary movement. Editors may have carefully monitored the information they included for conservative American readers—or perhaps more likely, the evangelistic ministries of most female Southern Baptist missionaries simply fell within the accepted mores of the day. Like female teachers and medical workers of many denominations, most Southern Baptist women engaged in evangelistic mission work appear to have understood their efforts to bring "uplift" to "heathen" women and children not as a limitation but as a special calling.

## Showing Social Concern at Home

While the woman's missionary movement elevated the call of women to "heathen" lands above all else, Southern Baptist women did not neglect mission work in the United States. From 1906 to 1918, *Our Mission Fields* and *Royal Service* described the ministries of missionaries and ordinary Southern Baptist women as they worked to combat social problems, minister to immigrants, and work in additional ways to help the poor and needy. These domestic missions roles were influenced not only by the woman's missionary movement but also by the social gospel movement.

The latter movement, which most scholars consider the religious wing of the broader Progressive movement, emerged in the North in the late nineteenth century in response to the unprecedented problems of urbanization and industrialization. It focused not only on saving individual souls but also on redeeming broken social structures. One of its prominent advocates, theologian Shailer Mathews, described the social gospel as "the application of the teaching of Jesus and the total message of the Christian salvation to society, the economic life, and social institutions such as the state [and] the family, as well as to individuals."[72] With this optimistic perspective of religion's role in societal progress, social gospel advocates emphasized humanitarian improvements such as reducing poverty, ending child labor, and fighting corruption. They focused their efforts on the burgeoning urban centers of the North, which were far more numerous than similar cities in the predominantly rural South and far more likely to be populated by impoverished immigrants. Social gospel influence, however, was felt in the South to varying degrees through organizations such as the Southern Sociological Congress, which assembled prominent Southern leaders to discuss social concerns.

Unlike most male Southern Baptists, WMU leaders were strongly influenced by social gospel thinking and incorporated key aspects of the social gospel into their home mission work.[73] WMU's Baltimore location, along with the ecumenical bent of its leadership, contributed to the organization's openness to the social gospel. In an urban area bordering the North, WMU staff members more frequently encountered the message of the social gospel than did their counterparts in the Deep South. Influential WMU leaders such as Heck, Annie Armstrong, and personal service chairman Lulie Wharton attended interdenominational conferences and lectures, worked with socially minded Southern Methodist women, and participated in the Southern Sociological Congress. Heck was even elected second vice president of this congress in 1914. These women, absorbing social gospel ideas from ecumenical interaction—and even from a few Southern Baptist seminary professors—led WMU leaders to espouse what Paul Harvey calls "a social consciousness that strode out in advance of the male progressives in the SBC."[74] WMU writers freely used the language of social Christianity in a way that few Southern Baptist men did.

The reforms that WMU leaders advocated to help the needy at home were similar to and likely stemmed from the social and spiritual "uplift" they desired for women and children overseas. Though the social gospel movement was distinct from the woman's missionary movement, both were shaped by the same Progressive ideology that influenced Protestant denominations (and broader American thinking) during this period. As Kendal Mobley notes, both movements aimed for the kingdom of God on earth, demonstrated interest in social and political reform, expanded women's sphere, and regarded American society as generally good.[75] Both probably also aroused interest among Southern Baptist women at least in part because of the dearth of leadership roles these women were permitted to hold in their churches and the SBC, apart from WMU. At home as overseas, women's lack of involvement in official church and denominational affairs led them to develop a more holistic missiology that focused on human welfare and social concerns as well as ecclesiology and conversion.

Without a doubt, female missionaries' achievements in the areas of education and health care for "heathen" women overseas influenced their mission work in America. Helen Barrett Montgomery even alleged that missionaries on the late nineteenth-century foreign mission field pioneered the same social ministry techniques that others adopted at home a generation later.[76] Patricia Hill calls the home mission movement the "biggest threat" to female foreign missions advocates;[77] however, this claim certainly does not seem to have been true for the SBC. Southern Baptist women's knowledge of mission work overseas evidently helped them become cognizant of the needs of lower-class women around them and carry out ministry strategies to meet those needs. Through their involvement with WMU and the SBC, most female Southern Baptist missionaries working among immigrants and the poor in America were probably at least initially more familiar with the ideology of the woman's missionary movement than that of the domestic social gospel movement, although their ministries combined elements of both.

The "separate sphere" missiology of "woman's work for woman" prevalent in women's foreign mission work was also evident in Southern Baptist women's missions efforts at home. Characteristic of evangelical womanhood in this period was the broadening of women's responsibility from mothers of the home to "mothers" of the community, and Southern Baptist women adopted this new role for the good of their communities. A few worked to combat the causes of social ills such as poverty; others ministered to immigrants; and even more aided the needy. In response to the hypothetical criticism that "this is not a woman's work," Wharton stated in the first issue of *Royal Service*, "No one can deny that her [woman's] work is primarily homekeeping, care of children and ministry to the sick and helpless. The facts that her house cannot be kept clean unless the neighborhood is clean; that disease finds its insidious way into her family through neglect and ignorance over which she has no control; that the moral standards of the vicinity of her home affect the character of her children; that 'the other woman' of few advantages and less intelligence and helpless little ones everywhere need her championship and guidance—these facts are forcing woman to reach out and take her share in preparing 'the home without walls,' in addition to fitting her own children for the new environment."[78] Such language reflected evangelical women's conviction that they were morally obliged to help their communities for the good of their families and others. The use of words such as "neglect," "ignorance," and "helpless" resembled characterizations of "heathen" women overseas, whom wealthy editors such as Heck felt also needed Southern Baptist women's "championship and guidance." Although such descriptions of needy women overseas were more frequent than those of women in America, both expressed the Progressive sentiment that middle- and upper-class Christian women had a responsibility to bring "uplift" to disadvantaged women and their children.

In addition, the ultimate motivation behind such "uplift," whether overseas or at home, was Christianization—first, of individuals, and second, of societies. WMU magazines carefully stated the priority of evangelism and personal conversion, sometimes amid almost contradictory claims about the importance of social change. The October 1910 issue of *Our Mission Fields* described options for mission service in American cities: "Whether teaching in a mission school, visiting the sick, visiting prisoners, gathering mothers into mothers' meetings, conducting sewing schools for children, or organizing and conducting neighborhood prayer-meetings for women—each [WMS] organization must decide this question for itself, *never losing sight of the fact that the end and aim of the work is the salvation of souls.*"[79] Southern Baptist women ministering in the United States, like their peers overseas, were careful to mention individual conversion as the primary goal of their work. And in the same manner as foreign missionaries, they engaged with Progressive optimism in a number of ministries designed to effect change upon societies as well as individuals. In both instances, women negotiated distinct roles in bringing personal and social "uplift" to women and children whom they felt were in desperate need of their guidance and compassion. The driving motivations of the woman's missionary movement were at work at home as well as abroad.

As the woman's missionary movement and the social gospel movement developed, WMU leaders sought new ways to involve both female missionaries and laywomen in mission work across the South. In 1909 WMU developed a new emphasis called personal service: "social service with the Gospel as its motive and conversion as its aim."[80] This emphasis was strongly shaped by Heck, whom historian Delane Tew calls "the most liberal leader of WMU."[81] WMU magazines also demonstrate the ongoing influence of personal service chairman Lulie Wharton. Wharton acknowledged that personal service was created in part "to live up with the most progressive thought and movements of the day" but also asserted that such ministry was "as old as the Gospel itself."[82] In their writings, Heck, Wharton, and other WMU leaders interspersed biblical teachings about "sick [people] to be cheered" and "strangers to be welcomed"[83] with oblique references to social gospel ideas in order to convince readers of the importance of personal ministry to the needy.

Present-day scholars discuss at length the connections between WMU's personal service program and the social gospel. Carol Holcomb convincingly demonstrates that the program's leaders "utilized social science methodology, embraced Progressive Era reforms, and called upon social gospel ideas to carry out its work."[84] Even WMU members who were unfamiliar with the social gospel learned some of its ideology through personal service, which writers soon portrayed as the primary form of home mission work for Southern Baptist women. According to *Our Mission Fields*, personal service represented not a usurping of but a "deepening" of home missions: "Home missions does not mean the spiritual care of ourselves and our children in elegant houses of worship. . . . It means ministering to the destitute and neglected. It means mothering the unmothered. . . . It means the prayerful study of sociological conditions. It means willingness to take hold of the unesthetic [*sic*], bald needs of sinful humanity with none of the romance and indefiniteness of distance."[85] In accord with this expanding understanding of home mission strategies, WMU soon developed leaflets and a manual with further instructions for personal service work. Personal service was added to WMU's organizational aims in 1911, and it was included the following year in the Standard of Excellence, a checklist of requirements for high-performing Women's Missionary Societies. In her characteristically bold manner, Heck even claimed that personal service was "without doubt one of the largest, if not the largest, and most significant movements begun not only by the Union, but, as far as I am aware, by any other of the large woman's missionary organizations in recent years."[86]

In contrast to previous home mission strategies, personal service could be undertaken not only by professional missionaries but also by laywomen, whether individually or in groups. Beginning in 1909, *Our Mission Fields* and later *Royal Service* frequently emphasized the importance of each woman's finding "some personal service to the poor, the sick, the degraded as an expression of her love."[87] Instead of relying on a handful of missionaries to minister in the United States, Heck explained, WMU could become "a vast company of women" engaging in similar efforts in their own communities.[88] Ever mindful of their denominational commitments, WMU leaders promised HMB and FMB that personal service would "in no way interfere with or overlap the work the societies are now doing and the far larger things they expect to do" to support missions; women would simply multiply their efforts through personal service of their own.[89] WMU's fulfillment of this promise, through continued sacrificial levels of giving to home and foreign mission work, probably kept its personal service program from closer scrutiny by SBC leaders.

As part of their personal service emphasis, writers for *Our Mission Fields* and *Royal Service* frequently discussed women's role in combating social problems, using language similar to that of social gospel leaders. Articles highlighted social ills such as liquor use, child labor, urban slums, "disregard of the Sabbath," and similar "destroyers of public health and purity."[90] Heck, Wharton, and other writers urged WMU members to work to eliminate these problems. Beginning in 1914, WMU adopted a "declaration of sympathy" as part of its plan of work and began printing it in the organization's annual *Year Book*: "As a body of women, we declare ourselves in sympathy with all that makes for the spiritual and physical uplift of our country—peace, prohibition, Sabbath observance, the family altar and the crusade against poverty, illiteracy, vice, disease and crime."[91] This statement clearly reflected Progressive concerns—issues that were of greater importance to groups such as the Southern Sociological Congress than to conservative religious organizations such as the SBC, which were more interested in personal conversion. Of all the roles that WMU magazines of this period suggested for women, combating deep-seated social problems was the most divergent from broader SBC interests.

Yet writers and editors did not hesitate to voice concern for what Wharton called the "wide scope of Christ's redemption,"[92] which incorporated societies as well as individuals, as well as the importance of discovering and altering the underlying causes of social evils. The March 1916 issue of *Royal Service* even quoted Samuel Batten's address before the Southern Sociological Congress: "They [churches] must teach men that it is just as wicked a thing to kill a family by renting them an unsanitary tenement as to throw strychnia in the milk bottle. . . . It is well enough to take the sickly child out of the slums; but it is more sensible to abolish the slums."[93] Similar statements appeared throughout WMU magazines, with special emphasis on urban areas. Writers urged their readers to help the city find "salvation from the un-Christlike spirit of selfish commercialism," reminding them of their "new responsibility" to warn young women who moved to cities for wartime employment of "dangers of which they never knew at home."[94] Articles accordingly discussed the problems of alcohol, urban housing, industry, working conditions in mills and factories, and public health, alongside arguments against foot binding and other social evils that affected women overseas. Clearly editors and other WMU leaders hoped to expand women's understanding of social problems and to encourage them to take action not only by helping victims but also by righting the injustices that led to victimization.

Throughout these discussions, women's role in ameliorating unjust conditions was often stated or implied. Although many of the problems that were mentioned could also be addressed by men, the omission of such topics from most SBC magazines, newspapers, and annual meeting minutes demonstrated male denominational leaders' lack of concern about them. WMU leaders, however, worked to convince women of the rightness of their role as "mothers" of society. A 1914 writer claimed, "Every city presents a housing problem. For the friendly visitor, there are several lines that may be definitely and tactfully pursued and women are preeminently fitted for this."[95] Because of their nature, their domestic experience, and their gradually expanding roles, such writers argued, women were well prepared to address social ills. Articles about poor working conditions often focused on women and children, as did features about social problems overseas. Writers sometimes included specific examples, such as this excerpt from the poem "Bargains" about an article of clothing: "Your price is right, and we do not fail / To buy. But what of the girl who works / In the gloom and the grime and the great wheels' whir? / The fear is there, and it lurks and lurks— / Just what was the cost to her?"[96] Such personalization of widespread social problems encouraged the magazines' female readers to identify with the women and children affected by these problems and thus to increase their efforts to end them.

From excerpts such as this, a casual reader of *Our Mission Fields* or *Royal Service* might have concluded that the majority of Southern Baptist women worked to combat large-scale social problems. This assumption is likely unjustified. Although WMU magazines addressed social issues, they did not usually describe related ministries in which Southern Baptist women were involved. Ministry reports from church groups were strangely absent; articles were generally confined to exhortation or explanation. As Holcomb explains, local women's societies that were involved in personal service often "utilized the methods and programs but ignored the more liberal ideas of the literature."[97] Although WMU leaders sought to portray Southern Baptist women as leading the cry against social injustice, most WMU members were probably not on the front lines of such a battle. Some of these women, however—especially in urban areas—were probably involved in personal service work that aided immigrant families.

Ministry to recent immigrants and "those far off, historically and racially," was at the heart of the "new home missions," an article in the March 1915 issue of *Royal Service* claimed.[98] During this period, thousands of immigrants streamed into the United States, some with little more than the clothes on their backs. *Our Mission Fields* and *Royal Service* included frequent references to what Mrs. Alex Beale in 1918 called the "teeming millions of foreigners who have poured into our country."[99] Although these immigrants were not as numerous in the South as in Northern urban centers, Beale reminded women that there were at least "a few families of these aliens" in every Southern community.[100]

Most WMU members viewed immigrants—like the women they encountered overseas—not as equals but as souls in need of the "uplift" that they believed would occur through Americanization and Christianization. Using language similar to the characterization of "heathen" women in other countries, a 1915 article spoke of "sad, crushed women and girls, boys and men" who were "casting off the shackles of bondage to sin and coming forth into the light and liberty of the sons of God."[101] One 1910 writer seemed surprisingly open-minded for her context, referring to the "blindness of prejudice," in this case against Native Americans.[102] But more frequently writers agreed with Laura Whitfield, who in 1915 discussed the "danger of social equality" for other races—a problem she called the "devil's bugaboo."[103] A few writers, such as Victor Masters of HMB, demonstrated seemingly contradictory attitudes within the same article. In a 1910 program, Masters wrote of the "obligation to preach the gospel to the black race . . . and to behave toward them with kindness and helpfulness," but a page later he warned of the impending danger to the "wholesome American blood . . . threatened by the swarms of polyglot people."[104] Most white Southern Baptists of the time—members of the race dominant in American society—felt themselves superior to immigrants. Still, WMU members' Christian compassion and allegiance to the gospel (as they understood it) would not allow them to exclude other races as unworthy of the message of Christ.

WMU magazines during this period described women's involvement in numerous ministries to immigrants, including Bible distribution, kindergartens, good will centers, and industrial schools that taught skills such as sewing and cooking. As with women's foreign missions efforts, such roles encouraged women's efforts in domestic and charitable work rather than in male-dominated institutions. Articles frequently mentioned Marie Buhlmaier, who ministered among new arrivals at the port of Baltimore, often through Bible distribution.[105] Bertha Lee Mitchell, who worked in a kindergarten for Italian immigrant children in Tampa, Florida, was also commonly named and on occasion submitted letters to the magazines herself.[106] Similar letters detailing laywomen's ministry to immigrants revealed that local missionary societies—especially in urban areas—were more frequently engaged in this type of work than in efforts to combat social problems.

Perhaps the quintessential form of women's ministry to immigrants included in *Our Mission Fields* and *Royal Service* involved settlement houses, later renamed good will centers. Clearly modeled after the social settlement houses established by Progressive leaders such as Jane Addams, these centers demonstrated WMU leaders' commitment to broader social gospel trends. Adopting the Progressive idea of community "uplift," good will centers additionally made "every effort . . . to bring souls to Christ."[107] Beginning in the mid-1910s, the centers established a Christian presence in numerous impoverished urban communities, usually ones populated by immigrants. The most well-known good will center in the South was in Louisville, Kentucky, where WMUTS students implemented the social service ideas they learned in their coursework. As Whitfield expressed in typical Progressive language, this center and others across the region aimed for the "general uplift of the neighborhood, the regeneration of individuals, and the development of the children" through training programs, women's and girls' clubs, and a variety of other efforts.[108]

WMU magazines frequently included features claiming that the centers' work often transformed individuals, if not communities. In 1915 the Canton Baptist Mission in Baltimore reported that "twenty-four mothers were converted" and that mission participants gave $23.87 to missions.[109] Such descriptions revealed that center workers transmitted to participants their Southern Baptist priorities of salvation and mission work. In 1917 leaders of the good will center in Meridian, Mississippi, similarly rejoiced that because of the center's influence, a young woman "who had become content with working in the knitting mill and was gradually losing her self-respect" began college, became "a devoted Christian," and aspired to

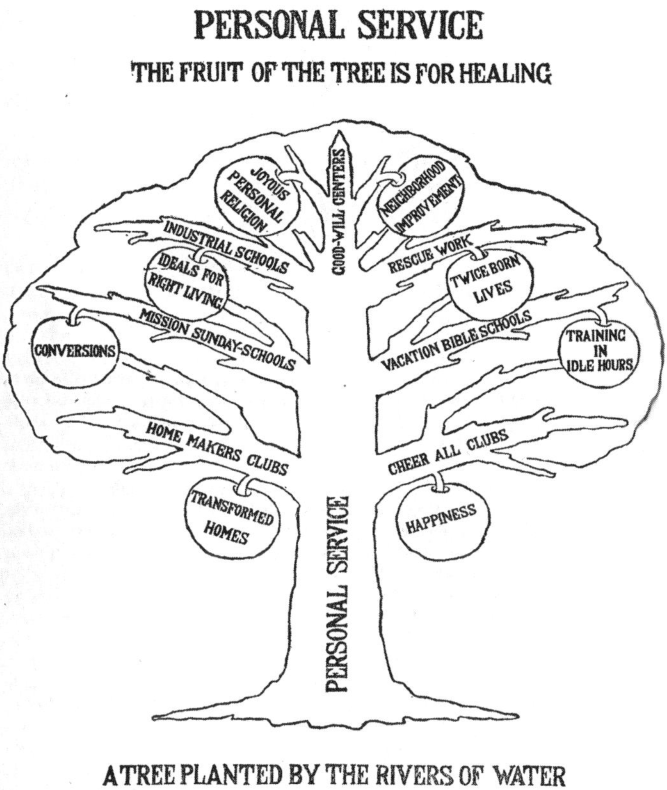


7. Illustration used to represent personal service in multiple WMU publications. (Used by permission of WMUA.)

be a teacher.[110] Leaders of other centers happily recounted to readers of *Royal Service* stories of women's success—as they regarded it—and encouraged these readers to establish new good will centers.

Women's role as "mothers" of their communities was evident in the work of good will centers. While government agencies often focused on male "heads of households," centers offered Homemakers' Clubs and Mothers' Meetings that empowered neighborhood women within their own realm of influence as they voiced concern for "problems of everyday life" and considered the need for "educated motherhood."[111] Programs in cities such as Louisville, Baltimore, Houston, Richmond, Norfolk, and Atlanta reached out especially to immigrant women—often the last members of their families to be touched by American influence—in order to bring about "a home more quickly and accurately adjusted to the unfamiliar environment of America."[112] For immigrant girls, centers provided "a great helpful sisterhood" through Cheer-All Clubs.[113] Girls learned from Baptist workers traditional Southern women's roles and etiquette, such as playing the piano and demonstrating table manners (a "most popular lecture" in Louisville),[114] as well as personal service techniques. Leaders of good will centers, like other Southern Baptists of the day, believed that Americanization was essential for immigrants to integrate into their new communities.

Center workers doubtless received satisfaction from the unique role they played in the "uplift" of their communities as they ministered primarily, though not exclusively, to women and children. The expanding scope of evangelical womanhood afforded these women the opportunity to add community ministry to the roles regarded as appropriate for their gender, and WMU magazines indicated that they pursued this new role with enthusiasm. Like female missionaries serving overseas, Southern Baptist women working with immigrants to the South advocated not only personal but also social change, convinced with Progressive optimism of the rightness of both their religion and their culture. As WMU's 1918 annual report put it, "Can there be any nobler, more Christ-like service than to minister to the stranger in our midst and win her allegiance to America and to Christ?"[115]

Although good will centers were generally located in urban areas, even the many WMU members living far from a city center could engage in a variety of ministries to help other women. WMU magazines portrayed such women as undertaking general ministry efforts to help the poor and needy. Many local societies that did not report work to combat social problems or to help immigrants did describe in *Our Mission Fields* and *Royal Service* their personal service efforts among their neighbors. In 1917 women in Georgia wrote about visiting "sick, prisoners, hospitals"; a group in a small town in Kentucky collected clothes for needy children and began a "flower fund" to cheer the sick; and South Carolina women led devotions with shut-ins and visited a children's home.[116] Still other groups conducted Vacation Bible Schools, distributed tracts, and knitted items for soldiers. WMU leaders in some states even employed female missionaries to engage in such ministries full-time. For example, missionary Ollie Cowles led women in southeast Missouri to minister on the "productive mission field" of mining towns.[117] Such types of personal service were clearly popular in many different settings.

These forms of ministry were likely prevalent among local societies because they conformed to traditional roles for Southern women.[118] They also continued efforts that Ladies Aid Societies had begun years earlier, "mak[ing] it easy in many churches for such [Ladies Aid] societies to unite with the Woman's Missionary Society."[119] Women embraced these ministries because they focused on the home and involved a compassionate, feminine response that male leaders found nonthreatening. As one writer stated, "The home life of the people, which they [female home missionaries] touch so beautifully and so constantly, is where the seed planted in the church service must be watered and fostered."[120] Few Southern Baptists doubted that ministry in the home was part of women's sphere.

Although editors dedicated a significant amount of space in *Our Mission Fields* and *Royal Service* to discussing social woes and reporting on ministries to immigrants, other forms of aid to the poor and needy appeared in reality to be the mission strategies most commonly reported by laywomen. All of these approaches—no matter the frequency with which they were enacted—reflected women's concerns for improving the social and spiritual conditions of other women in their neighborhoods and across their country. Influenced to varying degrees by social Christianity, WMU members' domestic mission work demonstrated the goals of Christianizing and "civilizing" women and children that were also evident in the woman's foreign missions movement.

## Supporting Missions

From 1906 to 1918, *Our Mission Fields* and *Royal Service* recounted stories of women who were actively ministering to other women overseas and in the South, including laywomen involved in personal service efforts. But these magazines also portrayed mission support as a vitally important role for local women's societies. A 1915 Bible study quoted the Central Committee's book *The King's Business*: "Every Christian woman must have part in this work personally or by proxy. Christ does not say to a part of the Church, 'Go ye into all the world,' and to the remainder 'Stay at home and study Browning and Ibsen, enjoy good music, play bridge, and give to Me the time which you may have left.'"[121] Although writers acknowledged that not everyone could go, they asserted that every Southern Baptist woman had an important role in praying for, learning about, and giving money to help missionaries—especially women—serving in other countries as well as in the United States. These mission support roles, frequently discussed in WMU magazines, reflected the emphases of the broader woman's missionary movement.

Prayer was a foundational part of the mission support role urged upon all WMU members. Since the beginnings of the woman's missionary movement in the nineteenth century, women had faithfully gathered to pray for missionaries and mission work around the world; Helen Barrett Montgomery claimed that the movement had been "born and nurtured in prayer."[122] *Our Mission Fields* and *Royal Service* indicated that Southern Baptist women continued this tradition through both individual and group prayer for missions. Multiple WMU writers expressed the importance of prayer, especially in the second half of this period. Writers described prayer as the "force" missionaries desired most, the most important channel for "self-expression in service," the "most powerful instrument" church members had, and "the very life" of missions.[123] Although because of lack of experience "very few [women] in each society . . . [would] lead in public prayer,"[124] these women slowly developed their skills and their voice through WMS meetings, whose programs always included prayer. Women enlarged their understanding of how to pray as they interceded for female missionaries "by name, and as though it were your own precious sister you were naming."[125] Southern Baptist women gradually joined with other female missionary supporters in praying for women's missions efforts around the world.

WMU members also observed weeks of prayer for foreign and home missions each year and prayed individually through the "Missionary Calendar of Prayer for Southern Baptists." This calendar, which included daily prayer requests for WMU workers and specific missionaries (usually women), was similar to calendars produced by other denominations involved in the woman's missionary movement. However, it failed to mention the World Day of Prayer in which other women's groups participated, perhaps in deference to male SBC leaders' suspicion of ecumenical efforts. The request for January 25, 1918, was typical: "[Pray] for the Misses Bertha Mitchell, Fannie H. Taylor, Nell Dekle, and Martha A. Dabney, working with Italian children in Tampa."[126] Readers prayed for other women as they ministered within—and simultaneously expanded—the sphere deemed acceptable for Southern Baptist women. WMU first published a prayer calendar as a stand-alone piece in 1907; it began to be included as a regular feature in *Royal Service* in 1918.[127]

Although these prayer emphases were evident in WMU magazines, prayer was not as frequent a topic as mission study or giving. As Patricia Hill explains, the fewer words devoted to prayer were likely a result of the growing secularization of American society, which affected not only WMU but other women's missionary groups as well.[128] WMU materials, as well as publications of other women's groups, depicted prayer as an important role for women in missions. However, their dearth of features about prayer revealed that other areas of mission support—such as mission study—probably took precedence for women during the early twentieth century.

According to *Our Mission Fields* and *Royal Service*, studying about missions was a key role for Southern Baptist women during this period. The importance of education, an emphasis of the broader Progressive movement, was reflected in the growing trend toward mission study among women's groups, including WMU. WMU leaders apparently agreed with leaders of the wider woman's missionary movement, who claimed that the idea of missions would gain "very little permanent hold" without mission study.[129] Just like women's missionary magazines of other denominations, *Our Mission Fields* and *Royal Service* assigned mission study a place of primary importance. Several pages in each issue were dedicated to programs sharing information about topics such as "Japan—the new world power," and "great missionary movements of the last three decades."[130] Local Women's Missionary Societies used these programs during their monthly meetings. Accordingly, the editors of *Our Mission Fields* urged readers to purchase "one [copy] to cut [for use in meetings] and one to keep."[131] Subscriptions grew rapidly as societies followed the recommended programs.

Led by Fannie Heck, WMU also joined other women's missionary organizations in encouraging the reading and group study of books related to missions. This type of "intensive education" through mission study became a part of WMU's Standard of Excellence; societies were encouraged to hold at least one mission study class a year.[132] In 1916 writer Laura Whitfield promoted the benefits of such classes: "Besides the general educational value of this study the mind broadens to a world outlook. . . . Prayer is made more effective because more intelligent and specific. . . . It trains leaders for better methods of missionary finance, and it makes people more ready to give for missions. . . . People are more willing to render service in community and church. . . . Some will hear the call to service in the mission field."[133] Although not all Southern women had the opportunity to pursue formal higher education, writers and editors explained, they all could profit from the many advantages of mission study. Well-educated WMU editors created for their generally less privileged readers a new role as "missionary expert[s]."[134]

Though WMU magazines promoted mission study goals similar to those of other women's missionary organizations, WMU declined to participate fully in the interdenominational Central Committee on the United Study of Missions (later renamed the Central Committee on the

United Study of Foreign Missions). This program began as a result of the Ecumenical Conference on Foreign Missions held in New York in 1900, which—surprisingly—most key WMU leaders did not attend. Although the reason for their absence is not entirely clear, perhaps they deferred to male SBC leaders, who were hesitant to support a conference whose women's program included men as "a goodly portion of the audience."[135]

Through the Central Committee, thousands of women across many denominations studied the same missions book each year. Between 1900 and 1921, the committee sold approximately two million mission study volumes.[136] Although WMU materials often referred to the books published by the Central Committee, they did not formally promote study of the recommended works, probably because of anti-ecumenical pressures from SBC leaders, who sometimes exhibited sectionalist sentiment and "Baptists only" Landmark tendencies. This stance revealed the way that the women navigated denominational power structures without completely distancing WMU's efforts from the broader woman's missionary movement. Even though *Our Mission Fields* and *Royal Service* did not advocate annual study of the Central Committee's books, they portrayed mission study as a key role for committed laywomen, just as other women's missions materials did.

*Our Mission Fields* and *Royal Service* likewise joined other publications of the woman's missionary movement in emphasizing giving to support mission work and female missionaries. Whitfield quoted the Central Committee's book *The King's Business*: "To awaken and develop in all the women of the church a true and complete view of the stewardship of life and life's possessions is but one step beyond its program of education and prayer in the definite responsibility of the woman's missionary society."[137] In this spirit, WMU leaders stressed the importance of women's roles in giving of themselves and their possessions to support mission work at home and overseas. They especially emphasized the necessity of "stand[ing] back of the work" during World War I, when one writer lamented "the withdrawal of men and means by the demands of the war."[138] While these women were often excluded from formal employment, during this period they realized the influence that their combined sacrificial gifts could have upon the SBC's home and foreign missions efforts.

Although WMU, unlike many women's missionary groups, did not send its own missionaries, it did espouse the same "separate sphere" ideology, primarily supporting female Southern Baptist missionaries who worked with women and children. As early as 1890, FMB recommended that WMU financially support all of its female missionaries.[139] WMU also contributed to "all the forms of work" carried out by HMB's female missionaries.[140] Around 1915 *Royal Service* began regularly featuring names of new female Southern Baptist missionaries appointed to serve overseas. The November 1915 issue, for example, included this list: "Miss Clara Keith, trained nurse to Africa; Miss Cora Hancock, educational work in the Girls' School at Abeokuta; Miss Lora A. Clement, to Kong Moon, China; Miss Carrie Hooker Chiles, kindergarten work at Fukuoka, Japan; Miss Grace McBride, trained nurse to China; and Miss Helen F. Eustis, to Sao Paulo, Brazil."[141] Printing such names encouraged the special responsibility Women's Missionary Societies felt to support "their" missionaries serving around the world—and posed no threat to male denominational leaders, whose efforts benefited from the women's contributions. Female missionaries' appeals for new workers only heightened the urgency with which society members gave.

Rarely did *Our Mission Fields* and *Royal Service* discuss the relatively small financial assets of most Southern women, compared to those of men. Instead of focusing on this inequity, editors and writers encouraged women to give back systematically a portion of everything they had been given, "planning in advance that your gift may be worthy of the One to whom you give it."[142] Although *Our Mission Fields* and *Royal Service* did not frequently encourage women to give their "butter and egg money," as earlier publications had, they still emphasized the need for women to give sacrificially. A 1906 writer described how even a Native American convert committed to "give him [God] little money, all I got," setting aside seventy-five cents for missions.[143] Substantial sums pooled from "mites" given by women such as this were a hallmark of the woman's missionary movement, and WMU magazines accordingly encouraged women to consider the value of their combined gifts—which editor Elia Nimmo in 1918 called a "tremendous force for both home and foreign missions."[144] Such statements quickly became reality for WMU; as the women's financial contributions increased, their influence within the denomination grew as well.

Although small donations were the norm, writers challenged women with guilt-inducing pleas for larger sacrifices, especially for annual offerings for international missions and domestic missions. A poem from William Vories questioned a woman's spending "eleven cents for missions and a dollar bill for lace"; similarly, Mary Faison Dixon compared the cost of Easter bonnets with missions giving.[145] A 1914 editorial reminded women, "We have trained the [Foreign Mission] Board to expect a large Christmas Offering. The missionaries are buoyed up by it each year. Shall we disappoint them this Christmas?"[146] And a 1917 article noted that world missions efforts cost much less than America's expenditures in World War I—and, the writer apparently believed, were an even more worthy cause.[147] The responsibility of supporting female missionaries led to continual appeals for money from all women who did not want to "leave the Lord"—or the SBC—"out."[148]

WMU magazines described the ways that women gave not only money but also supplies to support missionaries. Early issues of *Our Mission Fields* described women's efforts in assembling and mailing "missionary boxes" across the United States, primarily to missionaries on the western frontier. Each box contained supplies such as food, clothing, and books, which helped local societies form a "tender, binding link" with missionaries on the field.[149] A chart in the July 1909 issue of *Our Mission Fields* demonstrated that in the early years of the twentieth century, the cash value of women's box contributions was actually higher than the dollar amounts they donated to HMB and FMB.[150] The hundreds of boxes sent by Women's Missionary Societies demonstrated their determination—like that of other women's missionary groups—to give of their money and possessions to support female missionaries and missionary families as they brought "uplift" to non-Christians.

SBC leaders quickly recognized the potential of women's gifts, as FMB corresponding secretary R. J. Willingham acknowledged: "The women have a mighty influence."[151] Perhaps in response to such leaders' urging, *Our Mission Fields* and later *Royal Service* began to emphasize funds that did not pay missionary salaries, but supported missionaries more indirectly. As early as 1907, a writer encouraged giving to the Church Building Loan Fund, which helped provide "houses for the churchless churches of the West."[152] A 1916 editorial from Nimmo discussed the importance of supporting the Judson Centennial Fund, which helped build overseas institutions such as "our own special new responsibilities[,] the Sao Paulo and the Kumamoto schools for girls."[153] And with growing frequency, writers and editors encouraged giving to relieve FMB's debt. As Nimmo explained with fascinating logic, even though WMU consistently came close to its giving goals for foreign missions, the board's debt was WMU's responsibility in "a deep moral sense," since informed WMU members had encouraged the board to expand the scope of its mission work.[154] WMU members' mission support efforts thus only increased their institutional commitments.

WMU's enthusiastic giving to these causes soon led FMB corresponding secretary J. F. Love to maintain that the women had saved the board from "humiliating failure."[155] Such sentiments contributed to a growing sense of WMU's importance within the denomination as a whole and in turn to WMU members' commitment to the SBC. By 1915 WMU members, who made up less than 8 percent of the SBC's membership, gave more than 30 percent of the total funds raised for home and foreign missions; women in most other denominations did not give nearly as much.[156] WMU's creation of an "emergency women" program in 1918—to respond to "emergency call[s]" for denominational financial support—demonstrated the women's growing dedication to broader SBC causes and foreshadowed the role of denominational support that would become primary in *Royal Service* in the years that followed.[157] SBC leaders, who years earlier had questioned the wisdom of a separate organization for women, grew increasingly aware of the power of the women's financial support. WMU magazines' emphasis on giving not only reflected the concerns of the wider woman's missionary movement; it also demonstrated WMU leaders' growing commitment to supporting myriad denominational causes.

According to a 1915 *Royal Service* writer, multiple readers testified that their involvement in WMU made them "a better and a broader woman."[158] During the Progressive Era, when women's roles were gradually expanding outside the home, and when optimism and imperialism provided impetus for evangelism and social change, WMU magazines suggested challenging new options for their readers. While remaining mostly within the bounds of contemporary Southern Baptist norms, editors clearly identified with the woman's missionary movement. Influenced by this movement, from 1906 to 1918 *Our Mission Fields* and *Royal Service* portrayed women as involved in the "uplift" of non-Christians overseas and at home.

WMU editors Fannie Heck, Edith Crane, Claris Crane, and Elia Nimmo pitied "heathen" women in other countries, using language similar to that of women's missions advocates across many denominations. These editors described female foreign missionaries—primarily single women—as engaging in the same kind of work highlighted in other women's missionary publications: teaching, administering health care, and evangelizing. WMU magazines were similarly concerned with improving the spiritual and physical circumstances of women and children in the United States. Reflecting a confluence of the woman's missionary movement and social gospel thinking, writers urged both appointed missionaries and laywomen to aid the needy in their communities through a variety of personal service efforts. Such ministries reflected the woman's missionary movement's emphasis on women's unique roles in Christianizing and "civilizing" other women and children. Like women of other denominations, WMU leaders developed far-reaching ministries that gradually expanded their own sphere of influence.

Just as other women's missions publications, *Our Mission Fields* and *Royal Service* also discussed women's part in supporting missions through prayer, mission study, and giving. Although WMU did not fully embrace interdenominational mission support efforts, the organization's emphases generally mirrored those of other woman's missionary organizations. In this way, WMU leaders adopted a more ecumenical position than did most male Southern Baptists. WMU magazines also indicated that the women's success at raising money for missions caused them to gain respect within their denomination and to diversify the objects of their giving. This development, coupled with the gradual (but potentially divisive) gains in women's status that WMU writers failed to mention, prepared Southern Baptist women for a new role in their denomination in the post–World War I period.

# 3
# Supporting the SBC, 1919–1945

Pay the Tithe

*There's a call comes ringing through your heart and mine,*
*Pay the tithe! Pay the tithe!*
*'Tis a call of duty from a voice divine,*
*Pay the tithe! Pay the tithe!*

Chorus
*Pay the tithe, the blessed Gospel tithe,*
*It will shine on every shore,*
*Pay the tithe, the blessed Gospel tithe,*
*It will bless you ever more.*

*May the grace of giving everywhere abound,*
*Pay the tithe! Pay the tithe!*
*And a host of tithers everywhere be found,*
*Pay the tithe! Pay the tithe!*

*Let us not grow weary with our gifts of love,*
*Pay the tithe! Pay the tithe!*
*Thus we'll gather jewels for our crown above.*
*Pay the tithe! Pay the tithe!*

—Myrtle Creasman
"Tithing," *Royal Service*, August 1926, 36

In the years following World War I, mission work declined in popularity as new ways of thinking arose among many Americans. The woman's missionary movement also gradually weakened. As "woman's work for woman" thinking evolved into an ideology of "world friendship," almost all Protestant women's missions organizations were absorbed into broader denominational structures. However, WMU continued to expand its influence among Southern Baptist women and within the SBC as a whole—a surprising fact that most scholars of the woman's missionary movement have overlooked.

Between 1919 and 1945, WMU's *Royal Service* magazine emphasized women's roles in spreading the gospel, supporting missionaries, supporting national women on mission fields, and, most important, supporting the Southern Baptist denominational program. True to its conservative SBC context, *Royal Service* portrayed evangelism as the primary goal of women's missions efforts. The magazine also encouraged WMU members to increase their denominational commitment by supporting both female and male Southern Baptist missionaries, as well as national women leaders overseas, whom editors considered the "golden sheaves" reaped from previous missions efforts among the "heathen." The best way for women to fulfill all of these roles, according to *Royal Service*, was to support the complete program of the SBC, especially through financial gifts. Article after article highlighted tithing, fund-raising campaigns, and denominational debt relief as priorities for WMU members. These new emphases reflected the denominational identity developing among Southern Baptists, providing the SBC with much-needed support and ensuring WMU members an ongoing position within the denomination.

## American Missions after World War I

In the aftermath of World War I, Southern Baptists and all Americans faced a world less certain than they had previously imagined. Progressivism, with its optimistic, world-changing spirit, quickly gave way to a more isolationist national climate. The United States tightened its immigration policies and looked inward as the economic struggles of the Great Depression followed initial postwar prosperity. In the predominantly rural South, cotton prices dropped precipitously, threatening the welfare of many farmers. Prewar ideals of progress and reform no longer seemed useful to most Americans. In addition, the rise of scientific inquiry and biblical criticism challenged the Protestant consensus that had dominated the nation for the previous century. The highly publicized 1925 Scopes Trial in Dayton, Tennessee, highlighted the debate about the teaching of evolution in public schools—and the growing tension between conservative Christians and supporters of modern science. Around the same time, new methods of biblical study gained prominence among mainline religious scholars, casting doubt upon traditional interpretations of a wide range of biblical texts. Influenced by these methods and by their exposure to other cultures during World War I, some Americans questioned the traditional, exclusive truth claims of Christianity.

In reaction to this scientific and theological "modernism," some conservative Christians worked vigorously to return their denominations and their nation to what they believed were the fundamentals of their faith. These "fundamentalists" became prominent in the 1920s, especially through the opposition they mounted against trends in Northern mainline denominations, within which Progressive thought was most evident. Fundamentalists opposed not only evolution and biblical criticism but also cultural developments such as the emergence of "flappers," women who wore their hair and their skirts short and engaged in behaviors considered risqué. The effects of fundamentalism were also felt to some degree in the South, including among Southern Baptists. Within the SBC, fiery J. Frank Norris—pastor of First Baptist Church of Fort Worth, Texas—decried modernism, arousing anxiety about this threat among a minority of Southern Baptists. Unlike in most Northern denominations, though, the SBC's overwhelming conservatism prohibited much significant controversy from developing. One *Royal Service* writer did voice concern that Southern Baptist youth would be "eclipsed in the whirlwind of modernism which is sweeping through our schools and even through some of our churches."[1] The topic, however, was mentioned few other times in the magazine's pages. *Royal Service* editor and WMU corresponding secretary Kathleen Mallory largely left the debate over modernism in the SBC to the handful of men who suspected there was danger of such influence. As was their tendency throughout the century, WMU leaders avoided theological controversy, evincing their socialization as Southern women who prioritized harmony over conflict. Instead of discussing divisive issues that interested some male Southern Baptists, WMU leaders attempted to unify their constituency around the subject of world missions.

But among some Protestants, even mission work became a topic of debate during this period. After World War I, nations as diverse as India, Morocco, and the Philippines gradually asserted their independence and expressed aversion to Western control, including Christian missionary activity. Some leaders overseas and in the United States accused mission boards of cultural imperialism, questioning the propriety of imposing Western Christianity upon people in other lands. In order to accommodate these questions, several mainline religious scholars—commissioned by John D. Rockefeller Jr.—prepared a 1932 report titled *Re-Thinking Missions*. This controversial project proposed that Protestant mission work focus almost exclusively on social issues and the ethical dimensions of the gospel instead of on personal conversion. The report declared that "the relation between religions must take increasingly hereafter the form of a common search for truth,"[2] a claim that sparked vigorous discussion throughout the nation.

Soon popular magazines such as *Ladies' Home Journal* and *Atlantic Monthly* published articles debating the necessity of traditional mission work. At the same time, mission boards in mainline denominations such as the Methodist Episcopal Church and the Presbyterian Church worked to redefine missions as development work carried out in partnership with national leaders. Although fundamentalists and less militant conservatives continued to affirm the importance of evangelistic efforts, such work lost popularity among many Protestants, especially in the North. For the first time, influential leaders in the United States argued that traditional Protestant mission work was unnecessary or outdated. The "great century" of Protestant missions had come to an end.

Despite this controversy over mission strategies, most Protestant women's missionary groups continued to emphasize missions efforts, working to maintain their historic balance between evangelistic and socially oriented ministries. However, the polarization of opinions about missions made this task more difficult than it had been in previous years. As Dana Robert observes, in many denominations—such as the Northern Baptist Convention—fundamentalists did not want women to be involved in any type of mission work or ministry, especially social ministry, while modernists downplayed the need for evangelistic missions efforts at all. Facing criticism from both sides, female missions leaders such as Helen Barrett Montgomery struggled to maintain a moderate stance, emphasizing missions needs rather than arguing about doctrine.[3]

But such leaders in both the North and the South found that their traditional motivation of "woman's work for woman" was no longer relevant for much of their missions effort. Descriptions of pitiful "heathen" women did not attract many American women to the missions enterprise after World War I; instead, they increasingly provoked accusations of imperialism and archaism. In addition, the emergence of female Christian leaders on the mission fields prompted women's missions organizations to reframe their efforts as partnerships with the women of the world, using a new missiology of "world friendship." This emphasis, popular especially among women's groups in mainline denominations, highlighted women's work for peace and justice worldwide. It relied less on an appeal to women's unique capability to help other women than on women's general sense of benevolence and global "sisterhood"—significant topics in the wake of a world war. Children's materials produced by women's missions organizations often shared a similar theme: WMU's *World Comrades*, a monthly publication for boys and girls, was promoted as "a magazine to girdle the world with friendliness."[4] This shift in thinking from specialized mission to friendship eliminated some of the urgency many women felt to take the gospel to women and children around the world.

By this time some women also found the idea of a unique women's sphere restrictive instead of empowering. With the passage of the Nineteenth Amendment in 1920, American women were no longer excluded from the franchise—although in practice, this privilege was often extended only to white women. The National Women's Party, originally a suffragist organization, even proposed a comprehensive Equal Rights Amendment in 1923. In addition, women's employment, while still limited, increased slightly during and after World War I, even in the South—where a *Royal Service* writer observed "young women in practically every line of industrial work . . . [and] in nearly every profession."[5] Faced with such new opportunities, Christian women less frequently participated in single-gender missions organizations and social clubs. And like others across the nation, they invested less energy in old Progressive community reforms, instead becoming preoccupied with their own homes and families. The missions movement of their mothers and grandmothers failed to capture the attention of many American women after World War I.

The women who did continue to participate in the woman's missionary movement probably noted a change not only in its missiology but also in its leadership. Groups that had begun through the efforts of a few grassroots volunteers gradually established urban headquarters filled with highly educated, paid staff. In addition, most women's missions publications exchanged their chatty, conversational tone for more formal language—for example, discussing missions as "a science"[6]—that likely proved less interesting to many laywomen. This approach neglected the piety and preferences of the everyday women who undergirded the movement. Gradually women's missionary leaders found themselves to some degree distanced from their own constituency.

The same movement toward professional leadership and corporate structure that influenced female mission supporters also affected male denominational leaders in the post–World War I period. In many denominations, this trend manifested itself in a desire for greater efficiency and centralization. Male leaders began to question the necessity of women's missions organizations, which they claimed often duplicated the efforts of their denominations' primary mission boards. Without a distinctive "woman's mission for woman" motivation, women's missions groups were forced to justify their existence or merge into existing denominational structures. The responses of female leaders varied. Many agreed with Montgomery: "Cannot we cooperate all the better in joint undertakings, for having the separate work which each does better alone?"[7] Others, though hesitant to change, were reassured by the men's promises that women would for the first time become equal members of denominational boards instead of functioning as subordinates to male leaders.

Despite some women's misgivings, most women's missionary organizations were absorbed into larger denominational structures over the course of several decades. This occurred in the United Brethren Church in 1909; the Methodist Episcopal Church, South in 1910; the Disciples of Christ in 1919; the Protestant Episcopal Church in 1919; the Presbyterian Church in 1923; the Congregationalist Church in 1927; the American Baptist Convention in 1955; the Episcopal Church in 1958; and the Methodist Church in 1964.[8] After these mergers, women's missions efforts never regained their previous prominence; despite male leaders' promises and perhaps their good intentions, denominational mission boards failed to provide equal representation to women at home or overseas. Female missions leaders who had once worked to liberate "heathen" women now found themselves confined, in part because their own successes had reduced the perceived need for "woman's work for woman." Ironically, these women—removed from leadership in their own organizations—were poised to advocate broader roles for themselves in their churches and denominations in the decades to come.

In the SBC, however, WMU maintained its auxiliary status with little difficulty throughout this period—a significant and surprising fact that few have noted. While women and men of other denominations questioned conversionist sentiments, WMU's *Royal Service* maintained its focus on spreading the gospel, true to conservative Southern Baptist ideals. In addition, the magazine emphasized women's roles in supporting not only female but also male Southern Baptist missionaries, as well as national women who emerged as leaders on SBC mission fields. These new tasks enabled WMU members, unlike women in mainline denominations, to continue their missions efforts despite the decline of "woman's work for woman" missiology. More important, such roles provided WMU with a new emphasis that increased the organization's influence within the denomination: supporting the complete program of the SBC. *Royal Service* portrayed this denominational support as women's primary role in missions from 1919 to 1945.

## Spreading the Gospel

During this period, *Royal Service* first emphasized evangelism as an important role for women, demonstrating a conservative missiology that dismissed modernist doubts about mission work. Editors Elia Nimmo (1914–1920) and Kathleen Mallory (1920–1948) did occasionally acknowledge that a growing number of women and men were asking, "Is the day of foreign missions over?"[9] One writer lamented that after World War I, "even the churches seemed to lose their world vision."[10] But writers and editors unswervingly encouraged women to pursue traditional mission work. While the controversial *Re-Thinking Missions* opined that "there is little disposition to believe that sincere and aspiring seekers after God in other religions are to be damned,"[11] *Royal Service* encouraged its readers to reframe the conversation: "It is not a question if the heathen can be saved without Christ. It is a question if we can be saved if we keep Him to ourselves."[12] And even this statement—which downplayed theological discussion about the eternal destiny of the "heathen"—represented a more moderate position than that of most *Royal Service* writers. These women did not appear ashamed to assert that leading others to faith in Christ was a primary role of both the missionary and the woman's missionary society.

Indeed, *Royal Service* portrayed conversion as the ultimate goal of women's (and men's) foreign mission work. While multiple articles discussed medical and educational projects overseas, writers emphasized the evangelistic impact of these efforts more frequently than they had in prewar years. In a 1919 article, Isa-Beall Neel not only affirmed that "whether in hospital, dispensary or school, the main purpose of the missionary effort is to evangelize"; she went on to quote missionary R. T. Bryan: "Any work that does not directly or indirectly assist evangelism has no part in our [Southern Baptist] program."[13] Perhaps in reaction to modernists' postwar "re-thinking" of the purpose of missions—or in response to fundamentalists' emphasis on "soul-winning"—Neel affirmed the primacy of evangelism in all missions efforts, displaying strong support for this task in the denomination's work.

Similarly, frequent program writer Myrtle Creasman relayed the sentiments of the group of FMB missionaries serving in Nigeria: "You understand that all of our work is *evangelistic*. . . . Our schools, hospitals and dispensaries—everything has as its central purpose the saving of the souls of the people."[14] Careful to clarify the goal behind their institutions and actions, missionaries such as these confirmed the April 1931 program's conclusion that "evangelism and missions are different names for the same child."[15] Efforts such as educating girls and treating ailing women were no longer presented as essential ways to bring "uplift" to the helpless "heathen"; instead they were considered means to the greater goal of world evangelization that Southern Baptists increasingly emphasized after World War I. Clearly *Royal Service* writers expected Southern Baptist women around the globe to make "doing missions" synonymous with "sharing the gospel."

This emphasis on evangelism was even more prevalent in *Royal Ser-*

*vice*'s references to home missions and personal service work. The magazine suggested that sharing the message of Christ with other women was an important role not only for vocational missionaries but also for WMS members. As a 1923 writer affirmed, "We cannot . . . enjoy the senses of sight and hearing and be unaware of the great need for evangelization in our midst."[16] Frequent targets of women's evangelistic work in the South included immigrants, Jews, "Negroes," Indians, impoverished mountaineers, and urban slum dwellers—all of whom middle-class white Southerners considered members of a lesser race or social class. Writers detailed personal service efforts designed to reach these groups for Christ, sometimes using the same gender-based charitable strategies that had made the personal service program successful before the war. Women in Chattanooga built a good will center; the center in Louisville continued its Mothers' Club and Cheer-All Club; missionary Mildred Bollinger led a Daily Vacation Bible School in East St. Louis; and a WMS in Louisiana reached out to "the stranger, shut-ins, [the] hungry and [the] cold."[17]

Immediately after World War I, some social gospel influences were still evident in *Royal Service*'s Personal Service articles. Two 1919 features highlighted the Southern Sociological Congress, and a 1920 article expressed concern for "the child in industry."[18] Likewise, writers continued to discuss WMU's "moral standards": "world peace; patriotism; enforcement of national prohibition; Sabbath observance; sacredness of the home; maintenance of the family altar; high womanly ideals of speech, dress and conduct; better industrial conditions for women and children; public health; Christian education; and Americanization."[19] Women were frequently encouraged to promote these standards in their own communities. During the interwar years, articles supporting "peace on earth"—instead of "mutilating, starving, impoverishing, desolating" war—also appeared in the magazine.[20]

However, most personal service efforts detailed in *Royal Service* beginning in the 1920s were more evangelistic and less overtly related to the social gospel than those of previous years. As the fundamentalist-modernist controversy developed, social gospel thinking became increasingly suspect among many Southern Baptist leaders. Victor Masters of HMB accused social gospel leaders of association with "pantheism and evolution," modernist belief systems that most Southern Baptists abhorred.[21] Without a leader as socially minded and influential as Fannie Heck, who had died in 1915, and with the Progressive impulse waning in broader American society after World War I, WMU and *Royal Service* editors Nimmo and Mallory began to focus on the evangelistic dimension of women's personal service work. This action shifted women's efforts from the primarily female sphere of domestic and charitable work to the more male-dominated realm of evangelism—a significant change that did not occur in other woman's missionary movement organizations. Since no evidence indicates that WMU members had ever undertaken significant work to combat social ills in their local communities—despite the urgings of prewar *Royal Service* writers—they probably welcomed the new direction of the personal service program.

Evangelism, then, quickly became a priority for WMU, whose leaders were apparently more influenced by this conservative Southern Baptist emphasis than by the missiology of "world friendship" popular among many other women's missionary organizations. In 1920 the WMU Executive Committee voted to add soul-winning to the organization's list of fundamental aims, explaining in language similar to that of male SBC leaders that "the chief aim of all Christian work is the saving of souls."[22] The following year, writer Mary Livermore asserted that "nothing but personal saving of human beings is going to satisfy Him [God]."[23] A 1923 program similarly claimed that "Godly women have always expressed their love for their Lord by bringing others to Him."[24] While *Royal Service* never mentioned women formally preaching to groups of women or men, writers did not hesitate to challenge women to share the gospel informally with friends and neighbors. Personal service's principal aim, as a 1926 writer explained, was to "make those around us acquainted with Jesus by our lives, our deeds and our words."[25] Individual salvation, not friendship or social development, was the ultimate goal.

By 1929 *Royal Service* asserted that "personal service is a progression, the highest type being soul-winning"; a 1932 program again emphasized that soul-winning was the "highest expression" of personal service.[26] Without departing completely from their earlier theme of personal service, writers significantly reshaped their discussion of this topic to incorporate the more conservative ideal of soul-winning. "Saving" individual souls took precedence over transforming society, and a verbal testimony of one's Christian faith was regarded as the most useful method to effect this conversion. Later personal service articles confirmed this perspective, calling soul-winning the "most important task" and encouraging local societies to undertake evangelistic activities.[27] Reports of women handing out tracts and distributing New Testaments to Jewish friends confirmed that many societies were indeed focusing on evangelism.[28] In 1942 Mallory even led WMU to change the term "personal service" to "community missions," indicating a clear break from the emphasis's social gospel origins as well as an increased focus on evangelism, which contemporary WMU leaders believed was the "real purpose and heart" of the work.[29]

*Royal Service*'s attention to evangelism during this period aligned well with broader Southern Baptist interests, as WMU leaders implicitly agreed to use their influence to further denominational causes—and in turn gained increased respect from male leaders. While Congregationalists, Episcopalians, Methodists, Northern Baptists, Presbyterians, and the Dutch Reformed deemphasized conversion as a result of their work on *Re-Thinking Missions*, conservative Southern Baptist leaders were happy to hear of women's sharing the gospel one-on-one with friends and neighbors. WMU editors began printing in *Royal Service* letters of gratitude from SBC leaders such as J. B. Lawrence, executive secretary-treasurer of HMB, who praised WMU's evangelistic focus: "Through all the years Woman's Missionary Union has remained true to the missionary ideals of the New Testament. In many places and in many denominations the emergence of the immediate social order as a neglected field of Christian operation has somewhat eclipsed the missionary movement. But . . . Woman's Missionary Union has [maintained] . . . its devotion to missions at home and abroad."[30] Leaders such as Lawrence regarded WMU's evangelistic purposes as biblical and effective—and soon enlisted WMU leaders to promote convention-wide evangelistic efforts among their constituency.

WMU leaders, eager since the founding of their organization to support and not usurp the SBC's efforts, were satisfied to continue in their auxiliary position while increasing their own role in denominational affairs at the same time. During 1939, for example, *Royal Service* frequently emphasized the Southwide Baptist Revival, assuring Roland Leavell, HMB's superintendent of evangelism, of the "complete and continual cooperation of the Women's Missionary Societies and their auxiliaries" in this denominational "soul winning campaign."[31] The following year, the SBC's Nation-Wide Baptist Evangelistic Crusade was mentioned repeatedly in the magazine, often by male denominational leaders who expressed appreciation for the women's support. And in 1945, the SBC's one-hundredth anniversary, writers encouraged all women to participate in the Centennial Evangelistic Crusade, with its "titanic task of winning a million souls to Christ."[32] Increasingly, *Royal Service* commended participation in broader denominational emphases as an effective means of evangelizing others.

WMU writers portrayed women's roles in these revivals and crusades as supportive but significant. Singer Lee explained that no group had "greater possibilities for personal soul winning" in the Nation-Wide Baptist Evangelistic Crusade than did WMU. Women's compassionate nature, Lee argued, predisposed them to witnessing.[33] Likewise, Fred Eastham, HMB's secretary of evangelism, claimed that "woman out-distances man in the field of soul-winning" because of her "power to give herself to a person or a cause in a greater degree than a man." According to Eastham, the "finest traits" of women's femininity were glorified through their soul-winning efforts.[34] Emphasizing gender-based characteristics and roles, these writers echoed the "separate sphere" theories of an earlier era without relegating women to their own efforts entirely. They clearly regarded women's contributions to denominational crusades as important, though the crusades themselves were led by men.

Similarly, seminary professor Inman Johnson reminded WMU members, "One does not have to occupy a pulpit to be a great soul-winner. In many cases the great evangelists with their multitudes of converts have only to tip the scales of religious experience already laden by the influence of some woman or women."[35] In the roles that were appropriate for them, Johnson explained, women could have great influence. The pages of *Royal Service* indicated no disagreement with this sentiment. Most Southern Baptist women—who were by this time allowed to participate freely in missionary organizations and to vote in convention meetings—apparently did not feel restricted by their accepted roles in the denomination, as many of WMU's founders had. Instead the women regarded these roles as appropriate, evaluating them from within the framework of their culturally conditioned gender expectations. As WMU president Laura Armstrong noted in 1937, "Fifty years ago the place and position of women were vastly different from what they are today."[36] Armstrong and most Southern Baptist women of her day, like American women as a whole, generally remained content with the gains in status their foremothers had achieved for them. Instead of embarking upon their own unique tasks, these women participated gladly in denomination-wide evangelistic efforts in ways that male leaders regarded as appropriate.

Like other WMU leaders, then, *Royal Service* editors Elia Nimmo and especially Kathleen Mallory considered evangelism to be an important role for Southern Baptist women during this period, whether on the foreign mission field or through personal service and evangelistic crusades at home. Unlike women in mainline denominations, WMU members were motivated for missions in a new era and connected with the broader purposes of their denomination through their soul-winning focus. Supporting the SBC's efforts, WMU leaders and editors decided, was an effective way to help evangelize their nation and their world while at the same time gaining approval within their denomination.

## Supporting Missions

Acknowledging the importance of evangelistic work at home and abroad, a 1921 *Royal Service* writer urged readers to support Southern Baptist missions efforts: "Thousands of . . . men and women, with spirits aflame with love for God and humanity, have gone forth as witnessing of the 'light of the glorious Gospel of Christ.' The candles of the Lord are alight all over a darkened world. Let us keep them burning by praying with true desire 'Thy kingdom come'; by laying our gifts on His altar; by being faithful home lights ourselves, knowing that the world He died to save will be saved throughout our obedience to the Great Commission."[37] Women could spur on mission work around the world, this writer suggested, by praying for missions, learning about missions, and giving to missions. Editors Nimmo and Mallory continued to portray such efforts—which had been essential components of the early woman's missionary movement—as important roles for Southern Baptist women, even after their emphasis among other women's groups had waned. However, *Royal Service* writers, influenced by male SBC leaders' concerns, encouraged WMU members to support not only female but also male SBC missionaries—and the complete SBC program—through their prayers and mission study efforts. Most women who fulfilled these roles strengthened the SBC through their giving as well.

In WMU's early years, *Our Mission Fields* and *Royal Service*, like other women's missionary publications, had focused more on female than on male missionaries. But with the decline of "woman's work for woman" missiology, missions leaders proposed fewer roles that only female missionaries could fill. Thus many women's mission groups, organized as sending agencies for women only, found it difficult to justify their separate existence. Because of its conservative Southern Baptist context, though, WMU's situation was different: it had organized and continued to operate as an auxiliary to the SBC, supporting the efforts of the denomination. As a result, *Royal Service* was able to adapt to the changing interwar missions climate simply by featuring a variety of articles about denominational missionaries and encouraging its readers to support them all. WMU leaders thus renegotiated their position in the SBC by exchanging their "separate sphere" work for a denominational support role. While female workers continued to be of special interest to WMU, the organization's magazine began to highlight numerous ministries carried out by male Southern Baptist missionaries as well.

Before and immediately following World War I, *Royal Service* frequently featured on its cover the names of female missionaries newly appointed by FMB. But after 1925, this list was no longer included in the magazine. In addition, by the mid-1920s a few letters from male Southern Baptist missionaries began to appear in the magazine's From Our Missionaries page alongside notes from women serving on the mission field. The February 1930 From Our Missionaries page included four letters, all of which were written by male missionaries—a significant change from previous years.[38] While WMU still recognized female missionaries at its annual meeting and likely felt a special sense of sisterhood with these workers, the organization began to focus more on male missionaries as well. With their earnest efforts to promote all SBC missionaries, the women relinquished their unique realm of influence but subtly increased the importance of their organization to SBC leaders.

The majority of *Royal Service*'s monthly program suggestions after World War I likewise mentioned little about the unique needs of women in a specific location, a topic that had appeared in numerous articles about "heathen" women in previous years. These programs focused instead on general Southern Baptist evangelistic efforts and institutions in each place, reflecting the concerns of the male leaders of an enlarging denomination. The February 1922 program, for example, titled "Our New Foreign Mission Fields," included an impressive collection of facts about countries into which FMB was expanding but no specific information about women's work in any of these places, even though by this time female missionaries outnumbered males two to one.[39] Similarly, a December 1940 program on "The Orient" devoted much more space to describing the SBC's evangelistic institutions in China—schools, hospitals, a publishing house, and a broadcasting station—than to discussing ministries in which female missionaries were participating there.[40] Undergirding the denomination's complete missions program—and thus gaining an enduring place within it—had evidently become a more important role for WMU members than supporting female missionaries.

One way for women to assist with denominational work, according to *Royal Service*, was through prayer, which had been an important aspect of WMU's earlier "woman's work for woman" efforts as well. As a result of expanded opportunities for small group prayer, after World War I most Southern Baptist women were able to pray aloud "without the 19th century anguish"[41] that their grandmothers had experienced when praying in front of others for the first time. And because of their conservative beliefs, Southern Baptist women did not doubt the efficacy of prayer as women and men in some mainline Protestant denominations did. Believing that "prayer is the power that moves the world,"[42] WMU members fervently interceded for both the unevangelized and denominational work.

Multiple *Royal Service* writers discussed the importance of prayer for evangelism, a key emphasis among Southern Baptists during this period. Myrtle Creasman, for example, explained that prayer was "the greatest of all things we can do for the spread of the Gospel."[43] Although many Southern Baptist women participated in soul-winning efforts in their own communities and even overseas, writers indicated that this work was in vain without prayer. In 1934 Mrs. W. H. Gray challenged readers, "Will you not go secretly to the mercy seat at least once every day and implore the Father in behalf of those dying without a Saviour?"[44] Her plea was formalized in 1938 with the creation—through Laura Armstrong's influence—of the "Nine O'clock Prayer Hour," a time each day when WMU members were encouraged to pray for mission work around the world.[45] Beginning in 1934, Armstrong also led WMU to designate prayer as the first of its fundamental aims; to publish a booklet titled "Prayer, the Golden Chain"; and to institute cottage prayer meetings and an Intercessory League of Shut-ins.[46] During this era of secularization and professionalism in wider American society, local WMU members no doubt appreciated Armstrong's emphasis on the simple discipline of prayer, which had permeated their grandmothers' early missions efforts and in which any woman—trained or untrained—could participate.

But many requests for prayer in *Royal Service* during these years were perhaps more complex than the prayer concerns of early WMU members. Not only did writers discuss praying for the unconverted; they also frequently asked readers to pray for broader denominational causes. Beginning in late 1918, the magazine's Calendar of Prayer no longer requested prayer primarily for female missionaries—it included male missionaries and convention emphases as well. Each month's calendar focused on a different denominational concern; the March 1919 calendar, for example, highlighted "The Value of Mountain Schools" for underprivileged Appalachian children, while November 1936 discussed "Our Christmas Offering and Kingdom Building."[47] Features requesting prayer for women's work disappeared as denominational concerns took precedence.

Numerous articles throughout *Royal Service* affirmed the importance of praying for specific denominational projects as well. A 1924 writer encouraged a week of prayer for the Seventy-Five Million Campaign, the SBC's new financial plan; in 1945 community missions leader Mrs. W. T. Waring explained the necessity of cottage prayer meetings for the Centennial Evangelistic Crusade.[48] The magazine also continued to feature information about annual weeks of prayer for home and foreign missions, which focused largely on HMB and FMB. Although donating money to the boards was a significant emphasis during this time, at least one writer claimed that women's "greatest contribution" was not giving but private prayer.[49] Clearly writers and editors expected Southern Baptist women to persist in their significant support role of prayer during these years, extending their prayers not just to female missionaries but also to the entire convention program. Through such emphases, WMU members apparently hoped to contribute to broader SBC efforts—consequently securing their role in the denomination as supportive and essential.

Editors Elia Nimmo and Kathleen Mallory also continued to promote mission study as an important role for readers of *Royal Service* in this period. During and after World War I, interest in such study declined among women in mainline denominations; *World Missions and World Peace*, published in 1916, was the first book from the influential Central Committee on the United Study of Foreign Missions that lost money.[50] But at the same time, record numbers of Southern Baptist women expressed interest in mission study, with more than fifteen thousand study classes reported in 1922 alone.[51] Conservative Southern Baptist women still believed strongly in the importance of traditional mission work and had by this time adopted mission support as one of their unique roles in a male-dominated convention. WMU members, who probably had fewer opportunities for outside activities than did many Northern women, continued faithfully to devote their time to learning about missions, usually through studying books about missions work in a specific country or region. This emphasis on study led Creasman to remark in 1932, "Southern Baptist printed pages, how they fly! Millions of them are flying all over the southland."[52]

As in previous years, *Royal Service* editors and writers continued to recommend mission study books published by the Central Committee on the United Study of Foreign Missions—although in deference to SBC leaders' concerns about ecumenical efforts, WMU was not an official participant in the committee's study program. A 1920 reviewer, for example, endorsed Helen Barrett Montgomery's "unusually fine study book" *The Bible and Missions*.[53] Other books from the Central Committee, such as *Eastern Women Today and Tomorrow* and *Women under the Southern Cross*, were praised during the years they were published.[54] And as late as 1944, the magazine printed a favorable review of Montgomery's 1931 volume *The Preaching Value of Missions*.[55] Even after most women of other denominations had abandoned the woman's missionary movement, *Royal Service* encouraged Southern Baptist women to learn as much as they could about missions from the movement's publications—"always supplement[ing] with material concerning our own W.M.U. and S.B.C. work."[56] In this way, WMU leaders deftly promoted denominational institutions and appeared to submit to SBC leaders' concerns while in reality they were endorsing books from an organization that these men found questionable.

As the Central Committee's publishing business declined and eventually ceased, *Royal Service* writers recommended a number of mission study books by Southern Baptist authors, in accord with their growing commitment to denominational causes. The magazine's April 1923 issue, for example, featured both *The Bells of the Blue Pagoda*, published by FMB, and *From Strength to Strength*, published by HMB.[57] In addition, in the mid-1930s WMU leaders successfully requested that the mission boards publish annual mission study books featuring their efforts in a certain region or through a specific type of ministry.[58] In this way, the women demonstrated their ability to use their growing influence to effect change within the denomination, albeit in a manner that did not threaten male denominational leaders.

Around the same time, WMU leaders became interested in expanding the study of missions beyond WMU members, since "such a splendid array of mission books now being published makes one crave for the whole church the privilege of studying them."[59] The Church School of Missions, a cooperative effort with other SBC entities, was the result. Denominational leaders urged all church members—even men—to participate in this school, since "they need to know about missions" too.[60] Mission study, which had once been the unique domain of Southern Baptist women reading women's books about women's ministries around the world, now involved all Southern Baptist church members reading books by denominational publishers about the convention's complete missions program. Again the women renounced their "separate sphere" of influence for a broader commitment to the SBC—an emphasis that surely pleased SBC leaders.

This trend toward the study of wider denominational efforts was evident in programs published in *Royal Service* as well. The magazine not only included information about Southern Baptist missions efforts in a variety of regions; it also began to emphasize denominational causes that, strictly speaking, did not involve missions. For example, the May 1934 program plans instructed, "The leader should have a bowl of tulips or of other flowers on the table before her. She may explain that way back in 1814 our Baptist great-great grandparents planted a garden for us. It held but one bulb—the Triennial Convention. . . . In 1845 the bulb was dug up and divided, forming two flower borders, the Northern Baptist Convention and the Southern Baptist Convention."[61] Understanding denominational history was, to this writer, as important as learning about Southern Baptist mission work. Other writers apparently felt the same way about convention emphases, encouraging mission study leaders to use teaching techniques such as labeling candelabra with the seven objects of the Cooperative Program, the SBC's giving plan.[62] No longer was mission work the primary focus of women's study; Southern Baptist history and programs were just as important to mission study writers and probably to WMU members as well. Like prayer, the study of denominational programs was portrayed as an important role for Southern Baptist women in the pages of *Royal Service*. Unlike women in other denominations who had emphasized their own endeavors, the women who participated in SBC mission support activities were likely to support the complete program and leadership of their denomination—including female Baptist leaders who emerged on foreign mission fields.

## Supporting National Women

*Royal Service* encouraged its readers to support both female and male Southern Baptist missionaries, but it also promoted the women's special affinity with women from other countries. After World War I, descriptions of the plight of women overseas became less frequent in the magazine's pages than they had been in previous years. However, such descriptions did not disappear entirely until well into the 1930s, several years after most women's groups had ceased using similar language. A 1922 poem echoed sentiments from years past as it spoke of ". . . women bound in evils vast / Where flowers of joy can never blossom, / Of tired child-mothers, holding fast / A puny babe to shrunken bosom."[63] Three years later, another writer called attention to the great need of the "heathen with us": unchurched immigrants in the United States, she believed, also suffered greatly without the gospel.[64] A 1932 writer—perhaps influenced by missionary material from her younger years—described a Chinese girl "with bound feet and life bound by the superstition of a heathen home."[65] And the same year, Creasman mourned the plight of unreached African tribes "sitting in the darkness of heathen degradation," using terms that had been more common decades earlier.[66] While most leaders of mainline Protestant women's organizations during this period refrained from using such language, which they regarded as antiquated and insensitive, a few WMU writers apparently continued to view themselves as the liberators of needy non-Christian women.

But most attitudes toward national women displayed in *Royal Service* during this time were more complex. A May 1924 program, for example, was titled "Sisterhood of the Americas," using terminology that resonated with the emerging missiology of "world friendship." However, it also voiced sentiments popular in previous years, encouraging its white American readers to use their "better inheritance . . . to uplift the social, moral and home life of our sister continent."[67] Mixing ideologies of sisterhood and superiority, this program reflected WMU members' changing and often inconsistent attitudes toward women around the world. On one page, writers might describe a foreign people group as "superior in intellect and moral character"; on the next, as "ignorant, diseased, poverty-stricken, degraded, sinful."[68] Only through stories of national Christian women were writers' perspectives completely transformed.

Reflecting the changing climate of world missions, Mrs. Taul White commented in 1928 that "pioneer days are just closing."[69] As "separate sphere" ideology declined, brave female missionaries who had dared to take the gospel to "heathen" women were replaced by missionary generalists—and by well-trained national Christian women whom pioneer missionaries had converted. Numerous writers described the "new woman" who was emerging in newly Christianized cultures. Women in Mexico had "increasing freedom and influence"; women in Cuba led a "more fully occupied and highly cultivated life"; educated women in China were "studying law, entering medical ranks and becoming nurses"; and modern Japanese women were "as competent and 'all around' as . . . sisters in America or Europe."[70] Female missionaries who met these women, as well as WMU leaders who participated in BWA women's meetings, bore witness to their character and development. Stories of these women's good works soon replaced descriptions of their "heathen" counterparts who had not yet heard the gospel.

Testimonies about national women's leadership filled multiple pages of *Royal Service* during these years. A 1921 missionary letter introduced an abused Chinese mother who had become a Bible woman; the following year, missionary Mrs. G. A. Bowdler commended the efforts of female Argentine teachers at the Buenos Aires Baptist Boys' Academy.[71]

By 1923 a national woman was profiled in study materials for the Week of Prayer for Foreign Missions: missionary Mrs. J. W. McGavock described Claudia Villaneuva's exceptional ministry of "mothering" Santa Elena Baptist Church in Santiago, Chile, into existence through her prayers.[72] Missionaries related similar stories of national women again and again in the years that followed. Names such as Zung Ta Ta of China, Ludovica Cristea of Romania, Maria Magdalena Sampaio of Brazil, Kiyoko Shimose of Japan, Aurelia de Brando of Chile, and Adelaide Fasulo of Italy became familiar even to Southern Baptist women who had never traveled outside their own states.[73] Demonstrating *Royal Service*'s growing emphasis on national women leaders, a 1938 article series featured a female Christian leader from a different country each month—the "golden sheaves" that had resulted from missionaries' "harvesting" efforts.[74] Before long, national women themselves wrote directly to readers of *Royal Service*, describing how they became Christians, led mission studies, and participated in itinerant work to spread the gospel. No longer "heathen," these women worked diligently to spread the gospel among other women in their own countries.

*Royal Service*'s inclusion of numerous features about national women was not particularly remarkable in itself; most women's missionary publications that were still in existence during these years were filled with testimonies from non-Western women. However, editor Kathleen Mallory led *Royal Service* to highlight the women's evangelistic efforts in a way that was distinctive. While most mainline Protestant women's magazines discussed social issues, world friendship, and peace, WMU writers had a narrower focus. They often presented women's stories of evangelism and conversion, again demonstrating their support for significant Southern Baptist emphases during this period. One writer even remarked in 1920, "Get a man converted and you have a unit; get a woman converted and you have a multiplication table."[75] Stories of national women's evangelistic efforts demonstrated at least the second half of this statement, as Chinese Bible women, Brazilian field workers, Nigerian "helpers," and many other Christian women around the globe realized the results of their work to spread the gospel. Miss Poon of China led twelve women in a Bible study only three months after arriving in a remote village; Alake in Nigeria postponed her wedding to encourage village women to share Christ; and Dalila in Colombia distributed tracts and told Bible stories to children living in poverty.[76] A 1936 program reported that the SBC employed more than 2,500 such "native workers" on foreign mission fields.[77] Although statistics are not available, many of these were probably women.

*Royal Service* sometimes described these national women's efforts with terms not used for female missionaries' work. In 1923 Chinese Bible women testified to readers about their "call to preach."[78] Mallory, however, was careful to put the word "preach" in quotation marks both times it occurred, without elaborating further. A few years later, a woman who attended a BWA meeting remarked on a Chinese woman who "appeared in a status of full equality with her male co-workers in the task of the church."[79] Similarly, a Japanese deacon's wife was called a "second pastor" for her evangelistic efforts; and a missionary letter mentioned a Brazilian woman who "teaches the Bible and . . . leads all of the service" in her church, although "they do not call this preaching."[80] Mallory and *Royal Service*'s editorial committee apparently understood—and did not openly challenge—the restrictions on women's roles in their own Southern Baptist context but did not mind occasionally sharing stories about national women who fulfilled expanded roles in their own cultures. On the mission field, they felt, women might more freely adopt responsibilities that were not acceptable in the conservative American South. Descriptions of these women's ministries might have prompted some readers to support their efforts even more.

*Royal Service* readers were likely also encouraged by articles about national women who participated in denominational mission work. Editors Nimmo and Mallory included multiple features on this topic, seeking to impress upon readers the importance of denominational institutions in any context. As early as 1919, missionaries in various countries reported organizing local women into Women's Missionary Societies, which they linked to form national Women's Missionary Unions "patterned as nearly as possible after our own organization here in the homeland."[81] Just like groups in the United States, these societies held missions meetings, studied missions publications, and saved money for missions. By the mid-1920s, almost every Nigerian Baptist church boasted a WMS, and Brazil's WMU had its own headquarters and magazine.[82] Around a decade later, WMU in Japan reported hosting a Daily Vacation Bible School and a Young Woman's Auxiliary camp, in addition to operating a training school and good will center.[83] Similar developments were true of WMU organizations in many other countries. National leaders, trained by missionaries, multiplied the efforts of evangelism and women's work in their countries, even after some Southern Baptist women no longer felt an urgent call to minister specifically to women. While twenty-first-century missiologists may object to the use of Western organizational models in non-Western contexts, contemporary readers were probably pleased with the "Christianization" of each culture—and were encouraged to support the work of WMU and the SBC more fully.

Some national women even participated in the efforts of WMU and the SBC themselves. To the excitement of *Royal Service* readers, Mabola Ayorinde of Nigeria attended WMU meetings in the United States in 1938.[84] Women from many other countries also contributed to the SBC's financial efforts: a group from north China donated money to the Seventy-Five Million Campaign, and women in Nigeria gave $225 to the Lottie Moon Christmas Offering (LMCO), which supported FMB.[85] *Royal Service* reported that national women also wholeheartedly assisted in the work of the Baptist conventions emerging overseas, just as WMU members did in the SBC. Brazilian women, missionary Minnie Landrum enthused, tithed regularly to their young denomination and supported six Brazilian missionaries and five missionary students as well.[86] Clearly WMU leaders felt that such women were to be commended—and assisted. Southern Baptist women, writers pointed out, helped build the Baptist WMU Training School of Japan, the Brazilian WMU headquarters, and probably other ministry centers through their donations.[87] In addition, women's gifts to the SBC enabled more national workers and missionaries to evangelize women in many countries around the world. As Myrtle Creasman stressed, "These native leaders themselves are pleading all the time for more help from southern Baptists."[88] Supporting the SBC's denominational program, *Royal Service* writers suggested, was an essential way to provide for the national women leaders—no longer "heathen"—whom the magazine's readers had come to cherish.

## Supporting the Denominational Program

Spreading the gospel, supporting missions, and supporting national women: from 1919 to 1945, *Royal Service* suggested that Southern Baptist women could best fulfill all of these roles by supporting the complete program of their rapidly developing denomination—especially with their tithes and offerings. While most other women's missions organizations focused on their own endeavors and were eventually absorbed into larger denominational structures, *Royal Service* emphasized WMU's status as an auxiliary to the SBC and encouraged its readers to tithe to SBC programs, save money for denominational missions offerings, and give sacrificially to relieve convention debt. As the women adopted this denominational focus, they also subtly exercised increasing influence over SBC institutions, which came to rely on WMU's financial contributions. Denominational support, not power, was the women's primary goal; however, both eventually resulted from their endeavors. Although men retained ultimate control of the SBC, the women's efforts proved vital to the success of the convention and of WMU.

The SBC was organized as a convention, but in its early years it relied on a society method of giving, with individuals and churches funding whichever denominational entities they pleased. In 1916 only half of all Southern Baptist churches donated money to any denominational cause.[89] Programs such as WMU, Baptist Young People's Union, and Sunday School provided some uniformity to Southern Baptist churches, but the SBC was not yet a denomination in the modern sense of the word. Bolstered by the national trend toward efficiency and bureaucratization, though, the SBC gradually began to explore centralizing its efforts. In 1917 the convention formed an Executive Committee to coordinate its work between annual sessions, an important step in the SBC's development.

Just as significant was the cooperative giving plan the SBC approved two years later. At this time, encouraged by the success of fund drives during World War I, multiple denominations undertook enormous financial campaigns. The Methodist Episcopal Church, South, for example, financed "greatly enlarged plans of the denomination" through its Centenary Movement in 1919.[90] That same year, the SBC created its own Seventy-Five Million Campaign, optimistically expecting donations of that many dollars to pour in from churches and individuals across the South within five years. Due to a variety of factors, including an economic recession, only $58 million was collected by the campaign's end. However, the convention continued coordinating its efforts, launching in 1925 an ongoing funding plan called the Cooperative Program. Through this program, all giving was centralized, with individual donations divided among local, state, and national Southern Baptist entities. This approach revolutionized SBC life. For the first time, the denomination had a financial plan that supported its rapidly expanding programs and agencies. With an Executive Committee and a cooperative giving program, the SBC became a centralized, modern denomination in every sense.

As the SBC developed its denominational framework, WMU leaders faithfully supported convention programs. WMU president Laura Armstrong especially emphasized the relationship stated in the organization's official name: "Woman's Missionary Union, Auxiliary to Southern Baptist Convention." As an auxiliary, Armstrong and other WMU leaders believed, WMU was "a sharer in the ventures and victories of the Convention"; "a helper, an assistant, a supporter of the work of the S.B.C."[91] Armstrong emphasized that WMU supported the SBC because of WMU's "utter singleness of purpose . . . the promotion of missions."[92] She and other WMU leaders considered missions the primary reason for the SBC's existence, so—unlike women's leaders in many other denominations—they did not hesitate to lead WMU members to participate in a wide range of the SBC's work. As SBC director of promotion J. E. Dillard claimed (perhaps hoping for further donations), WMU's name could be changed to "Woman's Missionary Union Auxiliary to *Every* Southern Baptist Cause" because of the women's enthusiastic support of multiple convention programs.[93] Rather than maintain their separate tasks, the women adopted the emphases urged by male SBC leaders, subordinating their efforts to those of the larger denomination—but eventually gaining a new degree of influence within the SBC as a result.

As Delane Tew demonstrates, WMU was able to unite its members around denominational causes because the organization had already developed its own hierarchical "para-denominational" structure by this time.[94] Through its local, state, and national networks, and the pages of *Royal Service*, WMU was able to affect the actions of women throughout the convention. WMU also retained its influence among its grassroots members by relocating its national office from Baltimore to Birmingham, Alabama, a move the organization's Executive Committee approved in 1921.[95] According to *Royal Service*, Birmingham was not as "unduly influenced" by Northern thinking as some women feared that Baltimore was. The new location also allowed more space for WMU's expanding operations and brought the organization closer geographically to the majority of its members.[96] WMU's leadership accordingly shifted from Baltimore elites to mostly middle-class women from across the South. These middle-class women were less likely than their predecessors to follow controversial ecumenical trends such as social Christianity, instead emphasizing traditional SBC programs and gender roles that were accepted throughout the South.

Many of these leaders, then, may have been eager to take on a supportive role within the SBC because of their socialization as gracious, obliging Southern women—and because of their exclusion from other roles in their churches and denomination. When Helen Barrett Montgomery was elected president of the Northern Baptist Convention in 1921, for example, no female leaders were considered for elected positions in the SBC; women had first been allowed to vote in that denomination only three years earlier. Despite the WMU Executive Committee's 1921 request for increased female representation on convention committees, SBC leadership remained overwhelmingly male.[97] In addition, no woman gave a major address to the convention until 1929. As WMU president Minnie James remarked, Southern Baptist women in reality had "but little share in the administration of the affairs of the denomination."[98] The women's influence, though increasing, remained subordinate to that of male SBC leaders.

For this reason, at the same time that some women in mainline Northern denominations began to question their need for separate organizations, Southern Baptist women found that WMU was the primary way for them to participate in SBC life. Because of their conservative context, these women still benefited from their own auxiliary organization, through which they could support SBC efforts. Articles in *Royal Service* indicated that most WMU writers during this time were satisfied with their role as a "real helpmate"[99] to the convention, receiving accolades—and eventually increased influence—as a result of their ancillary efforts. Like most American and especially Southern women of the day, WMU members spent little time working to expand their rights. Instead of crusading for new roles within their denomination, these women used their energy to support burgeoning Southern Baptist programs and the enormous financial needs that soon resulted from them.

Accordingly, editors Elia Nimmo and especially Kathleen Mallory included in *Royal Service* a growing number of articles focused on denominational programs and institutions: "Our State's Part in the Campaign for Denominational Education"; "Ministerial Relief, Orphanages, and Hospitals"; "Our Convention: Its Organization and Purpose"; "Duty and the Denomination"; and "S.B.C. Calendar of Denominational Activities," among others.[100] Pages that had once been filled with information about women's special mission to other women now discussed women's essential role of supporting the SBC. Even the Calendar of Prayer included leaders such as I. J. Van Ness of the SSB alongside HMB and FMB missionaries.[101] One 1931 program plan disparaged "uninformed Baptists," to whom "names of [SBC] boards are a jumble," and encouraged its readers to become like "Mrs. Experienced Baptist," who understood the denominational program fully.[102] Pastor Ryland Knight verified the effectiveness of such features as he considered—and discounted—Paul's admonition for husbands to teach their wives privately: "Imagine the president of our Woman's Missionary Society seeking to gain from her husband additional information with regard to our denominational program[!]"[103] Such a casual dismissal of a biblical passage previously favored by male Southern

Baptists demonstrated the significance of women's new role in the SBC. Prohibited from leading their denomination, Southern Baptist women found their place in their churches and the entire convention not by establishing independent efforts but instead by becoming experts about denominational emphases.

WMU's support of the Seventy-Five Million Campaign, one writer suggested, strengthened its emphasis on the complete program of the convention. This campaign—which raised funds not only for home and foreign missions but also for causes such as ministerial relief and Christian education—"obligated the Union to a participation [*sic*] in every phase of denominational work."[104] Male convention leaders, eager to fund this new endeavor, urged the cooperation of WMU and other SBC entities. They soon appointed Mallory and James to the committee responsible for the campaign—one of the first times that WMU leaders were included on an official SBC committee unrelated to women's work. Such an action demonstrated male leaders' acknowledgment of WMU's growing power, as well as the men's desire to leverage WMU members' voice—and dollars—to support broader SBC causes. The women apparently felt flattered and not abused by this move. James rejoiced, "Never has its [WMU's] co-operation been so graciously and spontaneously sought and so gladly utilized."[105] Pleased that male convention leaders had requested their assistance, WMU leaders readily supported the Seventy-Five Million Campaign.

The women agreed to use their influence to raise $15 million of the needed $75 million, a goal that WMU promoted heavily throughout the pages of *Royal Service* and ultimately met. Beginning in 1919, the magazine was filled with article after article about the campaign, focusing with the convention in July of that year on preparation, in August on information, in September on intercession, in October on enlistment, in November on stewardship, and in December on victory.[106] The entire April 1922 Calendar of Prayer focused on the Seventy-Five Million Campaign; women were also encouraged to pray for its success each day in September during their prayer hour at 9:00 A.M.[107] Reflecting on these and other efforts by WMU members, one writer heralded "the opening of a new chapter in W.M.U. history"; another emphasized that during the campaign WMU was "prov[ing] . . . conclusively its *right to be*."[108] By promoting the campaign wholeheartedly, *Royal Service* writers demonstrated WMU's increasing commitment to support the complete program of the SBC.

In order to stimulate more women's support, WMU leaders often emphasized in *Royal Service* the ways that the Seventy-Five Million Cam-

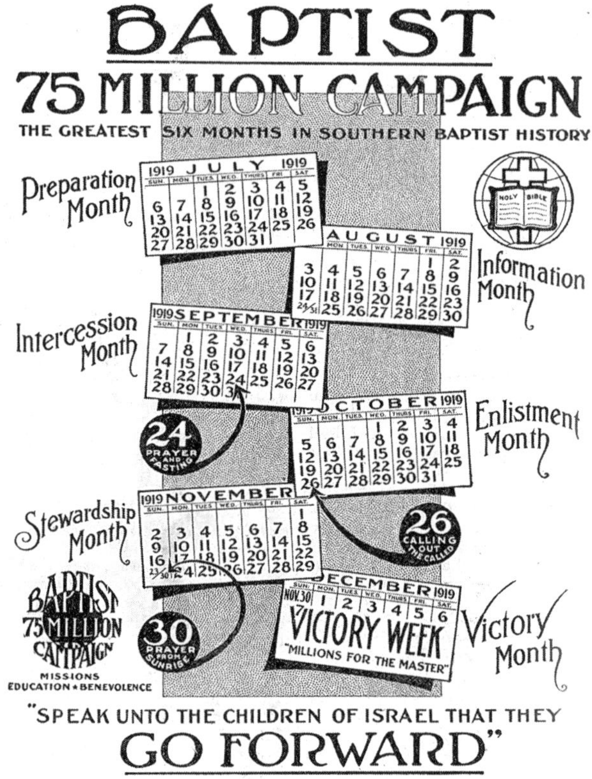


8. Back cover of September 1919 *Royal Service*. (Used by permission of WMUA.)

paign and its successor, the ongoing Cooperative Program, benefited mission work. A 1919 writer called enlistment for the campaign "the echo of the cry of need from our foreign missionaries," evoking the women's concern for foreign missions to encourage them to pledge their money.[109] Similarly, the back cover of the December 1919 issue of *Royal Service* was titled "Mathematics of China's Millions and 'Millions for the Master.'" If $75 million were given to the campaign, the writer demonstrated, 330 new missionaries (210 of them women), "many" native helpers, 8 mission stations, 29 church buildings, 4 church building loan funds, 93 missionaries' homes, equipment for 79 schools, 18 hospital buildings, and improvements for present mission stations would be added to the Southern Baptist missions effort in China. This would "win thousands of converts in China" and lead to "the winning of [all of] China for Christ."[110] Several years later, WMU president Laura Armstrong concurred that the Cooperative Program was the "Southern Baptist interpretation" of Christians' "world-wide obligation" to spread the gospel found in Acts 1:8.[111] Supporting efforts such as the Seventy-Five Million Campaign and the Cooperative Program, writers emphasized, would have greater impact on the mission field than would the women's giving alone. As Opal Osborne put it, "Your dollar does more through the Cooperative Program!"[112] By working together with other members of the SBC, WMU members could gain "that high degree of strength and success" that was possible only through cooperation.[113] Writers did not discuss, however, whether WMU would retain its autonomy and authority in such cooperative ventures.

But WMU leaders appeared to be mindful of this issue at times, at least in relation to their annual offerings for home and foreign missions, which they did not want to be subsumed into the Cooperative Program. Contending that "the special seasons [for home and foreign missions] are the times for special prayer and special over-and-above gifts," the women agreed to support the Cooperative Program only if their offerings were not included in it.[114] Annual missions offerings, *Royal Service* writers explained, were "a sacred and symbolic tradition" that "each year . . . [became] dearer to the hearts of the women."[115] These offerings supported causes for which HMB and FMB would otherwise be unable to provide—and that the women themselves usually selected. In a 1929 statement to the SBC's Executive Committee, members of the WMU Executive Committee voiced concern over what they considered the SBC's efforts to "control and restrict the individual freedom in giving that has characterized the very life of our denomination."[116] That the men heeded this criticism demonstrated the growing financial power of the women's organization. Because of the degree to which they controlled SBC contributions, WMU leaders were able to successfully maintain their seasonal offerings. Moreover, as the women continued to promote their offerings, the mission boards grew dependent on this income. WMU's unique role in the convention accordingly became more secure. Unlike other women's organizations that were merged into larger denominational structures, WMU used its denominational support role and fund-raising power to ensure its continued importance within the SBC.

In order to maintain their organization's financial strength for convention causes, *Royal Service* editors Nimmo and Mallory frequently printed articles to motivate women to tithe their money. While in 1895 the SBC had approved a resolution favoring tithing,[117] most convention entities devoted little attention to the topic in the years that followed. Giving was not the priority for these organizations that it was for WMU, which had been established in part to provide financial support for SBC missions efforts. WMU alone stressed tithing as a key role for Southern Baptists—especially for Southern Baptist women, who had traditionally prioritized personal sacrifice for denominational causes. The goal, WMU writers emphasized, was for every Southern Baptist woman to "pay into His [God's] treasury at least a tenth of her own personal income or outlay on personal expenses and pleasures";[118] offerings above this tithe were also encouraged. In order to encourage generous financial support, the magazine included regular features such as My Alabaster Box and Stewardship Suggestions, which provided practical advice about giving. WMU members and a few Baptist women from other countries also wrote in with "tithing testimonials" that described how they baked and sold cakes, assumed extra sewing projects, or taught music lessons to earn money to tithe. Such features—and the tremendous sums of money they generated—demonstrate that the women clearly prioritized financial support of the SBC.

Moreover, *Royal Service* editors promoted a tithing essay contest for young women, a church-wide Tithers' Fellowship League, lapel pins for tithers, tithing covenant cards, tithers' boxes, and tithing stickers.[119] For several years, a back page or pages of the magazine's January issue also included lines for women to sign as a reminder of their pledge to tithe. Because of WMU members' dedication to denominational causes, one of their main concerns apparently was tithing—a spiritual commitment that according to writers' theology often included temporal rewards. Myrtle Creasman even suggested that if all Christians had tithed, there "would have been no American depression," since God blesses those who tithe; and "the wars now raging through Europe and China might have been averted," because a Christian atmosphere would prevail.[120] Any woman who read even a few pages of *Royal Service* during this period would have been convinced that Creasman and other writers believed tithing was an essential role for Southern Baptist women.

Building upon this concern for tithing, during these years *Royal Service* also frequently emphasized stewardship—the use of not only money but also personality, talents, influence, time, opportunities, and possessions for Christ.[121] A 1928 writer remarked that working women, who had recently been organized into Business Women's Circles, had a "wide scope" for the practice of stewardship in their careers.[122] During World War II, stewardship chairman Alma Wright cautioned women against using too much of their time in Red Cross activities, reminding them that their lives belonged not to the government but to "God and His service."[123] In Wright's estimation, women's commitment to their faith—

and their denomination—took precedence over national concerns. Accordingly, writers repeatedly encouraged all women to be good stewards so that "there would be no lack of time or talents or money or personalities to carry on the work of Jesus"—or of the SBC.[124] In the 1930s, a Stewardship Covenant Card promoting stewardship and tithing appeared in *Royal Service*; by 1942 Creasman declared that stewardship was "the heart of W.M.U."[125] As writers and editors highlighted ways women could more effectively support the SBC, tithing and stewardship became priorities for WMU members.

By 1936 WMU reported 75,369 adult tithers, one-fourth of the organization's adult membership.[126] While annual per capita missions giving among SBC supporters was only $1.87—less than half a percent of the average monthly household income—among WMU members the figure was $4.49.[127] WMU members contributed more money to denominational causes than did most Southern Baptist men, although the great majority of WMU members during this period did not hold full-time jobs. Because of WMU's emphasis on giving, the organization's members diligently raised money through special projects considered appropriate for Southern women, such as those involving cooking and sewing, or by setting aside money from the "allowances" their husbands gave them for household expenses.[128] Such efforts enabled thousands of women to contribute small offerings that together amounted to a considerable force within the SBC.

Constantly reminded of their denominational support role through the pleas of SBC leaders and especially the pages of *Royal Service*, WMU members provided significant funding for the Seventy-Five Million Campaign and later the Cooperative Program, annual offerings for home and foreign missions, and other Southern Baptist causes such as the Fannie E. S. Heck Memorial, Christian Education Commission, Board of Ministerial Relief and Annuities, Church Building Loan Fund, and Henrietta Hall Shuck Memorial Fund. In the 1930s and early 1940s, WMU members also promoted the Every Member Canvass, a campaign to enlist every Southern Baptist in "financial support of local work of the church and all denominational causes."[129] J. E. Dillard remarked approvingly, "W.M.U. . . . should help in every worthy cause in each church and in the denomination. *And it does help*."[130] By giving faithfully to each emphasis the SBC created, WMU members and leaders alike demonstrated their growing influence within the convention; the women's cooperation was becoming essential to the success of SBC tasks.

The women's support continued to prove invaluable as SBC agencies slid into debt in the late 1920s and 1930s. During this time, economic depression and financial mismanagement plagued both HMB and FMB, leaving the two entities with a combined debt of nearly $3 million and a tenuous future. Numerous other convention agencies also accumulated debts they were unable to repay, totaling almost an additional $3 million.[131] Upon learning of this crisis, WMU leaders sprang into action. Mallory created a new feature in *Royal Service*, Pray Ye, to solicit prayer for debt relief. To arouse women's sympathies, writer after writer discussed the plight of missionaries affected by the debt, who "trusted us, depended on us, and we are failing them."[132] An unusually long From Our Missionaries page in the magazine's January 1926 issue presented maudlin pleas from needy mission fields: "Heavy Hearts in Bello Horizonte," "Pressed Down in Pernambuco," "Yearning Over Jerusalem," "Pingtu's Plight," and so forth.[133] Even the principal of WMUTS lamented that because of the debt, the school's graduates had to apply to other denominations' mission boards for appointment.[134] By including in *Royal Service* emotional appeals to readers' concern for missions, Mallory clearly hoped to encourage the women to give more money toward the convention's debts—in a sense also indebting convention leaders to the women's organization.

In 1933 WMU endorsed the Hundred Thousand Club, a new program to eliminate SBC debts. Although WMU leaders had originally created a separate debt-reduction strategy, they "relinquished their cherished plan"[135] in order to advance the program promoted by SBC leaders. The women began wholeheartedly promoting the Hundred Thousand Club after it was approved by the convention, choosing to reserve their veto power for more significant concerns such as separate missions offerings. Throughout the pages of *Royal Service*, writers encouraged women to join the hoped-for one hundred thousand Southern Baptists who would pay $1 each month to help eliminate denominational debts. Mrs. J. A. Anderson reminded readers, "Praying is fine. People ought always to pray. But if we want to pay our debts *we must plank down the cash*."[136] And "plank down the cash" the women did. By 1936 60 percent of Hundred Thousand Club members were women—"undoubtedly" WMU members.[137]

Four years later, with $3 million in debt still lingering, WMU promised the SBC that it would raise $1 million of the needed funds. Writers challenged every WMU member to give in 1940 double the amount she had given the previous year, "for a debtless denomination."[138] Appealing to wartime anxieties, HMB leader J. B. Lawrence urged readers to help the SBC become financially prepared for "a depleted and disillusioned, morally and spiritually enervated world [to] come to America for a blood-

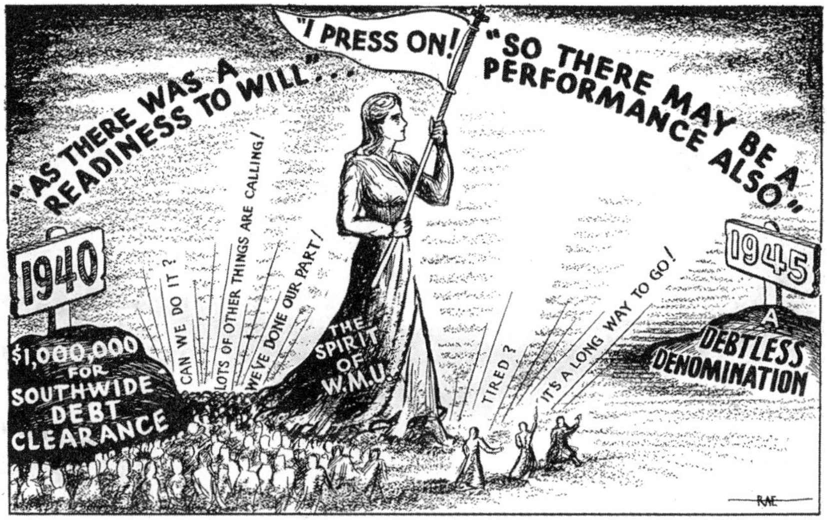


9. Cartoon from April 1942 *Royal Service.* (Used by permission of WMUA.)

transfusion" after World War II.[139] Creasman also regularly mentioned debt relief in monthly programs, reminding the women in 1942,

> What a horrible thing is debt!
> It is so binding, so grinding, so blinding!
> It is so wearing, so tearing, so ensnaring, so despairing!
> It is so harassing and so embarrassing!
> It is so stressing, so distressing!
> It is so pressing, so oppressing and so depressing!
> We worry, fuss and fume and fret
> And lie awake in grim regret,
> When we're in debt, when we're in debt![140]

"A Debtless Denomination by 1945" (the SBC's one-hundredth anniversary) soon became a familiar refrain in *Royal Service*'s pages—until the women's unprecedented giving caused convention leaders to anticipate being "Debt-Free in '43."[141] Their goal soon became reality: both mission boards' debts were finally paid off in the first half of 1943, and the remaining convention debts were cleared in the months that followed. This "most glorious victory" could not have been achieved without WMU; altogether the women gave more than $1.6 million.[142] Such a remarkable accomplishment reinforced women's significant role in supporting the SBC and convinced convention leaders that WMU's support was essential for any denominational cause to succeed.

Missionaries, pastors, and denominational leaders soon wrote to *Royal Service*, humbly thanking the women for their invaluable assistance. Men and women serving on the mission field declared that WMU members' gifts were like the "widow's meal" that never gave out, and pastors from across the South affirmed that "it really pays" to involve WMU members in efforts such as the Baptist Hundred Thousand Club.[143] Convention leaders were even more enthusiastic about WMU's work. Thanks poured in from the Relief and Annuity Board, the SSB, the Executive Committee, chairmen of SBC campaigns, and especially HMB and FMB. HMB leaders were "grateful beyond measure" and "under increasing obligation" to WMU; they had "no better friend."[144] FMB admitted that its "work would [have] collapse[d]" if WMU had not "saved our foreign mission cause in this tragic hour"; its leaders were "humbly and profoundly grateful."[145]

Leaders from across the convention agreed with J. E. Dillard, who spoke of how "W.M.U. came to the rescue" when SBC agencies were plagued with debt, likely saving them from ruin.[146] The women's organization, which was officially an auxiliary to the denomination, used its influence not just to support the SBC's institutions but also to prevent their demise. Male leaders quickly stated it was "impossible" to think about denominational causes without thinking of WMU.[147] By giving enthusiastically to denominational efforts, the women negotiated a new role for themselves within the SBC—one that convention leaders not only approved but increasingly required. Unlike other women's missionary groups, WMU transformed the old paradigm of women's work for other women into a broad support role that was integral to their denomination's success.

Through their denominational support, WMU members were involved in "the most interesting chapter in all our eventful history," the 1943 WMU *Year Book* proclaimed.[148] Indeed, from 1919 to 1945 *Royal Service* portrayed supporting the SBC as the most important missions role for WMU members, reflecting the denominational identity and culture developing among Southern Baptists. Participating in and giving to the SBC's programs, editors Elia Nimmo and Kathleen Mallory claimed, were the most effective ways for women to fulfill all of their essential missions roles. Women could assist with evangelistic efforts overseas and at home, enhance their prayer and mission study efforts for female and male missionaries, and increase their aid to emerging national women leaders by supporting the SBC.

This emphasis on denominational support provided WMU with clear focus and increased influence as traditional woman's missionary movement ideology fell out of vogue, leading to an important new role for WMU members. At the same time many other women's missionary organizations were merged into larger denominational structures, WMU began to occupy a significant auxiliary role in the rapidly developing SBC. The women's loyal denominational support and enormous financial contributions increased their organization's influence, as SBC leaders realized that their convention could not thrive without WMU's efforts. Instead of ignoring or even eliminating WMU, then, these officials praised the women's cooperative work. WMU members embraced their new denominational support role, ensuring the continuity of both their organization and the SBC during this period and in the years that followed.

# 4
# Cultivating a Christian Influence, 1946–1967

## My Hostess Was So Gracious

*My hostess was so gracious*
*That as we talked awhile,*
*I waited to discover*
*The secret of her smile.*
*Her home was very busy*
*With many a transient guest;*
*She surely had a secret—*
*Her spirit had such rest!*
*Then one day she told me*
*That when she swept the hall*
*She listened for the Master,*
*To hear his footsteps fall!*
*With many interruptions*
*She was patient all the more,*
*For she was always watching*
*For the stranger at the door.*
*Each time she set the table*
*With simple, wholesome meat,*
*She did it that the Master*
*Might come with them and eat,*
*And when she did the guest room*
*And daily made the bed,*
*She whispered to the Master—*
*"Lord Jesus, rest thy head!"*
*And so, I soon discovered,*
*In all things, great and small,*
*She did them for the Master—*
*The secret? That was all!*
*It filled her soul with sweetness*
*Though days in toil were spent,*
*She saw him in each duty,*
*Life became a sacrament!*
*But—did he come? you ask me,*

*With half indulgent air—*
*Ah, yes! he came for often*
*I've come and found him there,*
*I've felt him, heard him, seen him,*
*He ate there—we were three,*
*And when I left that morning*
*He laid his hand on me!*

—Eleanor Ruth Stephens
*Royal Service*, September 1951, 15

"An informed woman reads *Royal Service*," the back cover of that magazine's February 1962 issue proclaimed. And read—or at least subscribe—the women did. Subscriptions to *Royal Service* rose from around two hundred thousand in 1946 to nearly five hundred thousand in 1965,[1] as WMU and the SBC enjoyed their years of greatest strength. During this period, the magazine also celebrated its fiftieth anniversary, expanded to as many as ninety-six pages per issue, and included more features on "a wide range of subject matter of interest to Baptist women."[2]

*Royal Service* was heavily influenced by the domestic focus of American culture in these years. From 1946 to 1967, the magazine portrayed women's most important role not as bringing "uplift" to needy women or children or as supporting the denomination financially but as simply cultivating a Christian influence, most notably in the home. Aiding their families' faith development, editors and writers indicated, was an inestimable privilege—and responsibility—for Christian women. These women could extend their influence not through direct ministry efforts or heroic giving but by modeling Christian homes and sending their children as missionaries. Editors and writers likewise urged WMU members to use their positions as wives and mothers to address social problems they felt threatened the home, including racial inequality. The same editors, however, failed to critique gender inequality, which they did not consider problematic. Instead, throughout this period *Royal Service* reflected postwar American culture, emphasizing women's important role in the home.

## Southern Baptist Missions in a Changing World

Significant societal changes occurred in the United States in the years immediately following World War II. After the war, a generation of young men returned home from tours of duty, attended college as a result of the GI Bill, and settled down to comfortable lives with their growing families. Technological advances led to interstate highways and affordable suburban housing—as well as the nuclear arms race. The flourishing postwar economy contributed to an emphasis on comfort and convenience: by 1955 the United States, the new global power, consumed over one-third of the goods and services in the world.[3] Members of the growing American middle class bought cars and appliances such as clothes dryers to embellish their homes, which became increasingly important as centers of family life. The "baby boom" of seventy-six million children born between 1946 and 1964 demonstrated the value placed on family during this period and reflected the favorable economy that allowed many women who had worked during the war to return home and care for their families. In these years, the majority of the nation's residents turned inward, focusing on their family roles instead of on the uncertain world situation.

During this period, the South shared in the country's economic advance and cultural climate as never before. The growth of industries during the war caused the average Southerner's income to more than double, and many of the region's previously rural inhabitants moved to cities to find work in what C. Vann Woodward calls the South's "Bulldozer Revolution."[4] Hundreds of factories and businesses relocated from the North to the South, benefiting from the region's inexpensive labor, low taxes, and abundant resources. In addition, air conditioning made Southern homes comfortable and allowed families to spend hours indoors in front of their new television sets, absorbing programming from mainstream American culture. During these years some elements of Southern life—including racial attitudes—remained distinctive, but the region's uniqueness began to diminish. Removed from their impoverished rural lifestyles, many Southerners became more like other postwar Americans, although not always without a sense of nostalgia for the bucolic existence they had left behind. As *Royal Service* writer Irene Curtis lamented in 1949, "The South has passed from the simple life to the complex."[5]

In addition to changing lifestyles in the South, the postwar years witnessed the rise of evangelical religion throughout the entire United States. Popular evangelist Billy Graham was one of a number of "new evangelicals"— Christians who departed from their fundamentalist roots and engaged with American culture, bringing increased respectability to conservative American religion. The founding of the National Association of Evangelicals in 1942, Fuller Theological Seminary in 1947, the Evangelical Theological Society in 1949, and *Christianity Today* magazine in 1956 demonstrated the growth of new evangelicalism.[6] This emerging religious expression was especially popular in the North and the Midwest, the regions that had been most affected by fundamentalism in the 1920s. But throughout the entire nation, conservative churches experienced tremendous growth, and an increasing number of their members moved into the middle class. The rising influence of religion in American life was evident in 1954 when Congress added the phrase "under God" to the nation's Pledge of Allegiance; in the following year, "In God We Trust" was inscribed for the first time on all American currency. By 1965 almost two-thirds of American citizens were church members.[7]

This increase in religious sentiment, along with the prosperous economy, advances in airline transportation, and veterans' experiences in many nations, bolstered postwar evangelical missions efforts. A 1946 *Royal Service* program quoted a navy officer: "I don't believe anybody will come back from this war without being one hundred percent for foreign missions."[8] While many mainline Protestant denominations continued to question the necessity of evangelistic mission work at home and overseas, international missions became increasingly popular within the growing evangelical subculture. Dozens of North American parachurch missions organizations were rapidly founded, including Mission Aviation Fellowship in 1944, Far Eastern Gospel Crusade in 1945, Greater Europe Mission in 1949, and Overseas Crusades in 1950.[9] Many of these organizations experimented with nontraditional approaches to mission work, employing Bible translation, agriculture, radio broadcasting, music, and aviation as evangelistic tools. Evangelicals, highly motivated and optimistic about converting the world's peoples, joined these missions efforts in record numbers. By the mid-twentieth century, the mission force sent by evangelical organizations exceeded the declining numbers of cross-cultural workers affiliated with mainline Protestant denominations—and more missionaries went out from the United States than from any other country.[10] Female missionaries such as Elisabeth Elliot, who ministered among the South American people who had killed her husband, became heroes for thousands of American evangelical women.

During these years, the SBC and its mission boards experienced growth similar to that of other evangelical groups. Although Southern Baptists, steeped in Southern culture and wary of interchurch cooperation, have hesitated at times to call themselves evangelicals, the expansion of the SBC in many ways paralleled the rise of new evangelicalism. The denomination's churches increased in membership from fewer than six million individuals in 1946 to more than ten million in 1964, leading SBC historian Jesse Fletcher to call this period "the great advance."[11] Similarly, adult

WMU membership grew from four hundred thousand at the end of World War II to more than seven hundred thousand during much of the 1950s and 1960s. As many American families became more mobile, a number of Southern Baptists moved outside of the South for the first time, and soon the influence of the SBC spread into what had previously been considered the territory of the Northern Baptist Convention. By 1962 the SBC had churches in all fifty states.[12] Five years later, the total membership of SBC churches surpassed that of the United Methodist Church, making the SBC the largest Protestant denomination in the United States.[13] The SBC also sent more missionaries overseas than did any other Protestant group during this time.

In this era of growth and prosperity, Southern Baptists rapidly expanded their reach, building numerous new institutions both at home and overseas. FMB executive secretary Theron Rankin proposed in 1948 a bold new "program of advance" that led the board to double its missionary ranks and to begin work in more than a dozen new countries.[14] In the same period, HMB efforts expanded by 20 percent, as that board's missionaries began "pioneer missions" in thirty new states.[15] Convention leaders lauded this growth without realizing that it—along with the weakening of Southern identity—threatened the unity of a denomination based so strongly on a regional culture. Controversy over seminary professor Ralph Elliott's commentary on Genesis in 1961 provided the first rumblings of discord within convention ranks, as some conservatives expressed alarm at the book's use of modern historical-critical methods. However, the SBC's numerical and programmatic strength largely eclipsed this incident at the time.

As in previous years, WMU members during this period expressed strong support for their denomination, maintaining the position of influence that they had negotiated for their organization within the SBC. Editors Kathleen Mallory (1920–1948), Juliette Mather (1948–1957), and Ethalee Hamric (1957–1969) frequently included in *Royal Service* information about the convention's expanding institutions and emphases, including colleges and seminaries, the *Baptist Hour* radio program, the sesquicentennial Baptist Jubilee Advance, and even the National Conference of Southern Baptist Men.[16] As in the previous period, some issues of the magazine included a calendar titled "S.B.C. Coordinated Denominational Activities," while others recommended reading "our denominational periodicals"—publications of HMB, FMB, and state Baptist conventions—alongside *Royal Service*.[17] Clearly editors and writers expected WMU members to take an informed interest in broader denominational causes.

Indeed, one writer reflected in 1948: "From the beginning of its history Woman's Missionary Union has been together with the denomination, not something separate, but a part of the Southern Baptist Convention participating in all of its work. . . . How wise were the women leaders of that day who thus fixed the relationship of the W.M.U. to the S.B.C. on the 'together' basis! It was not so with the women's organizations of northern Baptists and other denominations, who chose the independent way, appointing their own missionaries and purchasing and holding their own property on mission fields. We are glad that we have stayed close by the Convention and its Boards and have been true to our name, Auxiliary, through all the years."[18] True to their upbringing as Southern women, WMU leaders emphasized their support of SBC structures, a role that they considered not restrictive but instead superior to Northern women's autonomy. Unlike other organizations in the woman's missionary movement, WMU had survived and even gained influence during the previous period by loyally assisting its denomination. Thus WMU leaders continued to stress this auxiliary role as the SBC expanded after World War II.

However, WMU's support of the SBC changed in what WMU stewardship chairman Amy Hickerson described as "a world of plenty, with war clouds lifted and a denomination free of debt."[19] Because of the SBC's more stable financial situation in these years, WMU members no longer claimed as essential a role in supporting the denomination through their giving. While denominational leaders still occasionally expressed that they were "overwhelmed with gratitude for the faithfulness [in giving] of Southern Baptist women,"[20] the women's sacrificial gifts were no longer required to save the SBC from ruin. Giving, especially to the Annie Armstrong Offering (AAO) and the LMCO, remained an important role for WMU members, but *Royal Service* no longer conveyed the financial urgency it had in earlier years. The number of articles featuring tithing, the Cooperative Program, and other forms of monetary support diminished significantly after SBC institutions transitioned from debt to prosperity. Adapting to this changing SBC climate, WMU editors no longer considered giving to support the denomination to be women's primary role in missions.

Likewise, rescuing "heathen" women in other countries, a task that had already fallen out of favor in *Royal Service* during the previous period, was no longer depicted as a viable role for WMU members in the postwar era. During these years, patronizing descriptions of women and men overseas disappeared almost entirely, replaced by reports of "the zeal and devotion of women in younger churches" that "often puts us to shame."[21] One Christian young woman from India reversed the language of the woman's missionary movement entirely, exclaiming to complacent American Christians, "You have wept many times for the heathen in my land; now I, from that heathen land, weep for you."[22] Unlike in earlier years, *Royal Service* writers understood that female American missionaries were not the sole source of salvation for needy women and children around the world. Instead, writers joined missions leaders from many denominations in explaining how female—and male—missionaries worked in partnership with national leaders to evangelize many lands, including the United States. Writers even discussed the transfer of mission responsibilities in some countries to national workers; the July 1965 issue of *Royal Service*, for example, praised the "move toward Nigerianization" of the Nigerian Baptist Convention.[23] As Southern Baptist women's pressing role in helping nationals diminished—and as American culture focused on comfortable domesticity—the magazine's writers began to simply inform their readers about Baptist work around the world rather than encouraging the women to action that only they could take.

In addition, by this time WMU members' tireless promotion of SBC missions efforts had made both women and men in their churches, on the whole, more aware of the denomination's work. WMU president Marie Mathis exclaimed in 1959 that God "hath done great things for us because our pastors have helped us. . . . Our church members have responded! . . . The denomination has responded!"[24] Many pastors, she enthused, had begun preaching missions sermons and promoting weeks of prayer for home and foreign missions because of WMU's influence. Ironically, however, this development weakened the women's role as missions advocates within their congregations. No longer did WMU members have a unique voice in presenting their churches with information about Southern Baptist missions; now male church leaders sometimes highlighted such emphases while women listened from the pews. Not only female but also male church members and leaders worked to support missions.

A similar shift was evident at the convention level, where WMU was respected for its financial support and emphasis on SBC programs. Alma Hunt, WMU executive secretary beginning in 1948, promoted close relationships with SBC leaders, speaking frequently of the "possibilities in co-operative planning."[25] In 1955 Hunt even became president of the

SBC Inter-Agency Council,[26] evincing the degree of authority her cooperative spirit gave her among male denominational leaders. Believing that WMU's position within the SBC was secure, Hunt led WMU to transfer some of its programs that had broadened in scope to denominational entities the women trusted.

WMU had already begun to reassign its good will centers to HMB, and during this period center workers became employees of the board, which WMU felt was better able to meet the needs of these missionaries.[27] Under Hunt's leadership, WMU gradually relinquished its control of the increasingly complex allocations of the AAO and the LMCO, allowing HMB and FMB to determine which missionaries and programs the monies would support. True to their emphasis on cooperation, the women's leaders also began encouraging "the entire church" to contribute to these offerings, in the hopes of securing greater donations.[28] In 1957 WMU voluntarily completed the transfer of its boys' organization, Royal Ambassadors, to the SBC's Brotherhood Commission, which the women felt was better equipped to provide male mentors. During the same year, WMU passed the ownership of its coeducational Carver School of Missions and Social Work, formerly the all-female WMUTS, to the SBC—in this instance facing pressure from male denominational leaders who argued that the school no longer had a distinct purpose related to WMU. All of these initiatives, begun by dedicated women seeking new ways to support the SBC, were so successful that they were incorporated into the denomination's broader structures, leaving few unique roles for women.

By 1964 WMU's church "task" statements involved the whole congregation, making no special mention of women: "teach missions; lead persons to participate in missions; provide organization and leadership for special mission projects of the church; and provide and interpret information regarding the work of the church and the denomination."[29] WMU staff member Elaine Dickson explained that by making many of its emphases church-wide, WMU "helps strengthen the mission interest of the church and helps the church fulfill its mission in today's world."[30] WMU tasks, Alma Hunt affirmed, were "portions of the church's tasks."[31] Accordingly, Hunt led WMU staff members to cooperate with leaders of other SBC programs to create a "correlated church curriculum" in which church members studied related themes not only in WMU organizations but also in Sunday School, Training Union, Brotherhood, and Music Ministry. In many ways, these changes reflected WMU's success in raising missions to a higher level of visibility within the SBC. But perhaps not coincidentally, WMU membership and subscription numbers began to decline around 1966. In a sense, the women had begun to work themselves out of a job. Although their mission support role in the SBC continued to be significant, it was no longer unique. Local congregations and even the entire denomination were working for the causes for which the women's grandmothers had pioneered support.

As a result, *Royal Service* during this period began to publish articles that urged a new role for women in missions. Though WMU members continued to support denominational efforts, as did many other Southern Baptists, they were also encouraged to adopt a different role that was theirs alone: cultivating a Christian influence in the home. Informed strongly by women's roles in postwar American culture and following models set by female missionaries years earlier, *Royal Service* editors and writers glorified women's domestic influence. Retreating into this gender-specific role provided women with what many must have felt was a satisfying purpose and a secure, domestic task amid a changing world.

## A Christian Influence in the Home

After the turmoil of World War II, many Americans embraced a remarkably conservative perspective regarding women's roles. The majority of middle-class white women married by age twenty and settled down in the expanding suburbs, where they cared for their families. During these years, average family sizes grew significantly: the birthrate for third children more than doubled, and births of fourth children nearly tripled.[32] Colleges began offering courses in subjects such as home economics—but the majority of female college students dropped out to get married before completing their studies. In addition, most women and men indicated in opinion polls that they favored a clear division of gender roles both in the home and in the workplace.[33] Feminist Betty Friedan critiqued this "feminine mystique" in her controversial book of the same name: "Millions of women lived their lives in the image of those pretty pictures of the American suburban housewife, kissing their husbands goodbye in front of the picture window, depositing their station-wagonsful of children at school, and smiling as they ran the new electric waxer over the spotless kitchen floor. . . . Their only dream was to be perfect wives and mothers; their highest ambition to have five children and a beautiful house, their only fight to get and keep their husbands. They had no thought for the unfeminine problems of the world outside the home; they wanted the men to make the major decisions."[34] While Friedan's description was hyperbolic and perhaps one-sided, the rapid sales of her book demonstrated the relevance of her words in the mid-twentieth-century American cultural milieu.

This domestic role for women was also reinforced by popular television shows such as *Leave It to Beaver* and *Father Knows Best*, which portrayed Caucasian families with strong, working fathers; fulfilled, homemaker mothers; and multiple happy, well-adjusted children. Likewise, popular women's magazines, though diverse in their focus, included numerous articles glorifying traditional women's roles. A 1949 *Ladies' Home Journal* writer, for example, proclaimed that "the homemaker, the nurturer, the creator of childhood's environment is the constant recreator of culture, civilization, and virtue."[35] This sentiment—and others like it—echoed lofty language that had been popular before the Civil War to describe women's roles in the home. As they had been more than a century earlier, American women were encouraged to dedicate their energies to the care of their families, wielding their benevolent, maternal influence to cultivate happy homes. Perhaps the greater freedoms and comforts that these twentieth-century women enjoyed allowed them consciously or unconsciously to return to old domestic roles with a sense of nostalgia instead of hardship or constraint. While recent studies demonstrate a diversity of attitudes toward women in this complex era, few scholars disagree that women's role in the home was a key emphasis in American culture during these years.

This strongly domestic focus was also evident in *Royal Service* from 1946 to 1967. The magazine's editors did not directly acknowledge the influence of postwar American culture on their ideology, but the number of articles they penned during this period on "the Christian home" demonstrated the importance of this topic in their thinking. *Royal Service* articles conveyed understandings of the home, motherhood, and family that were similar to those of mainstream U.S. culture, though always presented from an overtly Christian perspective. Editors Kathleen Mallory, Juliette Mather, and Ethalee Hamric urged the magazine's readers to use their influence primarily within the domestic sphere, leaving most public affairs for men to handle. *Royal Service* suggested that cultivating a Christian influence in the home was one of the most important roles for women during this period.

As might be expected, the magazine's writers justified their emphasis on the home by referring to the Bible, which Southern Baptists have traditionally cited as their foremost authority. Instead of admitting that the home was a topic of contemporary American interest, the women appealed to what they considered its timeless biblical basis. Prolific WMU program author Myrtle Creasman, who had written extensively about stewardship in previous years, adopted the domestic sentiments popular in this period without acknowledging their origin in broader American culture. Instead she claimed in 1948 that "home was the first institution given by God."[36] Similarly, missionary Deane Maynard in 1952 explicated the "heavenly home" of God the Father and the Son, after which she believed "the homes of earth" were to be patterned.[37] While these claims were based on biblical texts, *Royal Service* articles written in earlier years had not included such statements.

Nor had previous articles focused so strongly on the biblical mothers Hannah and Mary. According to religion professor Gilbert Guffin, writing in *Royal Service* in 1965, Hannah's role as the mother of Samuel established that "the first step of importance in our Christian mission to the world is what we do at home."[38] Similarly, former WMU president Ethlene Cox explained that Mary's example demonstrated that "a woman and a home and a child have mightily influenced the world."[39] Christian women who wanted a model for daily living, these writers emphasized, needed to look no further than the maternal examples of these two biblical characters, as they interpreted them. Even P. K. Dagadu of Ghana confirmed, "Christianity is a family religion. Jesus came to earth as a baby in a home."[40] Clearly, writers asserted, the home was important to God—and should be a priority for WMU members as well.

Although they did not directly acknowledge the influence of postwar American culture on this belief, the editors and editorial committee of *Royal Service* probably felt that their emphasis on the Christian home made the magazine more appealing to Southern Baptist homemakers not previously affiliated with WMU. Beginning in 1948, editor Juliette Mather expanded the magazine's contents to include more general articles not directly related to WMU's program; many of these new features focused on the home. Mather's successor, Ethalee Hamric, explained that she shaped the magazine's content to meet "the interests of a wide range of women . . . [both] the women in my city church [and] those in my sister's rural church."[41] This broadening audience was suggested by the tagline Hamric included in *Royal Service* from 1957 to 1963: "the missions magazine for Southern Baptist women."

These women, encouraged by their culture to serve as consummate homemakers, likely appreciated the numerous references to Christian homes in the pages of *Royal Service* during these years. A 1954 book reviewer instructed readers that "it is the mission of every married WMU member to have a Christian home"; similarly, a WMU Executive Board

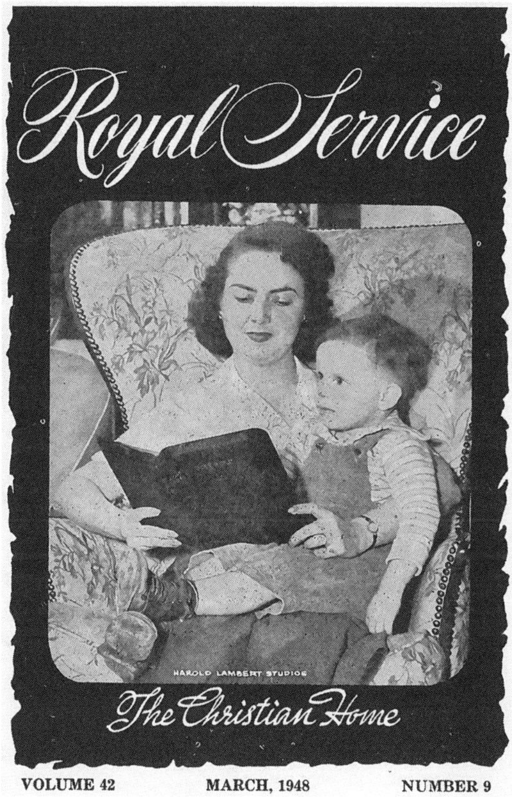


10. Cover of March 1948 *Royal Service*. (Used by permission of WMUA.)

member claimed in 1966 that nurturing better homes was "the biggest business in the world."[42] Like many other middle-class white women throughout the United States, these writers narrowed their focus to home and family—even reappropriating the traditional Southern Baptist language of "mission" to refer to domestic tasks. Dozens of other writers expressed similar opinions in *Royal Service*, occasionally alongside concern over "nation-wide family breakdown" that gave their ideas more urgency.[43] In accordance with this emphasis, the magazine's cover began occasionally to display photographs of mothers reading to their children, praying with their families, or performing other domestic duties. Article writers were sometimes pictured smiling alongside their husbands and children. And the magazine's pages frequently included photographs and illustrations of Christian families enjoying church together, participating in family devotions, and chatting happily over meals. Such dramatic changes to the content of *Royal Service* demonstrated the growing importance that editors and other WMU leaders placed upon cultivating a Christian influence in the home during the postwar years.

At least one *Royal Service* writer, like her secular contemporaries across the United States, idealized nineteenth-century gender roles, encouraging women to emulate their predecessors not for their bold missions work but for their domestic virtues. Recalling female Baptist missionaries whom readers revered, former FMB missionary Mrs. Roswell Owens claimed, "Ann Hasseltine Judson and Henrietta Hall Shuck saw that enlightened Christian women hold the key to Christian homes."[44] According to Owens's interpretation, Judson and Shuck were not only model missionaries, as they had long been considered, but model Christian homemakers as well. Owens did not mention the legacies of later, single women such as Lottie Moon or Annie Armstrong to support her claim; instead, she referred to two married women who had served during the early nineteenth century, when females' roles on the mission field had been more closely tied to their homes and families. Mid-twentieth-century women, she believed, would do well to espouse the domestic, Christian values of this earlier era of American life.

Other *Royal Service* articles likewise promoted gender roles popular in the nineteenth century and recurring within their contemporary context. Writers and editors urged women to pursue a "separate sphere" of activity in the home, although without using this exact phrase. In 1949 Mallory quoted an unnamed poet: "The men of the world build houses, ships, and domes; / But the women of the world, / God knows— / The women build the homes."[45] Emotion-laden words were used to describe women's roles in their distinctive realm of influence: here, to "build the homes"; elsewhere, to serve as "queens" in their homes, creating "havens" for their families.[46] Most readers probably agreed with a 1961 *Royal Service* writer: "It is in the home and in the church that women exert telling influence."[47] Similar statements throughout the magazine disprove for this period Dana Robert's claim that the Christian home was "the source of women's empowerment" and equality in missions.[48] While women did maintain a unique role in the home, this role did not promote equality as much as a return to hierarchical, gender-based spheres of influence.

Accordingly, multiple *Royal Service* writers—especially in the first half of this period—discussed a role they felt Christian women should prioritize: providing support to their husbands. Valeria Rankin, the wife of FMB executive secretary Theron Rankin, declared in 1946, "My place is here in Richmond helping make it possible for my husband to serve in his broader capacity."[49] Similarly, a 1965 writer explained that "a major part of the explanation of [the success of] Baker J. Cauthen," Rankin's successor, was not only "the Christian home in which he was reared" but also the influence of "Eloise Glass Cauthen, his life's companion."[50] Such women's virtuous influence in the home, writers felt, furthered their husbands' accomplishments. Being a wife was regarded as a significant commitment of service. As one writer commented, "When a girl marries[,] naturally her interests and schedule of life change to fit home and husband."[51] Similarly, the president of WMUTS—which was adjacent to SBTS—explained that most wives of seminary students spent their time not studying at the school but attending to the concerns of "pressing household duties and the care of little children."[52] Such writers apparently considered tending to their husbands' and children's needs to be one of the most important roles for married women.

Although many WMU leaders—including Mallory, Mather, and Hamric—were not married, few articles mentioned the viability of singleness for Christian women, an unpopular topic during this period. Apparently editors felt that their marital status was unusual, enabling them to produce materials to encourage Southern Baptist women's more common roles as wives and mothers. Implying that marriage was the appropriate course for Southern Baptist women, these editors generally excluded from *Royal Service* discussions of women who had never married, whose husbands had died, or who were divorced. Such women did not fit the stereotype presented in the magazine's articles. Writers assumed that marrying and supporting their husbands' efforts—not preparing for their own ministries or mission work—were women's priorities.

Rearing and guiding children were also important tasks for *Royal Service*'s readers during these years, writers emphasized. Under the editorial guidance of Mallory, Hamric, and especially Mather, the magazine highlighted the joys and responsibilities of motherhood. As with other domestic activities, caring for children was instilled with a sense of divine importance, and writers often used emotionally charged religious language to describe this role. Mothers, they opined, were "peculiarly blessed"; held "a divine task second in importance to none"; and enjoyed the "most sacred privilege" of leading their children to Christ.[53] Mrs. Ernest Pierce reminded readers that Ruth Graham, wife of the renowned evangelist, called herself "a homemaker by divine appointment."[54] And a 1952 photo caption even reappropriated the language of the beatitudes for mothers: "Blessed are the mothers of the earth, for they have combined the practical and the spiritual into one workable way of human life. They have darned little stockings, mended little dresses, washed little faces, and have pointed little eyes to the stars, and little souls to eternal things."[55] Clearly writers believed that the homemakers who constituted 80 percent of *Royal Service*'s readership[56] should feel not just happy but also blessed—as women of an earlier generation had been—to devote a large part of their time to raising their children.

Many articles during these years, then, detailed how women might go about the important task of child rearing and exhorted mothers to instill godly characteristics in their offspring. From 1948 until 1951, *Royal Service* included a feature called Why, Mommy?, which offered advice for mothers of young children and accompanying activity suggestions "for the sand-pile set." Writer Ruth Matthews answered questions such as "How early should parents begin their child's religious training?" Her response: "As soon as they start talking to their baby."[57] Numerous other writers also discussed the importance of "prepar[ing] spiritual food" for one's children.[58] As cartoonist Charles Wells reminded the women, "Vitamin pills will not make up for the patient guidance to a deep and resourceful faith."[59] Nurturing children's spiritual growth became as important to these writers as evangelizing the "heathen" had been in previous years.

Similarly, missionary Virgil McMillan did not urge mothers to serve on the mission field like he did but instead advised them to lead their children to Christ, pray together before meals, take their children to church, and "live a consistent Christian life" in their homes.[60] Additional features such as the "Ten Commandments for Modern Parents" and a list of characteristics titled "A Real Home" provided parenting suggestions for readers and reminded them that "the best thing parents can give to a child is a Christian home."[61] Such articles, though not addressing missions concerns as directly as most pages of *Royal Service* did, met readers' felt needs—and demonstrated the importance the magazine's writers and editors, influenced by postwar American culture, placed on the home. For the first time in *Royal Service*'s history, these leaders implied that women with families could not be effective in their worldwide impact unless they focused primarily on their role of supporting their own husbands and children. Reversing the sentiments of WMU writers from the early twentieth century, mid-century writers narrowed women's principal sphere of influence from the world to the home.

Writers in this period likewise placed new emphasis on the role they felt Christian parents had in creating "family altars" through regular times of worship and prayer with their children. These altars, the "highest expression of a Christian home," had been included among WMU's "moral standards" for years but began to be heavily promoted in *Royal Service* after

World War II. The magazine's June 1950 issue, for example, included two separate articles extolling family altars; the June 1940 issue had not mentioned this topic. Family altars even became a convention-wide emphasis in 1949, in part through WMU's influence.[62] *Royal Service* writers recommended that for family altars—also called "family worship"—parents and children set aside time together each day to read the Bible, pray, sing hymns, and discuss current missions events.[63] These activities, while seemingly routine, were imbued with great importance, as were other elements of Christian homes. Editors did not shy from hyperbole as they featured articles proclaiming family altars "the soul of a home," "cement that holds marriages together," a "sounding board for family problems," a "tie that binds," and part of a "child's most precious heritage."[64] Clearly WMU leaders believed that cultivating a Christian influence within the nuclear family should be a Southern Baptist woman's priority. For *Royal Service* readers during this period, unlike in the magazine's previous years, the home came first.

*Royal Service* wholeheartedly encouraged women to participate in family altars, but the magazine's writers apparently felt that leading this worship time was a Christian father's responsibility. True to the domestic ideal popular for American women after World War II, and reflective of their conservative Southern Baptist context, these writers portrayed women's appropriate role as supporting men's leadership, even in the home. A father's leading family worship, according to homemaker Sue Smith, resulted in "family solidarity which makes the home a place of security and blessing." The husband, she explained, "truly sets the pace for family activities."[65] Other writers agreed, though allowing that a wife might need to lead this worship time "in the absence of [her] husband" or if her husband were not a believer.[66] (In that case, "an attractive, well-kept home, well-prepared meals, and an abundance of love and happiness" could help lead the husband to faith, homemaker Mrs. Pat Clendinning explained.)[67] Although most husbands were at work during the day while their wives cared for the children, when the men returned home they were expected to resume their authority as family leaders. Their wives, perhaps recalling Owens's description of Judson and Shuck, apparently felt not only content but also blessed to assume what they believed was an important support role in their Christian families.

Such an emphasis on cultivating Christian homes was evident even in the metaphors *Royal Service* writers used to discuss a variety of topics. Instead of merely talking about sin hidden in a woman's life, Alabama WMU leader Mary Essie Stephens described sinfulness in terms of "an ugly streak of dust" that sunlight revealed on a hostess's table.[68] Hermione Jackson, a Birmingham pastor's wife, associated WMS programs with recipes requiring "teaspoons of witness," "cupfuls of understanding," and "bowls of knowledge."[69] She also compared enlistment for missions to—in turn—a tape measure, mixing bowls, measuring spoons, measuring cups, and canning jars.[70] The kitchen, not the mission field, was the prevalent image. Similarly, in a series of articles Alice Routh discussed how items in her pantry—a can of pineapple, a package of coconut, a can of coffee—reminded her of mission work around the world.[71] Several other writers introduced their articles by mentioning domestic topics such as peeling potatoes, cleaning house, or giving birth. These women probably hoped that such descriptions would resonate with their readers, most of whom spent a large portion of their time engaged in similar tasks. In addition these writers, like many others in *Royal Service* during this time, aspired to encourage readers to cultivate a distinctly Christian influence in their own homes. While this role naturally began with an inward focus—exploring the basis and importance of the Christian home, and wives' and mothers' tasks—many *Royal Service* writers also extended the role from the home into the world, in keeping with WMU's historic emphasis on missions.

## From the Home to the World

"To make homes," the May 1949 issue of *Royal Service* proclaimed, quoting nineteenth-century Scottish evangelical Henry Drummond, "that is what we are all here for." The magazine went on: "For the home / makes the town, / the town makes the city, / the city makes the country. / He who makes the home makes the world."[72] This sentiment captured well a missions philosophy popular among *Royal Service* writers and editors between 1946 and 1967. Southern Baptist women, they affirmed, both at home and abroad, should use their primary role in the home to influence their own families and neighbors—and eventually the world—for Christ. In this perspective, caring for children was not just a routine task; it involved the spiritual development of potential missionaries. And creating a Christian home meant not only domestic work; it also provided a witness to neighbors and friends. Leading other homes to become Christian was thus considered the ultimate goal of missions-minded homemakers. *Royal Service* writers transferred the high value their culture placed on the home not only to their own families but also to homes around the world. During this period, even the women's discussion of mission work was domestic in focus.

"Using the home as a center of witness" was a priority for WMU members, a 1966 program reminded readers.[73] Whereas previous generations of women had ventured into their communities or into the confines entrapping "heathen" women—or had wholeheartedly evangelized and "denominationalized" women in their towns and around the world—*Royal Service* editors in the mid-twentieth century narrowed the locus of women's mission work to one primary site: the home. Instead of urging women to venture out and become "mothers" of their communities, Mallory, Mather, and Hamric encouraged the women to use their influence inside the home as a "most natural and appropriate setting for sharing the gospel."[74] Like the New Testament Christians, these leaders explained, families could "open their homes for others to hear the gospel and to share testimonies."[75]

Examples of such ministry abounded in the magazine's pages. The Lucas family of Birmingham, Alabama, testified that the home had "unlimited possibilities" for witnessing: sons David and Darrell led two of their friends to become Christians after visiting with them, and as a result David "dedicated his life to special Christian service."[76] The Burress family invited a visiting Chinese engineer into their home in Hutchinson, Kansas, giving him a Bible to take back to his family.[77] Similarly, homemaker Helen Davis demonstrated a "real love for her lost neighbors," many of whom she evangelized in her house. At the same time, the writer was quick to add, Davis "did not neglect her own home, her children, or her husband."[78] Such stories modeled for readers a new paradigm of missions focused on the home, which was considered women's natural sphere of influence. According to *Royal Service*, no longer did women need to step outside the doors of their homes to share Christ's love; they could simply encourage their families to consider "our home as a place for witnessing for Christ."[79]

For this reason, writers encouraged homemakers not to be discouraged if they felt they had left unanswered a call to missions from their youth. Writer Sara Martin addressed the question, "Did God call you long ago to special service and have you somehow been sidetracked? Should you now be an appointed missionary?" Instead of encouraging the reader to apply for missionary service, as writers in previous years might have done, Martin counseled, "It may be that God called you to be a missionary-hearted wife and mother right where you are."[80] Women's roles in the home, she believed, were just as important as becoming a full-time missionary. In this way, Martin attempted to validate the domestic experiences of the majority of *Royal Service* readers, who did not have the opportunity to serve overseas. Such writers reprioritized their values to support the contemporary cultural emphasis on women's role in the home. In their estimation, cultivating a "missionary-hearted" Christian influence in the home was an appropriate way to fulfill God's call to serve.

Similarly, Juanita Wilkinson described a woman who had prayed that she would be a missionary but instead had married and called herself "just a housewife." This woman, Wilkinson indicated, witnessed to Mormons who came to her door—and, in Wilkinson's view, fulfilled her desire to become a missionary without ever leaving home.[81] As late as 1967, Irene Bark recounted that another mother went from tears to "beaming" as she discovered that God's call to mission service did not require living overseas; God simply "wanted her to be a missionary in her own home and community."[82] Bark—herself a pastor's wife who probably spent many of her days carrying out homemaking tasks to support her husband—prioritized Southern Baptist women's role in the home, likely pleasing readers by acknowledging the potential significance of the domestic duties that consumed much of their time. Such attitudes displayed a marked shift from previous paradigms of women's missions, which had encouraged going and giving. While editors did not relinquish their respect for traditional mission work, they apparently felt that many women could witness most effectively from their own homes.

According to *Royal Service* writers, this domestically focused missions strategy had as its goal not only the conversion of non-Christians but also the formation of more Christian homes. "Through missions," Myrtle Creasman claimed in 1948, "she [a Christian woman] helps to build Christian homes around the world."[83] The Christian home ideal, strongly influenced by American society, was in Creasman's view an appropriate outcome of evangelistic efforts in every country. Other writers felt that the same was true for each home in the United States. One women's group in South Carolina reported happily that the "best result" of their Thanksgiving mission project was not only "the twenty-nine conversions" but also "the many spiritual betterments that have made happy homes."[84] Unlike women in the previous period, members of this group regarded changed homes as nearly—or equally—as important as converted souls. A 1963 writer urged women to desire a similar outcome as they "pray[ed] that . . . women in Baptist churches will send the sweet perfume of Christ's encompassing love to permeate" not women's and men's lives but "the homes."[85] Influence a home for Christ, this writer probably felt, and multiple lives would be changed. As Drummond claimed, "All depends on the home."[86] Earlier *Royal Service* writers, with their emphasis on evangelism, had made such statements only about individual souls. But during this period, the motif of the home influenced even what WMU members hoped to accomplish through their evangelistic efforts.

Editors and writers also encouraged women to extend their influence from the home to the world by cultivating their own families' awareness of missions. Not only should mothers share Christ and their Christian homes with neighbors, they asserted; mothers should also help their sons and daughters learn about mission work from an early age. Raising missions-minded children during women's "glorious, fruit-bearing years"[87] became as important a task for women as serving on the mission field themselves, a marked change from earlier periods. Writers clearly elevated the home above more active public ministry. Even Edna Dawkins, one of the few women on FMB's professional staff, did not challenge mothers to apply for service overseas. Instead she urged them to "[lead] daily family prayer for missionaries, invit[e] missionaries . . . to your home, [and] mak[e] missionaries real by telling stories about them and their work."[88] Dawkins, like many WMU staff members, apparently felt that her singleness permitted her to pursue a ministry career that was not an appropriate priority for married women.

For such wives and mothers, writers prescribed "missionary reading," displaying missions pictures, discussing the missionary Calendar of Prayer, and giving to missions offerings in order to "create a strong missions influence in our homes" and to "make the voice of missions very real to sons, daughters, [and] grandchildren."[89] Sue Smith even described how her family marked missionaries' countries of service on a world map during their daily worship time.[90] Such features indicated that influencing children for missions was an important role for Christian mothers during this period—and one that readily combined the women's historic interest in missions with their contemporary emphasis on the home. As Hermione Jackson reminded readers, quoting Baker Cauthen, "The greatest school for missionary training is a devoted Christian home."[91]

Above all, writers advised, Christian mothers should encourage their children to commit their lives to mission service. A missionary "call"—such as God's calling of Samuel—was considered the most important instruction parents could help their children understand.[92] Missionary Alta Lee Lovegren reminded readers, "It is the parents' responsibility before God to provide such a spiritual atmosphere in the home that their children can hear God's voice"—and many parents, she felt, were failing at this task.[93] Lovegren and other writers urged mothers and fathers to redouble their efforts to teach their children about missions, not only so that girls and boys would gain missions knowledge but also so that they might eventually become missionaries themselves. A series of photographs of missionaries, children, and parents in the March 1961 issue of *Royal Service* reinforced this message, with the question "Is God calling your son or daughter?" prominently displayed across the page.[94] During these years, as many pages of the magazine encouraged parents to help children recognize God's call as challenged parents to consider a call to missions themselves.

No writer, however, acknowledged the inconsistency of guiding girls to a church-related vocation while urging their mothers to focus almost exclusively on family. Some of the girls of this period accordingly became young women in the 1970s who felt God's call not to mission service but to ordained Baptist ministry, to the dismay of many of their mothers. Based on the content they read in *Royal Service* between 1946 and 1967, these mothers may well have believed that becoming the parent of a missionary (but not of a clergywoman) was a more achievable and perhaps even more laudable role than becoming a missionary oneself.

Indeed, dozens of missionaries and missionary candidates inspired *Royal Service* readers with sentimental testimonies about how their own mothers had influenced their lives for missions. Hallie Neal, an FMB missionary to Mexico, described her mother's teaching and tenacity; missionary Elizabeth Hale of China reminisced about her mother's missions bedtime song; Mrs. A. P. Pierson in Mexico thanked God for her mother's prayers; and seminary student Mildred Plauchi testified to her grandmother's influence on her salvation.[95] Such features reinforced the gender ideology dominant in the postwar period, exalting women's role in the home and leaving public affairs to men. Editors probably believed that godly mothers wielded a greater influence on individual lives than any law or institution could provide.

A few mothers of missionaries related their own feelings as well, focusing again on the home. In articles such as "A Mother's Answered Prayer," "My Second Son Is a Missionary Doctor," and "Our Daughter Is a Missionary," women proudly discussed not their own mission work but their children's—and the atmosphere of support for missions that these mothers had provided in their homes years earlier.[96] Mrs. E. A. Gillis, whom Juliette Mather lauded for being named the 1949 "American Mother-of-the-Year," described the "sweetness of the presence of Christ in the home" in which she had raised her son Carroll, who became a missionary to Mexico.[97] And Sadie Crawley claimed that a "still small voice" told her, "To this end were you born, and for this purpose you came into the world—to be the mother of a missionary."[98] Serving as a missionary's mother, a role that had scarcely been mentioned in *Royal Service* before World War II, during this period became a mark of a devout, successful homemaker—and perhaps even the primary purpose for a woman's life. That women found fulfillment in this domestic support role instead of in more active missions tasks confirmed the value they placed on homemaking, in accordance with contemporary American gender constructs. For the first time, WMU members considered cultivating a Christian influence in the home one of their most important roles.

Like many mothers in the United States, women raising children on the mission field during these years were portrayed in *Royal Service* as committed to creating Christian homes for their own families in order to influence their children and the non-Christian families around them. Missionary Mrs. Claud Bumpus explained to readers, "Before we leave the States for our various fields of service, missionary wives are reminded that our most important place is in the home. With small children to care for, meals to plan, and all the other 'musts' of homemaking, a missionary wife cannot always go with her husband or take part in all of the activities she would like to. We are told that by making, as nearly as possible, an ideal Christian home in the community where we live, we are rendering our greatest service."[99] Apparently FMB leaders, who like WMU leaders were influenced by the domestic ideology prevalent in the postwar period, encouraged female missionaries to make creating Christian homes their priority. Instead of working tirelessly with national women, as exemplary missionary women had in the past, these female missionaries were expected to influence nationals indirectly, through their primary ministry with their families.

Missionary women—like many mothers in the United States—appeared to be content with this more restricted role, according to articles written by and about them. One missionary mother explained, "I want you to know [that] when I am caring for my children, I am doing Christ's service."[100] Another "missionary homemaker," Betty Cummins, had as her goal "demonstrating through the witness of her home the difference Christ makes"[101]—as did many Christian homemakers in the United States. Missionaries in the United States appeared to have similar priorities: a 1951 writer praised the "real home" of the Sieg family, missionaries who began every day with devotions together.[102] And photographs in multiple issues of the magazine showed happy missionary families—like other American Christian families—smiling together and enjoying time in their homes. Such images reinforced the gender ideals dominant in postwar American society, stressing women's role in the home—even when that home was overseas. Probably because of such an emphasis on family, the number of single women serving with FMB dropped precipitously, from 31 percent of the total missionary force in 1945 to only 13 percent in 1965.[103] Not only did American culture encourage every woman to marry and have children, but WMU editors as well as FMB and HMB leaders also apparently considered the most meaningful role for female Southern Baptist missionaries to be nurturing a family, not pioneering new missions endeavors.

Because of this emphasis on home and family, many missionary women discussed in *Royal Service* the influence that their Christian homes had on the people whom they hoped to convert. Although these mothers were generally more preoccupied with domestic roles than their bold "woman's work for woman" predecessors had been, they did continue to voice concern for non-Christian women and children, the primary audience they desired to reach through their Christian homes. Mavis Hardy reported that Japanese women peered through her windows "trying to find out what makes your home so different from others."[104] A national woman remarked about another missionary family, "I heard their prayer, their devotions; and, most amazing of all, even the children took part, asking questions and praying. . . . I became very much interested."[105] Apparently, a Christian home—and perhaps more significant, an American home—was an unusual and attractive sight to many non-Christian women overseas. Many female missionaries and their families likely joined one writer in praying, as did mothers in the United States, that "our home would become a place of positive witness for the Lord."[106] Witnessing, they agreed, was a "happy family affair"[107]—not simply a matter of personal evangelism, as it had been in previous years, but a task that relied strongly on the influence of the Christian home.

As part of this emphasis on Christian homes, missionaries often praised national Christian families whom they observed emulating their own domestic ideals. Communicating his own cultural values as well as Doña Consuela's, missionary Clark Scanlon remarked that this Guatemalan mother "ministers with healing hands in her own neat home" and raised five children who were "first-rate examples of the value of a Christian home."[108] Another missionary conveyed her joy in observing a young Israeli couple, whom she commended not for specific witnessing attempts but for forming a "Christian home shining as a light in this darkened city."[109] Similarly, writers praised a woman in Panama for "striving to build a Christian family"; a Japanese widow for courageously raising five Christian children; and Mrs. J. T. Valfor in the Philippines for maintaining daily family devotions, despite four years of war.[110] Missionaries, sensitized to the American cultural ideal of the Christian home, were quick to laud what they saw as its manifestations among nationals and to encourage these men and women to adopt other elements of the same ideal. As a result, many local women on SBC mission fields came to espouse an understanding of the home similar to that of the culturally dominant—though usually well-meaning—American missionaries who taught them. Señora Ceferina from Chile spoke as strongly as any FMB missionary when she declared that woman was "the center of the home." She continued, "If we can reach her, we can help her maintain a Christian home, help her educate her children, help her win her husband, and co-operate with him in creating a more complete work in the kingdom of God."[111] For Ceferina, as for the missionaries from whom she had learned some of her values, Christian mothers were an essential element of godly homes and families.

While the home was of primary importance to these nationals and missionaries, some Southern Baptist women did continue serving overseas in vocations that earlier female missionaries had pioneered: working as doctors and nurses, ministering in good will centers, teaching in schools, leading WMU organizations, and undertaking evangelistic work with women and children. Other female missionaries accepted the challenge of new roles, in accordance with the broadening scope of postwar evangelical missions efforts: publishing religious materials, bookkeeping, working at Baptist camps, ministering in children's homes, and serving as "house mothers" for Baptist students. But the majority of Southern Baptist missionary women mentioned in *Royal Service* during this period made homemaking for their own families a priority. A 1962 article profiling FMB missionary couples in Pakistan, for example, described five of the eight featured missionary women as homemakers—and did not mention two of the women's roles at all.[112] The magazine indicated that when such female missionaries were not busy maintaining their homes, they spent their remaining time on a variety of tasks traditionally considered "women's work": teaching sewing, leading music, writing letters, completing secretarial tasks, assisting in church activities, and homeschooling their children when they felt that good local schools were not available. Their roles mirrored those of the majority of the magazine's readers in the United States.

In *Royal Service*, many of these women were introduced by their husband's name and then by their own responsibilities in the home, revealing editors' prioritizing of domestic roles over even the missionary task. Mrs. William Clawson was a "homemaker and missionary"; Mrs. Wyatt Lee had "three children and assists her husband in the Boys' Student

Home"; and Mrs. W. L. Medcalf was a "mother and homemaker for her doctor-husband."[113] The phrase "missionary wife," which emphasized women's role in the home, became more popular than it had been in decades; readers were urged to pray for these women as they "strive to maintain exemplary Christian homes."[114] A few articles—even in this women's magazine—spent paragraphs detailing the work of "well-trained, aggressive" male missionaries but mentioned their "lovely wives" only in passing.[115] Such lengthy, stereotypical descriptions of male missions leaders, versus brief references to women's physical appearance, reinforced the idea that a woman's primary role was supporting her husband in the home.

In addition, photographs of female missionaries—not leading in churches or speaking in villages but "exchang[ing] cooking ideas" with national women and helping in the kitchen—also prioritized domestic tasks for women.[116] Many readers of *Royal Service*, homemakers themselves, doubtless identified with these wives and mothers who happened to be serving overseas. They understood from the magazine's pages that these missionaries' primary role was the same as their own: cultivating a Christian, missionary influence in their homes in order to impact families around the world. For many women, this task was imbued with great meaning. In their estimation, it was a role that only Christian mothers could fill.

## Civil Rights and Women's Rights

Because of their concern for the home, *Royal Service* writers and editors during the postwar period also encouraged women to use their Christian influence to affect the moral issues that they felt were endangering American homes and society as a whole. While caring for one's own family remained primary, writers for WMU's community missions emphasis—which had previously been called personal service and was repurposed as the more robust mission action in 1965—also urged readers to look beyond the sanctuary of their Christian homes in order to preserve them. Myrtle Creasman challenged WMU members in 1948 to "work not only for our own but for all American homes" by "stand[ing] for civil and moral conditions which will promote the safety and welfare of all homes."[117] Although readers probably regarded their own homes as their most important spheres of influence, they also inherited the community missions ideal from previous generations of WMU leaders and members. Since even before the time of Fannie Heck, WMU members had been ministering in their own communities. Women in this period did the same but often reinterpreted the motivation for their service as a desire to create and preserve Christian homes.

WMU national community missions director Edith Stokely reminded the women in 1952 that the need for Christian homes was "high on the list" of the "greatest needs in your community."[118] Because of this need, multiple WMU leaders urged readers not just to participate in family witnessing efforts but also to vote "to enact legislation that will protect her home from evil influences"; to combat salacious advertising that invaded "the sacred sanctuary of the home"; and to "enlist in the war against liquor evils" that threatened to destroy American families.[119] Guarding their own homes and the homes in their community from non-Christian influences was a priority for WMU members during these years, even if basic social action was required. Although sheltered in their homes, these women could not ignore the significant changes occurring in American society, including what they regarded as problems of "crime, gambling, divorce, alcoholic drinks, delinquency," racial prejudice, communism, materialism, and war.[120] These challenges only stimulated the women to work harder to cultivate a Christian influence within their families and their culture and thus "work for the Christian world mission" that they felt began at home.[121] If more Americans built truly Christian homes, one writer presumed, their children would have "the knowledge essential to maintain a good society" and to spread that knowledge around the world.[122] Such efforts, however, ultimately failed to reverse the changing American culture, which would contribute to turmoil in the SBC in the years to come.

But *Royal Service* writers were at least mildly successful in bringing attention to one social issue that the majority of WMU leaders apparently felt was important for Christian women and families to consider. Although the magazine rarely debated controversial topics during the time when Southern Baptists disagreed about them, it did include extensive discussions about racial inequality in the years following World War II. Guided by WMU's editorial committee, editors Kathleen Mallory, Juliette Mather, and Ethalee Hamric may have included numerous articles about the issue because it was on the mind of nearly every Southern woman, including the leaders of WMU. One writer called racism "the most acute world problem of today," and a national opinion poll likewise indicated that Americans thought civil rights was the most important issue facing the nation.[123] Lynchings, protests, Ku Klux Klan rallies, sit-ins, and even bombings filled Southern towns and evening news reports as the region experienced its greatest unrest since the Civil War.

Most Southern Baptists, unsettled by this turmoil and content with

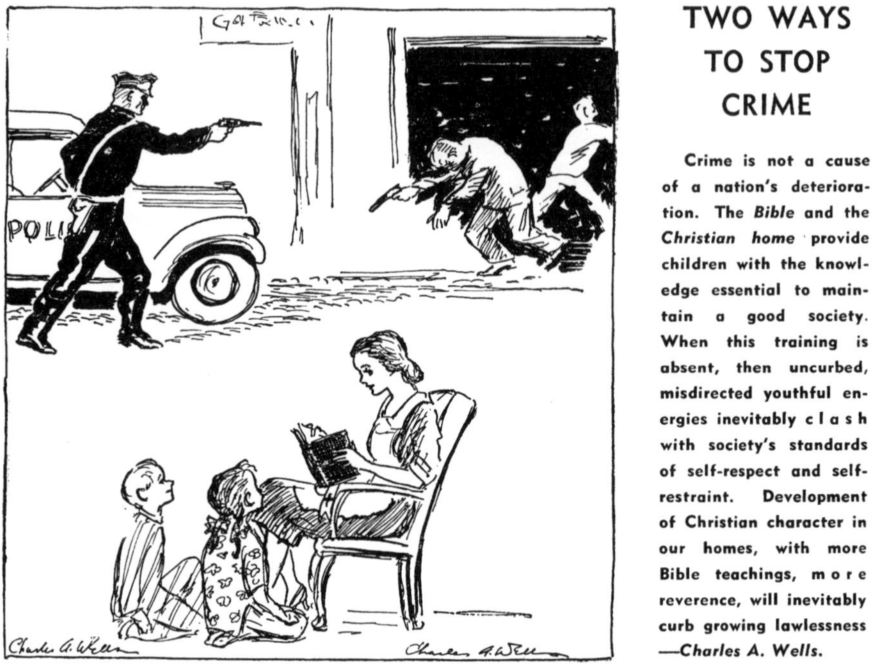


11. Cartoon from May 1957 *Royal Service.* (Used by permission of WMUA.)

their privileged position as Caucasians, opposed efforts toward racial equality, which the editor of the *Alabama Baptist* in 1956 deemed a "grave problem."[124] Opinions expressed in state Southern Baptist newspapers and convention meetings during these years were largely pro-segregation. A majority of laypeople as well as many pastors apparently agreed with leaders of Ephesus Baptist Church in Virginia: "Integration . . . is against the best interests and contrary to the wishes of the great majority of both races."[125] Several individuals worried that the racial crisis was an "invasion of states' rights" and "a communist-agitated move" that would destroy their way of life.[126] Clearly civil rights was a contentious and unpopular issue among Southern Baptists—and one with a growing impact upon the denomination.

Accordingly, *Royal Service* writers and editors could hardly avoid discussing race in the magazine's pages. Their attitudes toward African Americans, however, were significantly more progressive than those of most Southern Baptists. Appealing to their readers' maternal instincts, *Royal Service* writers urged women to consider "what every mother of whatever race wants for her child"—and in turn, to "teach our children that all people are born equal in the sight of God."[127] Such encouragement to consider other mothers' feelings above the opinions of other members of their own race posed a significant challenge to Southern Baptist women during this period but one correspondent to women's emphasis on the home. In teaching equality to their sons and daughters, writers averred, mothers would not only overcome racial stereotypes but also use their influence in the home to become "potentially one of the most powerful groups on earth as far as formation of attitudes and Christian character is concerned."[128] Helping children to view all races as equal, the women felt, was an appropriate and significant role for Christian homemakers.

*Royal Service* writers were also motivated to confront racism because of the global scope of their work. This idea was advanced by WMU staff member Mildred McMurry, who was probably WMU's strongest advocate of racial justice during this period. Influenced in her views by her studies at the University of Chicago, McMurry "hung on every word that [civil rights leader] Martin Luther King [Jr.] said," according to WMU president Helen Fling.[129] In her roles as WMU mission study director (1951–1954), department secretary (1954–1957), and division director (1957–1962), McMurry presumably had the opportunity to contribute ideas to WMU's magazine planning process during this period. McMurry explained her convictions to *Royal Service* readers in 1962: "As Christian women in a missionary organization, we cannot escape the responsibility laid on us to witness in our attitudes and acts to the fact that God is the creator of all men, who are equal in his sight. . . . The new urgency in these days demands serious study and discussion of Biblical teachings which give light on the world's greatest human problem."[130] As McMurry understood, WMU members' missionary commitment and desire to reach all people naturally made them more aware of their treatment of women and men of other races.

Indeed, a number of *Royal Service* writers called attention to the ways in which "race relations affect world missions."[131] Mary McCormick explicated, "We cannot expect the pagan peoples of the world, most of whom are dark-skinned, to have faith in our Gospel which teaches the fatherhood of God and the brotherhood of man when our actions deny our professions."[132] Many readers, with their desire to share the gospel—and their exposure to world cultures through WMU magazines—likely agreed. Unlike most other white Southern women (and men), WMU members frequently read about the conversion of Africans to Christianity and learned about the exemplary ministry efforts of Christian leaders from the same continent. The women's longstanding study of global mission work convinced at least some of them that "the command of Jesus to win all men leaves no room for race prejudice."[133] One Kentucky woman who read in *Royal Service* about mission work in Nigeria even invited into her family's home a Nigerian Baptist pastor who was studying in America. Although, as she explained, she was at first hesitant to extend this invitation, her previous mission study convinced her that "a true man of God would be all right whatever his race."[134] The woman reported that her family and the pastor had a delightful visit.

By this period, many WMU members had also been involved in work with African American Baptist women and children for years, which acquainted them with individuals of another race in ways most Caucasian women and men did not experience. Olive Powell, a student at WMUTS, testified in *Royal Service* that her work with an African American Bible school convinced her "that all men are the children of God and that a colored child should be treated with the same regard as a white child."[135] Mrs. C. W. Moseley from North Carolina remarked that interracial work was "one of the most worth-while projects" in which her missionary society participated.[136] Many other WMU members across the South reported that they trained leaders of African American Baptist women's groups, formed interracial leadership councils, led nursery schools for African American children, awarded scholarships to African American students, and led "Negro Vacation Bible Schools," among other endeavors.[137] These women's efforts, however, were still largely *for* African Americans, not undertaken *with* them.

WMU leaders, who had supported African American Baptist women's work since Annie Armstrong's day, even published a photograph of revered National Baptist leader Nannie Helen Burroughs on the cover of the June 1947 issue of *Royal Service*, edited by Kathleen Mallory. Mallory herself—along with more than one hundred other Southern leaders—had signed the 1943 Statement of Conference of White Southerners on Race Relations, which promoted "civic rights and opportunities" for African Americans, while not advocating racial integration.[138] Thus Mallory evinced WMU's relatively progressive thinking on racial issues while remaining within the bounds of attitudes considered acceptable among white Southerners of the day. Under the guidance of Mallory and later Alma Hunt, WMU members through their interracial work gained a different perspective on race relations than was prevalent among their neighbors who never ventured beyond their segregated streets. Unlike many other Southerners, some WMU members learned to "view the American Negro without prejudice"[139]—or at least to make progress toward such a view.

Immediately after World War II, however, a few *Royal Service* writers adopted the more common Southern—and Southern Baptist—defense of segregation, which even the 1943 Statement of Conference of White Southerners on Race Relations had failed to condemn. Writer Myrtle Creasman, quoting fundamentalist SBC leader E. P. Alldredge, in 1946 called segregation "the simple and natural right of the individual or the group or the race to separate its homes and schools and churches and business enterprises and professions and its social life from other individuals or groups or races as it may choose."[140] Thus Creasman articulated a widespread perspective among white Southerners who feared forced contact with African Americans. Other writers, while nominally advancing the cause of racial equality, used paternalistic language that African Americans surely found troubling. One pastor's wife reminded readers to "not be discouraged or disgusted if they [African Americans] forget to be humble, or when they flounder in their newly-given freedom. They will need unusual love and patience and help and guidance as they attempt to catch up."[141] In her perspective, African Americans were not yet true equals of Caucasians; they still needed sympathy and ministry from their more experienced white counterparts. A few similar prejudices, common in wider Southern society, were evident in *Royal Service*, especially during the early years of this period—including in a minority of the correspondence from readers featured on the We Get Letters page.[142] Such sentiments reflected the complex and sometimes contradictory attitudes about race prevalent among white Southern Baptists during this time, even among relatively forward-thinking leaders such as Mallory.

The overwhelming majority of *Royal Service* articles on the topic, however, advanced racial stances that were progressive for the period. Writer Lucy Grace rebuked the Ku Klux Klan, the white supremacist group popular among some Southern males: "How can intolerance reflect the spirit of Calvary? How can superiority find room at the cross?"[143] Similarly, McMurry proclaimed in 1963, "From the beginning of the Christian era, it has been the duty of Christians to protest error, and injustice. . . . The world is looking to us for moral leadership and for a clear cut interpretation of Christianity."[144] McMurry's sentiments echoed the language of civil rights leaders, voicing a concern for justice that was unfamiliar and uncomfortable to many Southern Baptists. An anonymous group of *Royal Service* readers protested to editor Ethalee Hamric that McMurry's

1963 article "could certainly have been eliminated from this or any other issue"[145]—revealing the prejudices of some Southern Baptist women in this period and the criticism that WMU editors received as a result.

Still, McMurry and other writers persisted, sometimes creating quizzes that challenged readers to examine their own prejudices with probing questions such as "Would you want them [people of other races] to live in your neighborhood? Would you like them as your personal friends?"[146] In July 1967, *Royal Service* even included a lengthy article on race relations by John Cross, the pastor of Birmingham's predominantly African American Sixteenth Street Baptist Church, which had been bombed in a racially motivated attack in 1963. Cross described how Birmingham "sought to come to grips with its racial dilemma" and urged readers to help improve conditions in the city.[147] Clearly the magazine's editors did not hesitate to challenge the attitudes and actions of many white Southern Baptists. Perhaps the women's experience with male-dominated Southern culture subconsciously contributed to their empathy with African Americans, another marginalized group. Certainly their Birmingham location meant that these WMU leaders could not ignore the civil rights struggles that were taking place virtually at their doorstep.

Mrs. Bradley Allison perhaps best summarized WMU leaders' views on the topic as she asserted, "Failing to share in solution of racial problems automatically makes us a part of the problem."[148] Indeed, McMurry demonstrated such an outlook by serving on a local committee for school desegregation, although she and other WMU leaders did not participate in Birmingham demonstrations related to race.[149] Within the pages of *Royal Service*, several writers suggested similar practical actions that women could take to combat racial injustice. They encouraged readers to advocate equal health care and education, cooperate with African American churches, write letters to report discrimination, "take a stand" against segregation, and lead group discussions about race relations.[150] Though the number of WMU members who actually participated in these activities is unknown, it is notable that within their conservative context writers provided such specific suggestions.

Editors and writers made no mention, however, of more controversial techniques of civil disobedience, such as sit-ins or marches. One writer did discuss what *not* to do: "picketing and boycotting"—or on the other extreme, "send[ing] used hymnbooks and worn benches to colored churches"—were ineffective techniques, she asserted.[151] Although some civil rights leaders may have held different opinions or advocated more direct involvement on the part of every Southern Baptist woman, the magazine's abundance of articles about race relations—unlike its avoidance of other controversial topics—was significant. *Royal Service* editors could have dismissed race as not related to missions, espoused prevailing racist views, included only a few half-hearted articles, or ceased discussing the topic after "hate mail" began arriving daily from some of the magazine's subscribers.[152] Instead they printed page after page of material that contemporary readers likely found thought-provoking. WMU leaders obviously felt that using their influence for racial equality was a role that all missions-minded Southern Baptist women should fill.

This emphasis, while noteworthy, was not unique to WMU publications. The organization's editors joined leaders of a handful of other SBC entities, including HMB, FMB, the Christian Life Commission (CLC), and the Social Service Commission, in espousing more progressive ideas about race than most Southern Baptists held. In 1947, influenced by these leaders, the SBC issued a Charter of Principles on Race Relations, which affirmed the equality of all people and called for justice without recommending specific actions. Within the next few years, WMUTS and all of the SBC's seminaries accepted their first African American students. These institutions integrated earlier than most other Southern denominational schools did, as well as before the Supreme Court's 1954 *Brown v. Board of Education* decision made school segregation unconstitutional.[153]

In 1964, the same year the national Civil Rights Act was passed, the CLC proposed a resolution supporting civil rights and integrated churches. After extended debate, however, messengers to the SBC failed to approve it. But the following year, messengers approved a similar statement, and the SBC officially instituted an annual Race Relations Sunday.[154] Moreover, in 1967 FMB appointed its first African American missionary since the 1880s; HMB already employed African American missionaries.[155] Even though many individual Southern Baptists were prejudiced against interracial cooperation or integration, some convention leaders advanced the cause of racial equality with their words—and sometimes with their actions. This outlook was especially true of WMU, which had the "most directly challenging approach [in the SBC] to the whole area of race," according to Southern Baptist ethics professor T. B. Maston.[156] Guided by leaders such as McMurry, Mather, and Hamric, *Royal Service* frequently advocated racial equality.

The plethora of material about race in *Royal Service* during these years was in marked contrast to the magazine's dearth of information about gender equality, however. Upon initial examination, this omission seems unusual for a magazine written by and for women, in an era when women's roles were beginning to undergo significant change. While the homemaker ideal, as previously described, was predominant in postwar American culture, during these years increasing numbers of women also added "paid employee" to their list of roles. By 1960, 40 percent of American women worked in part-time or full-time jobs outside their homes—twice as many as only twenty years before.[157] A few of these women began in the 1960s to advocate gender equality in the workplace and in the nation as a whole. Their concerns attracted the attention of President John F. Kennedy, who in 1961 established the Commission on the Status of Women. Two years later, the publication of the best-selling *Feminine Mystique* expanded the influence of Betty Friedan and others who believed that women's traditional roles in American society needed reform. In 1966 Friedan was selected as the first president of the National Organization for Women, the first new women's rights organization in the United States in many years and a harbinger of the modern women's rights movement. Leaders of this emerging movement championed equality for women in all aspects of American life.

During the latter years of this period, several mainline Protestant denominations began to engage in their own discussions about women's roles. In 1956 both the Methodist Church and the United Presbyterian Church in the USA sanctioned the ordination of female ministers. The predominantly Southern Presbyterian Church in the United States did the same in 1964—the year that the first Southern Baptist woman was ordained for pastoral ministry. Addie Davis's ordination by Watts Street Baptist Church in North Carolina was not the cause of serious discussion among SBC leaders, who probably viewed this event more as an anomaly to be dismissed than a trend to be resisted. Because of the denomination's conservative nature, Davis was not able to secure a pastorate in a Southern Baptist church and eventually relocated to Vermont. This situation reinforced Mather's observation in the 1958 *Encyclopedia of Southern Baptists*: "Southern Baptist women do not preach and are not pastors."[158]

In 1963, though, WMU president Marie Mathis was elected second vice president of the SBC, perhaps out of respect for WMU's seventy-five years of influence within the denomination. However, no other significant changes occurred with regard to women's official status in the convention during this time. No resolutions about women were adopted at SBC annual meetings in this period. Correspondingly, few SBC publications discussed women's roles in much detail. As in many other conservative evangelical denominations—especially in the South—women's primary influence was still assumed to be in the home. Female subordination, most Southern Baptists felt, was part of the appropriate ordering of society. The women's rights movement had not yet generated significant interest in the SBC, whether positive or negative.

Given this context, then, it is not surprising that *Royal Service* devoted little space to discussing gender equality. Editors Mallory, Mather, and Hamric continued to spend more time emphasizing the Christian home than they did the "modern woman."[159] Multiple writers throughout the period did acknowledge the growing number of "girls in gray flannel"—working women—many of whom, WMU staff member Billie Pate claimed, were "our finest, most consecrated and capable women."[160] WMU leaders evidently had little trouble with these women who did "double duty"[161] in the workplace and the home, as long as they continued to prioritize their families and cultivate a Christian influence in whatever context they found themselves. Accordingly, writers' discussions about working women tended to be more pragmatic than philosophical. Few articles debated the propriety of businesses' employing women; most simply recognized working women as a growing segment of the American population—and emphasized the necessity of including these and other "busy, busy women" in WMU.[162] For several years, *Royal Service* included a regular feature on the efforts of these working women, whom Alma Hunt emphasized were "just as important" and "just as valuable" as other WMU members.[163]

By the 1960s, as new roles emerged for women in American culture, the magazine's writers occasionally began to discuss the expanding roles of "today's woman," which Hamric enumerated as first "wife-mother: comforter, counselor, teacher, guider, arbiter, confidant, prodder, minder" and then "money-earner: typist, pastry-maker, teacher, salesperson, scientist, politician, lawyer, seamstress."[164] Even the order of this list revealed the priority that WMU leaders placed on women's tasks in the home. A few writers did acknowledge that through their increasingly varied roles, "modern women" often had "influence and position unknown in previous generations."[165] Instead of encouraging women to use this influence to seek their own equality, however, writers challenged them to appropriate it for "broader, more constructive Kingdom work"[166]—especially through WMU.

Thus WMU president Helen Fling reminded *Royal Service* readers in 1963 that WMU provided "the opportunity of maximum Christian service" for every Southern Baptist woman, especially "today's 'woman in transition.'"[167] Enlisting gifted women, especially professionals, "who are not so busy pursuing secondary matters that they fail to live in companionship with God" was apparently more important to *Royal Service* writers than was encouraging laywomen to advocate their own rights—probably a "secondary matter" to most writers.[168] As WMU enrollment gradually began to decline at the end of this period, Hamric and other WMU leaders did not focus their efforts on advancing new roles for women. Instead they used their influence to attempt to involve all Southern Baptist women—both traditional and "modern"—in WMU.

Perhaps the magazine's editors and editorial committee also felt that women's rights, like other controversial topics, provoked widely differing opinions among their readers, and thus they avoided mentioning the issue during these years. But the absence of even letters to the editor on the subject seems to indicate that unlike racial equality, gender equality was not a primary concern of the conservative Southern homemakers who comprised the majority of the magazine's readers and who were busy cultivating a Christian influence in their homes and communities. The lack of serious discussion of women's rights in the pages of *Royal Service*, as in the halls of SBC meetings, most likely indicated not that leaders suppressed dialogue about the topic but that it had not yet aroused widespread interest among Southern Baptist women. Few of these women could have predicted how significant gender roles would become in American society in the following years—and the dramatic effects that this issue, and accompanying societal changes, would soon have on the SBC.

Marie Mathis, reminiscing in 1963 on the bold struggles of pioneer WMU leaders, acknowledged that "this vision seems to have dimmed with victory. It is as though we have accepted the status quo—even slipped backward in some areas."[169] Her words accurately reflected the conservative roles that *Royal Service* portrayed for women in missions from 1946 to 1967, a period in which such insights were scarce as writers focused not on expanding women's roles but on encouraging women to cultivate a Christian influence in their homes and, in turn, their communities.

Strongly informed by—though not frequently acknowledging the influence of—postwar American culture, *Royal Service* writers and editors in these years highlighted the importance of nurturing a missions-minded Christian family, departing from the outwardly focused themes of "woman's work for woman" and sacrificial denominational support that had been significant in the magazine during previous periods. With woman's missionary movement ideology obsolete, and many church members supporting the SBC as a result of WMU's efforts, editors Kathleen Mallory, Juliette Mather, and Ethalee Hamric claimed a new role for WMU members in the home. Throughout *Royal Service*'s pages, they adulated Christian homemakers—adapting this popular cultural image to their own tradition—and expressed a new awareness of mothers' crucial roles in missions.

In addition, WMU editors and writers attempted to protect "sacred" homes by encouraging Southern Baptist women to rectify social problems that threatened them. These writers urged their readers to address racial inequality—a pressing problem in the South during these years—and demonstrated a comparatively progressive attitude about the issue. However, in keeping with their conservative Southern Baptist context, writers were silent regarding gender equality, a topic that would emerge as significant in the denomination only in the years that followed.

# 5
# Almost Unlimited Possibilities, 1968–1983

Woman's Psalm

*You have called me Woman,*
*O Lord.*
*You have created,*
*and made me female.*
*You have drawn me*
*into a kinship of the ages,*
*And into sisterhood*
*with those before me:*
*Ruth, Deborah, Esther*
*are my sisters,*
*Eve and Mary share my name.*
*Like a flower*
*springing up to live,*
*Like a fragrant blossom*
*growing in the field,*
*You have called me forth*
*in beauty*
*And counted me worthy*
*of honor.*
*I will praise you with my life.*

*Into a troubled time*
*you have called me*
*And I have heard.*
*Into a weeping people,*
*and into an evil day*
*Have I come.*
*With gifts sufficient*
*to my calling*
*You have favored me.*
*You are my strength,*
*you have not left me powerless:*
*You have given healing*
*and mercy into my hands,*

*And loving kindness to my touch.*
*You have filled my mouth*
*with truth,*
*Your name is on my tongue,*
*O Lord.*
*I will praise you with my life.*

—B. Joyce Clayton
*Royal Service*, March 1974, 31

Antiwar demonstrations. The assassination of civil rights leader Martin Luther King Jr. Protests against sexism in the Miss America pageant. All of these events dominated American news headlines in 1968, introducing to the United States a new climate of activism, liberation, and reform. Many middle-class American women breathed this air of change and abandoned full-time homemaking roles for remunerated professions, petitioning for equal pay and equal rights. Even Southern Baptist women found themselves seeking new roles in an atmosphere quite unlike that of their grandmothers in the early twentieth century or of their mothers in the years following World War II.

In an attempt to "match the spirit of a new decade" and "capture the mind and heart of every Baptist woman," as writer Kathryn Bullard put it,[1] executive director Alma Hunt led WMU to launch revised organizational structures in 1968 and to create several new magazines and organizational names in 1970. *Royal Service* became the monthly magazine for Baptist Women, which was a new, simplified organization for women ages thirty and above. *Contempo*, a monthly magazine introduced in October 1970, was intended for women ages eighteen to twenty-nine who were involved in the new Baptist Young Women organization. Features in these two magazines reflected the women's rights activism prevalent in American culture, replacing *Royal Service*'s earlier theme of maternal influence with that of nearly boundless roles for women. In marked contrast to the previous period, writers during these years discussed numerous opportunities for their readers, including a variety of employment and marital options. They also portrayed mission action as an important task for WMU members. Without espousing overly controversial positions on women's liberation, WMU writers and editors consistently described expansive roles for women in missions and in the church—roles strongly influenced by the changes occurring in American society.

## Women in a Changing World

"This is an explosive, revolutionary, wonderful time to live," declared Ethalee Hamric in 1968, recognizing the dawning of a new era more than ten years after she had begun editing *Royal Service*.[2] Hamric and millions of other Americans were gripped by the images of activism and counterculture emblazoned across television screens and newspaper pages during this period. Southerners and non-Southerners alike witnessed—and sometimes participated in—social movements that arose across the country as a new generation came of age. Race riots indicated that civil rights legislation had failed to procure full equality for African Americans. Women likewise drew attention to their maltreatment and petitioned for equal rights. A seemingly interminable war raged in Vietnam, and demonstrations against this conflict swelled almost daily. Students and activists took to the street to protest injustice and promote peace; thousands also experimented with drugs and anti-establishment "hippie" lifestyles. A new spirit of change replaced the inwardly focused, comfortably domestic post–World War II period.

During this period, groups such as the National Organization for Women—whose membership rose to 250,000 in the early 1970s[3]—sought to reform the gender discrimination inherent in many American laws and public policies. Influenced by the spirit of the time, a number of women began to advocate equality in employment opportunities, government representation, child-rearing responsibilities, and all other realms of American life. A younger generation of female activists, however, found such political advocacy too gradual and cumbersome. These women's liberationists, frequently called "women's libbers," adopted strategies similar to those used in the civil rights and antiwar movements. Seeking nothing less than a revolution in American culture, "libbers" participated in various forms of "consciousness raising" and social action, such as protests against beauty pageants, which they criticized for judging women by their physical appearance. Such endeavors were quite successful: 40 percent of American women in 1970 supported "efforts to change and strengthen women's role in society," and 57 percent affirmed the same statement in 1974.[4] This movement, often referred to as the second wave of American feminism, soon became arguably the largest social movement in U.S. history.

Within a short period of time, such reforms helped effect significant changes in many women's lives. As birth control became socially acceptable and most forms of abortion were legalized, the birthrate declined. For some American women, motherhood was no longer a primary goal.

Women who did have children increasingly sought employment: preschool enrollments rose dramatically, and soon almost half of all American women worked outside the home. More women also attended and completed college, with female enrollment in institutions of higher learning climbing 450 percent between 1950 and 1974.[5] Title IX of the Education Amendments of 1972 prohibited educational programs from discriminating against women, resulting in dramatic growth in the numbers of female athletes at high schools and universities across the United States. These women joined millions of others around the world in celebrating the United Nations' International Women's Year in 1975, which was soon extended to the United Nations Decade for Women. Even many Southern women, traditionally more conservative than their Northern and Western peers, participated in this movement, with Houston hosting the National Women's Conference in 1977. However, opposition from Southerners—and an emerging antifeminist movement—helped prevent the ratification by state legislatures of the long-proposed Equal Rights Amendment (ERA) to the U.S. Constitution, which Congress passed in 1972. While popular with many Americans, the women's liberation movement remained controversial throughout this period.

Churches were by no means immune from the debate over women's liberation. During this period, discussions about the roles of women in church life dominated American Protestantism. In 1971 the status of women in religion was even selected as the top religious news story of the year.[6] Methodist and Presbyterian denominations had already sanctioned the ordination of female ministers, and in the 1970s groups such as the Lutheran Church in America, American Lutheran Church, and Episcopal Church USA followed suit. Within a few years, more than eighty denominations had ordained eleven thousand American women, to the delight of a growing number of church members but to the chagrin of others.[7] Other denominations elected female leaders, resurrected women's organizations, created women's task forces, or held consultations on women's issues. American Baptists, for example, in 1970 conducted a study on women in executive staff positions and in 1974 convened a gathering of women serving in vocational ministry. During these years denominational women's magazines published article after article about women's roles, including the United Methodist women's "Celebration of Women in Ministry" and the United Presbyterian women's "Adam's Rib or the Singer of the Magnificat? What Is Woman in the Biblical Tradition?"[8] Thousands of Protestant women also pursued vocational ministry, enrolling in theological seminaries in record numbers to train not only for the pastorate but also for chaplaincy, teaching, and other ministry careers. Some of these women enlisted for overseas mission service, but that option was not as popular as it had been in the past, when fewer church-related careers had been available to women. To many female seminary graduates, pioneering in a pastoral role in the United States was more attractive than becoming a missionary.

Young women who did choose to serve as missionaries likely noticed that their mission agencies also began to explore issues of gender inequality. Many evangelical missions organizations reconsidered the undefined domestic roles that female missionaries had assumed in previous decades, calling these women an "underused asset" on the mission field.[9] The single-sex ministry promoted by "woman's work for woman" missiology—long past its prime—became even less popular as many female missionaries aspired to be "fully recognized equal partners" with their male counterparts.[10] Women such as Patricia Mortenson, who served with the interdenominational Far Eastern Gospel Crusade, urged mission boards to "view women as suited for roles besides just 'nurse, teacher, secretary, [and] children's worker,'"[11] and many organizations accepted this challenge. Although most female missionaries did not attain complete equality with men, the women who were interested in this goal succeeded in raising discussion about gender issues and consequently achieved real gains in status.

Other evangelical women likewise reconsidered their roles in a rapidly changing world—and in churches where change was often more gradual. While scattered conversations took place throughout the late 1960s and early 1970s, the first national statement on what came to be known as "evangelical feminism" occurred in 1973. In that year, the Chicago Declaration of Evangelical Social Concern was issued by a group of several well-known evangelicals, including Southern Baptist leaders Foy Valentine and James Dunn. This declaration acknowledged, among other things, that "we have encouraged men to prideful domination and women to irresponsible passivity" and called both sexes to "mutual submission and active discipleship."[12] The Evangelical Women's Caucus was formed the following year by evangelicals who believed that the Bible empowered women, not oppressed them. Also in 1974, discussion of Jesus's "liberation [of women] from the chains of custom" filled the pages of the influential evangelical feminist book *All We're Meant to Be: A Biblical Approach to Women's Liberation* by Letha Scanzoni and Nancy Hardesty. Although opposed by many in their churches, evangelical feminists had launched a viable movement.

Even prominent evangelical publications such as *Christianity Today* debated women's roles; like mainline Protestants, evangelicals could not ignore the women's movement.

The SBC was no exception. As Leon McBeth posits, Southern Baptists were "culturally conditioned" by their changing society to discover biblical support for women in ministry.[13] A number of Southern Baptists, like many other evangelicals, began to reexamine scriptural passages about men's and women's roles, often concluding that the two sexes' gifts were "complementary and mutually important" to the church.[14] Leaders of many SBC entities embraced egalitarian views more readily than did many of their constituents, with institutions such as CLC and SBTS advancing the most progressive ideology. A few Southern Baptist churches began ordaining women, and New York City's Christ Temple Baptist Church—an African American congregation with a female pastor—was admitted to the SBC in 1972.[15] Although precise figures are unavailable, it is likely that more than one hundred Southern Baptist women were ordained to ministerial roles by 1981.[16]

In addition, WMU president Marie Mathis was nominated for the SBC presidency in 1972 but lost the election to businessman Owen Cooper. In 1976 the convention chose laywoman Myra Bates as its second vice president. The following year, laywoman Marian Grant became the first woman to chair a major SBC board or committee—the Convention Committee on Order of Business.[17] Outgoing WMU president Christine Gregory became first vice president of the SBC in 1981, although she privately complained that she was "so completely ignored" in that role "because I was a woman."[18] By 1982 women comprised 10 percent of the SBC Executive Committee, 24 percent of FMB trustees, and 5 percent of the SBC seminaries' boards.[19] McBeth and sociologist Sarah Frances Anders carefully documented such statistics throughout this period, noting that although the percentage of women in SBC leadership roles was increasing, figures were still low in comparison with those of other denominations.

Supporters hailed these new roles for Southern Baptist women as "fundamental" and "far-reaching"[20]—but opponents protested that "God's chief assignment to women" was to assist their husbands.[21] The typical Southern Baptist's view fell between these two extremes. In surveys conducted among SBC church members in 1978, fewer than 20 percent of respondents indicated support for women serving in pastoral roles, but 75 percent approved of women's ordination to youth ministry, social ministry, or Christian education.[22] Letters to the editors of SBC publications alternately favored and opposed new roles for women. These editors printed a remarkable number of articles on the topic, often supporting women's rights.

Indeed, several Southern Baptist magazines dedicated an entire issue to women in ministry, including winter 1975 *Review & Expositor* and January 1977 *Baptist History & Heritage*, which *Royal Service* recommended to its readers. In November 1974, FMB's monthly magazine *Commission* claimed that women were "one of the unused potentials of modern missions" and reported on the expanding roles of female foreign missionaries.[23] HMB's May 1972 issue of *Home Missions* went even further, profiling three ordained Southern Baptist women and discussing the "subconscious female subjugation practiced by most Southern Baptist congregations."[24] These and other SBC publications in the 1970s overwhelmingly advocated women's equality in both church and society,[25] although many Southern Baptist laypeople held a different opinion. The growing divergence between SBC leaders and church members threatened the broad consensus that had prevailed in the denomination in previous years.

This increasing interest in—and controversy over—women's roles was evinced during the SBC's annual meetings. In 1973 pastor's wife Jessie Sappington presented a resolution affirming "distinctive roles" for women in submission to their husbands, which the Resolutions Committee rewrote to support women in leadership but messengers ultimately adopted with Sappington's original wording.[26] The following year, messengers rejected multiple proposals from CLC leaders favoring gender equality.[27] Undeterred, CLC sponsored a conference titled Christian Liberation for Contemporary Women; the SBC's Broadman Press soon published the proceedings in a book titled *Christian Freedom for Women and Other Human Beings*. These denominational leaders continued to champion the cause of women's equality, despite many church members' hesitation to consider such an issue.

In addition, in 1978 eleven SBC entities sponsored a three-day Consultation on Women in Church-Related Vocations—led by WMU's Catherine Allen—in order to "develop a body of findings for use by all denominational agencies in employment, policymaking, education programs, and vocational guidance."[28] The consultation's three hundred participants discussed the status of women in Southern Baptist life, with many voicing frustration over inequality. As a result, a few SBC entities vowed to eliminate sexism from their hiring practices and publications. Two years later, however, Joyce Rogers—wife of prominent Southern Baptist pastor Adrian Rogers—attracted four thousand women to her Mid-

Continent Women's Concerns Conference, which "encourage[d] women in fulfilling their traditional roles as wives and mothers."[29] Southern Baptists were clearly divided by conflicting views of gender.

Debate over women's roles—along with other controversial topics such as abortion and homosexuality—continued at SBC meetings, but the convention failed to declare an official position on the women's issue. Conflict persisted for Southern Baptists at the local and state levels as well, with some local associations refusing to seat messengers from churches with female deacons, seminary students adopting a resolution in support of women's rights, at least two state conventions passing resolutions against women in ministry, and female clergy encountering few opportunities and plentiful opposition. In 1980 and again in 1981, the SBC addressed this sensitive issue with the same carefully nuanced resolution that affirmed women's "immeasurable contributions" but also supported "the biblical role which stresses the equal worth but not always the sameness of function of women."[30] Influenced by their conservative Southern Baptist traditions, messengers hesitated to affirm full gender equality.

In 1983, when the SBC annual meeting took place in Pittsburgh instead of in the South, women's rights advocates in the convention finally claimed a victory with a resolution that encouraged "maximum utilization" of women's gifts, based on biblical passages such as Galatians 3:28.[31] That same year, Women in Ministry, SBC, was formed to "provide support for . . . and affirm" Southern Baptist women who felt called to vocational ministry.[32] WMU executive director Carolyn Weatherford arranged for WMU to supply meeting space and financial support for this new organization, and she (and later other staff members) served on its steering committee. This service, although never publicly emphasized by WMU leaders, demonstrated WMU's openness to exploring new positions for women in SBC life. Female Southern Baptist ministers appeared hopeful that their view would prevail at last.

However, around the same time new forces of conservatism arose in American religion and culture. In 1976 *Christianity Today* editor Harold Lindsell published his influential book *The Battle for the Bible*, which asserted that a strict understanding of biblical inerrancy was essential for Christian faith. Two years later, nearly three hundred evangelical leaders crafted the Chicago Statement on Biblical Inerrancy, a seminal affirmation that "Scripture is without error or fault."[33] Southern Baptist signers of this statement included prominent conservatives W. A. Criswell, former president of the SBC, and Paige Patterson, president of Criswell's Institute of Biblical Studies in Dallas. Influenced by such conservative evangelical views, these men played key roles in the controversy that wracked the SBC during the 1970s and 1980s.

Just as a growing number of evangelical leaders in these years viewed biblical manuscripts as wholly inerrant, many others believed that the Bible contained absolute statements mandating conservative social positions—and felt responsible to carry out these commands within American society. This emerging evangelical subgroup, known as the Christian Right (or Religious Right), labored to rid American society of what they considered to be a range of evils, including abortion, homosexuality, pornography, humanism, and "the fractured family."[34] Like-minded organizations were founded in rapid succession, including Focus on the Family in 1977, Concerned Women for America in 1979, the Moral Majority in 1979, and the Traditional Values Coalition in 1980. Of these, the Moral Majority was the most prominent. This organization wielded considerable influence in American religion and politics under the leadership of Jerry Falwell, pastor of Thomas Road Baptist Church in Lynchburg, Virginia, which at the time was not affiliated with the SBC. The Moral Majority's success was evinced in part by the election of conservative Republican Ronald Reagan as president in 1980. Conscious of his constituency, Reagan proclaimed 1983 the Year of the Bible and enacted legislation consistent with the Christian Right's aims. Conservative movements such as the Christian Right had clearly emerged as a significant influence in American society.

Opposition to feminism was an important issue for members of the Christian Right. Demands for gender equality, these Christians felt, were both unbiblical and dangerous. Dozens of women's leaders, including Joyce Rogers, hosted conferences and gave speeches (but not sermons) about "biblical womanhood." Best-selling books by authors such as Elisabeth Elliot and Marabel Morgan promoted the idea of women's submission.[35] And in broader American culture, a few women launched an antifeminist movement, with Phyllis Schafly's Stop ERA campaign as its most successful effort. Such ideology found a particularly welcoming home in the South, where conservative religion and traditional family systems prevailed. A 1980 study revealed that 46 percent of Southern Baptist ministers claimed to sympathize with the Moral Majority; a 1981 survey similarly showed that Falwell was the most influential preacher among Baptists in eighteen states.[36] The conservative countermovement in American society provided just the energy that a few concerned Southern Baptists needed to fuel their own conservative revolution—one whose effects would be felt for decades.

In 1973 a group of Southern Baptists, fearing that the denomination's theology was becoming increasingly liberal, formed the Baptist Faith and Message Fellowship and launched the conservative *Southern Baptist Journal.* Around the same time, other conservatives[37] created new educational institutions, including Luther Rice Seminary, Criswell Institute of Biblical Studies, and Mid-America Baptist Theological Seminary. Conservative influence gradually began to prevail at the Pastors' Conference that preceded the SBC's annual meeting. By the late 1970s, a number of conservatives—led by Patterson and judge Paul Pressler of Houston—began meeting to determine how to "secure the elected leadership of the convention from among those we know are committed to biblical inerrancy."[38] This group solidified their strategy by 1979, when they engineered Adrian Rogers's successful bid for SBC president. By assuming control of the presidency for several years, conservatives calculated, they could reshape the SBC's numerous committees and thus reposition the denomination theologically. Time would prove this strategy to be highly successful.

Rogers's 1979 election as SBC president heralded a new era for the denomination. In the years that followed, moderates struggled to retain power while conservatives attempted to "go for the jugular" of the convention, as Pressler infamously described efforts to gain control of trustee nominations.[39] "The Controversy," as many called it, soon overshadowed all other aspects of SBC life, attracting hundreds of pages of coverage from denominational and national media and consuming the attention of numerous pastors and convention leaders. Conservative candidates continued to be elected SBC president—a result, some moderates claimed, of hundreds of conservative church members being transported to each annual meeting in time to vote. Moderates, slow to develop a unified strategy, gradually understood the challenge facing them and took action. In 1980 North Carolina pastor Cecil Sherman assembled a "Gatlinburg Gang" of moderate leaders in order to "beat back the Fundamentalists" by "do[ing] serious politic."[40] Three years later, moderates founded the journal *SBC Today* and established a Forum as an alternative to the annual Pastors' Conference. Tensions continued to mount as moderates and conservatives alike realized that the future of the convention was at stake.

Moderates, largely supportive of the SBC and holding key administrative positions within it, pointed out that many conservative churches only nominally supported the Cooperative Program and other convention endeavors, such as the ambitious Bold Mission Thrust missions emphasis. Conservatives countered that the denomination's programs had become a "golden calf."[41] Moderates decried creedalism and the politicization of the convention; conservatives stressed the need to rectify what they considered errant theology. Central to the debate was controversy over women's appropriate roles in church and society.[42] Moderates emphasized men and women's equality and freedom in Christ, while conservatives believed the Bible mandated female submission. As SBC leaders debated their competing visions for women, the editors of *Royal Service* and *Contempo* included frequent—though less divisive—discussions of women's roles in their magazines' pages as well.

## WMU's New Woman

Between 1968 and 1983, both *Contempo* and *Royal Service* included numerous articles supporting a wide range of roles for women. When asked about their views on women's rights, however, WMU leaders consistently declined to respond, asserting as Carolyn Weatherford did in 1979 that their "singular purpose" was missions.[43] Unwilling to involve the organization officially in such a controversial issue, these leaders explained—as Catherine Allen put it—that WMU was interested in "anything that enabled women to do more for the cause of missions, or anything that hindered them from missions."[44] Everything else, they felt, was secondary. WMU president Christine Gregory agreed with this specific focus: "I never felt that you can be all things to all people. You just can't do it."[45] Aware of the diversity of strong opinions about women's roles among Southern Baptists, including WMU members, WMU leaders officially limited their organization's focus. These women negotiated their conservative SBC environment by generally remaining silent about their personal convictions on divisive issues. As in previous years, WMU leaders avoided theological debate, prioritizing instead the less contentious topic of missions.

But despite their efforts at neutrality, WMU leaders throughout this period personally—and sometimes publicly—affirmed women's service in a variety of ministry roles. In 1971 Hunt and WMU president Marie Mathis asserted, "Don't think we're not progressive. We're just not militant."[46] With such a declaration, these leaders associated WMU with the broad goals of the women's liberation movement while distancing the organization from the movement's more radical participants. This stance, although not articulated in WMU's official statements, was held by many WMU leaders during this time. For example, despite their claims that WMU did not promote women's rights, Weatherford led WMU to help form Women in Ministry, SBC, and Gregory took a "personal stand . . .

on [supporting] the ordination of women."[47] Neither of these actions appears to have been mentioned in *Royal Service* or *Contempo*, probably because of editors' desire to avoid advancing strong positions that the majority of their readers would have opposed. However, conservative SBC leaders had little doubt that WMU leaders disagreed with their views on gender roles. Joyce Rogers allegedly even told Gregory that she "had a notebook on" Gregory's and Weatherford's activities and knew what they were doing.[48] No matter what they discussed (or did not discuss) in their public statements, WMU leaders apparently supported views on women's issues that were progressive enough to be suspect among the denomination's growing conservative contingent.

Editors of *Royal Service* and *Contempo* during this period espoused the same broadly feminist ideology held by other WMU leaders, as well as by staff members at many other SBC entities. Guiding *Royal Service*'s efforts in these years were editors Ethalee Hamric (1957–1969), Rosanne Osborne (1969–1973), Laurella Owens (1973–1977), Lane Powell (1977–1978), Adrianne Bonham (1978–1981), Anne Leavell Mann (1982–1983), and Betty Merrell (1983–1985). *Contempo* editors included Owens (1970–1973), Ellen Dossett (1973–1974), and Mary Ann Ward (1975–1987). For a variety of reasons, including family responsibilities, relocation, and job promotions, the tenure of many of these editors was relatively short. However, throughout this period both *Royal Service* and *Contempo* displayed a surprising consistency in their discussions of women's roles. This indicated not only that the magazines' editors probably held similar opinions but also that WMU Executive Board members and upper-level staff members exerted a significant degree of control over the magazines' content.

Aware of the controversy surrounding women's rights, WMU throughout this period maintained its policy of what editorial director Gertrude Tharpe referred to as allowing "many people from many places [to] help plan and decide what will go in *Royal Service* each month."[49] Most important, editors continued to shape their magazine plans around the extensive proposal and review processes of the organization's Executive Board. In addition, editors sent manuscripts to "several people in the [WMU] building and around the country" for comment before publication in order to "assure that every . . . word can be counted on"[50]—or perhaps more realistically, that every word would not be too radical. Multiple issues of *Royal Service* even listed WMU's president and executive director as consulting editors. Without a doubt, the organization controlled its words carefully.

In order not to alienate its relatively conservative constituency, or get "too far ahead of the people in the churches," as Hunt described it, WMU did not publish statements that Owens called "too flaming."[51] But the words that the organization did print advocated a wide range of opportunities for women in church and society. While not explicitly championing the women's liberation movement, WMU editors repeatedly discussed many of the same roles for women that this movement emphasized, using what Allen describes as "language that left the sky as the limit as to what women could do."[52] Although editors and other WMU leaders avoided radical statements that many Southern Baptists would oppose, in their magazines these leaders repeatedly moved beyond their historic focus on missions to affirm new roles for women. As an auxiliary to the SBC, WMU was financially and editorially independent, with leaders elected by local WMU members and not by messengers to debate-filled SBC annual meetings. Thus WMU's executive director and president did not need to fear that conservative donors or trustees would reshape their organization's focus or its leadership. As Weatherford explained, tongue in cheek, "I'm not worried about my job. No man wants my job."[53] While they were conscious of the controversy that arose in the SBC during this period and exercised caution in the content they published, WMU leaders such as Weatherford felt secure enough in their organization's autonomy to include in their magazines opinions with which many conservative SBC leaders surely disagreed.

Thus in addition to supporting annual Southern Baptist emphases, *Royal Service* and *Contempo* promoted new, women-centered events such as Women's Day in the Church and Baptist Women Year in the Church. The organization's leaders—like many other Americans at the time—apparently considered womanhood itself something to celebrate. In contrast to Weatherford's and Gregory's rather disingenuous statements about WMU's "singular purpose," WMU staff member Aline Fuselier forthrightly declared, "WMU means involvement in women."[54] The March 1974 issue of *Royal Service* included reader Joyce Clayton's "Woman's Psalm"; the June 1978 edition of *Contempo* similarly advertised sheet music for Fannie Heck's "Woman's Hymn," which WMU had apparently resurrected.[55] Recurring features about women's roles in church and society filled page after page of both magazines in the mid-1970s: Womensphere and Reborn Free in *Royal Service*, On Womanhood in *Contempo*, and a number of similar emphases. As in the early years of the woman's missionary movement, articles about foreign mission fields discussed conditions for women: "Does a [West African] woman have money of her own?" "Is it difficult to be a woman in your culture?"[56] Writers implicitly—but not explicitly—challenged patriarchal SBC culture as they celebrated women's efforts in church and society.

Descriptions of women in these magazines diverged from those *Royal Service* had included during the previous period but aligned with contemporary cultural models. No longer was the ideal woman quietly maternal; WMU editorial director Lawrence Webb criticized the "bias . . . which puts women on pedestals" and separated them from the rest of the world.[57] Webb, the first male supervisor of professional personnel at WMU, espoused progressive views, perhaps in part as a result of his studies at SBTS. The writers selected by Webb and WMU editors accordingly portrayed women as "no idle stroller[s] on the sideline," "unordinary," "free," and full of "unique gifts and strengths."[58] The "greatest sin" a woman could commit was not failing to raise Christian children but—according to *Contempo* writer Rebecca Thompson—"not developing [her] potential."[59] A 1970 writer agreed that the tasks to which God could call women were "limitless."[60] Approximately twenty years after *Royal Service* had described the home as women's appropriate realm of influence, the magazine's pages were filled with references to women's empowerment, daring, and freedom—all emphases prominent in the women's liberation movement.

Although writers disapproved of what they regarded as the excesses of this movement, they largely affirmed its focus on women's equality. As Webb stated, "My wife . . . is not a radical feminist, but she is a liberated kind of person."[61] Several editors apparently felt that all women deserved to be treated as "liberated kinds of people": they experimented with gender-inclusive pronouns such as "(s)he" and "he or she," just as many other publishers did. And a number of articles for the first time identified women by their full names instead of by their husband's name—Sarah Wicker Smith instead of Mrs. Tom Smith, for example. Such adjustments reflected a conviction that women were defined by their own identities and not by their relationships to men, a sentiment that reflected changes occurring in American culture at the time.

In a more radical move, WMU writers and editors reinterpreted biblical passages to emphasize gender equality. In response to the Consultation on Women in Church-Related Vocations, Weatherford led WMU to pledge in a written statement to "show inclusively and specifically God's plan for Christian women to be bearers of the Good News"[62]—but such a commitment was already evident in the pages of WMU magazines. Bible studies in the postwar years had praised mothers such as Hannah and Mary; editors and writers throughout this period, however, demonstrated a proclivity for female leaders such as Deborah and Lydia. Instead of glorifying these women's domestic qualities, writers—both female and male—described the ways in which the women had "boldly challeng[ed] the beliefs and practices of a corrupt world" and "exercised their gifts of service."[63] Reviewing biblical narratives through a contemporary lens, writers claimed, for example, that Jochebed "must have been a strong personality"; Esther had "assumed leadership in direct opposition to the custom of that day"; and the woman Jesus met at the well had demonstrated "both faith and action."[64] Writers and editors described biblical women as powerful agents of change—the same role that many evangelical feminists desired for contemporary women.

Similarly, writers discovered themes of gender equality in Paul's writings—books that conservative Southern Baptists often quoted to support female subordination. Webb and Margaret Crawley were among those who drew attention to the story of Priscilla, whom they alleged had served as part of a "husband-wife partnership in ministry," thus refuting "the stereotype that 'a woman's place is in the home.'"[65] Seminary professor Hubert Drumwright asserted that Phoebe had been a deaconess in the church at Cenchrea,[66] a controversial claim amid debate over acceptable ecclesiastical roles for women. Numerous writers cited verses such as Galatians 3:28—which Velma Brown called Paul's "emancipation proclamation"—to affirm women's equality, excusing with surprising ease more restrictive passages in Paul's writings as "influenced naturally by the male-dominated society" of the time.[67] Literal readings of such apparently hierarchical Pauline passages were proposed primarily in letters from the magazines' readers, such as a Baptist Young Women group from Lawson, Missouri, who defended "God's chain of command in Ephesians 5:23."[68] Unlike these local WMU members, the writers secured by *Royal Service* and *Contempo* editors promoted biblical interpretations that favored gender equality.

Editors and writers for these magazines likewise presented outstanding historical female missions leaders as paragons of action and equality. Numerous articles described the contributions that "early adventurous, dedicated women" had made to the cause of missions—not by mothering missionaries but through their own "courageous conduct" on foreign mission fields.[69] Ann Judson, praised in previous years for being an exemplary mother, was now acclaimed as a woman who, as Lynette Williamson put it, had "participated as [a] partner" with her husband; her "intellectual capacity" was also noteworthy.[70] Annie Armstrong and Lottie Moon, whom many writers in the previous period had overlooked, were once again popular—Armstrong for what Weatherford called her "stubborn will to go forward" and Moon for having actually been "a 'women's libber' who threatened to resign unless FMB allowed her to participate in policy-making."[71] Writers refashioned these historic missionary heroes to fit contemporary ideals.

More than once, Weatherford even described the formation of missions organizations such as WMU as an early expression of the women's movement, although she noted that the women had organized in order to demonstrate missions concern and not to advocate their own rights.[72] Still, Weatherford stressed these women's boldness, which some contemporary readers doubtless found appealing. Seminary student Mary Harrison likewise discussed what she regarded as the "revolutionary roles" the first students at WMUTS had assumed in 1904.[73] Such writers worked to demonstrate that earlier generations of Southern Baptist women had displayed the very traits prized by American women in the second half of the twentieth century. Instead of emphasizing the women's domestic skills or piety, as editors and writers had done in the postwar years, writers in this period agreed with the sentiment expressed by Martha Nelson: "Never underestimate the influence of a woman!"[74]

In addition to adapting biblical and historical narratives to contemporary norms, writers profiled a number of "new, missioning women" whom they felt were worthy of emulation.[75] Women were no longer featured in *Royal Service* for being mothers or wives of missionaries; instead they were included for their own personalities and accomplishments. According to writer Nancy Carter, one Japanese woman was repeatedly introduced as Mr. Matsumura's wife—and wanted to reply, "I appreciate and I love and respect my husband, but I am Akiko Matsumura!"[76] Similarly, WMU member Bede Jeffords concluded that she was "liberated": she loved and supported her husband, but "I am my own person."[77] Such women—like "women's libbers"—felt that their true identities involved much more than their marital status. Unlike those profiled in *Royal Service* during the previous period, these women emphasized female autonomy instead of subordination.

For a few years in the late 1970s and early 1980s, *Royal Service* included a feature called She's a Baptist Woman Too. This series, written by Jacqueline Durham, carefully profiled a number of Southern Baptist women filling nontraditional roles: a college professor in Louisiana, the lieutenant governor of Kentucky, a pilot from Florida, and a bank vice president from Louisiana, among others.[78] Durham even introduced readers to Carmen Dorta, a Hispanic pastor's wife who had preached in forty-six countries; Mary Odell Littlejohn, a church staff member "known as a 'libber'"; and Pearl Holmes Duvall, an ordained chaplain who had felt that "her gifts were being wasted" at her previous secretarial missions jobs.[79] These women clearly did not typify the magazine's readers; however, they represented the diversity of leadership roles that Adrianne Bonham and *Royal Service* editorial committee members apparently felt were suitable for WMU members. As writer Minette Drumwright celebrated, "Women have more opportunities to participate in the whole of life today than ever before."[80] Readers, it seems, were expected to rejoice along with Drumwright and to "dare to make ourselves available"[81] for any number of roles to which God might call them. Not only mothers and missionaries but also businesswomen and female ministers had become appropriate role models for Southern Baptist women.

Editors also encouraged readers to look beyond the pages of *Contempo* and *Royal Service* for information about Christian womanhood. They reviewed several books about women's place in church and society, almost always supporting expansive roles. Instead of praising titles about the Christian home, as they had during the previous period, writers promoted books such as *Woman Alone: Confident and Creative* and *Speaking Up: A Book for Every Woman Who Wants to Speak Effectively*. In 1983 Joanne Lisk even recommended a book criticizing the same women that *Royal Service* would likely have praised in earlier years—those whom she said "retreat[ed] to the kitchen to try to catch the flavor of the good old days" and thus, in her opinion, abandoned the Great Commission.[82] Reviewers profiled multiple volumes by evangelical feminists, including Letha Scanzoni and Nancy Hardesty's influential *All We're Meant to Be*, which Pansy Webb found "refreshing" and "sane."[83] Writers also recommended similar books by Southern Baptist authors: Leon McBeth's *Women in Baptist Life* was "a stirring account of the contributions of women"; John Howell's *Equality and Submission in Marriage* (which favored equality) was "firmly grounded in biblical principles"; and WMU's own *The Woman I Am* series was "provoking" and "deeply spiritual."[84] Books by conservative authors such as James Dobson, however, were infrequently mentioned. Instead a number of reviewers praised works that affirmed equality between women and men, clearly aligning themselves with the aims of evangelical feminism, as well as to a lesser extent the women's liberation movement.

Despite the enthusiasm they expressed for women's expanding roles, editors—like other WMU leaders—stopped short of endorsing the women's liberation movement in its entirety. Writer Ruth Miller explained that although she liked the sense of sisterhood she observed among "libbers," she "disagree[d] with most methods of the women's liberation movement"[85]—a sentiment with which many *Royal Service* readers likely agreed. Writers and editors never urged readers to join the "libbers" advocating radical changes in women's social position, a move that most Southern Baptists would have regarded as extreme. But writers also never encouraged WMU members to join the growing conservative Christian women's movement, with which some readers surely agreed. Instead, *Contempo* editor Mary Ann Ward asserted that she "strongly dislike[d] the excesses of both groups."[86] Aware of their diverse constituency, editors were likewise careful to present balanced perspectives on controversial political issues such as the ERA, irrespective of their own preferences.[87] And rather than urging readers to seek ordination to Southern Baptist ministry, which would have been widely viewed as a divisive stance, editors and writers challenged readers more generically to "stir up the gifts God has given us" and become "free in Christ."[88] WMU editors almost certainly favored expansive roles for women, but they avoided strong statements that would likely have offended SBC conservatives. By so doing, WMU leaders also won the trust of some conservative readers, who may have thus unconsciously accepted the magazines' more oblique references to women's rights.

Indeed, while not officially supporting the women's liberation movement, multiple writers for *Contempo* and *Royal Service* used phrases prevalent in this movement to describe spiritual issues. In the same way that women in previous years had Christianized the domestic language admired at the time, writers and editors during this period used popular terminology to portray freedom in Christ as "the most exquisite liberation womankind can ever know" and invited readers to be part of a "spiritual revolution" through WMU.[89] Christianity, they implied, was even more fulfilling than the women's liberation movement; equal treatment and higher pay were not as important as "equal rights—to hear the gospel."[90] Utilizing a popular phrase for her own purpose, Aline Fuselier encouraged readers to "use woman power" not for their own advancement but "for missions"; Mary Ann Ward proposed that "the right to know Jesus Christ personally" was "a new women's issue for Christian women."[91] One denominational leader even referred to himself as an "activist"—not for women's rights but for the SBC's Cooperative Program.[92] Southern Baptist Christianity, writers implied, was just as contemporary as the women's liberation movement and served a higher cause. By reinterpreting women's liberation terms for their own purposes, writers and editors attempted to

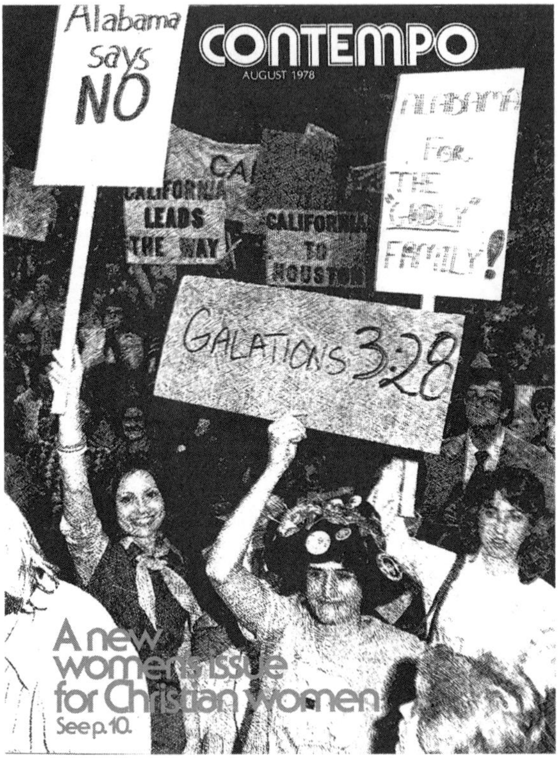


12. Cover of August 1978 *Contempo*. (Used by permission of WMUA.)

establish the relevance of their historic emphasis on missions. They also demonstrated their comfort with the vocabulary of women's liberation, revealing their loose affinity with the movement.

That editors of *Contempo* and *Royal Service* continued to prioritize missions over equal rights activism is unsurprising, considering their context and goals. But the degree to which they did embrace women's liberation ideals is remarkable. Page after page highlighting "liberated women" and endorsing evangelical feminist books encouraged readers to pursue unlimited opportunities and develop egalitarian relationships, in striking contrast to the roles *Royal Service* had suggested for women in earlier years. Without explicitly endorsing the women's liberation movement, WMU editors repeatedly affirmed many of its goals.

## Employment and Marital Status

*Royal Service* and *Contempo*'s emphasis on freedom and equality led these magazines to highlight a wide range of roles for women in the workplace or at home. A 1976 *Contempo* feature by seminary student Barbara Burkett asked, "Are You a Successful Woman?" and concluded that all the women profiled were successful: a dean of women at a seminary, a homemaker, an unmarried public health nutritionist, and a teacher who was also a mother.[93] No longer did writers portray one role—homemaker—as the most satisfying or significant for Christian women. Instead they enumerated what Burkett called the "almost unlimited possibilities" available to contemporary women.[94] Editors of *Royal Service* and *Contempo* apparently agreed with Christine Gregory, who used familiar women's liberation terminology to discuss employment and homemaking: "We do not have the right to judge women on their choices."[95] This sentiment diverged significantly from the attitudes of earlier WMU writers, who had implicitly criticized women who did not prioritize the home. Now, for the first time, WMU magazines presented such a variety of options for women that every reader could identify with at least one.

In marked contrast to the previous period, when women were not always strongly encouraged even to become missionaries, articles during these years explored the "world of church vocations" that women were beginning to fill.[96] Many WMU editors in earlier years had been graduates of WMUTS, absorbing the domestic ideology dominant among WMU leaders before their school merged with SBTS. However, during this period seven of the nine editors of *Royal Service* and *Contempo*—like many editors of other Southern Baptist publications—had studied at SBC seminaries and had thus been shaped by the broader currents of theological understanding popular among Southern Baptist scholars of the day. Many of the professors who had taught these women at SBC seminaries supported women in ministry, refused to ascribe to biblical inerrancy, and generally espoused views that made conservatives consider the schools bastions of liberalism. WMU editors' seminary training almost certainly helped foster their support for women in ministry, in contrast with the views of WMU magazines' readers, who typically had no formal theological education.

Editors' seminary studies also made them more likely to select other theologically trained women (and men) to write for WMU magazines. Several of these writers were also employed in ministry roles that utilized their seminary education. For example, Martha Woody was a former church planter and current minister of education at Clifton Baptist Church in Louisville, Kentucky, and Phyllis Merritt was the third woman to have received a Master of Divinity degree from SWBTS. Even Mary Frances Bailey, who described herself as a "wife, mother, homemaker, and freelance writer," held a Master of Religious Education in Church Social Work degree from SBTS.[97] Instead of pursuing only homemaking, as most writers in the previous period had done, women such as Bailey completed coursework in theological education before settling down to motherhood or careers. The influence of this training for ministry was evident in the roles such writers described for women in the pages of *Royal Service* and *Contempo*.

Multiple articles in these magazines—especially in *Contempo*—discussed the growing numbers of women who were involved in or preparing for vocational ministry, reflecting WMU's involvement with the Consultation on Women in Church-Related Vocations and with Women in Ministry, SBC. Reviewing this trend of women in ministry, HMB staff member Carl Hart prophetically remarked that "the Lord is getting ready to do something";[98] other writers felt the same way. "God speaks to women," the May 1980 issue of *Contempo* proclaimed, and profiled four women serving in ministry careers: a writer, a social worker, and two preschool ministers.[99] No female pastors or associate pastors were included, perhaps because these roles were more controversial—or because Southern Baptist women filling such positions were difficult to find. However, editors urged women to help church leaders become more open to hiring female ministers. For example, a 1975 article included a list of questions to help readers determine "how does my church rate?" in its inclusion of women.[100] Pages that in the postwar years had instructed women about raising children while their husbands pursued ministry careers now encouraged the women themselves to become involved in vocational ministry—a contrast indicative of the dramatic shift in attitudes toward women in American culture and among some Southern Baptists as well.

Articles about home missions demonstrated a similar commitment to the inclusion of women in a variety of ministry roles. Beginning in the 1970s, WMU editors joined leaders of HMB—and FMB—in advocating an expanding range of options for women in missions. HMB staff member Wendell Belew explained to *Royal Service*'s readers his conviction that "God wants me to speak with clarity and to act with courage regarding God's call to women";[101] his colleagues expressed similar sentiments. Numerous articles profiled women serving in diverse home missions roles, including Hettie Johnson, the first female director of an HMB division; Mary Archer, the director of a Baptist center (whose husband, the writer noted, provided a "strong support system"); and Joanne LeGette, a divorced church planter who felt the need to explain that she did not "preach from the pulpit."[102] A few female missionaries with the more common assignment of "home and church" were also highlighted, but editors apparently preferred to feature women who "blaze[d] new paths for others to follow."[103] Like HMB's *Home Missions* magazine, *Contempo* and *Royal Service* readily profiled female missionaries whose roles would have been unthinkable a few years earlier—and remained controversial among many Southern Baptists.

Church extension associate, which an HMB staff member described as "something like an assistant to a pastor," was another such role.[104] An article featuring Suzanne Coyle, a church extension associate who "drew her own [Southern Baptist] congregation" in inner-city Philadelphia, also frankly described the exclusion of many women from such positions because of "lack of money or lack of acceptance by state or local leaders."[105] With this statement, *Contempo* editor Mary Ann Ward implicitly criticized what she and several other SBC leaders considered the overly conservative ideology of the majority of grassroots Southern Baptists. Letters from the magazines' readers demonstrated such conservative beliefs. For example, Mrs. G. R. Ferrell protested in 1976, "This women's lib thing has gotten completely out of hand. . . . Why can't we . . . leave the assistant pastor title to the men where it rightly belongs?"[106] Judging from similar opinions published in the letters pages of *Royal Service* and *Contempo*, many readers' thinking differed significantly from that of WMU leaders.

But editors persisted in their efforts to broaden readers' perspectives through printing the testimonies of women who were involved in home missions. Like many moderate Southern Baptists, these women countered objections about "pleas[ing] man instead of God"[107] by appealing to God's gifting and call. "I know firsthand that a woman can be called," affirmed Deena Williams Newman in 1982, "because I have been."[108] Especially noteworthy was a feature about Mary Fran Hughes, an ordained chaplain intern who was also a member of the Women in Religion Task Force of the National Organization for Women.[109] Reader Mrs. Ed Keys "felt compelled to speak up" against the article; Mary Ann Ward responded with the editorial comment that WMU had "a responsibility to make readers aware of what is happening in our denomination . . . because this . . . affects missions."[110] Despite this assertion, however, editors were virtually silent about other denominational happenings, including the escalating controversy between conservatives and moderates and the rise of conservative women's groups that competed with WMU for members. Editors focused almost entirely on new roles for women, making dubious the claim that their sole interest was missions.

This emphasis on expansive roles for women was also evinced in *Con-*

*tempo*'s and *Royal Service*'s features about foreign missions. Leveraging the influence and cooperative relationships they had acquired within the denomination, WMU leaders asked FMB in 1974 to assign missionary wives their own job titles if the wives desired them. In an attempt to shape their readers' views of women's place in missions, WMU magazines repeatedly highlighted women filling nontraditional roles rather than the 40 percent of FMB missionaries who continued to serve in a "church and home" capacity.[111] Writers profiled the creator of the first Bible concordance in the Hausa language, the first female FMB vice president, the first woman appointed as an evangelist (although the article noted that she was reaching other women), and the first female editor of the Spanish Baptist magazine *El Eco*, among others.[112] FMB staff member Richard Styles wrote about the twelve female FMB board members, perhaps in an attempt to demonstrate that organization's growing openness to women.[113] And FMB writer Ruth Fowler even suggested that the SBC was moving toward full equality for women in "the total task of world missions."[114] Just as women were achieving many "firsts" in American society, such writers implied, they were also successfully filling an increasing number of new roles on the mission field.

At least two articles mentioned female foreign missionaries who assumed some pastoral duties. Kathryn Burns in Greece led Wednesday night prayer meetings when her husband was away, and Frances Greenway of Rhodesia called herself "a preaching missionary as much as a medical one," although stating that she did not preach from a pulpit.[115] However, the only female pastors named in these magazines were foreign nationals. As in previous years, editors more readily discussed controversial roles for Baptist women overseas than in their own context. A 1975 feature briefly described how a preaching point in Malaysia grew under the "guidance and earnest preaching" of a local young woman named Annie—leading reader June Ridens to denounce "Satan's tricks of slipping ideas into our minds until we just gradually accept them."[116] And Theo Sommerkamp wrote two pages about Merion Johansson, whom he called "just an ordinary pastor" in Sweden who happened to be a woman.[117] Out of fear of criticism or perhaps lack of subject matter, editors never profiled a female Baptist pastor from the United States. However, their decision to affirm women's preaching at all demonstrated their affinity with SBC moderates as well as with evangelical feminists.

Just as they emphasized vocational ministry, the editors of *Royal Service* and especially *Contempo* also included a number of articles about women who were pursuing secular employment. By this period, a significant percentage of Southern Baptist women worked outside the home, most in nonministry positions. Dot Sample, for example, who served as WMU president beginning in 1981, had a successful career as a psychologist. WMU editors, professionals themselves, had not previously criticized women for working, and during this period WMU magazines featured at least as many articles supporting women whom Mary Lane Powell called "Millie Moneymaker[s]" as they did "Hannah Homemaker[s]."[118] A full-page graphic in the April 1972 issue of *Contempo* detailed "opportunities for women in the 70's and 80's," including careers in male-dominated fields such as dentistry, physics, engineering, and architecture—but not motherhood, which had been so important in previous years.[119] Other articles mentioned marriage and family in relation to women's careers. Reader Dixie Meyer explained that her job brought her fulfillment and provided her children with "the opportunity to go to college."[120] Challenging earlier gender constructs, Catherine Allen—herself a working mother—argued that "working, married mothering" was an "economic, intellectual, survival, and social" necessity.[121] Like "women's libbers," these writers emphasized their own needs and quality of life, which earlier writers had subsumed to the needs of women's families. Writers and editors in this period did not oppose women's employment, as some Southern Baptists did, or merely tolerate this role; they encouraged it.

In order to support their working readers and retain them as WMU members, many *Contempo* writers offered advice about the workplace. Teena Andrews enumerated promising vocations for women, warned against gender discrimination, and challenged each woman to "use her God-given gifts to the best of her ability."[122] Mary Bowman offered advice on workplace etiquette and behavior.[123] And Kay Wheeler Moore recommended guidelines to help women "maintain a proper balancing act" between work, home, and church.[124] Influenced by cultural changes, WMU magazines were now filled not with advice about homemaking but with tips on interacting with coworkers and sharing domestic tasks with husbands. Ward even led *Contempo* to include a feature called Career Connection, which introduced readers to Christian women serving in vocations from sales to engineering.[125] Writers also urged young women to attend college in order to prepare for more challenging careers. Just as in broader American society, paid employment—not homemaking—became the favored role for women.

In the same way that earlier WMU writers had encouraged women to

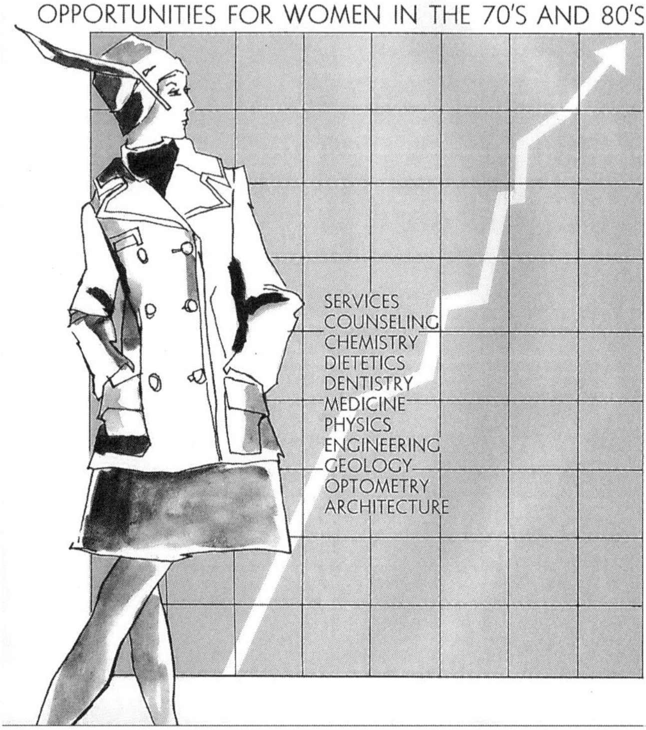


13. Illustration from April 1972 *Contempo*. (Used by permission of WMUA.)

take advantage of witnessing opportunities in their homes, writers during these years challenged readers to "witness on location through your vocation."[126] Perhaps to counter arguments against women's employment and to portray WMU as relevant, writers and editors sought to demonstrate that the workplace provided new ways for WMU members to carry out their historic purpose: missions. Writers explained that a career could be an "arena in which to live out your Christian witness," "part of God's will," and "a way to serve the Lord."[127] Multiple women testified about how they shared their beliefs with their coworkers: stockbroker Sonja Bass drank juice rather than alcohol at company parties, answering resulting questions about her faith; and journalist Kay Wheeler Moore served as the de facto chaplain for her office.[128] One article even described the Christian advice and "listening ear" that sex therapist Nancy Badgwell provided to her clients[129]—likely raising questions among readers about the propriety of Badgwell's occupation. To the magazines' editors, such "marketplace missionaries" exemplified contemporary WMU members.[130]

Ironically, though, many women stopped participating in Baptist Young Women and Baptist Women once they began working. Aware of this trend, WMU leaders exhorted groups to adapt their meeting times and formats to accommodate women who were employed outside the home. "Simplicity and flexibility," an article to pastors explained, were key.[131] However, reported membership in WMU women's organizations in 1980 was less than 75 percent of the 1963 total[132]—a significant decline. WMU's support of careers for women, alongside what the WMU Executive Board in 1970 called a "decided increase" in women's employment,[133] may have cost the organization members that it never regained.

Not all members of Baptist Women and Baptist Young Women went to work, however, or agreed with those who did. Some women, persuaded in previous years to consider homemaking the most important vocation, continued to espouse such a perspective. A majority of *Contempo*'s readers—employed or not—indicated that "being a good wife and mother" was among their primary concerns.[134] And six out of every seven *Royal Service* readers, whose views were probably more traditional than those of *Contempo*'s younger audience, felt that women with small children should not work outside the home.[135] A letter typifying this perspective, written by Mrs. Jim Ritter of Oklahoma, was printed in the August 1976 issue of *Contempo*: "In most circumstances, there is no real necessity for mothers to be working other than for their own selfish fulfillment. . . . If more women took the time to be mothers and wives, there would be less divorce, unemployment, and juvenile delinquency. . . . I cannot believe that the Southern Baptist Convention is for women's liberation."[136] Other readers similarly chided WMU for following a "worldly trend" and promoting "the work of one who has come to steal and to kill and to destroy."[137] Such arguments reflected not only statements that had been published in *Royal Service* in earlier years but also the teachings of conservative Christian women's groups and the emerging Christian Right. WMU members and leaders, influenced by disparate ideologies, no longer agreed on what the primary role of a Christian woman should be.

But not all homemakers who read *Royal Service* and *Contempo* expressed their opinions with such strong language; many simply described their preference in terms of personal freedom. Veteria Billingsley from Mississippi declared, "Let me be free to serve God and family."[138] Vickie Schull of North Carolina explained that as a homemaker, she was "free to be where I'm needed when I'm needed."[139] And Sharon Vanskike of Montana agreed: "As far as I can see, the home does not limit me."[140] These women defended homemaking not by using the "Christian home" arguments popularized in the previous period but by appropriating women's liberation terms for their own purposes. The use of such language demonstrated that the women's thinking was more strongly shaped by the surrounding culture than they may have liked to admit.

A few writers enlisted by WMU likewise utilized the concept of freedom, overlaying it with the Christian idea of calling in an attempt to broaden women's thinking. Aware that their readers espoused a variety of perspectives about women's roles but held spirituality in high esteem, editors and writers stressed God's guidance of women into many avenues of service. Catherine Allen encouraged every reader to "find and live God's will for her," which she explained was not limited to homemaking but might also include a career.[141] Such language built on readers' desire to follow God's will in an attempt to demonstrate that God could lead women into paid employment as well as domestic roles. Even homemaker Judy Abercrombie testified that "I have been called by God to do it [homemaking]" in the same way that other women had been called to the workforce.[142] Unlike earlier writers, Abercrombie regarded homemaking as simply one possibility among the many available to Christian women. Articles such as "The Decision to Marry" and "Parenthood: To Be or Not to Be" similarly presented readers with a variety of lifestyle options absent in previous years—always with an emphasis on "seek[ing] God's direction."[143] Apparently writers felt that God could guide women in ways that their predecessors had seldom considered.

Writers who did discuss women's roles in the home generally broadened their perspectives to fit the spirit of the time. An occasional article still urged readers to use their maternal instincts to "creat[e] a warm, loving Christian home" or to "establish family worship,"[144] often as one of many exhortations rather than as the article's sole focus. More frequently, however, writers acknowledged that mothers—even on the mission field—should not be "hallowed as some rare species of saint" but were "fully human," just as fathers were.[145] As domesticity became less popular in American culture, such women decided that maintaining a spotless home was not a priority. Sarah Ogle of Texas, for example, explained that her house was "not the showcase it was when we first got married" because "my calling as a Christian is to people, and things do not matter."[146] Writers praised this type of "home that became a mission" through families' efforts such as ministering to neighbors, welcoming underprivileged teens, and beginning house churches.[147] Influenced by contemporary culture, writers and editors considered helping individuals outside the home to be more important than cultivating an impeccable house and family.

Not only the home but also marital relationships were of interest to some writers. A few women advocated what they considered traditional Christian interpretations of male headship—the husband's "tremendous responsibility of leading your family in spiritual growth."[148] This hierarchical perspective, implicit in the domestic roles writers had proposed during the previous period, was popularized in the 1970s by conservative Christian leaders such as James Dobson and Bill Gothard. As might be expected, such a view was prevalent in letters from readers of WMU magazines. Arlene Grove of Maryland explained that "my husband is my head, as Christ is the head of the Church (only one head per body)"; an unnamed reader likewise asserted that "the Bible says to submit to your husband," even if his heart was not in the right place.[149] These women, influenced by the growing conservative evangelical movement in the United States, surely hoped that writers for *Contempo* and *Royal Service* would promote similar ideology.

However, most features in these magazines espoused egalitarian gender constructs similar to those promoted by evangelical feminists, if not "women's libbers"—again revealing the influence these movements had on WMU editors and leaders. Writer Phyllis Merritt scripted a ceremony for engaged couples that highlighted Ephesians 5:25, which commands husbands to love their wives—but omitted Ephesians 5:22, the corresponding admonition for wives to submit to their husbands.[150] Similarly, instead of urging women to support hierarchical marital roles, seminary professor C. W. Brister advised husbands and wives to "participate equally as partners."[151] Other writers encouraged couples to work together on household chores and family finances, an idea that would have been foreign to postwar writers, to whom women's domestic roles had been almost sacred. In a reversal of these roles, Jim Cox, a businessman whose wife was heavily involved in WMU, explained that he completed more household tasks than his wife, who was busy with meetings and mission projects.[152] No longer was the ideal WMU member a dutiful wife and devoted homemaker; instead, her active lifestyle and shared domestic tasks demonstrated her "liberated" perspective.

*Contempo* and *Royal Service* not only deemphasized homemaking; they also suggested that singleness was an option as valid for women as marriage. As the number of single Americans rapidly increased to nearly one-third of the adult population, writers rethought what one called the "biological myth that only as a wife and mother can a woman fulfill her role in society."[153] WMU leaders such as Carolyn Weatherford, themselves unmarried, no longer felt the need to consider singleness a unique aspect of their occupation; instead they led WMU to adopt the prevalent idea that singleness was just as conventional as marriage. Using language similar to that employed in descriptions of vocational choices, editor Mary Ann Ward explained in 1979 that "Christian marriage is a calling from God, but so is singleness."[154] Single missionaries stressed their obedience to God's specific call on their lives: "I am the way God wants me," Frances Greenway affirmed.[155]

Influenced by women's rights advocates, who emphasized unmarried women's independence, writers for the first time explored the benefits of the "adventure" of singleness: opportunities to befriend diverse people, time for ministry efforts, and freedom to change plans or locations, among others. As multiple women observed, Jesus himself had been single. Accordingly, articles urged churches and WMU members to realize that "single women are complete persons,"[156] ending their conscious or unconscious exclusion of such women. In contrast to the postwar years, when writers and editors had regarded singleness as an aberration from the ideal of marriage, during this period they portrayed singleness as an acceptable—and even celebrated—role, as it was among many other American women.

Even more significant, *Royal Service* and *Contempo* first broached the topic of divorce during these years. As the divorce rate rose among church members as well as among other Americans, the magazines' editors could no longer assume that their readers were happily married to their first husbands. More than one divorced woman was featured in She's a Baptist Woman Too. Barbara Pellici, for example, was a "woman with deep Christian commitment" whose first marriage simply "did not work out."[157] Influenced by a growing cultural permissiveness toward divorce, a few writers—like some other SBC moderates—reconsidered traditional Southern Baptist views on the topic, especially beginning in the 1970s. No longer was the Christian home a sacred institution never to be divided; pastoral counselor Andrew Lester avowed in *Royal Service* that Jesus's teachings on divorce were "guidelines" instead of "unalterable rules."[158] Writer Judy Holley likewise explained that divorce was in some situations "the most ethical choice that a Christian can make."[159] Many of the magazines' readers surely disapproved of such assertions, believing with Jerry Falwell that the "fractured family" was unbiblical and highly problematic.[160]

More common in *Royal Service* and *Contempo*, however, was the less controversial view that divorce was a sin—along with the corresponding platitude "hate the sin but love the sinner."[161] Divorce, as reader Nelda Gann affirmed, was "against Bible teachings," but writers urged churches to "communicate Christian concern" to divorced women and men.[162] Instead of emphasizing judgment and exclusion, as Christian Right leaders were prone to do, writers adopted more tolerant attitudes from broader American culture, alleging that Christians were "negligent" if dance clubs accepted divorcees more readily than churches did.[163] "She may have just gone through a divorce," Anne Leavell Mann challenged readers in 1980. "Would BYW welcome her?"[164] Accepting women from a variety of backgrounds, as evangelical feminists urged, had become more important than requiring all women to conform to a specific gender norm. Divorcees, singles, wives, homemakers, employees, missionaries, and ministers—for the first time, *Contempo* and *Royal Service* featured WMU members who filled all these roles. Influenced by women's changing place in American society and religious life, editors depicted a wide range of employment and marital options for Southern Baptist women.

## Mission Action

Writers for *Contempo* and *Royal Service* clearly spent many pages detailing the expanding roles that they believed women could fill. Aware of the controversy that was emerging in the SBC, however, editors and other WMU leaders measured their words carefully. A 1979 *Contempo* interviewer asked WMU president Christine Gregory, "What do you think about women's ordination?" Gregory did not answer the question directly but instead encouraged women to "stop worrying about how we can work out our own frustrations"—presumably over gender inequality and the SBC—"and just get busy. Use that energy to help hurting people."[165] Like several other SBC entities, WMU attempted to use the cause of missions to sidestep denominational conflict and call for unified action. Indeed, during this period *Contempo* and *Royal Service* emphasized hands-on mission action above the more passive mission support activities popular in previous years, with a focus on social issues that had not been evident since WMU's early days. Such features were shaped in large part by the activist culture in which the women lived.

WMU president Helen Fling designed the organization's mission action program in 1965 as a Christian response to "these times of controversial social issues."[166] The successor to WMU's programs of personal service (1909–1941) and community missions (1942–1964), mission action was apparently part of WMU's attempt to "be in our day the force it has been in other days," as executive secretary Alma Hunt desired.[167] At least in the area of mission action, WMU seemed to have succeeded in this goal. As HMB employee Elaine Furlow remarked, mission action during this period grew "like wildfire" among churches—as it also did in the pages of WMU magazines.[168]

In both *Royal Service* and *Contempo*, writers promoted numerous opportunities for "courageous women" to engage in "daring ministries and creative witnessing,"[169] again highlighting the expansive, exciting roles they felt were appropriate for contemporary women. Using language of call and gifting similar to that employed in their justifications of female ministers and unmarried women, writers urged Southern Baptist women to "dare [to] make ourselves available to God *here* and *now*."[170] Nearly every issue of both *Contempo* and *Royal Service* challenged the magazines' middle-class readers to minister to less privileged groups, such as migrants, the illiterate, the hungry, the deaf, foster children, and prison inmates. Unlike in previous periods, a few writers even described the needs of nightclub entertainers; individuals contemplating suicide; alcoholics and drug addicts; and those whom writers believed were adversely affected by homosexual practices, incest, and pornography. Like divorcees, the women felt, these individuals needed Christians not to condemn them but instead to "be the presence of Christ" in the midst of complex circumstances.[171] A "tremendous, hurting world" demanded mission action.[172]

And act the women did. Mrs. Judson LeCroy avowed that mission action groups were the most popular Baptist Women organizations in Savannah, Georgia,[173] and numerous features about groups' mission action projects demonstrated that other Baptist Women and Baptist Young Women embraced the concept as well. Indeed, *Contempo* and *Royal Service* included as many letters and articles from readers about mission action as they did about controversial women's rights issues. In one letter, missionary Mildred Blankenship described receiving more than two hundred inquiries about literacy missions in response to an article featuring her ministry.[174] Among many others, women from Spartanburg, South Carolina, explained how they led a Bible club for unchurched children; a church in Georgia highlighted its sponsorship of Laotian refugees; and Louisiana women reported befriending visiting seafarers.[175] Even ninety-year-old Edna Roach "was a missionary in her own right at the nursing home," inviting other residents to attend worship services and sewing sock monkeys to earn money for missions.[176] In contrast to the previous period, women of all ages and situations explained to other readers how they had discovered "areas overflowing with needs and possibilities" and had taken action.[177]

WMU members were hardly the only Americans acting on their convictions, however. As WMU leader Katharine Bryan acknowledged, "Involvement has been the 'in' word for several years now, and involvement is what mission action is all about."[178] Indeed, social activism was one of the primary components of the women's liberation movement; it was an essential feature of the civil rights and antiwar movements as well. Among Protestants, several prominent evangelicals signed the Chicago Declaration of Evangelical Social Concern; the BWA implemented a social emphasis called World Mission of Reconciliation through Jesus Christ; and many mainline denominations—including American Baptists—published materials that Gregory deemed "very strong on mission action."[179] Within the SBC, CLC encouraged churches to address a wide range of social issues, and HMB developed its own department of Christian Social Ministries. The Brotherhood Commission also agreed to work with WMU to lead churches in mission action, which Fling soon averred was "going great guns."[180] As was generally the case throughout this period, WMU worked cooperatively with other SBC entities, whose staff largely shared the same moderate sentiments as WMU leaders. Such relationships would later become more problematic for WMU as conservatives gained power within the SBC.

During these years, however, WMU leaders used their new emphasis on the popular cause of mission action to attempt to grow their membership. Editor Lane Powell, for example, challenged female Southern Baptists not involved in Baptist Women to "give this organization a second chance."[181] WMU leaders also urged these women's younger sisters to join Baptist Young Women, which members from Leesburg, Florida, explained was "not a social club but an active missions group."[182] Such an explanation revealed not only the affinity these Floridians had for WMU but also the reputation for dull, cliquish meetings that made some Southern Baptist women uninterested in Baptist Women and Baptist Young Women. With these organizations' new emphasis on mission action, many women did find WMU a fitting way to express Christian social concern—but others took advantage of similar opportunities both within and outside of the SBC. WMU leaders, strongly influenced by their activist culture, could not claim mission action as a role unique to their members.

But the emphasis on mission action in *Contempo* and *Royal Service* probably led these magazines' readers to be among the church members most active in such ministry. Editors replaced earlier years' articles about the Christian home with recurring features about mission action, including People Who Need People, Love Thy Neighbor, and Life-Changers Today. Advertisements for mission action books and workshops filled pages previously packed with child-raising tips. And even programs designed for use during Baptist Women and Baptist Young Women meetings urged women to take action rather than simply to cultivate a domestic Christian influence. A Current Missions Group program in *Royal Service*, for example, not only described the challenges facing illiterate individuals but also exhorted group members to "determine what step can be taken immediately toward participating in literacy missions."[183] Articles about prayer similarly challenged women not just to intercede for their own families but also to pray "that we will be more aware of needs around us and . . . find ways of communicating God's love through action prompted by concern."[184] Popular WMU speaker Stuart Calvert described how she asked a probation officer for initials of juvenile offenders for whom her group could pray—and changed her lifestyle in response to his question, "Have you ever thought about doing something after you prayed?"[185] Editors implied that even relatively passive mission support roles such as prayer and study, prominent in previous years, should lead to the women's primary new task: mission action.

Not since the early twentieth century had WMU members participated in such concerted social efforts. Mission action shared many similarities with its predecessor from that period, personal service—although community missions, the program promoted in the intervening years, had been less progressive. Both personal service and mission action emphasized women's role in ameliorating social ills and displayed the influence of broader societal reform efforts. Just as the turn-of-the-century social gospel movement had prompted Fannie Heck and Lulie Wharton to pioneer WMU's personal service program, the activist movements of the 1960s and 1970s encouraged Fling and other WMU leaders to champion mission action. Personal service writers in the early 1900s had exhorted readers to minister to immigrants, visit prisoners, and eliminate the causes of poverty. Decades later, mission action writers likewise urged women to "minister and witness to internationals," "help the prisoner and his family," and "lead our churches to make specific commitments of money for relief and development."[186] Both emphases encouraged more involvement in social issues than many Southern Baptists were comfortable with, although more male SBC leaders agreed with WMU's stance in the latter period than in the former. Still, critics in both periods charged the women with demonstrating "too much social gospel."[187]

Such criticism challenged both personal service and mission action writers to explain why women's appropriate realm of influence had spread beyond the home to encompass their communities and even their world. Although mid-twentieth-century men (and women) were more accustomed to women's involvement in many aspects of American life than their forebears had been, some conservative Southern Baptists still were uneasy about women's role in mission action. WMU writers defended this emphasis in one of the same ways that they supported women's rights in church and society: using the Bible. Writers pointed out that Ruth had cared for her mother-in-law, the Shunammite woman had met Elisha's needs, Dorcas had helped those outside the church, and Jesus himself had offered six "literal, practical suggestions" for mission action projects: feed the hungry, give drink to the thirsty, care for the stranger, clothe the naked, look after the sick, and visit the prisoner.[188] Other articles cited biblical passages about compassion, such as Isaiah 58:6–7, Matthew 7:16, Matthew 10:42, and Luke 10:25–35.[189] Writers thus appealed to selected verses from the Bible, which Southern Baptists considered their primary source of authority, in an attempt to convince women of the rectitude of their cause.

While conservative Southern Baptists could not deny these biblical commands to demonstrate Christ's love, some may have noted that editors infrequently mentioned verses about verbally testifying to the gospel or about being "born again," a phrase popular among conservative evangelicals.[190] In 1975 Weatherford did lead WMU to add direct evangelism to its task statements, in order, she claimed, to help women learn "basic witnessing skills"[191]—and perhaps also to satisfy the SBC's growing conservative contingent. As in the early twentieth century, WMU leaders and writers were careful to explain that the goal of social ministry was to "share my witness."[192] Despite such gestures, however, the ministry actions that these women suggested were often more closely aligned with contemporary social movements than with conservatives' evangelistic strategies. Seminary student Dale Helmbold even disparaged one strategy, averring that "just going to people, handing them a Bible, and leaving is not mission action."[193] Indeed, many more pages of both *Contempo* and *Royal Service* discussed mission action ideas than suggested witnessing techniques.[194] WMU editors thus joined other moderate SBC leaders in prioritizing social action over personal conversion.

Unlike their personal service predecessors, mission action writers emphasized the "worth and dignity" of every ministry recipient, especially during the first decade of the mission action program.[195] Like their evangelical contemporaries who were involved in social issues, writers warned against causing a person "to feel he was a project rather than an important individual in the eyes of God" and encouraged women to undertake long-term efforts in order to cultivate "deep relationships with persons" and avoid "hit-and-run ministry."[196] Aware of most readers' relative position of privilege as members of the white middle class, writers challenged women to "test your sensitivity-awareness": "Do I get pleasure and self-gratification from manipulating people?" "Can I accept these people as they are in the same way Christ accepts me?"[197] In striking contrast to the condescending descriptions of "heathen" women popular during personal service years, mission action articles in *Royal Service* and *Contempo* urged WMU members to view all people—Christians and non-Christians, upper class and lower class alike—as "basically the same, with the same deep needs."[198] Understanding, editors and writers felt, took precedence over conversion. Some writers even invited women to "empathetically experience the target person's experience" by touring a jail, eating a meal at a nursing home, or creating a budget from a welfare income.[199] Such an emphasis on equality and dignity revealed the influence of contemporary human rights movements and the corresponding cultural focus on self-esteem. Unlike patronizing personal service writers or disapproving members of the Christian Right, these women urged readers to identify with ministry recipients and regard them as their peers.

However, editors of *Contempo* and *Royal Service* did not frequently encourage women to address the underlying causes of social problems through organized political and social action, as personal service writers had done. Instead, they more often proposed solutions on an individual level, exhorting each woman to "be the Lord's representative in my home, my neighborhood, my classes, my job, any place that I am."[200] Editors and other WMU leaders were likely wary of taking divisive political stances during this turbulent period, much as they declined to state an official position on women's rights. Editors did, however, continue WMU's earlier emphasis on racial reconciliation. Carolyn Weatherford admitted that she could not explain why WMU focused on race but not other issues—such as abortion—that had captured evangelicals' attention; she concluded, "There's a fine line between what is missions and what isn't."[201] Rather than laboring to define each topic in relation to missions, however, perhaps a more realistic perspective would admit WMU's general reluctance to take a strong position on issues such as abortion, evolution, and school prayer that were more than "mildly controversial" among SBC leaders and members.[202] Readers, after all, could express their disapproval by unsubscribing.

By this time, many Southern Baptists publicly decried racial discrimination, even if vestiges of prejudice remained in their thoughts or actions. Multiple editors of *Contempo* and *Royal Service*, influenced by the civil rights movement—as were other moderate SBC leaders—challenged the magazines' readers throughout the period to eliminate all such prejudice and to begin to "'accept' and not just 'tolerate'" African Americans.[203] While occasionally denouncing "black power advocates who are belligerently anti-white," writers encouraged women to "develop some personal friends among Negroes."[204] *Contempo* editor Mary Ann Ward affirmed the SBC's progressive 1968 Statement concerning the Crisis in Our Nation, which Alma Hunt and dozens of other SBC leaders signed to demonstrate their commitment to racial equality.[205] Articles introducing African American role models and promoting integrated neighborhoods also continued WMU's tradition of racial concern. For the first time, such articles urged white middle-class readers to consider African American Baptists as "allies in missions, not as 'objects' of missions."[206] Instead of discussing how they used their privileged status to assist African Americans, as earlier women had done, writers described successful cooperative ventures between white and black churches: Connecticut congregations worshipped together, churches in Arkansas held a joint Bible conference, and youth worked together to lead a missions Vacation Bible School in Georgia.[207] Unlike their predecessors, the magazines' editors apparently believed that true collaboration between the two races strengthened efforts such as mission action.

This emphasis on partnership and action was also evident in the volunteer missions opportunities that *Contempo* and *Royal Service* described, especially during the second half of this period. While editors most frequently urged women to address social problems through local mission action projects, they also did not hesitate to explain that readers who were able could "offer my life" for a few weeks or years by serving alongside a career missionary.[208] True to their denominational commitment, both magazines often detailed volunteer opportunities available to readers through HMB and FMB: "Wanted: three dentists to work in Guyana for two weeks doing tooth extractions"; "A place for you . . . adult vocational teacher, Philippines."[209] Such a focus on hands-on missions involvement, influenced by the activism of American culture at the time, was increasingly common among other evangelical missions organizations as well. As overseas travel became more accessible and programs such as the Peace Corps emerged, Christians realized that volunteers of both sexes could multiply the efforts of career missionaries through short-term service.

Accordingly, WMU joined other SBC entities in highlighting testimonies from missions volunteers, many of whom claimed—as Karon Owen did in 1979—that their trip was "one of the greatest growing experiences of my life."[210] Like other women profiled in *Contempo* and *Royal Service*, these volunteers filled a wide variety of roles, most of which their mothers and grandmothers would probably not have attempted. Clara Pahl participated in her first construction project at age sixty-nine; Tani Murrah witnessed on ski trails in Wyoming; and Anna Adams "was not afraid" to serve as a mission treasurer for a year in Vietnam.[211] Again using language of gifting, writers challenged WMU members to consider missions opportunities aligned with their skills, explaining that "all you need is a willingness to try and to be used of God."[212] One volunteer even described the "importance and joy in giving myself rather than just giving my money"[213]—a striking contrast to *Royal Service*'s emphasis on finances during the 1920s and 1930s. Editors now encouraged women to express their Christian commitment not by donating money or raising Christian children but by personally taking action to demonstrate God's love among people around the world.

Appealing to contemporary women's sense of adventure, several writers also urged readers to involve their families in volunteer missions, "the best possible vacation."[214] As the home became less the locus of Christian nurture and more the base for family ministry efforts, numerous families accepted the challenge and shared their "most interesting missions activities" with WMU members.[215] Virgie Gill and her granddaughter led backyard Bible clubs in Arizona; the Goodgame family spent the summer ministering in Uganda; and Charles and Grace Coe served as chaplains at the Kentucky State Fair.[216] In keeping with their openness to diversity, writers encouraged even single-parent and one-person families, overlooked in earlier periods, to volunteer their time.[217] Writers also demonstrated their acceptance of women's leadership, explaining that "most often, the woman is the key" to her family's service; missions was "new and frightening" to many men, who were not involved in WMU.[218] While in previous years editors had exhorted wives to defer to their husbands' spiritual authority, they no longer hesitated to assign that leadership role to the women. Influenced by women's expanding roles and the activist bent in American culture, WMU writers and editors portrayed mission action as an essential task in which Southern Baptist women could participate in a variety of ways.

When the ideal of a "liberated" woman became popular in American culture beginning in the late 1960s, WMU editors and writers adopted a similar focus in *Royal Service* and soon *Contempo*. In contrast to the domestic tasks that these WMU magazines had emphasized for Christian women in the preceding period, editors now challenged readers to use their gifts in an almost unlimited number of circumstances. A working, unmarried mother; a homemaker involved in mission action; a seminary student pursuing vocational ministry—all were equally valued by writers, who used biblical and historical examples to encourage each woman to take advantage of the wide range of possibilities available to her. Such emphases reflected the influence of evangelical feminism and revealed an affinity with the women's liberation movement as well. Although WMU writers and editors eschewed the more radical ideas of "women's libbers," their affirmations of women's equality and social action were strongly shaped by contemporary cultural movements. Just as many American women hoped that their nation would soon achieve gender equality, so too did WMU writers appear optimistic about the full inclusion of women in the SBC in the years to come.

Fearful of criticism from some contemporary Southern Baptists, however, editors of *Royal Service* and *Contempo* at times employed a deliberate strategy of silence. They did not officially urge WMU members to be ordained or to advocate women's rights, as leaders in several mainline denominations—and even a few Southern Baptists—did. But, evincing their organization's editorial and financial autonomy, editors did feature women serving in a plethora of ministry positions, including a Swedish pastor and a member of the National Organization for Women. Such extensive discussion of women's new roles, especially in a magazine that ostensibly highlighted only missions, was remarkable. Clearly WMU editors and editorial committee members demonstrated more sympathy for moderate Southern Baptist views than did their typical readers—or the conservative leaders who were beginning to stir up dissent within the SBC. During this period, WMU leaders managed to avoid denominational conflict as they encouraged women to adopt nearly boundless roles in church and society. This situation, however, would soon change.

# 6
# Developing Spiritually in a Context of Division, 1984–2006

Traveling on My Knees

*Last night I took a journey*
*to ________________ across the seas;*
*I did not go by boat or plane,*
*I traveled on my knees.*
*I saw so many precious people there*
*with scars and wounds within,*
*But God told me I should go,*
*that there was oil to pour for Him.*
*But I said, "Lord, I cannot go*
*and work with such as these."*
*He answered quickly, "Yes, you can . . .*
*by traveling on your knees."*
*He said, "You pray;*
*I'll meet their need,*
*You call and I will hear,*
*Be concerned about their fate,*
*of those both far and near."*
*And so I tried it, knelt in prayer,*
*gave up some hours of ease;*
*I felt the Lord right by my side,*
*while traveling on my knees.*
*As I prayed on and saw them helped*
*and the badly wounded healed,*
*I saw God's workers' strength renewed,*
*while laboring on the field.*
*I said, "Yes, Lord, I have a job,*
*my desire Thy will to please;*
*I can go and heed thy call,*
*by traveling on my knees.*

—Sandra Goodwin (adapted)
*Missions Mosaic*, December 1995, E22

"Be it resolved," pronounced messengers to the 1984 annual meeting of the SBC, "that we encourage the service of women in all aspects of church life and work *other than pastoral functions and leadership roles entailing ordination*."[1] Thus began a new era for women in the SBC, including leaders and members of WMU. Debate and restrictions quickly replaced the "almost unlimited possibilities" that had emerged for Southern Baptist women during the previous period. Conservative women's ministry groups, begun in earlier years, exploded in popularity, while WMU struggled with declining membership. In an attempt to "focus on women's interests and life stages"[2] as these women's ministries did—and thus interest more women—WMU leaders in 1995 combined Baptist Young Women and Baptist Women into Women on Mission, which they promoted as a versatile organization for all women. Concurrently, *Missions Mosaic* replaced both *Royal Service* and *Contempo* as the WMU magazine for women. Yet subscriptions continued to decrease as WMU's influence among Southern Baptist women waned. Discord between WMU and SBC leaders during this period brought additional stress to the organization.

In such a climate, WMU editors declined to publicly voice any opinions about gender roles or SBC politics that would have been controversial among Southern Baptists. Instead the magazines' editors emphasized concepts popular among many American evangelical women, such as spiritual growth, prayer, and witnessing—encouraging women to develop a "missions lifestyle" through involvement in WMU. While WMU leaders during these years struggled fiercely with conservative SBC leaders, *Royal Service*, *Contempo*, and *Missions Mosaic* included material that editors hoped would appeal to not only moderate but also conservative Southern Baptist women, many of whom demonstrated a growing interest in personal spiritual devotion.

## Conservatism and Controversy

"Today's woman may head a large corporation, lead a scientific expedition to study baboons in Africa, or become an astronaut on a flight to outer space," writer Winona Cobb declared in the July 1984 issue of *Contempo*.[3] Benefiting from the effects of the women's liberation movement of the 1960s and 1970s, American women during this period enjoyed what one *Contempo* writer called "a tremendous amount of freedom" that had been unthinkable to many of their predecessors.[4] Although vestiges of inequality remained, the more than 70 percent of American women who were gainfully employed filled a wide variety of roles. Some women even served as surgeons, college presidents, nuclear scientists, and secretaries of state, filling one of the highest offices in the U.S. government. As a result of such progress, many women no longer made striving for parity a priority. Even the term "feminist" became politicized and unpopular, in part as a result of conservatives' influence. Consequently, by the 1990s fewer than 25 percent of American women considered themselves feminists.[5] Discussion of women's rights became less prevalent during this period as the nation settled into a prosperous, individualistic climate filled with numerous opportunities for most women.

Southern women were not impervious to these cultural trends; however, as in previous years, a somewhat more conservative attitude toward gender roles prevailed in their region. Evangelicalism remained prominent throughout the South, with increasingly conservative theology gaining popularity among many evangelical adherents. This development led some individuals—including many Southern Baptists—to espouse what they regarded as a biblical theology of male headship and female submission. The formation of the Council on Biblical Manhood and Womanhood (CBMW) in 1987 encouraged such a hierarchical position. Notably, Southern Baptists Paige and Dorothy Patterson were among CBMW's founders. In contrast, the egalitarian perspective of Christians for Biblical Equality (CBE), organized in 1988 with less SBC support, indicated that gender roles were still contested among American evangelicals. However, the growing influence of the Christian Right predisposed many white evangelicals to more conservative positions on moral and cultural issues than they had previously advocated. Christian Right leaders such as Pat Robertson and James Dobson mobilized thousands of evangelicals in "culture wars" to advance what they believed were traditional family values threatened by a secular society. By the end of this period, such leaders succeeded in making evangelicals a significant countercultural force—and one of the largest blocs of Republican voters in the country.

From this evangelical conservatism, with its emphasis on traditional gender roles, arose groups such as Promise Keepers. This organization, which was most influential in the mid-1990s, involved millions of Christian men in the United States—and later around the world—in claiming leadership of and commitment to their families. Within the SBC, many pastors and laymen "embraced the Promise Keepers ministry," according to a 1997 *Baptist Press* release.[6] Indeed, a survey conducted by Promise Keepers revealed that more than 30 percent of attendees at the organization's conferences were Southern Baptist.[7] This enthusiasm for Promise

Keepers demonstrated the SBC's affinity with conservative evangelical causes during this period.

While evangelical men attended Promise Keepers rallies, their wives may have participated in women's ministry events. In the 1980s, influential megachurches such as Chicago's Willow Creek Community Church began women's ministry programs, and this trend quickly spread to evangelical churches across the United States. These ministries sought to enrich women's lives through Bible study, prayer, mentoring, and special events. The nondenominational *Women's Ministry Handbook*, for example, published in 1992, included chapters titled "Organizing Great Bible Study Groups" and "Planning a Successful Women's Retreat."[8] Beginning in 1996, hundreds of thousands of evangelical women attended events hosted by the Women of Faith ministry, with themes such as "Outrageous Joy" and "Extravagant Grace." Many church-based women's ministries used similar language, along with images that they considered feminine: cursive scripts and pictures of pastel lilies accompanied metaphors comparing women's spirituality to "cultivating the garden" or "gathering a bouquet of flowers."[9] Instead of urging women to consider issues of gender equality that had previously been significant to a number of evangelicals, most women's ministries propagated conservative views about gender.

Among Southern Baptist women, women's ministries were an "exploding trend," as Georgia women's ministry leader Mary Frances Bowley put it in 1995.[10] By the mid-1990s, Southern Baptist author and speaker Beth Moore was wildly popular among women's ministry audiences within and beyond the denomination, with thousands completing her Bible studies, including *A Woman's Heart—God's Dwelling Place* and *Breaking Free: Making Liberty in Christ a Reality in Life*, among many others. In 1993 the SBC's SSB established an office of Women's Enrichment Ministry to "provide churches with the best, most relevant programs, sources, and services to meet the distinctive needs of women, enabling them to experience enrichment through their relationship with Christ."[11] This ministry was initially led by Denise George of Birmingham, Alabama.

While the establishment of Women's Enrichment Ministry outwardly appeared to be an innocuous move, it challenged WMU's claim that it served all Southern Baptist women. Although George lived within a few miles of the national WMU office, WMU leaders learned of SSB's plans only one day before they were made public, evincing the tense relationship between the two entities over their women's strategies. National WMU staff soon produced a white paper examining women's ministry, which they admitted "compounded" WMU's "discomfort over declining enrollment figures."[12] Unlike WMU organizations for women, Women's Enrichment Ministry proved highly popular during this period. In many SBC churches, women in their twenties and thirties flocked to women's ministry groups and events, often leaving aging WMU members feeling threatened and confused. As in some other denominations, long-established women's organizations declined as new groups—which appeared to be free from the constraints of tradition—appealed to the felt needs of contemporary women. In reality, however, the ideology such groups offered was deeply traditional but presented in attractive new ways.

The women's ministry model was especially well suited for the SBC, whose conservative contingent acquired more power with each passing year. The denomination's annual meetings became fierce battlegrounds between moderates and conservatives, with a record 45,404 messengers attending the 1985 gathering in Dallas. In an attempt to quell the controversy, the SBC established a Peace Committee, which included former WMU president Christine Gregory. This action, however, failed to bring lasting reconciliation between the two factions. Soon it became evident that conservatives had established a majority within the denomination—or, as conservative pastor Jerry Sutton put it, "Truth has triumphed!"[13] Moderates gradually acknowledged their defeat and formed their own institutions, which separated from the SBC in the years that followed. As early as 1987, more progressive moderates organized the Alliance of Baptists, while a centrist group formed the Cooperative Baptist Fellowship in 1991. New seminaries emerged as controversy transformed SBC schools; the moderate *Associated Baptist Press* countered the SBC's *Baptist Press*; and even the president of FMB, Keith Parks, resigned and accepted a similar position with CBF.

As a result of conservatives' influence in the SBC, by the 1990s both FMB and HMB no longer allowed ordained women to serve as missionaries. In 1998 messengers at the denomination's annual meeting approved an addition to the Baptist Faith and Message, the SBC's statement of faith, which affirmed husbands' "headship" in marriage and admonished wives to "submit . . . graciously" to them[14]—arousing the ire of both moderate Baptists and the mainstream media. A 2000 revision of the same statement—which international missionaries were soon required to sign—argued that "while both men and women are gifted for service in the church, the office of pastor is limited to men as qualified by Scripture."[15] Conservatives, clearly in control of the SBC, rapidly instituted what they believed were biblical precepts, many of which also aligned with the goals of the Christian Right. Indeed, by 2000 a survey revealed that a majority of Southern Baptist ministers either were members of or "felt close to" Christian Right organizations: 92 percent to Dobson's Focus on the Family, 55 percent to Don Wildmon's American Family Association, and 49 percent to Robertson's Christian Coalition.[16] No longer was a "Grand Compromise" among a variety of perspectives possible within the SBC; instead, the denomination cultivated a close relationship with the Christian Right.

As the SBC entered the twenty-first century, it continued on this conservative course, in 2004 withdrawing its membership from the BWA, the global fellowship for Baptists, because of the BWA's alleged liberalism. Two years later SWBTS, led by key conservative Paige Patterson, dismissed Sheri Klouda from her Hebrew professorship, leaving only men to teach pastoral ministry students. SWBTS, along with other SBC seminaries, also established certificate and degree programs for women—programs that encouraged women to embrace "the blessings and joys of homemaking and motherhood" and offered courses in hospitality, decorating, and serving as a minister's wife, among other areas.[17] By the end of this period, SBC leaders had taken an unarguably conservative stance on gender roles, for the first time opposing prevalent cultural norms instead of gradually accepting them.

As an auxiliary to the SBC, WMU was not immune to the conflict that wracked the convention during this period. Unlike in previous years, when WMU had managed to avoid entanglement in controversy, beginning in the late 1980s the autonomy of the women's group became a source of growing frustration for SBC leaders. WMU "identified too closely with moderates and with Women in Ministry in particular," according to conservative Southern Baptist journalist James Hefley.[18] Unable to control WMU's leadership because of the organization's auxiliary status, conservatives exercised their power indirectly. In 1988 Paige Patterson recommended that WMU become an agency whose leaders were selected by the convention, arguing that operating the women's organization differently from other SBC entities was "discriminatory toward women."[19] Thus Patterson deftly used the language of women's equality to advocate an action that would have subjected WMU to close control by conservative male SBC leaders. As might have been expected, WMU executive director Carolyn Weatherford opposed Patterson's suggestion, explaining to state WMU leaders that she "declined to respond."[20]

In 1990, just months after new WMU executive director Dellanna O'Brien pledged to keep WMU "above the convention controversy,"[21] the organization for the first time made a public statement about the conflict. "We regret that our silence . . . might have been construed as consent," the WMU Executive Board declared in a specially called meeting, and affirmed the right of individuals, churches, and state Baptist conventions to choose their plans for missions giving.[22] Conservative convention leaders thus took offense at what they regarded as WMU's support of alternate funding options promoted by moderates. Dorothy Patterson accused WMU in inflammatory language of "missions terrorism";[23] others wrote to O'Brien with similar opinions. What O'Brien and other WMU leaders claimed was a genuine attempt at neutrality, convention leaders viewed as thinly veiled support of the moderate cause.

Conflict between WMU and the SBC escalated in 1992, when CBF leaders approached WMU about producing missions education materials featuring CBF missionaries. "WMU is our only hope," CBF supporter Bee Garris King pleaded.[24] O'Brien assured CBF coordinator Cecil Sherman in a June 1992 letter that WMU was "most interested"; the WMU Executive Board likewise affirmed its "strong desire that we serve *all* churches in the Southern Baptist Convention."[25] Such willingness to cooperate with CBF—which most conservatives regarded as "a schismatic group that has set itself against SBC leaders"[26]—revealed WMU leaders' moderate affiliations, which many other SBC leaders in the previous period had shared. During these years, however, the denomination's conservative new decision makers were deeply troubled by such alignments. The SBC Executive Committee entertained a motion—later tabled—to "invite Woman's Missionary Union to initiate legal steps to become an agency of the Southern Baptist Convention rather than remain as an auxiliary."[27] And in an impassioned, three-hour dialogue, FMB executives questioned WMU leaders about their relationships with CBF and the SBC.[28] As the controversy continued unabated, O'Brien admitted that "it appears we are headed to a showdown."[29]

This fateful prediction was realized between 1993 and 1995, the years of the most heated conflict between WMU and the SBC. In January 1993 the WMU Executive Board asserted its autonomy—and demonstrated its growing distance from conservative SBC leaders—by unanimously adopting a new vision statement and core values for WMU, along with six controversial recommendations. These statements had been formulated by The Committee, a group of seventeen WMU Executive Board members appointed by WMU president Carolyn Miller. WMU agreed in its six recommendations to produce resources for various Southern Baptist groups, such as CBF, "at their request," and established a degree of independence from the SBC by committing to expand its own volunteer program, emphasize social issues, and accept direct financial gifts.[30] WMU subsequently mailed to all SBC pastors and missionaries—along with a number of denominational leaders—an "open letter" attempting to influence their view of these decisions. Instead of discussing WMU's actions in terms of the SBC conflict, WMU leaders in this letter appealed to Southern Baptists' concern for world evangelization, alleging that the WMU Executive Board's decisions would "empower WMU to be more effective in reaching the world for Jesus Christ."[31] However, denominational leaders considered WMU's actions threatening, not evangelistic. Chaos ensued.

In the next several weeks, SBC leaders confronted WMU in a variety of ways. FMB leaders mailed a videotape of their July 1992 dialogue with WMU to all SBC missionaries; Adrian Rogers denounced WMU's "feminization of missions"; FMB trustee chairman John Jackson called WMU an "adulteress"; and the SBC Executive Board called for WMU to "make clear its singular cooperation" with the denomination.[32] The same men who controlled the conservative transformation of the SBC were frustrated by their lack of official power over WMU—even more so because of their belief in women's functional subordination to men. Accordingly, these leaders vehemently protested what they believed was the breach of an implicit institutional marriage covenant between WMU and the SBC. Just as these men thought that a woman agreed at her wedding to a lifelong, submissive relationship to her husband, so they also believed that WMU at its formation had committed to support the SBC's programs and direction in perpetuity.

WMU leaders, however, refused to return fully to the denominational support role they had happily assumed during the mid-twentieth century, recognizing that the denomination's leadership had since changed significantly. Instead, WMU used its auxiliary status and the influence it had gained during previous periods to assert at least partial independence from the SBC. In the spring of 1993, WMU distributed a follow-up report to SBC pastors and leaders in order to "bring clarification and understanding" to their controversial actions, which the women termed their desire to "embrace all Southern Baptists."[33] However, anger and confusion—not understanding—prevailed.

WMU again encountered hostility in 1994 when its leaders voted to accept a $100,000 check from CBF, although O'Brien pointed out that other SBC entities had received financial gifts from that organization.[34] Keith Parks explained to O'Brien that CBF sent this unsolicited contribution to WMU "in deep appreciation for your ongoing strengthening of global evangelization and missions."[35] According to FMB president

Jerry Rankin, though, WMU's acceptance of this donation demonstrated a "divided focus and ambiguous loyalties" that he believed would diminish WMU's influence within the SBC.[36] However, WMU leaders understood Rankin's statement as a further attempt to control their organization. Months later, WMU discovered FMB's attempt to trademark the LMCO, which the women had created a century earlier to support the board's missionaries. FMB leaders soon apologized, but the damage had been done. After efforts to file jointly for the trademark proved unsuccessful for legal reasons, WMU trademarked both the LMCO and the AAEO, licensing these trademarks exclusively to the SBC mission boards.[37] This action ensured that WMU maintained a degree of control over both offerings and thus over the mission boards as well.

WMU's relationships within the SBC remained tense as O'Brien and her staff continued to cooperate with CBF. As part of a denominational restructuring plan, SBC leaders in 1995 again invited WMU to become an agency under the convention's control. When the WMU Executive Board again refused to allow their organization to become an SBC agency, its members found WMU "reduced to footnote status" in the denomination's new structure.[38] The SBC officially reassigned to HMB WMU's longstanding responsibility for missions education in SBC churches and similarly delegated women's ministry to SSB. While convention leaders could not control the women's efforts, they could attempt to marginalize WMU into insignificance. In the years that followed, these new SBC ministry assignments implied, WMU would have to carry out its endeavors without the convention's blessing.

Just weeks later, O'Brien led WMU to reassert its autonomy by announcing its decision to "produce materials in cooperation with the Cooperative Baptist Fellowship" without altering production of its traditional SBC resources.[39] This commitment enraged SBC leaders, who believed that it undermined WMU's pledge to support the SBC. Morris Chapman, president and chief executive officer of the SBC Executive Committee, found this action "astonishing"; Larry Lewis, HMB's president, deemed it "inappropriate."[40] Rankin went even further, mailing to the denomination's forty thousand pastors, WMU directors, and other leaders a letter sternly rebuking WMU for "promot[ing] a divisive missions program" and urging the organization's board to reverse its decision.[41] When O'Brien learned of this action, she asserted in a written public statement that she was "furious," calling Rankin's letter "inflammatory, misleading, and divisive."[42] She soon retaliated with an equal demonstration of power, mailing a "WMU special report" to the same audience that had received

Rankin's letter in order—as she put it—to "interpret for you the activities in which we are engaged."[43] Such fierce public debate demonstrated that the relationship between WMU and FMB had reached a new low.

Later dialogue sessions between WMU and FMB leaders helped preserve the working relationship between the two entities, although hard feelings remained. At WMU's 1996 Executive Board meeting, Rankin addressed the organization's response to the SBC conflict: "It is getting tiresome to talk about politics, power, and control after 16 years. This is the Southern Baptist Convention and this is where it is going. I think WMU needs to face [the question], 'Are we going to get on track and work together and support the leadership, the mission boards, and what the Southern Baptist Convention is doing?'"[44] WMU leaders, probably also weary of controversy, appear to have gradually adopted this cooperative spirit. Or perhaps the women decided simply to keep their objections to themselves.

Indeed, one WMU editor spoke of the organization's "underlying fear that the SBC could 'force' its churches not to use our materials."[45] Although WMU leaders had prevented WMU from becoming an SBC agency in order to maintain their organization's autonomy, in so doing they refused denominational funding and thus remained reliant on revenue from the magazines they sold to Southern Baptist churches. Anxious not to provoke further negative reactions, WMU leaders remained silent regarding the revisions to the Baptist Faith and Message in 1998 and 2000, with which they must surely have disagreed. Even this silence brought rebuke from Dorothy Patterson, who called it a "peculiar" stance for a women's organization and unsuccessfully urged WMU to affirm the conservative roles for women that the new Baptist Faith and Message described.[46]

The installation in 2000 of Wanda Lee as WMU executive director/treasurer marked a transition to a more amicable relationship between WMU and the SBC, although underlying tensions remained. In that year, WMU allayed conservatives' concerns by ceasing publication of materials for CBF as that organization grew and hired its own missions education staff. When the SBC withdrew from the BWA in 2004, however, WMU continued to support the BWA Women's Department, which it had helped found decades earlier. The following year, Lee addressed a gathering of the moderate Baptist General Convention of Missouri, despite criticism from conservative leaders. And in 2006 the SBC Executive Committee urged the convention once again to invite WMU to become an agency instead of an auxiliary—but messengers, weary of denominational conflict, defeated this recommendation. Ironically, WMU's auxiliary status, a result of women's subordinate role in the nineteenth-century SBC, allowed the organization to determine its own direction throughout the denomination's controversy a century later. Formed as an auxiliary in part to assure male convention leaders of their control, WMU later used its unique position in the SBC to thwart men's attempts to control it.

## Doing Missions through WMU

While WMU and SBC leaders fought bitterly over WMU's role in the denomination, WMU magazines included remarkably little criticism of the SBC or even information about the ongoing controversy. *Royal Service* editors during these years included Betty Merrell (1983–1985), Edna Ellison (1986–1993), and Cindy Dake and Laura Savage (1993–1995). Editing *Contempo* were Mary Ann Ward (1975–1987), Diana Woodcock (1988–1989), Eleanor Clay (1990–1991), Dake (1991–1993), and both Dake and Savage (1993–1995). Several editors shaped *Missions Mosaic* throughout the period: Dake (1995–1997), Becky Nelson (1997–1999), Joanne Parker (2000–2005), Sue Sprenkle (2005–2006), and Janet Erwin (2006). A variety of circumstances, including increased employee turnover throughout American society, contributed to the large number of WMU editors during this period. Multiple editors resigned from their posts to serve as career missionaries; others accepted new positions within WMU.

Of this group, Ellison, Dake, and Parker had the longest tenures, together serving for eighteen of the twenty-three years in this period. These three editors (and others) influenced the magazines' content in accord with their emphasis on spirituality—a topic that both seminary-trained WMU leaders and grassroots WMU members could embrace. These editors also apparently selected writers who supported such a spiritual focus, in contrast with the more controversial topics writers and editors had favored in the previous period. As before, the WMU Executive Board also had significant input into the subjects featured in *Contempo*, *Royal Service*, and *Missions Mosaic*. In addition, several WMU staff members continued to read manuscripts for each issue to ensure their "clarity, accuracy, and suitability."[47] Wary of the growing power of the SBC's new conservative leaders, these reviewers likely flagged any information they felt was too contentious for WMU to publish. Indeed, O'Brien admitted to historian Elizabeth Flowers in a 2006 interview that instead of taking a prophetic stance on the SBC conflict, in its publications WMU "avoided those areas that would be controversial."[48] More so than in the previous period, the organization's leaders were disinclined to publish articles that might arouse dissent among their members.

Thus WMU editors and writers used surprisingly little ink to describe the SBC conflict. Instead they prioritized their own organizational efforts, exhorting women not to be "sidetracked" from continuing their missions efforts through WMU.[49] Of the few articles that mentioned the convention controversy, most simply urged women to be informed. In 1986 WMU executive director Carolyn Weatherford did not advise *Contempo* readers to espouse a moderate position but instead encouraged them rather benignly to "find out all you can about the issues . . . then decide what you believe."[50] The same year, a two-page article about "how to attend a Southern Baptist Convention"—and the booklet from which it was excerpted—introduced women to SBC protocol and processes, without ever mentioning the significant topics under debate.[51] Concerned about alienating their subscribers, some of whom already suspected WMU of moderate leanings, editors intentionally avoided discussing the substantive issues involved in the denominational disagreement. These editors recognized that the majority of WMU members—like the majority of Southern Baptists—probably supported conservative positions in the SBC conflict, if they were aware of the debate at all. Thus, in a fascinating move, editors attempted to preserve WMU's voice within the SBC by generally remaining silent about WMU leaders' divisive stances.

A few writers did suggest that readers concerned about the denominational controversy should consider the primacy of missions in the SBC's efforts. "Ask [God] that the people elected be missions-minded," one 1985 article urged.[52] Weatherford similarly explained that at the denomination's 1985 annual meeting in Dallas, she would "evaluate decisions in terms of how they will affect world missions" and opined that "Southern Baptists must keep at the heart of our Convention strong missions concern."[53] These exhortations reflected WMU's historic priority of missions—and corresponded with many moderates' view that cooperation for missions superseded doctrinal uniformity. However, most WMU members, who supported missions but were unfamiliar with the intricacies of the convention controversy, probably did not understand the full implications of such statements. Instead of advancing clear positions on the SBC conflict, WMU editors—when they mentioned the topic at all—included general statements about missions with which their readers would surely have agreed.

WMU leaders did infrequently write features for *Contempo*, *Royal Ser-*

*vice*, and *Missions Mosaic* that addressed specific disagreements they had with SBC leadership. In two separate articles published in 1985, Weatherford decried "rumors" that WMU advocated the ordination of women through its involvement with Women in Ministry. She repeatedly emphasized that "the vast majority" of participants in that organization "are not ordained."[54] Such statements suggested that WMU was receiving increased criticism for its involvement with Women in Ministry—and demonstrated WMU leaders' growing reluctance to support female ministers publicly. WMU magazines also defended the organization's auxiliary status, a "104-year-old relationship that has worked,"[55] and in 1995 even included an insert explaining WMU's "great concern" at its exclusion from the SBC's restructuring plan.[56] A few 2004 articles likewise urged women to pray that "the Baptist family [the BWA] will not be split apart by the actions of a few" at the SBC meeting that year.[57] WMU editors and leaders apparently felt that these issues were significant and noncontroversial enough to report to their diverse readership. Otherwise, however, WMU magazines remained remarkably silent about the conflicts that were redefining the organization's relationships within the convention.

Although WMU's involvement with CBF was at the heart of its bitter dispute with SBC leaders, that organization appears never to have been discussed within the pages of *Royal Service*, *Contempo*, or *Missions Mosaic*. In an article describing the "new things on the horizon" as a result of the WMU Executive Board's momentous 1993 actions, O'Brien highlighted only three less controversial recommendations. She failed to mention WMU's decisions to create materials for diverse Southern Baptist groups (including CBF) and to accept contributions from individuals and groups (including CBF), commenting only that "space doesn't permit a full listing" of the board's recommendations.[58] Such a significant omission attempted to shield WMU members from the substantial issues involved in the organization's conflict with the SBC and thus to present an unarguably positive portrait of WMU. Realizing that "we have women of all theological persuasions in our organizations," as O'Brien put it,[59] WMU leaders carefully avoided revealing their moderate affiliations in their magazines. A 1994 article exemplified this strategy, as WMU staff member Joyce Mitchell urged a woman who had been asked about the SBC struggle simply to "confess . . . that the intricacies of denominational history are not your forte"—and to seek to involve the questioners in Baptist Young Women.[60] Loyal participation in WMU's missions efforts, not in the convention conflict, was the most important role for Southern Baptist women, such articles implied—although behind the scenes a massive SBC-WMU power struggle was taking place.

As in previous years, editors encouraged every reader to "commit to being a strong missions-minded/hearted woman . . . [through] learning, praying, giving, and doing"—WMU's historic methods of supporting SBC mission work.[61] But in the latter half of this period, Joanne Parker and other editors also guided *Missions Mosaic* to include new ways for women to be involved in missions: through WMU's ministries. These ministries, most of which began in the 1990s as a result of the WMU Executive Board's recommendations, encompassed everything from supplying clean water for missionaries to selling fair-trade international handcrafts. Such efforts provided ways for women to minister directly through WMU—not through HMB or FMB.

A variety of features in *Missions Mosaic* during the late 1990s and early 2000s detailed WMU's ministries. No longer did articles titled "A Place for You to Serve" enumerate volunteer missions opportunities available through FMB or HMB; instead they challenged readers to participate in WMU's MissionsFEST and FamilyFEST short-term mission trips.[62] Pages once dedicated to telling missionaries' stories now described how WMU's International Initiatives projects carried "the comfort of Christ to . . . women and children" around the world.[63] Throughout the early years of the twenty-first century, even the front cover of *Missions Mosaic* depicted not career missionaries but women such as Sandra Mitcham, a site coordinator for Christian Women's Job Corps, WMU's welfare-to-work ministry in the United States.[64] Such features implicitly encouraged readers to develop loyalty to WMU as an autonomous missions organization, not just as a means to support FMB and HMB. This new focus reflected WMU's increased independence from SBC emphases. While several pages in each magazine continued to highlight the denomination's missionaries, a number of articles detailing and soliciting funds for WMU's ministries urged women to become involved in missions directly through WMU.

But editors could no longer boast that WMU was the only way for Southern Baptist women to be involved in missions. O'Brien admitted in 1999 that as a result of the denomination's reorganization, WMU "lost . . . perhaps a part of our distinctive contributions" to the SBC.[65] In reality—partially at WMU members' urging—churches and convention agencies had increased their support of and involvement in missions over the previous several decades, thereby taking on the missions promotion role that

WMU alone had once filled in the SBC. Acknowledging these changes, Catherine Allen even controversially claimed in 2002 that "it is doubtful that WMU's historic reason for existence is valid today."[66] WMU writers conceded that "most Southern Baptists have the opportunity to do mission work without being a part of Woman's Missionary Union"—but they resolutely avowed that "the best means for women to participate in mission work is through WMU."[67] Disinclined to relinquish their rich century-long heritage, writers frequently challenged women to invite their neighbors, coworkers, and friends to participate in WMU organizations with them so that these friends could "have a life-changing experience" and "know what they are missing."[68] Articles emphasized enlisting new members for WMU organizations alongside learning about and doing missions.

Despite these efforts, throughout this period WMU's enrollment and revenue continued to decline, with fewer than half as many readers subscribing to the organization's magazine for women in the 1990s as in the 1960s. In addition, a 1996 survey revealed that the majority of Women on Mission members were above sixty-five years old.[69] As a result, editors and writers stressed the importance of involving younger women in WMU and dispelling what Dake called in 1995 the "inaccurate impression" of WMU as "an organization for very old women who were rather exclusive in their meeting habits."[70] Editor Sue Sprenkle maintained a decade later that the "million dollar question" for WMU was "How do we reach young women?"[71]—a question that many writers throughout this period attempted to answer. "See what types of activities interest them," Debra Berry advised.[72] Form a hands-on "action group," Betty Shoe testified.[73] "Meet their needs," Edna Ellison suggested.[74] Most writers did not propose that WMU members urge younger women to be involved in missions and ministry efforts through other organizations; instead they challenged readers to introduce "all women in the church" to WMU.[75]

In order to encourage more women to be involved in missions—and in WMU—a growing number of articles in *Missions Mosaic*, *Royal Service*, and *Contempo* emphasized that busy, working women of all ages should "set missions as a priority" and avoid letting their "commitment to God and missions get squeezed out."[76] Writers such as Arnette Smith explained how they found "a way to work and still be involved in the Great Commission," recommending that their peers read about missions while waiting at a doctor's office, listen to recordings of missionary biographies while driving, and pray for missions on their lunch breaks or in the shower.[77] Paid employment, these writers felt, was no excuse for a lack of involvement in WMU. Several articles also praised the work of missionary women who ministered beyond their homes, including Marilyn Prickett, a social ministries director serving with HMB in Washington, DC, and Rebekah Naylor, an FMB doctor in India.[78] However, during these years such features stressed not the women's employment status but their missions involvement.

Unlike in the previous period, then, when editors had devoted page after page to exploring working women's new roles, during these years writers merely accepted employment as "a fact of life" for most American women.[79] Although Dorothy Patterson feared that WMU magazines did not appropriately "lift up . . . the responsibility of homemaking," a WMU editor countered that ignoring working women would have been equivalent to "hiding our heads in the sand."[80] Just as they had done in earlier years, editors refused to criticize women's employment choices, attempting to provide material to meet the varying needs of homemakers and employees. Instead of encouraging these women to seek vocational fulfillment or increased rights, editors and writers encouraged both groups to become involved in missions through WMU.

Young and old, employees and homemakers, singles and marrieds, African Americans and Caucasians—WMU magazines no longer emphasized the inclusion of each type of woman but instead urged them all to focus on missions. As one missionary remarked, "I am a woman in missions who happens to be single. I do my job—my singleness is secondary."[81] Just as in broader American society, middle-class women's varied lifestyles were no longer a subject of debate but were simply an accepted reality. Joyce Mitchell accordingly described women's options as "formal education, challenging career, fulfilling marriage, child-rearing and nurturing, ministry or community service, and rewarding personal relationships"[82]—an almost overwhelming array of possibilities.

But one possibility WMU writers did not commonly mention was submission to male headship, a favorite topic of conservative groups such as CBMW and the Baptist Faith and Message revision committees. Neither did WMU writers spend time promoting gender equality in churches and homes, in contrast with egalitarian organizations such as Christians for Biblical Equality, with which some WMU leaders likely sympathized. While editors generally continued their policy of using gender-inclusive language, they did not experiment with inclusive language for God as groups such as Women in Ministry did. In addition, articles that earlier had described "liberated" women now avoided controversy by simply explaining that it was up to each woman to "determine what our own particular role is."[83] Prescribing gender roles—whether traditional or nontraditional—was apparently less of a priority to writers than was describing practical ways women could be involved in missions every day.

Women's participation in WMU and its ministries, then, was more important to editors and editorial committee members than was women's involvement in the SBC debate or assumption of specific gender roles. For many women, editors believed, such participation might well include spiritual development and prayer. In the hope of involving more women in their organization, WMU leaders appropriated these concepts—popular among women's ministries—into their missions model, infusing them with what one editor described as a "softened missions effect."[84] They added witnessing, an emphasis amenable to SBC conservatives and congruous with their own developing conviction that "all spiritual growth leads to a missions lifestyle."[85] Though editors did not highlight the themes of homemaking and "gracious submission" prominent among some conservative SBC women's ministries, they did incorporate such ministries' tenor of spirituality into the roles they portrayed for women in missions.

## Developing Spiritually toward a Missions Lifestyle

"*Every* woman" in the SBC, a 1995 *Missions Mosaic* article declared, should participate in Women on Mission—not just to learn about missions but to "become a better Christian witness and strengthen her daily walk with God."[86] Such an emphasis on spiritual growth was common among evangelicals during this period. Books such as Richard Foster's *Celebration of Discipline* and Henry Blackaby's *Experiencing God*—published by SSB—climbed the best-seller list, and courses on spiritual formation proliferated in evangelical churches and schools. With their inward focus, women's ministries stressed personal spirituality, encouraging women to pray, study the Bible, and develop a deep relationship with Christ. WMU evinced its interest in this trend in 1993 by adding "developing spiritually toward a missions lifestyle" to its official task statements, guided by Executive Board members' desire to reach women not currently involved in WMU.[87] WMU editors also demonstrated the organization's emphasis on spirituality by including numerous features on the topic in *Contempo*, *Royal Service*, and *Missions Mosaic* throughout this period.

A 1994 survey in *Royal Service* revealed similar priorities for WMU members as for women's ministry participants, with questions such as "How much time do I spend daily to study God's Word?" and "How have my Christlike qualities improved compared to ten years ago?"[88] No longer did editors portray WMU leaders as primarily a source of information about missions; instead these women—like women's ministry leaders—became "a catalyst for women to grow in their relationship with Christ."[89] Magazine pages that had once discussed mission action and liberation now featured topics from revival to spiritual disciplines, with Pat Sullivan even suggesting that cleaning toilets for others could "bring spiritual renewal."[90] Unlike earlier writers, who had stressed mission action's goal of justice and equality, Sullivan intimated that ministry efforts were valuable merely for their effects on the women who undertook them. Such an inward focus on spiritual growth reflected WMU leaders' willingness to appropriate this popular concept to convince women of the relevance of missions to their daily lives. Guided by the WMU Executive Board's desire for WMU to remain relevant and attract new members, each editor throughout this period filled a number of her magazine's pages with information related to spiritual growth.

Numerous features in *Contempo*, *Royal Service*, and *Missions Mosaic* exemplified this emphasis on women's spirituality, including the magazines' book reviews and ads. Editors promoted titles such as *Second Wind: Refreshing Pauses and Prayers for Women*; *Seeking Sabbath: A Planning Guide for Women's Retreats*; *Active Spirituality* by conservative pastor Chuck Swindoll; and Beth Moore's popular study *A Heart like His: Intimate Reflections on the Life of David*.[91] Other recommended books highlighted lifestyle issues on which women's ministry groups often focused, many of which were only tangentially related to missions. *Childless Is Not Less* explored infertility; *Engaged* featured engagement and marriage; and *Just Because They've Left Doesn't Mean They're Gone*, published by Focus on the Family, discussed relationships with adult children.[92] As women's ministry topics gained popularity—and expansive roles for women became suspect among Southern Baptists—references to conservative books on spirituality and Christian living replaced the evangelical feminist titles that WMU magazines had promoted during the previous period. Growing closer to God became a more important role for WMU members than exploring their call to minister to others.

Under Carolyn Weatherford's leadership, in 1985 WMU even formed its own trade publishing imprint to create general interest books for Christian women: New Hope Publishers. From 1989 to 1996, not only did WMU's involvement in Women in Ministry decline but through New Hope WMU also published *Magazette*. This newsletter was designed "to encourage, enable, and enrich" not female ministers but "Southern Baptist ministers' wives."[93] This newsletter, which WMU women's magazines sometimes promoted, on occasion featured as writers and guest editors the wives of prominent SBC conservatives, including Joyce Rogers, Rhonda Kelley, and Dorothy Patterson. While these women rarely wrote for *Royal Service*, *Contempo*, or *Missions Mosaic*, their inclusion in any publication produced by WMU, whose leaders publicly clashed with conservatives, was remarkable. Desiring "all women to be radically involved in the mission of God,"[94] the organization's leaders endeavored to gain an audience among even conservative ministers' wives, whose cause was thriving in the denomination and who were more likely to be involved in women's ministry groups than in WMU.

In addition, Dake, Parker, and other editors worked to dispel the common view—even voiced by president Marjorie McCullough—that WMU organizations and women's ministries were competing groups.[95] As Dellanna O'Brien explained in a letter to WMU member Dolores Davis, most women's ministry groups involved "good women who simply have not been exposed to a missions agenda"—women who might be led to a missions commitment more readily through affirmation than through criticism and division.[96] O'Brien and other WMU leaders thus maintained that their emphasis on spiritual development was not just a goal in itself but a step toward a missions lifestyle. In an attempt to improve relationships among church women's groups—and to introduce more women to this missions lifestyle through WMU—*Missions Mosaic* recommended in 1996 that WMU members host celebration experiences "for all the women in the church to come together to celebrate what God is doing."[97] In 2006 editor Sue Sprenkle also challenged each reader to "become an agent of reconciliation" among women's groups in her church, urging women to purchase a WMU book to learn more about this role.[98] The goal of Sprenkle and other editors, it appears, was not only to support a variety of women's efforts but also more pragmatically to increase WMU membership and sales. WMU leaders during this period realized that cooperation with women's ministry groups was more likely to augment women's missions involvement—and their own numbers—than was competition.

Accordingly, numerous articles in *Missions Mosaic*, *Contempo*, and *Royal Service* mirrored women's ministries' use of florid descriptions and designs to attract women's attention. Especially in the mid-1990s, several pages included stereotypically feminine artwork popular among women's ministry groups, such as hearts, cursive scripts, and pastel floral backgrounds. WMU editors and writers throughout this period used emotive language to describe women's "hunger for the deep things of God,"[99] prioritizing an individual's relationship with Christ just as women's ministries did. Sev-

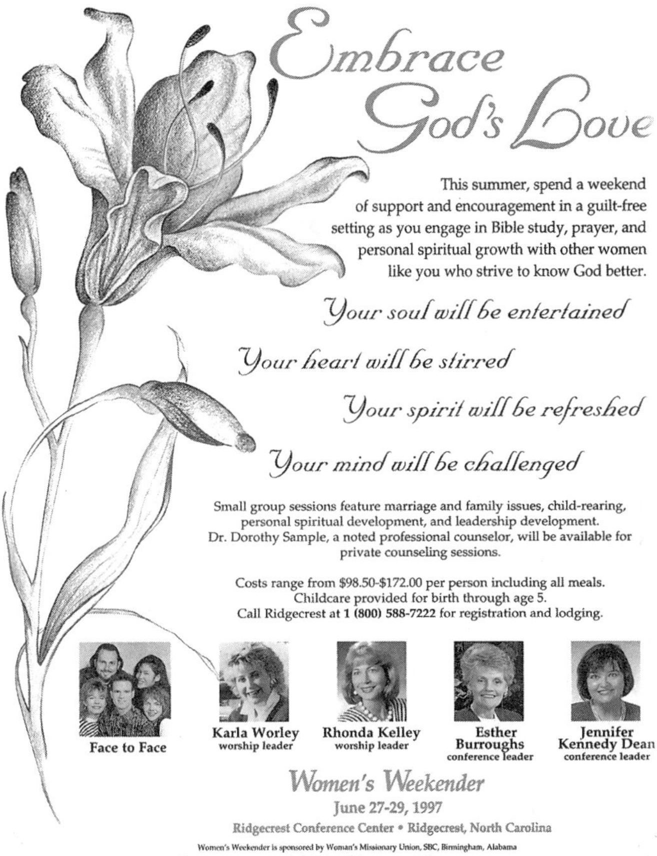


14. Page from May 1997 *Missions Mosaic.* (Used by permission of WMUA.)

eral writers expressively personified "the heartbeat of God," "the hand of Jesus," God's "whispers in your ear," and the "Father's everlasting arms."[100] Such phrases emphasized God's immanence and implied that following God would bring women a "sense of belonging and victory"[101] that was sometimes lacking in their earthly relationships. Some writers even described knowing God as "an intimate relationship" as precious as "intimacy between lovers."[102] God is "yearning over you, longing for you," declared popular writer and retreat leader Jennifer Kennedy Dean.[103] Like other evangelical women seeking to minister to their peers, such writers depicted God rather anthropocentrically as a faithful lover and friend intent upon meeting women's needs more completely than any human could.

Developing intimacy with God was a priority, both WMU editors and women's ministry leaders maintained; only then could women "allow the light of Christ's love to pour through" them onto others.[104]

Editors also reinterpreted their descriptions of ideal Christian women to reflect this emphasis on inner spirituality. Phoebe was no longer a biblical model of a deaconess, as *Royal Service* had asserted in 1970, but was instead "an effective spiritual investor."[105] Esther represented not just a daring, action-oriented woman, as earlier writers had claimed, but someone willing to seek out and follow "the hidden hand of God."[106] And missionary Lottie Moon was revered not as a radical, as she had been in the previous period, but as a woman who had spent her years in China "discovering the gift of love and getting to know God."[107] As before, writers' depictions of these historic women were strikingly similar to the language used to describe the roles that WMU magazines promoted for their contemporary readers. Such writers were probably more influenced by broader evangelical cultural ideals than they realized.

Descriptions of contemporary Southern Baptist women during this period likewise elevated piety above activism. Missionary Jan Johnsonius developed a relationship with God that was "so much more personal" after her husband's death; communications manager Janice Granger "nurture[d] the spiritual growth of each member of her family."[108] The July 1992 issue of *Royal Service*, in partnership with SSB, even asked readers to nominate "Christian women of excellence"—whom editors described as having "a growing relationship with Jesus Christ that exemplifies the fruits [*sic*] of the Spirit."[109] WMU editors, like women's ministry leaders, clearly valued women's private "grow[th] in their faith and commitment to Christ"[110] over earlier roles such as helping the "heathen," giving generously, cultivating a Christian home, or exploring women's possibilities. Editors also prioritized spiritual growth over involvement in the SBC controversy, ignoring the significant struggles occurring between WMU and SBC leaders in order to maintain their broad readership.

Correspondingly, numerous articles in *Royal Service*, *Contempo*, and *Missions Mosaic* encouraged readers not to renegotiate gender boundaries but to help other women grow spiritually. Advertisements for books by popular New Hope authors challenged women to aspire to "planting your life in another and releasing the fragrance of Christ" by "preparing yourself to mentor."[111] Influenced by broader American and evangelical culture, where mentoring was "all the rage," as Dake put it, writers in the second half of this period urged WMU members to mentor other women to "know God more deeply."[112] Just as women's ministry advisors exhorted group leaders to "encourage and nourish mentoring relationships," WMU writers such as missionary Susan Field encouraged women to "share in Christ's work through other women by mentoring."[113] Helping other women develop their relationship with God, editors intimated, was more important than urging them to challenge restrictions upon their roles in the SBC or in broader American society. As in the immediate post–World War II years, WMU magazines emphasized that their readers' most effective ministry occurred within the home, as they influenced their own lives and those of their family and friends.

Editors and writers also encouraged women to grow spiritually by "listening to the Spirit of God."[114] The Holy Spirit, whom writer Mary Langford in 1991 confessed that Baptists had "shied away from" in previous years, was portrayed as women's "source of spiritual empowerment" and gifting, as social worker Cindy Ketron put it.[115] This topic was especially prominent during the 1990–91 WMU year, when the WMU Executive Board approved *Empowered!* as WMU's annual emphasis, perhaps influenced by the growing charismatic movement that stressed the role of the gifts of the Holy Spirit in Christians' experience. Continuing the theme of personal fulfillment familiar to women's ministry groups, writers discussed "the blessings, benefits, and power that can be ours as we journey under the leadership of the Spirit."[116] This empowerment, however, now related to personal spirituality, not to expansive ministry roles as it had in the previous period.

Editors and writers stressed the individualistic dimension of the gospel by exploring the Holy Spirit's gifts to each Christian—gifts that WMU member Julia Sims Harris avowed were "as unique as our own fingerprints."[117] As in earlier years, writers affirmed that God distributed a variety of spiritual gifts that women could use to "go into the world" and minister or, as a 1991 writer put it, "be a channel of his grace."[118] This emphasis was probably stronger in WMU magazines, with their historic missions focus, than it was in women's ministry publications. But unlike in the previous period, WMU writers spent little time exploring how God's gifting could lead women to serve in ministerial positions that had traditionally been reserved for men. Instead they highlighted a variety of less radical gifts—not always mentioned in the Bible—that women could use "where you are right now," including hospitality, letter writing, flexibility, tutoring, and a "green thumb" for gardening.[119] Becoming attuned to God's Spirit and God's unique plan for each reader was more important than encouraging women with pastoral and leadership gifts, editors implied.

In accord with their emphasis on individual piety, WMU magazines also stressed the importance of "spending daily time with God."[120] Especially in the first half of this period, editors and writers joined other late twentieth-century evangelicals in prioritizing daily quiet times, a concept that one WMU editor vowed Southern Baptists had "never heard anything about" in earlier years.[121] By the 1980s, evangelical publishers—including the SBC's SSB—sold books such as *How to Have a Quiet Time*, and women's ministry leaders affirmed that an effective women's ministry should be "built on" Bible study, a key element of quiet times.[122] As women flocked to meetings of women's ministries and groups such as Community Bible Study and Bible Study Fellowship, WMU magazines similarly urged readers to "set aside a regular time and place to seek the Lord" through Bible study and prayer.[123] Regular features such as Prayer Patterns and Seek Him, Meet Him included material to help women "spend quality time with Jesus daily,"[124] and printed patterns called Thy Word Have I Hung on My Wall encouraged women to cross-stitch and display Bible verses. Instead of emphasizing only missions, these WMU editors emulated other evangelical leaders in their focus on a daily time of Bible study and prayer.

Like many of the magazines' features during this period, articles about quiet times prioritized both spiritual growth and personal satisfaction. Former editor Edna Ellison, for example, challenged women to evaluate themselves by considering statements such as "I am confident I have reached the peak of enjoyment in daily, consistent study of the Bible."[125] Writers expressed that having a regular quiet time would help women "build that special one-on-one relationship with God"[126]—developing their personal spirituality before concerning themselves with the world around them. This emphasis, incongruous with WMU magazines' activist bent during the previous period, displayed the unmistakable influence of late twentieth-century evangelical piety, especially as it was demonstrated among women's ministry organizations. Realizing that traditional missions work was not a compelling subject among many Southern Baptist women, WMU editors highlighted instead the popular topic of personal spirituality in an attempt to interest more women in their efforts—rarely mentioning the denominational struggles that might disincline women to participate in WMU. As *Missions Mosaic* reader Jan Kirkland confirmed in 2003, "Being a part of Women on Mission has helped me to grow spiritually."[127] She could have made the same comment about almost any women's ministry group.

## Praying

Throughout this period, editors of *Contempo*, *Royal Service*, and *Missions Mosaic* revealed their penchant for personal spirituality most clearly through the hundreds of pages they devoted to discussing prayer, which writer Anne Leavell Collingsworth called "the smartest thing any Christian can do."[128] This role, which had been included in WMU magazines since their inception, took precedence in these years as it never had before. As with general devotional emphases, the topic of prayer was popular among women's ministry groups and other evangelicals during this period. "An effective women's ministries program," a popular women's ministry guidebook explained, "will start with prayer."[129] Evangelical publishers produced dozens—if not hundreds—of books such as *Sacred Journeys: A Woman's Book of Daily Prayer* and *Talking with God: A Woman's Workshop on Prayer*. The SBC's SSB offered titles including *Prayer in Baptist Life* and *A Woman's Garden of Prayer*. And *Today's Christian Woman*, an evangelical women's magazine, included around ninety articles on prayer during a ten-year period alone.

In accord with WMU leaders' proclivity for promoting topics popular among other evangelical women's groups, editors included in WMU magazines a number of regular features on prayer, including Intercessory Prayer, Pray Today, Prayer, and Prayer Patterns. Many readers probably concurred with Cleota Lenert of Florida, who maintained that these features were "the single most important factor of my adult years in deepening my own spiritual growth."[130] Developing a relationship with God through prayer, both readers and editors implied, was a priority for Christian women. At least a few pages of every magazine included information about prayer, from inspirational quotes to suggestions to help readers "make prayer a habit."[131] Acknowledging women's busy lifestyles, articles advised that readers pray "on your way to work, school, or errands" or "while reading or doing routine chores."[132] Some writers recommended that women use a mnemonic such as ACTS (adoration, confession, thanksgiving, supplication) to guide their prayers; others offered "six keys to fervent prayer" and "four tips for getting focused."[133] Such features reflected the pragmatic, individualistic tendencies of contemporary American evangelicalism. A few articles also extolled the value of prayer retreats and of "prayerwalking and prayerdriving."[134] Editors intimated that there was no one correct way to pray; women's options for prayer—though not for vocational ministry—were nearly boundless.

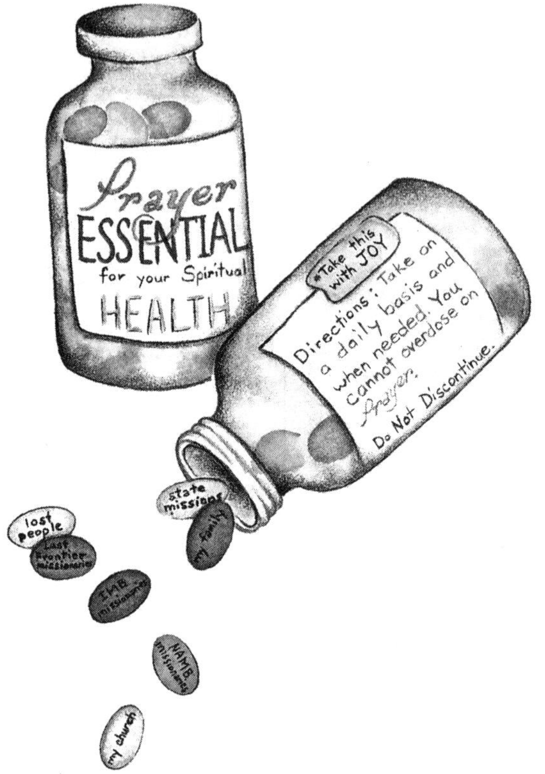


15. Illustration from November 2002 *Missions Mosaic*. (Used by permission of WMUA.)

WMU leaders, however, quickly codified these options into a number of prayer programs, including Baptist Young Women Prayer Projects, Missions Pray-ers for homebound Baptist Women members, Women on Mission prayer groups, and the SBC's National Missions Prayer Plan. Unlike most women's ministries, which were content simply to advise women about prayer and provide them with time to pray with others, WMU fit prayer into its programmatic structure. That the organization provided so many prayer programs—unlike in earlier periods—demonstrated the importance of the subject during these years. However, this programming of prayer may also have exemplified why many younger women bypassed WMU's traditional structure in favor of women's ministries' relational approach, as declining *Contempo* subscriptions and rising women's ministry involvement demonstrated.

In addition to promoting prayer programs, WMU editors included in their magazines multiple articles depicting biblical and historical figures as paragons of prayer. Deborah, who had been praised in the previous period for her bold leadership, was extolled in 1990 as "a model for the role of praise in prayer."[135] Hannah, who had exemplified Christian motherhood to writers in the post–World War II years, now demonstrated that "prayer is the real force for change in the status quo."[136] Writers clearly interpreted biblical passages using the themes that they believed were important for Christian women to understand. Several articles reminded readers that prayer had been an essential element of Jesus's earthly ministry—"Jesus loved to pray," according to Kathryn Grant—and urged readers to "pray like Jesus prayed."[137] However, such features did not discuss Jesus's aid to the needy or warnings against injustice, themes that had been more popular during the activist years of the 1970s. Editors similarly highlighted prayer—not just action—as a significant factor in the success of historical missions leaders such as William Carey and the Moravian Church, whose leaders "followed biblical teachings on prayer and saw God work in great and powerful ways."[138] As they did with biblical and historical exemplars of spirituality, writers lauded these men and women not for their active ministry but for their personal devotion to God—which, writers suggested, led God to act in ways greater than humans ever could.

Editors likewise commended contemporary women for their reliance on God's power through prayer. WMU magazines, with their aging readership, included a number of articles praising "octogenarian prayer warriors" such as Marguerite Babb, Lillian Middleton, and Esther Livengood—a homebound woman who explained that through prayer "I touched base with medical personnel in the cholera epidemic in Peru. I stood watch in a sailors' hospital in Charleston."[139] While editors continued to profile a few older women who had participated in volunteer mission trips, their new emphasis suggested that prayer was at least as important a role for this audience as was mission action. And younger women, whom editors in the previous period had strongly encouraged to participate in hands-on ministry, now also read about role models such as a homemaker who was a member of the National Prayer Corps and a mother who instead of starting or leading a church "prayed for a church."[140] Writers correspondingly lauded several female—and male—missionaries not for their bold actions or groundbreaking ministries but for their conviction that "prayer is the key to all that we do."[141] Even one *Missions Mosaic* editor chose as her byline "Joanne [Parker] loves to hear how God answers our prayers for missions."[142] Influenced by evangelical and national cultures that promoted quietism over activism, editors portrayed prayer as "the most important thing that one person can do for another."[143]

Unlike most evangelical women's ministries, however, editors and writers for *Missions Mosaic*, *Royal Service*, and *Contempo* spent little time discussing how prayer could enhance women's spiritual lives, in contrast to their depiction of quiet times in general. Instead they focused on prayer's efficacy as the "single most important factor in the advancement of God's kingdom on earth."[144] As missionary Sanan Brazzeal put it, prayer "inevitably" changed the person praying—but it changed "the lost millions of her world" more.[145] True to their historic missions purpose, writers challenged women to avoid "me-and-mine-centered" prayers, recommending instead intercessory prayer for "lost souls, broken homes, carnal Christians, weary ministers and missionaries, a complacent church, and a wayward nation."[146] By exhorting readers to "make our prayers less selfish,"[147] writers and editors added a countercultural dimension to this otherwise culturally influenced emphasis. They subtly refuted the contemporary American tendencies toward individualism and consumerism that often manifested themselves in egocentric religion among women's ministry participants and other evangelicals. While such individualism did shape articles about personal spirituality, editors dedicated at least as much attention to "chang[ing] the world through prayer."[148]

This emphasis on prayer as a "missionary role" distinguished WMU organizations from women's ministry groups, whose participants multiple WMU members criticized for not having "a biblical understanding of their personal responsibility for fulfilling the Great Commission."[149] Influenced by their century-long missions heritage, WMU leaders adapted the popular concept of prayer to their model of mission support. Never revealing WMU's conflicts with FMB and HMB leaders, WMU editors urged their readers to continue supporting FMB and HMB missionaries, whom editors probably felt were not responsible for the actions of the mission boards' leaders. Editors also understood that WMU had guided its members to hold HMB, FMB, and especially their missionaries in highest esteem; opposing the boards in WMU magazines would have angered many of the organization's members.

Thus editors and writers during this period simply provided their readers with innocuous advice about how to "pray more effectively and specifically for missions," denigrating nonspecific prayers such as "God bless the missionaries."[150] "When you go shopping," former WMU staff member Cathy Butler recommended, "think of the missionary wife and mother who is learning to cook new dishes with unfamiliar food items. . . . When you study your Bible or see a Christian television program, pray for the missionary translating Scriptures into a heart language."[151] Such advice imbued women's daily tasks not with sacred import to the Christian home, as in the post–World War II period, but with the possibility of providing "undergirding support" to SBC missionaries around the world.[152] Indeed, numerous missionaries testified to "how much the prayers of those in the United States have meant to me"—including Margie Callaway Pearson, serving in Ethiopia, who was convinced that Southern Baptists' prayers had saved her life during an emergency surgery on her birthday.[153] Prayer, such articles implied, was not primarily a means of spiritual growth but a denominational missions task as essential as active ministry.

In fact, some writers suggested that prayer was even more important than mission action (later called "doing missions"). In 1989 HMB staff member Ron Johnson discussed women's "opportunity to do something about their world" not through bold ministry efforts—praised by leaders of both HMB and WMU in the previous period—but by praying and witnessing.[154] And FMB staff member Randy Sprinkle later explained that "the closed places of the world" could be opened by intercessors—not by "woman's work for woman," as in earlier years, or by other mission action efforts.[155] Such writers, influenced by trends in contemporary American evangelical culture, regarded prayer as the "greatest force available to us today."[156] Writers in the previous period had been more likely to make such a statement about public social action.

But influenced by WMU's legacy of personal service, community missions, and mission action, WMU members did not avoid action altogether. Numerous pages of *Contempo*, *Royal Service*, and *Missions Mosaic* detailed groups' mission action projects, several of which resulted from women's prayers. Lynda Grimes of Garland, Texas, shipped supplies overseas after she learned of this need from reading a missionary's prayer letters.[157] Similarly, Baptist Young Women from Corinth, Mississippi, "were led to concrete action and direct missions involvement" in Idaho as they prayed for a missionary there.[158] As they had previously done, the magazines' writers discussed both prayer and mission action. However, during this period—unlike in earlier years—writers and editors explained that "you must begin with prayer."[159] Action, readers learned, was secondary.

Not only prayer for mission action but also prayer for witnessing was essential for Southern Baptist women, editors emphasized—a sentiment with which SBC conservatives could hardly disagree. As with other types of mission work, witnessing first required women to "smother in prayer" their plans.[160] Highlighting a belief in the importance of prayer over evangelistic strategies, African American writer Ethel Robinson reminded readers that "no techniques will be a substitute for prayer."[161] Former campus minister Ginny Ireland affirmed that prayer was "a strategy for reaching the lost" and "Jesus' first step in evangelism."[162] Such writers intimated that witnessing, like mission action, was possible only as a result of "a life of prayer";[163] prayer was the foundation upon which multiple planks of the Christian life could be built.

Even becoming a Christian, editors believed, depended on prayer. At least one issue of *Missions Mosaic* included a "sinner's prayer" that women could pray with individuals who wanted to "accept Jesus into their heart": "Dear Lord, I am a sinner," Edna Ellison coached readers. "I do believe that Christ alone can save me and that one day I will follow Him to heaven."[164] Such a prayer, increasingly common among contemporary evangelical groups, again demonstrated the influence of American evangelical trends upon WMU editors. Although they were sometimes more oriented toward missions, WMU magazines' frequent prayer emphases corresponded with the priority of prayer among other contemporary evangelical groups. WMU editors encouraged prayer as much as women's ministry leaders did.

## Witnessing

WMU magazines' focus on prayer for witnessing led naturally to discussions of witnessing itself. During this period, articles in *Contempo*, *Royal Service*, and *Missions Mosaic* demonstrated that an important role for Southern Baptist women was sharing with others "the greatest Gift of all—Jesus Christ."[165] This task, though not foreign to women's ministry groups, was most strongly influenced by other evangelicals, including Southern Baptist conservatives. With the rise of conservatism among American evangelicals, direct evangelism began to be emphasized more frequently than social ministry. Techniques such as Evangelism Explosion, created by megachurch pastor D. James Kennedy, and the Four Spiritual Laws tract, written by Campus Crusade for Christ founder Bill Bright, gained prominence. The SBC, as it was wont to do, soon created its own approaches, including Continuing Witness Training, Share Jesus without Fear, FAITH, and Crossover evangelistic events preceding SBC annual meetings. Beginning in the mid-1980s, HMB, led by conservative trustees, decreased its social ministry efforts and established programs its leaders called interfaith witness, mass evangelism, marketplace evangelism, personal evangelism, and ministry-based evangelism, among others. "Evangelism," affirmed HMB vice president Darrell Robinson, "is the consequence of the church being the church."[166] During this period, SBC leaders rarely made similar statements about social ministry.

In the 1990s, Esther Burroughs of HMB worked with Dellanna O'Brien and other WMU leaders to advocate women's evangelistic efforts with other women. This emphasis, probably inspired by the rise of ministries by and for women, in a sense returned women to the gendered sphere to which they had been restricted in the nineteenth century. WMU magazines promoted evangelism—but editors did not suggest that women should witness only to women. Instead they joined writer Barbara Davis in urging readers to "witness verbally for Christ"[167] to everyone who crossed their paths. WMU editors thus adopted a new focus on witnessing throughout this period, influenced by broader evangelical culture as well as by changes in the SBC. Such features were especially prominent in the first half of this period, when evangelicals stressed witnessing most strongly. While WMU leaders privately (and sometimes publicly) objected to many emphases of SBC conservatives, they generally agreed with this group on the importance of witnessing, which WMU had traditionally considered an important missions task.

Throughout this period, WMU editors maintained that witnessing depended upon a woman's relationship with God. Writers explained that witnessing should "naturally overflow from her personal relationship with the Lord"; devotional time and prayer were the "backbone of any attempt to witness."[168] Such sentiments demonstrated the influence of women's ministries' focus on individual spirituality. Preparation for witnessing, writer Barbara Donaldson asserted, included not only rehearsing a testimony of one's conversion but also personal spiritual disciplines such as "worship[ing] God daily, study[ing] God's word, [and] pray[ing]."[169] Thus spirituality assumed a role of prime importance in WMU magazines' descriptions of witnessing—a role not stressed by earlier WMU writers who had discussed the topic.

As they did with prayer, WMU editors and writers adapted a popular emphasis to promote their missions purpose: they encouraged readers to "depend upon the Holy Spirit," as most women's ministries did.[170] However, writers taught women to take this action not just for personal fulfillment but so that the Holy Spirit would "empower you to witness," as one writer put it.[171] To help WMU members recognize the difference between these two approaches, writers asked them to determine whether all "women's events and activities [in your church] have an intentional evangelistic focus."[172] If not, Women on Mission consultant and former editor Laura Savage urged readers to invite women's ministry participants to join them in evangelistic endeavors, such as block parties or summer witnessing projects.[173] Writers and editors challenged women to seek God's power to involve themselves and other women in personal witnessing, not in new ministry roles, as articles had advocated during previous years, or in denominational conflict, about which WMU magazines remained strategically silent.

Editors realized, however, that the thought of witnessing caused many women to become "paralyzed with fear,"[174] so they occasionally explicated the importance of this task. Why witness? Most important for bibliocentric Baptist women, because "Christ gave us the authority to witness and commanded us to do so."[175] Again biblical passages—as writers and editors interpreted them—formed the basis of a role that WMU magazines advocated for women. Writers also appealed to readers' emotions, explaining that their efforts could help determine the "destiny of someone's very soul" and relating what they believed was the tragic fate of individuals who died before they had been evangelized.[176] Such techniques were common among American evangelicals, revealing once more WMU editors' proclivity for incorporating broader trends into *Missions Mosaic*, *Contempo*, and *Royal Service*.

Interestingly, though, editors' most frequent argument for witnessing involved readers' individualism and sense of importance. As Mildred Patterson put it, "Deep down I know I am not ordinary. . . . I have a special place of service in witnessing."[177] Such sentiments appropriated the individualistic bent of contemporary evangelicalism and especially women's ministries in an attempt to make witnessing appeal to readers. Although a woman may not have been appointed by a mission board or ordained by a local congregation, homemaker Sharon Reece Neff asserted that she had been "divinely appointed when [she] accepted Christ."[178] This statement was probably intended to empower women, many of whom found it difficult to be ordained and sometimes appointed within the SBC during this period. However, such remarks—unlike earlier emphases—implicitly discouraged women from seeking recognition within the denomination, reminding them instead that their most important commission for witnessing and ministry came from a "higher authority."[179]

In a similar fashion, editors of *Missions Mosaic*, *Contempo*, and *Royal Service* praised biblical and contemporary women for their roles in witnessing endeavors, not for the groundbreaking ministries that writers had frequently mentioned during the previous period. Multiple Bible studies extolled "witnessing models in the Bible," such as Anna, Mary Magdalene, and the woman at the well.[180] Others explained "what the Bible says about evangelism,"[181] usually without equivalent descriptions of biblical teachings on social ministry. Page after page featured WMU members such as Mary Ann, who talked to an obscene phone caller about God; Melba Tiller, who shared her testimony "right there in the floral section" of a store; and Edna Ellison, a former WMU editor who "led a woman to Christ at a drive through window."[182] Such emphases revealed the priority that witnessing had become for both grassroots WMU members and the magazines' editors. These features implied that always being ready to testify to one's faith—not exploring new possibilities or seeking social justice—was a significant role for Southern Baptist women.

Even descriptions of missionaries' work focused on evangelism more than they had in the previous period, emphasizing that "all missionaries have the primary responsibility of evangelism that results in churches."[183] While this shift was due in part to the growing conservative influence at HMB and FMB, WMU leaders had historically regarded evangelism as an important task. In closed-door meetings with the mission boards' leaders, O'Brien and others may have voiced concern for social ministry, which WMU had also traditionally prioritized. However, in the less activist climate of this period, WMU editors did not appear reluctant to highlight missionaries' evangelistic work. Ellison, for example, published without comment an article by FMB staff member Anita Bowden expressing the "overwhelming, crushing necessity" that evangelism had become to some missionaries, who consequently left social ministry efforts in such fields as health care to devote their complete attention to people's "more critical need to know Christ."[184] During the previous period, when Southern Baptist social ministry approaches had been their strongest, WMU magazines had included no such features.

Revealing the significant changes that had occurred in WMU editors' thinking over the course of two decades, a 1991 article even attempted to convince readers that "though the Matthew 25 passage catalogs the needs for food, clothing, hospitality, health care, and prison ministry, we need to keep witnessing at the forefront."[185] This statement represented a surprisingly casual discounting of a biblical mandate for a Southern Baptist publication. By subordinating social ministry to witnessing, such articles deemphasized fields in which female missionaries had traditionally predominated, presenting an opposite perspective from what writers had offered during the previous period. Influenced by individualistic trends in broader American culture and by the increasingly conservative assignments that FMB and HMB gave their missionaries, editors suggested that witnessing was a vital role for Southern Baptist women at home and abroad. Though social ministry did not disappear from WMU magazines entirely, it became a secondary concern.

Editors affirmed that just as featured missionaries and WMU members sought every opportunity to give "verbal witness to the love and mercy of Jesus Christ," as Breena Paine put it,[186] so too should each reader of *Contempo*, *Royal Service*, and *Missions Mosaic* testify about her faith as frequently as possible. Magazine pages that had once detailed the variety of people to whom middle-class women could minister now enumerated groups with whom they could share Christ: family members, neighbors, coworkers, "yuppies," Mormons, immigrants, gas station attendants, hairdressers, waitresses, and postal workers, among many others. In addition to "spontaneous, uncalculated witnessing," writers recommended evangelistic strategies popular among many evangelical groups, such as distributing Bibles and tracts, inviting neighbors to church, and wearing Christian apparel.[187] Editors also urged women to employ the popular technique of "shar[ing] your personal testimony": they supplied multiple worksheets for readers to detail "my life and attitude before following Christ," "how I realized God was speaking to me," "how I became a Christian," and "what being a Christian means to me."[188] Such features revealed the influence of evangelical individualism upon the women's beliefs.

Demonstrating the priority they placed upon sharing one's faith, writers for WMU magazines avowed that no situation was exempt from Christ's command to witness. They explained that women had "abundant ways" to spread the gospel, although, unlike ordained male ministers, they practiced "evangelism with no pulpit."[189] Accordingly, editors rarely profiled female evangelists or church planters, probably because these roles were increasingly controversial and because Southern Baptist women were excluded from such ministries during this period. Instead of encouraging women to seek ordination for such positions—a move that would have brought criticism to WMU—editors were content to describe the witnessing opportunities of which "ordinary" women could avail themselves.

Just as editors in previous years had provided page after page of instruction about mission action, then, during this period they carefully advised women on their witnessing techniques, coaching them even on their clothing and demeanor. "Be relaxed . . . be friendly . . . establish eye contact," one writer urged.[190] Such features reflected the contemporary interest in witnessing among many evangelicals, including SBC leaders. Editors Edna Ellison, Cindy Dake, and Laura Savage—often in partnership with Esther Burroughs at HMB—also promoted training events and books about evangelism, including Dayspring, a conference "helping women learn to reach the world," and *LIVINGtouch*, a study of "your personal witness in an impersonal world."[191] These efforts demonstrated the priority of evangelism to WMU leaders. The mission action workshops and books of earlier years faded from the scene as "faith-sharing" became an esteemed—and noncontroversial—role for Southern Baptist women.[192]

WMU magazines did continue to suggest ideas for mission action, including participation in WMU's ministries, some of which involved more social ministry than programs of other SBC entities did. However, even mission action writers agreed with Sammie Jo Barstow, who stressed that women should "look for those opportunities . . . to tell them [mission action recipients] about Jesus" as they ministered.[193] "The biggest problem" in mission action, according to one writer, was not the inability to find a suitable project but the failure to share one's faith.[194] Although writers in the previous period had explained that a verbal witness was not always appropriate in mission action, reader Ruth Ward and others reversed this sentiment, unequivocally declaring that unevangelistic efforts were not really mission action at all.[195] Even an article featuring the "holistic missions" work of missionary Sandy Gustin quickly clarified that the primary purpose of such endeavors was "bringing lost people to God through Jesus Christ."[196] Editors, like other WMU leaders, were surely aware of the disfavor with which conservative SBC leaders regarded social ministry, and selected their words carefully. "The greatest ministry," they affirmed with writer Dorothy Godsoe, was not "deal[ing] with physical problems" but "bring[ing] someone to Jesus."[197]

Such evangelistically focused descriptions of mission action diverged from the activist sentiments prevalent in WMU magazines during the previous period, more closely resembling WMU's community missions work from the post–World War II years—when, one writer acknowledged, "women [had] felt the need to give stronger effort to personal evangelism, or soul-winning."[198] Clearly the emphasis on evangelism prevalent among conservative American evangelicals—including the SBC's new leadership—influenced WMU significantly. Though editors may have strategically downplayed social ministry during this period to avoid controversy, the hundreds of pages that they devoted to vigorous discussions of witnessing seem to indicate that WMU truly believed that this task was important. "Verbalizing your faith in Jesus Christ to . . . non-Christian[s]"[199] was an essential role for Southern Baptist women, the organization's writers and editors affirmed more strongly than they had ever before.

"Many women aren't interested in an 'organization,'" Laura Savage explained to *Missions Mosaic* readers in October 1997. "But they *are* interested in spiritual growth, Bible study, prayer, and personal fulfillment of God's will for their lives," she continued. "And Women on Mission is all that and more."[200] These words aptly summarized WMU editors' strategy to address women's interests and boost declining subscriptions to *Contempo*, *Royal Service*, and *Missions Mosaic* from 1984 to 2006. Rather than continuing to advocate new personal and professional roles for women, a cause that was less popular in American culture during this period, editors such as Edna Ellison, Cindy Dake, and Joanne Parker sought to imitate the conservative emphases of women's ministries that were rapidly gaining thousands of members among Southern Baptists and other evangelicals. Instead of activism and liberation, editors portrayed developing spiritually, praying, and witnessing—through participation in WMU organizations—as the most important roles for Southern Baptist women.

WMU magazines' conservative emphasis on spirituality is especially remarkable when considered in conjunction with WMU's decision to cooperate with CBF moderates, notwithstanding attempts by conservative SBC officials to control the women's organization. WMU leaders evidently understood that the majority of their magazines' readers were fairly conservative women who probably would have disagreed with WMU's moderate sympathies, had they been fully aware of them. Editors tailored their message accordingly, featuring only noncontroversial topics in *Contempo*, *Royal Service*, and *Missions Mosaic*, while reserving more thorough discussion of WMU's divisive stances for annual reports, press releases, and letters to churches. Working to maintain a broad subscriber base and thus to support WMU financially, editors included throughout WMU magazines conservative content that appeared to prove true the women's assertion that they were not liberals but simply wanted to provide all Southern Baptist churches with missions material. At least in the articles they published in their women's magazines, WMU leaders demonstrated a striking similarity to other evangelicals in the roles they suggested for women.

# 7
# Southern Baptist Women's Writings in Retrospect

The one unforgivable sin among American evangelicals, according to historian Margaret Bendroth, is "thoughtless capitulation to the secular standards of American culture."[1] More so than adherents of other Christian traditions, evangelicals pride themselves on relying upon what they consider to be the timeless truths of the Bible rather than upon changing cultural mores. Unfamiliar with their own history, many contemporary evangelicals idealistically suppose that their beliefs and practices are shaped solely by biblical principles, discounting the effects of the broader culture in which their faith has developed. These individuals fail to realize that their expressions of Christianity are necessarily culture bound, much as they themselves are confined to a particular human body in a specific location. As this study exemplifies, historically American evangelicals have been influenced by the culture in which they live more strongly than they might like to admit.

This influence is especially marked in the changing evangelical perspectives on women's roles. The typical white American woman underwent rapid transformation from "separate sphere" homemaker at the onset of the twentieth century to confident career woman a few decades later. A Southern Baptist leader present at the founding of WMU in 1888—when the women were reluctant even to speak to "mixed audiences"—would have scarcely recognized the organization in 2006, with its seminary-trained staff and emphasis on women's leadership. Such an observer would be astonished to read WMU leader Linda Clark's observation in a 1998 issue of *Missions Mosaic*: "In today's society, women are found in nearly every profession. We are attorneys, physicians, executive officers, and politicians."[2] The content WMU published in its women's magazines throughout the century reflected these rapid societal changes. *Our Mission Fields*

(1906–1914), *Royal Service* (1914–1995), *Contempo* (1970–1995), and *Missions Mosaic* (1995–2006) suggested a number of different roles for Southern Baptist women in missions over the course of a century. WMU editors continually—though not always consciously—reshaped their ideal of Christian womanhood to correspond with views of gender popular within American culture and Southern Baptist life.

From 1906 to 1918, WMU magazines clearly identified with the interdenominational woman's missionary movement, while remaining mostly within the bounds of contemporary Southern Baptist norms. Like other women's missions publications, *Our Mission Fields* and later *Royal Service* emphasized the importance of the "uplift" of "heathen" women into Westernized and Christianized societies. Writers stressed female missionaries' unique roles in ministering to women on foreign mission fields—usually through education, health care, and evangelism—under the rubric of "woman's work for woman." As a result of what they considered these female missionaries' noble efforts, WMU leaders believed that the lives of thousands of needy foreign women would be transformed. For example, a 1908 writer described a Japanese woman as formerly "most unpromising, very lazy and untidy, rough pimpled face, void of expression"—but celebrated the "joyous light on her face [and] a smile" after the woman became a Christian.[3] Likewise, articles portrayed missionaries in North America as improving conditions for "sick, sorrowing, and unconverted" women and children through social ministry.[4] Writers also encouraged thousands of women at home to participate in similar ministries in their own communities, as well as to pray, learn, and give "for the carrying forward of mission work among women and young people."[5] WMU magazines highlighted "separate sphere" efforts to aid other women as the primary role for Southern Baptist women in missions until around the end of World War I.

With the decline of the woman's missionary movement after World War I, WMU editors shifted their portrayal of their readers' roles from "woman's work for woman" to supporting the SBC. From 1919 to 1945, writers stressed the importance of "woman's contribution to the kingdom"[6] in spreading the gospel, supporting missionaries, supporting national women, and, most important, supporting the denominational program. Reflecting the denominational identity and culture developing within the SBC, article after article in *Royal Service* highlighted tithing, fundraising campaigns, and SBC debt relief as priorities for WMU members. As Myrtle Creasman explained in 1931, "When the tithe of our millions flows into the Lord's treasury[,] then will the funds measure up to the needs of the field."[7] This new emphasis provided WMU with a clear focus at the same time as traditional woman's missionary movement ideology fell out of vogue. The women's loyal denominational support and enormous financial contributions increased their organization's influence, as SBC leaders realized that their convention could not thrive without the efforts of WMU—which SBC Executive Committee member Walter Gilmore called "a life-saver for all of our missionary enterprises."[8] The financial support that resulted from the women's actions proved vital to the denomination's success.

After the SBC paid its debts, *Royal Service* writers adopted a new emphasis: encouraging women to cultivate a Christian influence in their homes and, in turn, in their communities. Strongly informed by—though not frequently acknowledging the influence of—postwar American culture, the magazine's writers and editors from 1946 to 1967 stressed the importance of nurturing missions-minded Christian families. Indeed, according to a 1950 *Royal Service* program, "A happy, peaceful world depends upon Christian homes."[9] Editors thus departed from the outwardly focused themes of "woman's work for woman" and sacrificial denominational support that had been significant in the magazine during previous years. With woman's missionary movement ideology obsolete and many church members supporting the SBC as a result of WMU's efforts, editors claimed a new role for WMU members in the home, leaving broader affairs to the men who controlled them. Throughout *Royal Service*'s pages, writers adulated Christian homemakers—adapting this cultural image to their own tradition—and expressed a new awareness of mothers' crucial roles in missions. As Kate Ellen Gruver maintained, "The influence of a Christian mother is eternal."[10] In addition, writers attempted to protect "sacred" homes by encouraging Southern Baptist women to rectify the social problems such as racial discrimination that threatened them.

When the ideal of a "liberated" woman became popular in American culture beginning in the late 1960s, *Royal Service* and soon *Contempo* quickly adopted a similar focus. In contrast to the domestic tasks they had stressed in the preceding period, editors from 1968 to 1983 challenged readers to use their gifts in an almost unlimited number of circumstances. Without espousing overly controversial positions on women's liberation, writers and editors consistently supported broad roles for women in missions and in the church "in order to meet the changing needs of changing times."[11] A working, unmarried mother; a homemaker involved in mission action; a seminary student pursuing vocational ministry—all were equally valued by writers, who used biblical and historical examples to encourage each woman to take advantage of her wide range of possibilities and undertake "liberated work"[12] in her community. Teresa Shields Parker explained to *Contempo* readers in 1979, "It's an age when a woman doesn't have to ask herself, Do I dare? She does. She dares."[13] Such an emphasis on bold action reflected the influence of evangelical feminism and demonstrated an affinity with the women's liberation movement as well.

From 1984 to 2006, however, instead of advocating expansive roles for women—a cause that was no longer prominent in American culture—WMU editors imitated the conservative focus of women's ministries that were gaining thousands of participants and by which some WMU groups felt "threatened," according to editor Sue Sprenkle.[14] Instead of activism and liberation, editors portrayed developing spiritually, praying, and witnessing—through involvement in WMU organizations—as the most important roles for Southern Baptist women. As writer Anna Kathryn Hardin challenged readers in 2004, "We must know that we, ourselves, are ready to present the gospel. Do we have a life of prayer, Bible study, and worship that will make us attentive to God's voice?"[15] WMU editors rarely mentioned their organization's fierce struggles with conservative new SBC leaders, realizing that many readers might disagree with WMU leaders' views. Instead, *Royal Service*, *Contempo*, and *Missions Mosaic* editors consciously reshaped their depiction of women in missions in an attempt to appeal to not only moderate but also conservative Southern Baptist women, many of whom demonstrated an increasing interest in what *Royal Service* called "growing in godliness."[16]

Clearly the gender constructs portrayed in WMU magazines from 1906 to 2006 were influenced by broader American culture. When Progressivism led many Protestant women to become "mothers" of their communities through social gospel activities, WMU magazines advocated a robust program of social ministry called personal service. Indeed, WMU leader Lulie Wharton acknowledged in 1912 that WMU created a personal service department in order "to be in line with this new phase of modern thought . . . believing that the religion of Jesus Christ applied to social problems is the only remedy that will heal."[17] But as American women began to idealize domestic roles in the mid-twentieth century, WMU editors promoted a more conservative community missions approach and discussed the importance of raising Christian children. "Women love home," proclaimed Creasman,[18] echoing a sentiment espoused not only by WMU magazines but also by secular women's magazines, television programs, and U.S. culture more broadly. WMU editors consistently appropriated images of womanhood popular in wider American society to interest their magazines' readers in tasks that WMU leaders of the day felt were important.

Thus when activist sentiments again prevailed throughout the United States beginning in the late 1960s, WMU magazines highlighted a plethora of social ministries and advocated new roles for women. *Contempo* editor Laurella Owens even surveyed readers in 1971 to see if they felt the magazine succeeded in "speaking to today's social problems as they relate to missions"[19]—clearly demonstrating the influence of broader cultural issues on WMU leaders' thinking. And at the turn of the twenty-first century, editors' focus on spirituality and witnessing reflected similar trends in American evangelicalism, as well as a propensity for self-fulfillment within U.S. culture. Noting this changed emphasis, longtime WMU member Edith Robbins complained in 2002, "You are trying to be all things to all people and it just isn't working. . . . Go back to in-depth articles about missions."[20] Although she did not respond to Robbins in the pages of *Missions Mosaic*, editor Joanne Parker may have been tempted to quote one of the multiple WMU leaders—such as former executive director Alma Hunt—who asserted that their organization "never veered from the purpose of missions."[21] However, the content of WMU magazines made this claim dubious. Popular gender roles and evangelical emphases found their way into multiple issues of *Our Mission Fields*, *Royal Service*, *Contempo*, and *Missions Mosaic*.

Instead of advancing radical views that challenged broader American or evangelical thinking, then, WMU magazines most often reflected the context in which they were written. In a sense, this is unsurprising: publications, like individuals, are naturally a product of their time. Savvy editors also recognize that articles on contemporary topics frequently sell more magazines. But WMU leaders were probably more cautious than other evangelicals in the opinions they advanced in their magazines. Neither vehement activists nor pious but uneducated laywomen, WMU editors and editorial committee members were conscious of the complexity of their SBC context and accordingly exercised temperance in the content that they published. WMU executive director Dellanna O'Brien, for example, explained that the organization's magazines "attempted to take the middle road" among the variety of opinions present within the SBC; a 1970 *Contempo* article similarly urged readers, "Don't vote with the extremists."[22] In addition, WMU's extensive magazine planning and review processes throughout the century revealed the attention that the organization's leaders and editors gave to every word before they printed it. Especially in the latter years of the twentieth century, content appeared to be shaped by editors' awareness that WMU was supported primarily by magazine sales and thus dependent on subscribers' satisfaction.

In addition, Southern Baptists' views of women's roles were often more conservative than those of other Southern evangelicals—who in turn tended to espouse new ideas about gender more slowly than did their Northern counterparts. Even WMU's status as an auxiliary to the SBC was subordinate to the position of most other denominational women's groups. According to WMU president Laura Armstrong, writing in 1945, this auxiliary role meant that WMU was a "helper, assistant, colleague, partner, cooperator, ally, associate, coworker, companion and comrade to the Convention of which it is a part."[23] WMU leaders such as Armstrong gladly subordinated their work to broader SBC efforts throughout most of the twentieth century, questioning this approach only when a contingent of conservative denominational leaders emerged at the end of the century. Thus the women wrote from within a conservative SBC framework, one known for its traditionalism and not for pioneering new stances on gender or other social issues. This context inevitably influenced the words and actions of both WMU leaders and members.

But within their Southern Baptist environment, WMU editors were at times cautiously progressive in their views. Although they generally shied away from controversy, editors occasionally presented perspectives that were prevalent among some Americans but with which most Southern Baptists disagreed. For example, WMU leaders, who were relatively open to ecumenism, adopted social gospel ideology more freely than most Southern Baptists did. A 1915 *Royal Service* program quoted Charles Thompson, a writer for the *Missionary Review of the World*: "The time has now fully come when the church must address herself to meet and repair the wrongs of society, to which she has long been measurably indifferent."[24] Such a statement, which many male SBC leaders would have hesitated to repeat, demonstrated the women's affinity with social gospel thinking. WMU's personal service program reflected Progressive trends in American society and religion that many Southern Baptists were more likely to reject than to embrace.

In addition, in the mid-twentieth century WMU editors frequently promoted racial and gender equality. Although these ideas were gaining popularity among some segments of the American population, they were largely disparaged by Southern Baptist laity at the time. As early as 1946, *Royal Service* writers such as Willie Jean Stewart called for WMU members to "put aside those prejudices of which they are tempted to be proud"[25]—a challenging admonition amid more prevalent Southern Baptist defenses of racism and segregation. And in the 1970s, Weatherford and other leaders guided WMU to advocate "greater and larger service" for "the women of the churches"[26] throughout the pages of *Royal Service* and *Contempo*, even when such sentiments found disfavor among many Southern Baptists. Perhaps as a result of their own marginalization within Southern society—and within their denomination—WMU editors and writers at times spoke up for the rights of groups considered subordinate, such as African Americans and women.

Editors doubtless realized that causes such as social reform, civil rights, and gender equality were unpopular among many grassroots Southern Baptists. Indeed, letters from readers occasionally expressed disapproval of WMU magazines' treatment of these topics. In response to a 1976 *Contempo* article on womanhood, for example, Mrs. John Love Jr. protested that "I even felt like throwing the whole magazine and my collection of them in the trash."[27] Conscious of this conservative Southern Baptist audience, editors and other WMU leaders never allowed discussion of such issues to dominate their magazines. From the carefully edited articles they published, it is impossible to ascertain WMU leaders' views fully, although a review of their personal papers may prove elucidating to future researchers.

Altogether, the women appeared to be—in the words of historian Paul Harvey—"neither fundamentalist nor feminist."[28] A product of the woman's missionary movement, WMU continued to prioritize mission work above ideology, avoiding denominational debates whenever possible. When "woman's work for woman" strategies became unpopular, WMU leaders reinvented their members' role in missions within the gender boundaries accepted in the SBC. Thus as other women's organizations were dissolved or absorbed into denominational structures in the first half of the twentieth century, WMU thrived by advancing for its members a denominational support role with which few Southern Baptist leaders could disagree. Maternal influence, an important focus of WMU magazines—and other American women's publications—in the years that followed, was likewise amenable to SBC leaders. With such emphases, WMU distinguished itself from other women's missionary organizations and provided women with one of their few opportunities for leadership in the SBC. WMU ensured its continued existence largely by adopting new roles popular within its denominational and the national culture.

This cultural adaptation, however, proved more troublesome for WMU during the second half of the twentieth century. SBC conservatives—influenced by the countercultural Christian Right—watched with disfavor as WMU joined the denomination's moderates in promoting expansive roles for women, a cause that many Americans advocated at the time. Soon conflict erupted between WMU and SBC leaders. Around the same time, fewer women expressed interest in traditional denominational organizations, and WMU's membership declined. In an attempt to interest more women, at the end of the twentieth century WMU editors acknowledged that they were emulating emphases popular among other American evangelicals. These editors intentionally incorporated multiple components of conservative women's ministries into their depiction of women's roles in missions. This approach, WMU leaders hoped, would help ensure a viable role for their organization among SBC audiences.

Of course, the views expressed in *Our Mission Fields*, *Royal Service*, *Contempo*, and *Missions Mosaic* were the result of WMU's editorial processes and did not represent the opinions of every woman in the SBC. However, they provide the most complete historical record of twentieth-century Southern Baptist women's perspectives anywhere available. From these magazines, it is clear that between 1906 and 2006 many Southern Baptist women—like other American evangelicals—were strongly shaped by their culture, alternately adopting roles of activism and quiet influence as such emphases waxed and waned in popularity. If a woman did not like a gender role included in a WMU magazine during the twentieth century, she needed only to wait a few years for a new role to emerge, just as it did in broader American culture. Perhaps this is what some Southern Baptist women are doing even today.

# Appendix A

## Editors of WMU Women's Magazines, 1906–2006

| | |
|---|---|
| *Our Mission Fields* | |
| Fannie Heck | 1907–1911 |
| Edith Crane | 1911–1912 |
| Claris Crane | 1912–1914 |
| *Royal Service* | |
| Elia Nimmo | 1914–1920 |
| Kathleen Mallory | 1920–1948 |
| Juliette Mather | 1948–1957 |
| Ethalee Hamric | 1957–1969 |
| Rosanne Osborne | 1969–1973 |
| Laurella Owens | 1973–1977 |
| Lane Powell | 1977–1978 |
| Adrianne Bonham | 1978–1981 |
| Anne Leavell Mann | 1982–1983 |
| Betty Merrell | 1983–1985 |
| Edna Ellison | 1986–1993 |
| Cindy Dake and Laura Savage | 1993–1995 |
| *Contempo* | |
| Laurella Owens | 1970–1973 |
| Ellen Dossett | 1973–1974 |
| Mary Ann Ward | 1975–1987 |
| Diana Woodcock | 1988–1989 |
| Eleanor Clay | 1990–1991 |
| Cindy Dake | 1991–1993 |
| Cindy Dake and Laura Savage | 1993–1995 |

*Missions Mosaic*

| | |
|---|---|
| Cindy Dake | 1995–1997 |
| Becky Nelson | 1997–1999 |
| Joanne Parker | 2000–2005 |
| Sue Sprenkle | 2005–2006 |
| Janet Erwin | 2006 |

# Appendix B

## WMU Executive Directors, 1888–2006

| | |
|---|---|
| Annie Armstrong | 1888–1906 |
| Edith Crane | 1907–1911 |
| Kathleen Mallory | 1912–1948 |
| Alma Hunt | 1948–1974 |
| Carolyn Weatherford | 1974–1989 |
| Dellanna O'Brien | 1989–1999 |
| Wanda Lee | 2000–2006 |

From 1888 to 1936, this position was called corresponding secretary.
From 1937 to 1975, this position was called executive secretary.
From 1976 to 2006, this position was called executive director.

# Appendix C

## WMU Presidents, 1888–2006

| | |
|---|---|
| Martha McIntosh | 1888–1892 |
| Fannie Heck | 1892–1894 |
| Abby Gwathmey | 1894–1895 |
| Fannie Heck | 1895–1899 |
| Sarah Stakely | 1899–1903 |
| Lillie Barker | 1903–1906 |
| Fannie Heck | 1906–1915 |
| Minnie James | 1916–1925 |
| Ethlene Cox | 1925–1933 |
| Laura Armstrong | 1933–1945 |
| Olive Martin | 1945–1956 |
| Marie Mathis | 1956–1963 |
| Helen Fling | 1963–1969 |
| Marie Mathis | 1969–1975 |
| Christine Gregory | 1975–1981 |
| Dorothy Sample | 1981–1986 |
| Marjorie McCullough | 1986–1991 |
| Carolyn Miller | 1991–1996 |
| Wanda Lee | 1996–2000 |
| Janet Hoffman | 2000–2005 |
| Kaye Miller | 2005–2006 |

# Notes

## Chapter 1

1. Joyce Rogers, "God's Chief Assignment to Women," *SBJ* 2, no. 1 (January 1974): 9.

2. "The Baptist Faith and Message," SBC, http://www.sbc.net/bfm/bfm2000.asp (accessed October 19, 2013).

3. P. H. Mell, "Why Is Woman Denied the Privilege of 'Preaching the Gospel'?" *AB*, July 23, 1883.

4. Walker L. Knight, "Equality and Stained Glass," *HM*, May 1972, 6.

5. "The Baptist Faith and Message."

6. See, for example, "The Woman I Am," *C*, August 1977, inside back cover.

7. H. Leon McBeth, "Perspectives on Women in Baptist Life," *BHH* 22, no. 3 (July 1987): 9.

8. Ann Braude, "Women's History *Is* American Religious History," in *Retelling U.S. Religious History*, ed. Thomas A. Tweed (Berkeley: University of California Press, 1997), 87–107.

9. Throughout this book, I will use David Bebbington's seminal definition of evangelicalism as Christian faith characterized by biblicism, crucicentrism, conversionism, and activism. See David W. Bebbington, *Evangelicalism in Modern Britain: A History from the 1730s to the 1980s* (London: Unwin Hyman, 1989), 2-17.

10. John Scudder, *An Appeal to Christian Mothers in Behalf of the Heathen* (New York: American Tract Society, 1840), 40.

11. "The W.C.T.U.," *AB*, January 2, 1890.

12. L. H. Daggett, *Historical Sketches of Woman's Missionary Societies in America and England* (Boston: L. H. Daggett, 1879), 137.

13. Patricia Ruth Hill, *The World Their Household: The American Woman's Foreign Mission Movement and Cultural Transformation, 1870–1920* (Ann Arbor: University of Michigan Press, 1985), 46–51; R. Pierce Beaver, *American Protestant Women in World Mission: A History of the First Feminist Movement in North America* (Grand Rapids: Eerdmans, 1980), 88.

14. Isabel Hart, introduction to Daggett, *Historical Sketches*, 6.

15. Beaver, *American Protestant Women*, 88.

16. Helen Barrett Montgomery, *Western Women in Eastern Lands* (New York: Macmillan, 1910), 3.

17. Ruth A. Tucker, "Women in Mission," in *Toward the Twenty-First Century in Christian Mission*, ed. Gerald H. Anderson, James M. Phillips, and Robert T. Coote (Grand Rapids: Eerdmans, 1993), 284.

18. Montgomery, *Western Women*, 268.

19. Ibid., 38.

20. Beaver, *American Protestant Women*, 222–23; Daggett, *Historical Sketches*, 144.

21. Mary Ellen Zuckerman, *A History of Popular Women's Magazines in the United States, 1792–1995* (Westport, CT: Greenwood Press, 1998), 3–99.

22. Helen Barrett Montgomery, *The Bible and Missions* (West Medford, MA: Central Committee on the United Study of Foreign Missions, 1920), 221.

23. Mrs. Elliott, "Story of a Native Woman," *Light and Life for Women*, October 1903, 480. I have preserved in the endnotes each woman's name as it was printed on the magazine's page.

24. Joan Jacobs Brumberg, "Zenanas and Girlless Villages: The Ethnology of American Evangelical Women, 1870–1910," *Journal of American History* 69, no. 2 (September 1982): 353.

25. Emma Raymond Pitman, *Missionary Heroines in Eastern Lands: Woman's Work in Mission Fields* (London: S. W. Partridge, 1884), v; Mrs. O. P. Moss, "Woman's Work for Woman," *HH*, December 1882.

26. Fannie E. S. Heck, *In Royal Service: The Mission Work of Southern Baptist Women* (Nashville: Broadman Press, 1948), 90.

27. Hart, introduction, 9.

28. Montgomery, *Western Women*, 8.

29. Julia D. Carrothers, *The Sunrise Kingdom, or Life and Scenes in Japan: And Woman's Work for Woman There* (Philadelphia: Presbyterian Board of Publication, 1879), 310, emphasis in the original.

30. Ibid., 329; Martha Foster Crawford, "Women in Church Work," *AB*, August 27, 1891.

31. Edwin Munsell Bliss, *Organization and Methods of Mission Work* (Chicago: Student Volunteer Movement for Foreign Missions, 1897), 31.

32. Maud Wotring Raymond, *The King's Business: A Study of Increased Efficiency for Women's Missionary Societies* (West Medford, MA: Central Committee on the United Study of Foreign Missions, 1913), 124.

33. John Albert Broadus, *Should Women Speak in Mixed Public Assemblies?* (Louisville: Baptist Book Concern, 1880), 14; A. McDowell, "Female Education," *BR*, August 26, 1868.

34. T. T. Eaton, *The Bible on Women's Public Speaking* (Louisville: Baptist Book Concern, 1895), 23.

35. M. E. Wilson, *BB*, May 28, 1885.

36. G. W. Hall, "Woman's Work," *HH*, March 1884.

37. Constitution, Minutes, Woman's Mission to Woman, SBHLA.

38. "Woman's Mission to Woman, of the Baptist Churches of Maryland," *BB*, April 14, 1887.

39. Minutes, Woman's Mission to Woman, October 7, 1873.

40. "Southern Baptist Convention," *WR*, May 18, 1872.

41. Annie Armstrong to T. P. Bell, December 13, 1893, http://xroads.virginia.edu/~ma02/harris/sbc/aa_1293.html (accessed October 19, 2013).

42. *SBCA 1872*, 42.

43. *SBCA 1878*, 32.

44. *SBCA 1878*, 41.

45. *SBCA 1882*, 25, 38.

46. J. W. R., "Progress in Missions," *HH*, May 1883; A. J. Holt, "Women's Work," *HH*, May 1885.

47. J. A. Hackett, "The Woman Question the Coming Question," *RH*, April 22, 1886.

48. John P. Shaffer, "To the Baptist Women of Alabama," *AB*, March 4, 1886.

49. Sarah Dobbins to Sarah Grimes, *RH*, March 22, 1888, emphasis in the original.

50. S. A. V., "A Woman's View of Woman's Work among the Baptists of Virginia and of the South," *RH*, January 26, 1886.

51. "Women and Home Missions," *BB*, May 15, 1884.

52. "A Position on Women's Work," *BR*, April 21, 1886.

53. M. E. Wilson, *BB*, May 28, 1885. Wilson was later dismissed from her position because of her negative view of centralized missions organizations.

54. J. J. D. Renfroe, "A Glance at the Convention," *RH*, June 4, 1885.

55. *SBCA 1885*, 14, 30. A woman *had* evidently been admitted as a messenger to the SBC in 1877 and again in 1882, using only her initials and last name.

56. *SBCA 1885*, 30, iv.

57. Heck, *In Royal Service*, 4.

58. "Sketch and Constitution of the Woman's Missionary Societies (Auxiliary to S. B. C.)," *WMUAR 1888*, 3.

59. Minutes, The Woman's Meeting in Richmond, Virginia, May 11, 1888, WMUA.

60. "Organized!" *Baptist Basket*, June 1888.

61. J. E. P., "The Woman's Committee," *WR*, June 7, 1888.

62. Minutes, The Woman's Meeting.

63. "Sketch and Constitution of the Woman's Missionary Societies," 5.

64. Raymond, *King's Business*, 74.

65. Lottie Moon to readers of the *Foreign Mission Journal*, September 15, 1887, in Lottie Moon and Keith Harper, *Send the Light: Lottie Moon's Letters and Other Writings* (Macon, GA: Mercer University Press, 2002), 223.

66. *WMUAR 1889*, 9. Although children were also encouraged to give to missions through WMU, the majority of WMU's "age-graded" organizations were not formalized until the early twentieth century.

67. Mrs. J. F. Pullen, "Treasurer's Annual Report," *WMUAR 1889*, 11–13.

68. "The Home Base of Missions," Program for January, *OMF*, January 1910, 18. Throughout this book, the names of individual articles published in WMU magazines are capitalized and enclosed in quotation marks ("The Home Base of Missions"). The names of columns or features that recurred throughout several issues of these magazines are capitalized, without quotation marks (Program for January).

69. In 1937 the title of corresponding secretary was changed to executive secretary; in 1976, to executive director. In 1957 the executive secretary and her staff assumed the duties of treasurer. Beginning the same year, the executive secretary was

no longer elected at the annual meeting, but was selected by a personnel committee or similar group. See appendixes B and C for a list of national WMU leaders from 1888 to 2006.

70. *SBCA 1889*, iii.

71. *SBCA 1893*, lxi.

72. H. Leon McBeth, "Role of Women in Southern Baptist History," *BHH* 12, no. 1 (January 1977): 6; Carolyn Weatherford, "The Role of Women in Baptist Missions," *BHH* 27, no. 3 (July 1992): 26; Carolyn DeArmond Blevins, "Patterns of Ministry among Southern Baptist Women," *BHH* 22, no. 3 (July 1987): 41.

73. Heck, *In Royal Service*, 4.

74. Sarah Dobbins to Sarah Grimes, *RH*, March 22, 1888.

75. *WMUAR 1893*, 14.

76. *HH*, November 1882.

77. Annie Armstrong to H. A. Tupper, January 9, 1888[?], in Annie Armstrong and Keith Harper, *Rescue the Perishing: Selected Correspondence of Annie Armstrong* (Macon, GA: Mercer University Press, 2004), 70.

78. "*Our Mission Fields*," *OMF*, July 1907, inside front cover.

79. "A Survey of the Year," *WMUAR 1907*, 35.

80. *WMUAR 1914*, 27.

81. "A Survey of the Year," *WMUAR 1907*, 35.

82. "The Treasuryship of Training," Program for July, *OMF*, July 1914, 12.

83. *SBCA 1916*, 60; "Round Table," Union Notes, *RS*, October 1916, 25.

84. "The Spirit of *Royal Service*," *RS*, July 1915, 29.

85. *WMUAR 1914–1969*.

86. *WMUAR 1970–1995*.

87. WMU continued to publish *Missions Mosaic* after 2006; however, this study concludes with that year.

88. *WMUAR 1995–2006*.

89. To avoid confusion, I will consistently refer to this group as the Executive Board.

90. Minutes, Executive Board, WMU, January 23–26, 1957, 9–13, 40, WMUA.

91. "Policy of Executive Committee," Minutes, Executive Committee, WMU, January 20, 1909, 31, WMUA.

## Chapter 2

1. T. P. Bell, quoted in W. W. Gardner, *The Heathen Lost without the Gospel* (Louisville: Baptist Book Concern, 1892), 32.

2. W. O. Carver, "Baptists and the Problem of World Missions," *R&E* 17 (July 1920): 327.

3. Henry W. Frost, quoted in Mrs. George Hillman Whitfield, "The New Patriotism," Program for March, *RS*, March 1915, 7.

4. "Annual Address of the President," *WMUAR 1910*, 11.

5. Edith Campbell Crane, "World Survey of Home and Foreign Missions," Program for September, *OMF*, July 1910, 46.

6. Hill, *The World Their Household*, 161; Dana L. Robert, *American Women in Mission: A Social History of Their Thought and Practice*, ed. Wilbert R. Shenk (Macon, GA: Mercer University Press, 1996), 256.

7. Nancy A. Hardesty, "The Scientific Study of Missions: Textbooks of the Central Committee on the United Study of Foreign Missions," in *The Foreign Missionary Enterprise at Home: Explorations in North American Cultural History*, ed. Daniel H. Bays and Grant Wacker (Tuscaloosa: University of Alabama Press, 2003), 109.

8. See Kenneth Latourette, *A History of Christianity* (New York: Harper, 1953).

9. "Two Notable Conferences," Editorial, *RS*, March 1915, 4; "The Southern Jubilees," *OMF*, January 1912, 19; "Foreign Mission Survey," Program for October, *RS*, October 1915, 9.

10. "Annual Address of the President," *WMUAR 1911*, 12.

11. Ethel Winfield, "Getting the Keynote," Training School, *RS*, April 1916, 23.

12. Magazine References, *OMF*, October 1911, 7.

13. *OMF*, October 1911, front cover.

14. Helen Barrett Montgomery, *Prayer and Missions* (West Medford, MA: Central Committee on the United Study of Foreign Missions, 1924), 168.

15. Montgomery, *Western Women*, 71.

16. Ibid.

17. Hill, *The World Their Household*, 56–57.

18. Brumberg, "Zenanas and Girlless Villages," 396.

19. "Japan—the New World Power," *OMF*, July 1906, 21; "Mexico," Program for June, *OMF*, April 1908, 41; "The Lands of Buddha, India, and Japan," Program for June, *OMF*, April 1909, 45; Loy J. Savage, "Stepping Upward," From Our Missionaries, *RS*, January 1915, 19; Evelyn C. Leonard, "The Old, Old Story," From Our Missionaries, *RS*, December 1916, 21; "Cuba and Panama," Program for March, *RS*, March 1918, 10.

20. Program for October, *RS*, October 1918, 14.

21. Ibid., 8.

22. Carrothers, *Sunrise Kingdom*, 307.

23. D. B. Wells, "A Glimpse of Old Mexico," *Woman's Work for Woman*, January 1904, 9.

24. Mrs. George Hillman Whitfield, "Building for the Future China," Program for December, *RS*, December 1914, 10.

25. Montgomery, *Western Women*, 45.

26. Lottie Moon to R. J. Willingham, November 7, 1901, cited in Paul Harvey, *Redeeming the South: Religious Cultures and Racial Identities among Southern Baptists, 1865–1925* (Chapel Hill: University of North Carolina Press, 1997), 212.

27. Gregory Vickers, "Models of Womanhood and the Early Woman's Missionary Union," *BHH* 24, no. 1 (January 1989): 47.

28. Heck, *In Royal Service*, 349.

29. Kate Cox White, "The Call of Latin America," From Our Missionaries, *RS*, February 1916, 19.

30. "Africa," Program for October, *OMF*, October 1907, 11.

31. Minutes of the Woman's Missionary Societies, Auxiliary to Baptist State Convention of North Carolina (Raleigh, 1892), 35, cited in Carol Crawford Holcomb, "Mothering the South: The Influence of Gender and the Social Gospel on the Social Views of the Leadership of Woman's Missionary Union, Auxiliary to Southern Baptist Convention, 1888–1930" (PhD diss., Baylor University, 1999), 51.

32. "Japan—the New World Power," 17; "Frontier Missions," *OMF*, October 1906, 26; "Two Republics—Brazil and Argentina," *OMF*, January 1907, 32.

33. Maud R. McLure, "*Thou* Crownest the Year," Training School, *RS*, October 1914, 23.

34. Maude Burke Dozier, "Missionary Women's Work in Japan," From Our Missionaries, *RS*, April 1915, 20.

35. "Foreign Missions," Program for February, *OMF*, January 1911, 30.

36. "Editorial Notes," *Woman's Work for Woman*, January 1904, 1; Mrs. B. J. Baughman, "A Girls' School in a Sultan's Residence," *Woman's Missionary Friend*, June 1917, 198.

37. Jane Hunter, *The Gospel of Gentility: American Women Missionaries in Turn-of-the-Century China* (New Haven: Yale University Press, 1984), 10.

38. "China, the Middle Kingdom," Program for December, *OMF*, October 1909, 45.

39. "Mexico," *OMF*, April 1907, 36.

40. "Mission Schools," Program for May, *OMF*, April 1908, 24.

41. "Mexico, Central America, and Cuba," Program for November, *OMF*, October 1909, 29.

42. "Mexico," Program for June, *OMF*, April 1908, 43.

43. "China, the Middle Kingdom," Program for December, *OMF*, October 1909, 45.

44. "Mission Schools," Program for May, *OMF*, April 1908, 25.

45. Ibid., 23.

46. "China, the Middle Kingdom," Program for December, *OMF*, October 1909, 44.

47. Alice M. Duval, "His Eye Seeth Every Precious Thing," From Our Missionaries, *RS*, May 1915, 20.

48. Mrs. George Hillman Whitfield, "Building for the Future China," Program for December, *RS*, December 1914, 12, quoting Margaret Burton, *The Education of Women in China* (New York: Revell, 1911), 5, 230, although without a direct citation.

49. "The Lands of Buddha, India, and Japan," Program for June, *OMF*, April 1909, 50.

50. Montgomery, *Western Women*, 105.

51. "Mission Schools," Program for May, *OMF*, April 1908, 24.

52. "Girls' Schools in China," *RS*, December 1917, back cover.

53. "China," Program for December, *OMF*, October 1907, 38.

54. "Mexico, Central America, and the Canal Zone," Program for October, *OMF*, October 1910, 22.

55. "Medical Missions," Program for June, *OMF*, April 1913, 47.

56. "Medical Missions," Program for August, *OMF*, July 1908, 26.

57. "Medical Missions," Program for June, *OMF*, April 1913, 47.

58. "Medical Missions," Program for August, *OMF*, July 1908, 30.

59. "China," Program for December, *OMF*, October 1910, 55.

60. "Medical Missions," Program for August, *OMF*, July 1908, 30.

61. "China," Program for December, *OMF*, October 1907, 37.

62. Edna E. Teal, "The Gift of Healing," From Our Missionaries, *RS*, August 1916, 21.

63. W. Richie Hogg, "The Role of American Protestantism in World Mission," in *American Missions in Bicentennial Perspective*, ed. R. Pierce Beaver (South Pasadena, CA: William Carey Library, 1977), 381.

64. "Medical Missions," Program for August, *OMF*, July 1908, 30.

65. Montgomery, *Western Women*, 132.

66. "Japan—the New World Power," 19.

67. Henrietta North, "Seeing We Have This . . . Ministry We Faint Not," From Our Missionaries, *RS*, June 1916, 21.

68. Maude B. Dozier, "From Sunshine Land," From Our Missionaries, *RS*, June 1916, 21.

69. "China," Program for December, *OMF*, October 1907, 37. This missionary is identified as Dr. G. W. Ayers.

70. "Cuba," Program for July, *OMF*, July 1910, 20–21.

71. Lottie Moon to H. A. Tupper, April 14, 1876, in Moon and Harper, *Send the Light*, 32.

72. Shailer Mathews, "Social Gospel," in *A Dictionary of Religion and Ethics*, ed. Shailer Mathews and G. B. Smith (New York: Macmillan, 1921), 416.

73. See Betsy Flowers, "Southern Baptist Evangelicals or Social Gospel Liberals? The Woman's Missionary Union and Social Reform, 1888 to 1928," *American Baptist Quarterly* 19, no. 2 (June 2000): 106–28; Gregory Vickers, "Southern Baptist Women and Social Concerns, 1910–1929," *BHH* 23, no. 4 (October 1988): 3–13; and Holcomb, "Mothering the South," among others.

74. Harvey, *Redeeming the South*, 214.

75. Kendal P. Mobley, "The Ecumenical Woman's Missionary Movement: Helen Barrett Montgomery and *The Baptist*, 1920–1930," in *Gender and the Social Gospel*, ed. Wendy J. Deichmann Edwards and Carolyn De Swarte Gifford (Chicago: University of Illinois Press, 2003), 168–70.

76. Montgomery, *Western Women*, 85–86.

77. Hill, *The World Their Household*, 56–58.

78. Mrs. H. M. Wharton, "The New Spirit," Personal Service, *RS*, October 1914, 24.

79. "City Missions," Program for November, *OMF*, October 1910, 41, emphasis added.

80. "Personal Service," *WMUAR 1915*, 65. A department of personal service was created at the national WMU office in 1909, but the program was not officially approved until the WMU annual meeting in 1910.

81. C. Delane Tew, "From Local Society to Para-Denomination: Woman's Missionary Union, 1890–1930" (PhD diss., Auburn University, 2003), 142.

82. Mrs. H. M. Wharton, "Beside Living Waters," *WMUAR 1915*, 60; Mrs. H. M. Wharton, "Report of Personal Service Department," *WMUAR 1912*, 66.

83. Heck, *In Royal Service*, 207. See Matthew 25:35–36.

84. Holcomb, "Mothering the South," 115.

85. "World Survey of Home and Foreign Missions," Program for September, *OMF*, July 1910, 44.

86. Fannie Heck, "By Way of Remembrance," Personal Service, *RS*, December 1915, 28.

87. "World Survey," Program for October, *OMF*, October 1909, 19.

88. Heck, "By Way of Remembrance," 28.

89. Mrs. George Hillman Whitfield, "At Our Own Door," Program for February, *RS*, February 1915, 8.

90. "World Survey," *OMF*, October 1909, 12; "The Southern Sociological Congress," Personal Service, *RS*, May 1915, 26.

91. "Personal Service," *YB 1916–1917*, 38.

92. Mrs. H. M. Wharton, "Southern Social Problems and the Home Mission Board," Program for March, *RS*, March 1916, 12.

93. Ibid.

94. "The Salvation of the City," Program for July, *OMF*, July 1909, 9; "Program for November," *RS*, November 1917, 12; "Planning for the Convention Year," Program for July, *RS*, July 1918, 16.

95. "Home Lights," Personal Service, *RS*, December 1914, 25.

96. "Bargains," Personal Service, *RS*, August 1915, 26.

97. Holcomb, "Mothering the South," 249.

98. Mrs. George Hillman Whitfield, "The New Patriotism," Program for March, *RS*, March 1915, 12.

99. Mrs. Alex W. Beale, "The Stranger in Our Midst," Personal Service, *RS*, October 1918, 26.

100. Ibid.

101. Mrs. R. W. Hooker, quoted in Mrs. George Hillman Whitfield, Program for August, *RS*, August 1915, 10.

102. "Indians," Program for May, *OMF*, April 1910, 30.

103. Whitfield, "The New Patriotism," 9.

104. Victor Masters, quoted in "Southern Problems for Southern Baptists," Program for March, *OMF*, January 1910, 42.

105. See, for example, "Our Bible Work," *OMF*, January 1907, 12.

106. See, for example, Bertha Lee Mitchell, "The Kindergarten in Tampa," From Our Missionaries, *RS*, February 1915, 19.

107. Mrs. George Hillman Whitfield, "At Our Own Door," Program for February, *RS*, February 1915, 10.

108. Ibid.

109. Mrs. H. M. Wharton, "Homemakers' Club of Canton Baptist Mission, Baltimore," Personal Service, *RS*, November 1915, 25.

110. Mary Faison Dixon, "In Jerusalem," Program for August, *RS*, August 1917, 11.

111. Whitfield, "At Our Own Door," 12.

112. "Social Problems and Their Challenge," Program for June, *RS*, June 1918, 15.

113. Whitfield, "At Our Own Door," 11.

114. "The Cheer-All Club at the Training School Good Will Center," Personal Service, *RS*, June 1915, 25.

115. Mrs. James Kirkman, "In Service," *WMUAR 1918*, 57.

116. Kathrina C. Quick, "Personally Conducted," Personal Service, *RS*, November 1917, 26.

117. "State Missions," Program for September, *OMF*, July 1908, 47.

118. See Tew, "Local Society to Para-Denomination," 131, 142.

119. *Manual of W.M.U. Method* (Nashville: SSB, SBC, 1917), 13.

120. "Missions East of the Mississippi River," Program for November, *OMF*, October 1911, 31.

121. Mrs. James Pollard, "Our Country for God," Bible Study, *RS*, March 1915, 6, quoting Raymond, *King's Business*, 88, although without a direct citation.

122. Montgomery, *Prayer and Missions*, 200.

123. "Foreign Missions," Program for February, *OMF*, January 1911, 35; Mrs. George Hillman Whitfield, "Our Local Organization," Program for January, *RS*, January 1915, 12; "China," Editorial, *RS*, December 1917, 4; "Round Table," Union

Notes, *RS*, March 1918, 28. The 1915 article quoted Raymond, *King's Business*, 216, although without a direct citation.

124. *Manual of W.M.U. Method*, 128.

125. *OMF*, January 1911, 35.

126. "Missionary Calendar of Prayer for Southern Baptists," *RS*, January 1918, 5.

127. Minutes, Executive Committee, WMU, December 10, 1907, 30, WMUA.

128. Hill, *The World Their Household*, 148–49.

129. Montgomery, *Western Women*, 254.

130. "Japan—the New World Power," 13–25; "Great Missionary Movements of the Last Three Decades," Program for January, *OMF*, January 1909, 6–17.

131. "*Our Mission Fields*," *OMF*, July 1906, inside front cover.

132. "Annual Address of the President," *WMUAR 1909*, 11; "Planning for the Convention Year," Program for July, *RS*, July 1918, 11.

133. Mrs. G. H. Whitfield, "Reading for Missions," Program for July, *RS*, July 1916, 13.

134. "Foreword," *OMF*, January 1911, 9.

135. Ecumenical Conference on Foreign Missions, *Ecumenical Missionary Conference, New York, 1900*, vol. 1 (New York: American Tract Society, 1900), 6.

136. Robert, *American Women in Mission*, 261.

137. Mrs. George Hillman Whitfield, "Our Local Organization," Program for January, *RS*, January 1915, 12, quoting Raymond, *King's Business*, 232, although without a direct citation.

138. "Foreign Mission Survey," Program for October, *RS*, October 1915, 9.

139. *WMUAR 1890*, 25.

140. "*Royal Service*," Editorial, *RS*, October 1914, 5.

141. "Round Table," Union Notes, *RS*, November 1915, 27.

142. "China," Editorial, *RS*, December 1917, 5.

143. "Frontier Missions," *OMF*, October 1906, 21.

144. "Home Mission Survey," Editorial, *RS*, January 1918, 7.

145. William M. Vories, "Missions and Lace," quoted in Mrs. George Hillman Whitfield, "Japan of Today," Program for April, *RS*, April 1915, 13; Mary Faison Dixon, "The Home Base," Program for May, *RS*, May 1917, 10. Vories's poem first appeared in the *Missionary Review of the World*.

146. "Christmas Courage," Editorial, *RS*, December 1914, 4.

147. "The World Field," Current Events, *RS*, January 1917, 22.

148. "China," Editorial, *RS*, December 1917, 5.

149. "Round Table," Union Notes, *RS*, October 1916, 25.

150. "Cash and Box Contributions of the Woman's Missionary Union," *OMF*, July 1909, back cover.

151. "The Passing of Our Good Friend," Editorial, *RS*, February 1915, 4.

152. "Missions in the Southwest and State Missions," Program for September, *OMF*, July 1907, 51.

153. "January's Opportunities," Editorial, *RS*, January 1916, 4.

154. "Remember July 22!" Editorial, *RS*, July 1916, 6.

155. "Round Table," Union Notes, *RS*, October 1916, 24.

156. Victor I. Masters, *Baptist Missions in the South* (Atlanta: HMB, 1915), 153–54.

157. "Emergency Pledge," *RS*, November 1918, back cover.

158. "How One Girl Helped Another," Home Department, *RS*, June 1915, 29.

## Chapter 3

1. Mrs. C. D. Creasman, "Youth: Tomorrow's Messenger of the Word," Program for June, *RS*, June 1933, 22.

2. Laymen's Foreign Missions Inquiry and William Ernest Hocking, *Re-Thinking Missions: A Laymen's Inquiry after One Hundred Years* (New York: Harper & Bros., 1932), 69.

3. Robert, *American Women in Mission*, 308–9.

4. "Let *World Comrades* Be My Valentine," *RS*, February 1926, 35.

5. "The Joy of Work," Book Reviews, *RS*, June 1920, 31.

6. Raymond, *King's Business*, 18.

7. Montgomery, *Western Women*, 272.

8. Beaver, *American Protestant Women*, 184–90; Robert, *American Women in Mission*, 302–3.

9. Mrs. W. C. James, Current Missionary Events, *RS*, October 1930, 33.

10. Mrs. W. C. James, "Our Unchanging Task in a Changing World," Program for November, *RS*, November 1929, 17.

11. Inquiry and Hocking, *Re-Thinking Missions*, 19.

12. From Our Missionaries, *RS*, May 1921, 27, quoting an unnamed author.

13. Mrs. W. J. Neel, "What the Baptist 75 Million Campaign Will Mean to China," Editorial, *RS*, December 1919, 8.

14. Mrs. C. D. Creasman, "The Challenge of Modern Conditions to Uplift the Banner of the Cross in Africa," Program for July, *RS*, July 1935, 27.

15. Mrs. C. D. Creasman, "They That Turn to Righteousness," Program for April, *RS*, April 1931, 19.

16. "Evangelistic Agencies of the Home Mission Board," Program for August, *RS*, August 1923, 16.

17. Margaret Buchanan, "Chattanooga Good Will Center," Personal Service, *RS*, June 1923, 30; "The Summer School at Louisville," Personal Service, *RS*, May 1921, 30; Virginia Hill, "Settlement Work in Louisville," Training School, *RS*, March 1922, 29; Mrs. C. D. Creasman, "A Summer Cruise through Home Mission Fields," Program for August, *RS*, August 1936, 25; Mrs. Eureka Whiteker, "The Work Goes Forward," Personal Service, *RS*, July 1940, 7.

18. Mrs. H. M. Wharton, "The Southern Sociological Congress," Personal Service, *RS*, August 1919, 26; Mrs. H. M. Wharton, "The Southern Sociological Congress," Personal Service, *RS*, September 1919, 27; Mrs. J. Clyde Turner, "The Child in Industry," Personal Service, *RS*, December 1920, 30, 33.

19. "W.M.U. Fundamentals for New S.B.C. Year," *RS*, August 1925, front cover.

20. "Christianity and World Peace," Peace on Earth, *RS*, September 1931, 7.

21. Victor I. Masters, "The Press and Christianity," *RH*, January 16, 1919, 8.

22. *WMUAR 1920*, 15, 64. Fundamental aims were also called "chief aims."

23. Mary Livermore, Personal Service, *RS*, October 1921, 28.

24. "Evangelistic Agencies of the Home Mission Board," Program for August, *RS*, August 1923, 16.

25. "The Aim of Personal Service: By All Means Save Some," Program for September, *RS*, September 1926, 14.

26. Mrs. C. F. Creal, "The Gift of Self," Personal Service, *RS*, August 1929, 29;

Mrs. C. D. Creasman, "Entrusted with the Gospel," Program for September, *RS*, September 1932, 20.

27. Mrs. P. B. Lowrance, "Aim of Personal Service," Personal Service, *RS*, February 1936, 8; Mrs. C. D. Creasman, "The Great Commission and W.M.U.—Chief Aims: 'Enlistment and Personal Service,'" Program for September, *RS*, September 1939, 22.

28. Mrs. Eureka Whiteker, "The Work Goes Forward," Personal Service, *RS*, July 1940, 7.

29. Mary Christian, "Report of Southwide Personal Service Chairman," *WMUAR 1942*, 90; Mrs. George E. Davis, "Crusading for Christ in a Cottage," Community Missions, *RS*, March 1945, 6.

30. J. B. Lawrence, quoted in Mrs. C. D. Creasman, "Southern Baptists: Sheaves—with Rejoicing," Program for January, *RS*, January 1938, 21–22.

31. Roland Q. Leavell, "The Southwide Baptist Revival for Which We Pray," Southwide Baptist Revival, *RS*, January 1939, 5; Arthur Fox, "The W.M.U. in the Soul Winning Campaign of 1939," Southwide Baptist Revival, *RS*, May 1939, 5.

32. M. E. Dodd, Centennial Evangelistic Crusade, *RS*, October 1944, 5.

33. Singer E. Powell Lee, "Personal Evangelism," Evangelistic Crusade, *RS*, March 1940, 5.

34. Fred C. Eastham, "Aiding Centennial Crusade to Successful Conclusion," Centennial Evangelistic Crusade, *RS*, September 1945, 10.

35. Inman Johnson, "Women Soul-Winners," Evangelistic Crusade, *RS*, March 1941, 10.

36. Mrs. F. W. Armstrong, "Message of W.M.U. President: A Compelling Heritage," *WMUAR 1937*, 17.

37. "Foreign Mission Outlook," Program for January, *RS*, January 1921, 9–10.

38. From Our Missionaries, *RS*, February 1930, 7–10.

39. "Our New Foreign Mission Fields," Program for February, *RS*, February 1922, 7–13.

40. Mrs. C. D. Creasman, "Pressing on through Difficulties (Orient)," Program Material, *RS*, December 1940, 23–25.

41. Ella Broadus Robertson, "Learning to Pray," Bible Study, *RS*, February 1939, 10.

42. Mrs. F. W. Armstrong, "Why the Offering?" Editorial, *RS*, December 1935, 4.

43. Mrs. C. D. Creasman, "Entrusted with the Gospel," Program for September, *RS*, September 1932, 20.

44. Mrs. W. H. Gray, "The Ninety and Nine," Bible Study, *RS*, October 1934, 12.

45. See "W.M.U. Plan of Work for Calendar Year of 1938," *YB 1938*, 24.

46. Mrs. F. W. Armstrong, "Prayer—Power," Editorial, *RS*, August 1934, 4.

47. "The Value of Mountain Schools," Calendar of Prayer, *RS*, March 1919, 4–5; Maud McLure, "Our Christmas Offering and Kingdom Building," Calendar of Prayer, *RS*, November 1936, 11.

48. "Round Table: 'O, Zion, Haste,'" Union Notes, *RS*, September 1924, 31; Mrs. W. T. Waring, "Woman's Part in the Centennial Evangelistic Crusade," Community Missions, *RS*, May 1945, 29.

49. Mrs. C. D. Creasman, "An Urgent Gospel Where We Live," Program Material, *RS*, January 1941, 26.

50. Robert, *American Women in Mission*, 274–76.

51. *WMUAR 1923*, 33.

52. Mrs. C. D. Creasman, "The Power of the Printed Page," Program for August, *RS*, August 1932, 18.

53. "The Bible and Missions," Book Reviews, *RS*, August 1920, 28.

54. Mrs. Julian P. Thomas, "Eastern Women Today and Tomorrow," Book Reviews, *RS*, July 1933, 31; Mrs. Julian P. Thomas, "Women under the Southern Cross," Book Reviews, *RS*, May 1935, 33.

55. Willie Jean Stewart, "The Preaching Value of Missions," Book Reviews, *RS*, January 1944, 6.

56. Mrs. Eugene Levering, "Mission Study," Editorial, *RS*, July 1920, 5.

57. Book Reviews, *RS*, April 1923, 32.

58. Una Roberts Lawrence, "Report of Southwide Mission Study Chairman," *WMUAR 1935*, 96.

59. Ida M. Stallworth, "The Annual School of Missions," Church School of Missions, *RS*, April 1932, 8.

60. Mrs. C. D. Creasman, "Schools and the Kingdom," Program for September, *RS*, September 1936, 28. Men's mission study classes were probably taught by other men.

61. Mrs. T. M. Pittman, "With the Program Committee," Program Plans, *RS*, May 1934, 17.

62. Inabelle Coleman, Business Women's Circles, *RS*, February 1936, 15.

63. "Making a Home in a New Land," Program for July, *RS*, July 1922, 16.

64. Mrs. Guy Waldrop, "The Task That Is Nearest," Personal Service, *RS*, November 1925, 27.

65. "Christian Education Imperative at Home and on Mission Fields," Program for June, *RS*, June 1932, 30.

66. Mrs. C. D. Creasman, "Entrusted with the Gospel," Program for September, *RS*, September 1932, 25.

67. "Sisterhood of the Americas," Program for May, *RS*, May 1924, 16.

68. Mrs. C. D. Creasman, "Africa: Waiting for the Word," Program for July, *RS*, July 1933, 18, 19.

69. Mrs. Taul B. White, "Woman in Missionary History," Program for May, *RS*, May 1928, 23.

70. "Mexico," Program for January, *RS*, January 1924, 14; "A Cuban Courtship," Home Department, *RS*, February 1924, 31; "New Movements in the Orient," Program for April, *RS*, April 1927, 17, 19.

71. Mrs. E. T. Snuggs, "Tak Yan," From Our Missionaries, *RS*, July 1921, 25; Mrs. G. A. Bowdler, "The Buenos Aires Baptist Boys' Academy," From Our Missionaries, *RS*, February 1922, 25.

72. Mrs. J. W. McGavock, "For Week of Prayer: Mothering a Church in Chile," *RS*, December 1923, 30.

73. Kathleen Mallory, "Zung Ta Ta Still Lives," *RS*, April 1924, 10–11; "A Rumanian Heroine," Home Department, *RS*, April 1925, 29; Mrs. A. B. Christie, "A Church Builder," From Our Missionaries, *RS*, January 1932, 9; Mrs. T. M. Pittman, "A Golden Sheaf in Japan," Program Plans, *RS*, May 1938, 19; Mrs. James W. McGavock, "Aurelia V. de Brando," From Our Missionaries, *RS*, January 1942, 31–32;

Mrs. Dewey Moore, "Faithful Mothering of Italian Orphans," From Missionaries, *RS*, October 1945, 8.

74. For example, see Mrs. T. M. Pittman, "A Golden Sheaf in Africa," Program Plans, *RS*, April 1938, 17.

75. "Survey of Foreign Missions," Program for October, *RS*, October 1920, 14.

76. Floy Hawkins, "Finding Faithful Women," From Our Missionaries, *RS*, February 1939, 32–33; Mrs. C. D. Creasman, "Think on These Things: Whatsoever Things Are of Good Report," Program Material, *RS*, June 1942, 29; Helen Meredith, "They Also Serve," From Our Missionaries, *RS*, June 1944, 23.

77. Mrs. C. D. Creasman, "Signs of Kingdom Progress," Program for June, *RS*, June 1936, 26.

78. "Testimonials from Chinese Women," From Our Missionaries, *RS*, September 1923, 33.

79. Mrs. W. C. James, Current Missionary Events, *RS*, September 1928, 33.

80. Mrs. C. D. Creasman, "The Japanese," Program for September, *RS*, September 1937, 24; Rev. and Mrs. S. S. Stover, "Strengthening the Churches," From Our Missionaries, *RS*, June 1943, 31.

81. "Greetings from Our Mission Fields," *WMUAR 1919*, 51–57; Mrs. W. Harvey Clarke, "Southern Baptist Missionaries in Japan," Program for July, *RS*, July 1928, 19.

82. "African Womanhood," Program for July, *RS*, July 1924, 18; Mrs. W. E. Allen, "Activities of South American Churches," Program for August, *RS*, August 1928, 17.

83. Mrs. C. D. Creasman, "Lifting the Banner in the Land of the Rising Sun," Program for August, *RS*, August 1935, 27.

84. Mabola Ayorinde, "Some Impressions of the Jubilee Meeting in Richmond," Our Golden Jubilee, *RS*, August 1938, 7.

85. Irene Carter Stephens, "A Joyful Noise," From Our Missionaries, *RS*, March 1920, 22; Mrs. C. D. Creasman, "Good News of Kingdom Progress," Program for July, *RS*, July 1936, 24.

86. Mrs. C. D. Creasman, "Think on These Things: Whatsoever Things Are of Virtue," Program Material, *RS*, July 1942, 23.

87. Inabelle Coleman, "Schools and the Kingdom," Business Women's Circles, *RS*, September 1936, 17; Edith O. West, "Brazilian W.M.U. Headquarters," From Our Missionaries, *RS*, December 1936, 11.

88. Mrs. C. D. Creasman, "Miracles of the Word in Other Lands," Program for April, *RS*, April 1933, 28.

89. Harvey, *Redeeming the South*, 87.

90. Mrs. E. B. Mathews, "How the Methodists Did It," *RS*, December 1919, 25.

91. Mrs. F. W. Armstrong, "Centennial Commitments," Editorial, *RS*, January 1945, 3; Mrs. F. W. Armstrong, "Auxiliary," Editorial, *RS*, September 1933, 4. As an auxiliary to the SBC, WMU did not (and still does not) receive any Cooperative Program funds.

92. Mrs. F. W. Armstrong, "Message of W.M.U. President: A Royal Diadem," *WMUAR 1934*, 19.

93. J. E. Dillard, "Woman's Missionary Union, Auxiliary to Southern Baptist Convention," Editorial, *RS*, November 1945, 4.

94. Tew, "Local Society to Para-Denomination."

95. *WMUAR 1921*, 17–19.

96. Mrs. F. S. Davis, "Regarding the Removal of W.M.U. Headquarters," and Eliza S. Broadus, "Some Reasons against Removal of W.M.U. Headquarters," Editorial, *RS*, November 1920, 4–5.

97. Mrs. W. C. James, "Address of W.M.U. President," *WMUAR 1921*, 29; "Women and the Southern Baptist Convention," Editorial, *RS*, July 1922, 4–5.

98. Mrs. W. C. James, "Address of W.M.U. President," *WMUAR 1922*, 27.

99. Mrs. C. D. Creasman, "Sheaves—with Rejoicing," Program for January, *RS*, January 1938, 23.

100. "Our State's Part in the Campaign for Denominational Education," Program for September, *RS*, September 1920, 10–13; "Ministerial Relief, Orphanages, and Hospitals," Program for July, *RS*, July 1921, 10–15; "Our Convention: Its Organization and Purpose," Program for May, *RS*, May 1927, 17–24; Mrs. F. W. Armstrong, "Duty and the Denomination," Editorial, *RS*, April 1938, 4; Mrs. F. W. Armstrong, "S.B.C. Calendar of Denominational Activities," Editorial, *RS*, February 1941, 4.

101. Maude McLure, "Miracles of the Word in Other Lands," Calendar of Prayer, *RS*, April 1933, 17.

102. Mrs. T. M. Pittman, "With the Program Committee," Program Plans, *RS*, May 1931, 15–16.

103. Ryland Knight, "My W.M.S. and I," Society Methods, *RS*, August 1941, 10. See 1 Corinthians 14:34–35.

104. "Christian Education," Editorial, *RS*, February 1921, 4.

105. "Planning for Convention Year," Program for July, *RS*, July 1920, 11.

106. "Baptist 75 Million Campaign," *RS*, September 1919, 32.

107. "Baptist 75 Million Campaign," Calendar of Prayer for Southern Baptists, *RS*, April 1922, 7; "Round Table," Union Notes, *RS*, September 1919, 28.

108. "W.M.U. Plans for 1921–1922," Program for October, *RS*, October 1921, 15; "Planning for Convention Year," Program for July, *RS*, July 1920, 11, emphasis in the original.

109. "Foreign Mission Survey—Holding the Ropes," Program for October, *RS*, October 1919, 12.

110. "Mathematics of China's Millions and 'Millions for the Master,'" *RS*, December 1919, back cover.

111. Mrs. F. W. Armstrong, "In All Judea," Editorial, *RS*, September 1941, 4.

112. Opal Osborne, Business Women's Circles, *RS*, April 1945, 12.

113. Mrs. C. D. Creasman, "An Urgent Gospel Summons States . . . 'To Enlarge . . . Lengthen . . . Strengthen,'" Program Material, *RS*, September 1941, 22.

114. Mrs. C. D. Creasman, "Laborers Together with God in Kingdom Tasks," Program for February, *RS*, February 1936, 21.

115. Mrs. W. J. Cox, "Practice and Prayer," Editorial, *RS*, November 1931, 4; Mrs. T. M. Pittman, "With the Program Committee," Program Plans, *RS*, December 1935, 21.

116. Minutes, Executive Committee, WMU, May 6, 1929, 32, WMUA.

117. *SBCA 1895*, 18–24.

118. Mrs. Walter H. Hunt, "Bring Ye All the Tithes," *RS*, September 1923, 8.

119. Juliette Mather, "Best Y.W.A. Tithing Story in Southwide Contest," Our Young People, *RS*, July 1929, 27; Mrs. G. R. Martin, "The Tithers' Fellowship League," Tithing, *RS*, September 1931, 5; "Tithing Pin Ceremony," Editorial, *RS*,

June 1926, 5–6; Mrs. Carter Wright, "A Stewardship Revival, Our Greatest Need," Stewardship Suggestions, *RS*, January 1944, 4; *RS*, September 1926, 5; "W.M.U. Plan of Work for Calendar Year of 1930," *YB 1930*, 9.

120. Mrs. C. D. Creasman, "The Great Commission and W.M.U. Chief Aims—'Tithes and Offerings,'" Program for October, *RS*, October 1939, 24; Mrs. C. D. Creasman, "God's Unchanging Plan of Stewardship," Program Material, *RS*, October 1940, 26.

121. See Mrs. C. D. Creasman, "Lifting the Banner through Stewardship," Program for September, *RS*, September 1935, 18–22.

122. Mrs. T. V. Herndon, "Stewardship for Business Women," Business Women's Circles, *RS*, January 1928, 30.

123. Mrs. Carter Wright, "Caesar's . . . and . . . God's," Stewardship Suggestions, *RS*, May 1942, 33.

124. Creasman, "Lifting the Banner through Stewardship," 18.

125. Mrs. C. D. Creasman, "An Urgent Gospel, Free or Bound?" Program Material, *RS*, February 1942, 22.

126. Mrs. C. D. Creasman, "The Blessed Grace of Giving," Program for October, *RS*, October 1936, 22; *WMUAR 1937*, 42.

127. Mrs. W. C. James, Current Missionary Events, *RS*, January 1936, 12.

128. "Tithing Testimonials," *RS*, October 1922, 9–10.

129. Mrs. W. C. James, Current Missionary Events, *RS*, November 1931, 33.

130. J. E. Dillard, "The W.M.U. and the E.M.C.," Stewardship Suggestions, *RS*, November 1943, 17, emphasis in the original.

131. Catherine Allen, *A Century to Celebrate: History of Woman's Missionary Union* (Birmingham: WMU, 1987), 131.

132. Mrs. W. J. Cox, "Go Forward, Slack Not," Editorial, *RS*, November 1932, 4.

133. From Our Missionaries, *RS*, January 1926, 27–31, 35.

134. Carrie U. Littlejohn, "With the Alumnae," Training School, *RS*, April 1931, 28.

135. Mrs. F. W. Armstrong, "Denominational Debts Decrease," Editorial, *RS*, February 1936, 4.

136. Mrs. J. A. Anderson, "Planking Down the Cash," Stewardship Suggestions, *RS*, October 1936, 5, emphasis in the original.

137. Armstrong, "Denominational Debts Decrease," 4.

138. Mrs. Carter Wright, "What Will Your Vote Be?" For a Debtless Denomination, *RS*, August 1940, 5; Mrs. Carter Wright, "Equivalent of Double the Memberships," For a Debtless Denomination, *RS*, April 1940, 7.

139. J. B. Lawrence, "Appeal for the March Week of Prayer and Annie Armstrong Offering," *RS*, February 1942, 5.

140. Mrs. C. D. Creasman, "An Urgent Gospel, Free or Bound?" Program Material, *RS*, February 1942, 22.

141. Mrs. Carter Wright, "A Gourd Vine versus Nineveh," Stewardship Suggestions, *RS*, January 1943, 6; Mrs. F. W. Armstrong, "'Debt-Free in '43'—If," Editorial, *RS*, July 1943, 4.

142. Walter Gilmore, "Every Member Canvass," *RS*, November 1934, 12; *WMUAR 1934–1944*.

143. Mrs. C. D. Creasman, "Lifting the Banner of the Cross through Our Christ-

mas Offering," Program for December, *RS*, December 1935, 30; Frederick S. Porter, "Yes, It Really Pays," Appraisal by Pastors, *RS*, July 1937, 9. See 1 Kings 17:8–16.

144. J. B. Lawrence, "The Value of the 1934 Annie W. Armstrong Offering for Home Missions," *RS*, August 1934, 6; J. B. Lawrence, "Appeal for the March Week of Prayer Offering," *RS*, February 1937, 5; J. B. Lawrence, "From the Home Mission Board," *WMUAR 1932*, 124.

145. Charles E. Maddry, "Good Tidings," *RS*, July 1934, 5; Charles E. Maddry, "Appeal to Southern Baptist Women and Young People: A Crisis Averted," *RS*, December 1934, 31; Charles E. Maddry, "Greetings from the Foreign Mission Board," *WMUAR 1944*, 144.

146. J. E. Dillard, "Good News for the W.M.U.," For a Debtless Denomination, *RS*, January 1943, 7.

147. J. E. Dillard, "The W.M.U. and the Baptist Hundred Thousand Dollar Club," Stewardship Suggestions, *RS*, January 1939, 7.

148. "For a Debtless Denomination," *YB 1943*, 56.

## Chapter 4

1. *WMUAR 1946–1967*.

2. "Cover Story," *RS*, January 1966, 4.

3. David Edwin Harrell, *Unto a Good Land: A History of the American People* (Grand Rapids: Eerdmans, 2005), 1036.

4. C. Vann Woodward, *The Burden of Southern History* (Baton Rouge: Louisiana State University Press, 1968), 6.

5. Irene Curtis, "Christ the Answer in City Streets," Program, *RS*, February 1949, 26–36.

6. Douglas A. Sweeney, *The American Evangelical Story: A History of the Movement* (Grand Rapids: Baker, 2005), 172–75.

7. Harrell, *Unto a Good Land*, 1044.

8. Myrtle Creasman, "Evangelical Witness to the World," Program, *RS*, April 1946, 23.

9. Gerald H. Anderson, "American Protestants in Pursuit of Mission: 1886–1986," in *Missiology: An Ecumenical Introduction: Texts and Contexts of Global Christianity*, ed. Frans J. Verstraelen et al. (Grand Rapids: Eerdmans, 1995), 400.

10. Joel A. Carpenter and Wilbert R. Shenk, eds., *Earthen Vessels: American Evangelicals and Foreign Missions, 1880–1980* (Grand Rapids: Eerdmans, 1990), xii–xiv.

11. Jesse C. Fletcher, *The Southern Baptist Convention: A Sesquicentennial History* (Nashville: Broadman & Holman, 1994), 179–218.

12. "In the Heart of District 48," *RS*, January 1962, 26.

13. Mark A. Noll et al., eds., *Eerdmans' Handbook to Christianity in America* (Grand Rapids: Eerdmans, 1983), 464.

14. William R. Estep, *Whole Gospel—Whole World: The Foreign Mission Board of the Southern Baptist Convention, 1845–1995* (Nashville: Broadman & Holman, 1994), 277–78.

15. "Pioneer Missions in 30 States," *RS*, May 1960, 1.

16. Mrs. Ralph Smith, "Aiming High," Program, *RS*, February 1951, 29; S. F.

Lowe, "Use Your Baptist Hour," *RS*, May 1947, 7; Alma Hunt, "Woman's Missionary Union and Baptist Jubilee Advance Plans," *RS*, July 1958, 6–8; George W. Schroeder, "Free Men through the Ages," *RS*, September 1957, 14–15.

17. "S.B.C. Coordinated Denominational Activities for 1947," *RS*, January 1947, 30–31; Mrs. Louis L. Dabney, "Worship through Intercessory Prayer," Circle Program or for Second WMS Meeting, *RS*, November 1964, 24.

18. "Laborers Together in Our Denomination," Program, *RS*, May 1948, 21.

19. Mrs. Clyde V. Hickerson, "The Perils of Prosperity," *YB 1947*, 53.

20. M. Theron Rankin, "You Can Find Yourself in the Lottie Moon Christmas Offering Goal," *RS*, November 1949, 1–2.

21. Carrie U. Littlejohn, Call to Prayer, *RS*, May 1960, 17.

22. Mrs. Marse Grant, Call to Prayer, *RS*, June 1962, 24.

23. I. N. Patterson, "On the Threshold," *RS*, July 1965, 3.

24. Mrs. R. L. Mathis, "Labourers Together, Writing a New Chapter," *RS*, February 1959, 40.

25. Alma Hunt, "Report of Executive Secretary," Minutes, Executive Board, WMU, May 16, 1964, 110, WMUA.

26. Catherine Allen, *Laborers Together with God: 22 Great Women in Baptist Life* (Birmingham: WMU, 1987), 203.

27. Allen, *Century to Celebrate*, 224.

28. Minutes, Executive Board, WMU, September 6, 1956, 116, WMUA.

29. "The Tasks of Woman's Missionary Union in a Church," *RS*, July 1964, inside front cover.

30. Elaine Dickson, "WMU . . . Helping the Church Fulfill Its Mission," Circle Program or for Second WMS Meeting, *RS*, August 1964, 28.

31. Alma Hunt, "A New Leaf," *RS*, October 1964, 7.

32. Page Smith, *Daughters of the Promised Land: Women in American History* (Boston: Little, Brown, 1970), 298.

33. William H. Chafe, "The Paradox of Progress," in *Our American Sisters: Women in American Thought and Life*, ed. Jean E. Friedman and William G. Shade (Boston: Allyn and Bacon, 1982), 567.

34. Betty Friedan, *The Feminine Mystique* (New York: W. W. Norton, 1963), 18.

35. Dorothy Thompson, "Occupation—Housewife," *Ladies' Home Journal*, March 1949, 11. See also Flowers, *Into the Pulpit*, 42, and Nancy A. Walker, *Women's Magazines, 1940–1960: Gender Roles and the Popular Press* (Boston: Bedford/St. Martin's, 1998).

36. Mrs. C. D. Creasman, "The Christian Home, Our Immediate Task," Program, *RS*, March 1948, 19.

37. Deane Maynard, "The Multitudes Need Christian Homes," Program, *RS*, May 1952, 25.

38. Gilbert L. Guffin, "The Kingdom Is Coming, O Tell Ye the Story," Bible Study, *RS*, December 1965, 13.

39. Mrs. W. J. Cox, "How Far Is It to Bethlehem?" Program, *RS*, December 1954, 38.

40. P. K. Dagadu, "God Works through Families," *RS*, May 1957, 13.

41. Ethalee Hamric, quoted in Catherine Allen, "Where's Ethalee?" *RS*, October 1969, 7.

42. Anne Crittendon Martin, "*The Recovery of Family Life* by Elton and Pauline Trueblood," New Books to Read, *RS*, April 1954, 13; Mrs. J. Winston Pearce, "Our Witness Begins at Home," *RS*, May 1966, 13.

43. George Lewis Bailes, "Housing Shortage or Home Shortage?" *RS*, June 1950, 11.

44. Mrs. Roswell E. Owens, Call to Prayer, *RS*, May 1963, 32.

45. *RS*, May 1949, 3.

46. Mrs. C. D. Creasman, "The Christian Home, Our Immediate Task," Program, *RS*, March 1948, 23; Mrs. Howard Butt, "Except the Lord Build the House," *RS*, February 1958, 9.

47. "Life Committed," *RS*, April 1961, inside front cover.

48. Dana L. Robert, "What Happened to the Christian Home? The Missing Component of Mission Theory," *Missiology* 33, no. 3 (July 2005): 332–33.

49. Mrs. M. Theron Rankin, "Why I Volunteered for Mission Service," *RS*, November 1946, 6.

50. Roberta E. Hampton, "Baker J. Cauthen: Man of Prayer," *RS*, November 1965, 1.

51. Is This Your Question? *RS*, January 1950, 15.

52. Emily K. Lansdell, "Many Kinds of Preparation," W.M.U. Training School, *RS*, February 1952, 22.

53. Mrs. Milton Tyler, "Stewardship, Ways in Which Women Can Tithe," *RS*, May 1948, 6; Mrs. Howard Butt, "Except the Lord Build the House," *RS*, February 1958, 11; Reitha Hight Coggins, "Am I My Brother's Keeper?" Program, *RS*, March 1950, 27.

54. Mrs. Ernest H. Pierce, "The Missionary Home," Circle Program, *RS*, April 1960, 38.

55. William L. Stidger, *RS*, May 1952, 19. See also Matthew 5:3–12.

56. Elaine Dickson, "Here's How *Royal Service* Subscribers Look in Statistics," *RS*, June 1965, 10.

57. Ruth Latuille Matthews, "Tell Me about God," Why, Mommy? *RS*, July 1948, 14.

58. Marjorie Lou Stump, "There Is a Child Here," *RS*, February 1963, 24–25.

59. Charles Wells, "The Mothers Men Remember," *RS*, May 1956, 36.

60. Virgil McMillan, "An Open Letter to Baptist Mothers," *RS*, June 1955, 5.

61. "Ten Commandments for Modern Parents," *RS*, March 1954, 24; "A Real Home," *RS*, May 1957, 37; Sibyl B. Townsend, "Broken Cisterns," Program, *RS*, May 1957, 33.

62. Joe W. Burton, "A Family Altar Campaign," *RS*, March 1949, 15.

63. "A Family Worshiping Together," The WMU Leader, *RS*, December 1967, 61; Hermione Dannelly Jackson, "Christian Worship in the Family," At Your Circle Meeting, *RS*, February 1958, 40.

64. Helen Fling, "Spiritual Life Development," *RS*, March 1963, 4; Anne Crittendon Martin, "Happily Ever After," *RS*, January 1949, 4; Mrs. Joe W. Burton, "The Family Altar—a Cornerstone for the Christian Home," *RS*, May 1949, 11; Charles A. Wells, "Parental Love Is Not Enough," *RS*, May 1955, 25.

65. Sue Smith, "The Stronghold of Family Life," *RS*, June 1965, 32.

66. Joe W. Burton, "Women and Family Worship," *RS*, April 1949, 13.

67. Mrs. Pat Clendinning, "My Family: Witnessing to Each Other," Circle Program or for Second WMS Meeting, *RS*, April 1966, 30.

68. Mary Essie Stephens, "Christ in You, the Hope of Glory," Week of Prayer for Foreign Missions, *RS*, December 1958, 87.

69. Mrs. Lamar Jackson, "Combining Our Missions Gifts," Circle Program, *RS*, August 1959, 28–30.

70. Mrs. Lamar Jackson, "Measure Your Success at Enlisting Women in Missions," In Your Circle, *RS*, January 1959, 25.

71. Alice Routh, "On My Pantry Shelf," *RS*, May 1953, 6; Alice Routh, "Names from My Pantry Shelf," *RS*, August 1953, 10; Alice Routh, "Coffee Time," *RS*, September 1953, 17.

72. Henry Drummond, "To Make Homes," *RS*, May 1949, 28.

73. Mrs. Pat Clendinning, "My Family: Witnessing to Other Families," Circle Program or for Second WMS Meeting, *RS*, May 1966, 31.

74. "Your Family in Mission Action," *RS*, May 1966, 19.

75. Ibid.

76. Howard Lucas, "Family Witnessing: Unlimited Possibilities," *RS*, June 1966, 29.

77. Mrs. C. J. Burress, "Missions and Salt," *RS*, January 1956, 8–9.

78. Mrs. Dorothy Smith, "Two Circles That Grew into Two Churches," *RS*, March 1950, inside back cover.

79. George L. Ewting, "Out of the Mouths of Boys," *RS*, February 1966, 9.

80. Sara Hines Martin, "Are Home Missionaries Needed?" Circle Study or Second WMS Meeting, *RS*, March 1967, 30–31.

81. Juanita Morrill Wilkinson, "A Study of Major Cults: The Mormons," Circle Program or for Second WMS Meeting, *RS*, July 1966, 31.

82. George and Irene Bark, "We Went Home Again!" *RS*, March 1967, 4.

83. Mrs. C. D. Creasman, "The Christian Home, Our Immediate Task," Program, *RS*, March 1948, 24.

84. Mrs. George E. Davis, "Eleven Thanksgiving Baskets," Community Missions, *RS*, November 1949, 19.

85. Mrs. B. Lloyd Parsons, "Arise, and Go into the City," Week of Prayer for Home Missions, *RS*, March 1963, 57.

86. Henry Drummond, "To Make Homes," *RS*, May 1949, 28.

87. Carol Hunt, "The Glorious Years," *RS*, June 1960, 8.

88. Edna Frances Dawkins, "The Missions Volunteer in My Church," *RS*, May 1956, 5.

89. "Do You 'Foster' a Missionary Family in Your Own Home?" *RS*, June 1957, inside back cover; Mrs. A. L. Aulick, "On the Rock or on the Rocks?" Program, *RS*, June 1950, 30; Mrs. Davis C. Woolley, "Family Worship at Our House," *RS*, April 1960, 8; Carolyn Rhea, "With Songs in Our Hearts," *RS*, November 1966, 9; Victor and Joan Varner, "What Is Missionary Education?" Circle Program or for Second WMS Meeting, *RS*, January 1966, 32; Mrs. Ralph Gwin, "Missionaries Are Needed," Program, *RS*, April 1962, 25.

90. Sue Smith, "The Stronghold of Family Life," *RS*, June 1965, 33.

91. Mrs. Lamar Jackson, "Heralds of the King," Week of Prayer for Foreign Missions, *RS*, December 1964, 52.

92. Robert A. Watts, "Preparing Youth to Hear God's Call: Children Need Parental Guidance," *RS*, May 1964, 15. See 1 Samuel 3:1–18.

93. Alta Lee Lovegren, "Her Parents Failed Her—and God," *RS*, June 1957, 18 19.

94. "Is God Calling Your Son or Daughter?" *RS*, March 1961, 8–11.

95. Deane Gregory Maynard, "The Multitudes Need Christian Homes," *RS*, May 1952, 26–30; Sibyl B. Townsend, "Broken Cisterns," Program, *RS*, May 1957, 34; Mrs. L. F. Maynard, ed., "I Remember Mother," *RS*, May 1957, 2–3.

96. Nina Holaday Gunn, "A Mother's Answered Prayer," *RS*, February 1952, 8–9; Mrs. Lee Dorrough, "My Second Son Is a Missionary Doctor," *RS*, June 1957, 1; Mrs. Tom M. McCullough, "Our Daughter Is a Missionary," *RS*, June 1949, 6–7.

97. Mrs. E. A. Gillis, "Christ in Your Home," *RS*, May 1950, 2.

98. Sadie T. Crawley, "My Son Is a Missionary," *RS*, January 1949, 1–2.

99. Mrs. Claud Bumpus, "Dollies by the Dozens," *RS*, December 1956, 12.

100. Unnamed missionary, quoted in Rosalee Mills Appleby, Call to Prayer, *RS*, April 1964, 20.

101. "8 Missionary Couples in Pakistan," *RS*, June 1962, 9.

102. Louise Woolfolk, "A Real Missionary Home," *RS*, September 1951, 13.

103. Martha Skelton, "Women in Foreign Missions," *Commission*, January 1985, 21.

104. Mrs. Lamar Jackson, "Carest Thou Not?" Program, *RS*, June 1960, 34.

105. Ibid.

106. Mrs. Andrew Coltharp, "Tidings of Redemption," Week of Prayer for Foreign Missions, *RS*, December 1961, 57.

107. Carolyn Rhea, "The Lord's Song in a Strange Land," Program, *RS*, January 1959, 34.

108. A. Clark Scanlon, "Christianity Is a Family Affair," *RS*, March 1957, 10–11.

109. June Petty, "A Dream Fulfilled," *RS*, November 1960, 28.

110. "It Takes Christian Living," *RS*, September 1951, 10; Maude B. Dozier, "Things Don't Just Happen," *RS*, January 1949, 7; Mrs. Lamar Jackson, "Children of the King," Week of Prayer for Foreign Missions, *RS*, December 1964, 59.

111. Georgia Mae Ogburn, "More Stimulating than Tea," *RS*, May 1964, 30.

112. "8 Missionary Couples in Pakistan," *RS*, June 1962, 8–11.

113. Mrs. James Stertz, "Songs in the Night," *RS*, August 1959, 35; Mrs. Mickey R. Johnston, Call to Prayer, *RS*, November 1962, 20.

114. Saxon Rowe Carver, Call to Prayer, *RS*, May 1958, 30; Hannah Reynolds, Call to Prayer, *RS*, October 1961, 18–19.

115. Gertrude Tharpe, "Hawaii Convention Leadership," *RS*, May 1959, 5; Kate Ellen Gruver, "We Proclaim Christ," Week of Prayer for Home Missions, *RS*, March 1964, 42.

116. "What Else Do Missionaries Do?" *RS*, April 1958, 26–27; *RS*, January 1954, front cover.

117. Mrs. C. D. Creasman, "Sixty Years in Royal Service," Program, *RS*, January 1948, 24.

118. Edith Stokely, "To Community Missions Chairmen," Hints to Committee Chairmen, *RS*, November 1952, 19.

119. Mrs. William McMurry, "Did You Read It?" *RS*, April 1961, 18; "Report of Resolutions Committee," *WMUAR 1957*, 97; W. Earl Hotalen, "Ten Effective Strategies against Liquor Evils," *RS*, March 1948, 5.

120. Mrs. C. D. Creasman, "Living Up to Our Moral Standards," Program, *RS*, June 1946, 21; Mrs. Joe W. Burton, "The Continuing Price of Freedom," Program, *RS*, July 1951, 26.

121. Marjorie Moore Armstrong, "Choosing the Most Excellent Way," Program, *RS*, October 1952, 29.

122. Charles A. Wells, "Two Ways to Stop Crime," *RS*, May 1957, 34.

123. Mrs. C. D. Creasman, "The World Significance of Justice and Cooperation among the Races of the South," Program, *RS*, May 1946, 20.

124. Leon Macon, "The Segregation Problems," *AB*, March 8, 1956.

125. Ephesus Baptist Church, "Preserve Segregation," Resolutions, *RH*, February 3, 1955.

126. Davis Lee, "The Negro in the South," *AB*, September 3, 1964; W. H. Prescott, "Letter to the Editor," *BS*, March 29, 1961.

127. Saxon Rowe Carver, "Anna's Journey in Understanding," *RS*, September 1961, 15; Jonnabelle Truitt, "Interracial Justice," *YB 1949*, 69.

128. Katharine Parker Freeman, "Christ the Answer to Racial Tension," *RS*, March 1949, 26.

129. Helen Fling, interview by Catherine Allen, February 14, 1985, transcript, tape 104, page 12, WMUA.

130. Mrs. William McMurry, "When Your Circle Studies *The Bible and Race* by T. B. Maston," *RS*, April 1962, 17.

131. Mrs. Bradley Allison, "Race Relations—Determining Factor in World Missions," Program, *RS*, September 1964, 37.

132. Mary R. McCormick, "Saviour for the Negro in Africa and in America," Program, *RS*, September 1948, 25.

133. Ross Coggins, "The Ins and Outs of Race Prejudice," *RS*, September 1964, 6.

134. Mrs. Frank W. Chase, "A Wise Man out of the East," *RS*, December 1951, 10.

135. Olive Powell, "Field Work—an Avenue of Growth," Training School, *RS*, August 1946, 12.

136. Mrs. C. W. Moseley, "Claiming Opportunities in the Master's Name," Community Missions, *RS*, February 1948, 6.

137. Mrs. John M. McGinnis, "Jack and Jill Go up the Hill," *RS*, March 1951, 9–11; Mrs. Fred Watts, "They Learned to Lead," *RS*, February 1954, 4–5; Eva Berry, "Together in Missouri," *RS*, March 1950, 8–9; Hermione Dannelly Jackson, "Our Ministry to Other Races and Nationalities," Circle Program, *RS*, June 1958, 15; Sam Olive McGinnis, "The Harvest Is Right at Hand," *RS*, February 1955, 4–6.

138. John LaFarge, *The Race Question and the Negro* (New York: Longmans, Green, and Co., 1943), 149; Allen, *Century to Celebrate*, 253.

139. Mary Christian, Business Women's Circles, *RS*, June 1947, 17.

140. Mrs. C. D. Creasman, "The World Significance of Justice and Cooperation among the Races of the South," Program, *RS*, May 1946, 23.

141. Mrs. Chester F. Russell, "A Newly-Given Freedom," *RS*, August 1954, 21.

142. See especially the unsigned letter "A Comment to Ponder," We Get Letters, *RS*, April 1964, 28; and letters of response in subsequent issues.

143. Lucy Grace, "Reflections," *RS*, March 1949, 1.

144. Mrs. William McMurry, "Our Freedoms," *RS*, June 1963, 13.

145. We Get Letters, *RS*, December 1963, 10.

146. Mrs. William McMurry, "Attitude Test," Hints to Committee Chairmen, *RS*, February 1952, 19.

147. John H. Cross, "Birmingham, 1967," *RS*, July 1967, 9, 43.

148. Mrs. Bradley Allison, "Race Relations—Determining Factor in World Missions," Program, *RS*, September 1964, 37.

149. Alma Hunt, interview by Catherine Allen, August 28, 1984, transcript, tape 14, page 144, WMUA.

150. Mary R. McCormick, "Saviour for the Negro in Africa and in America," Program, *RS*, September 1948, 28–29; Katharine Parker Freeman, "Christ the Answer to Racial Tension," *RS*, March 1949, 27; John E. Mills, "Are You Helping?" *RS*, June 1956, 15; Ross Coggins, "Race Relations Sunday," *RS*, February 1965, inside back cover.

151. Mrs. W. B. Pittard Jr., "Liberty and Justice for All," Program, *RS*, July 1952, 27.

152. Fling interview transcript, tape 103, page 41, WMUA.

153. Alan Scot Willis, *All According to God's Plan: Southern Baptist Missions and Race, 1945–1970* (Lexington: University Press of Kentucky, 2004), 158–59; Emily K. Lansdell, Carver School, *RS*, May 1954, 16.

154. *SBCA 1964*, 88–89; *SBCA 1965*, 244–47.

155. Mrs. Ralph Gwin, "Developing Race Relations," Study in Circle or Second WMS Meeting, *RS*, June 1967, 44.

156. T. B. Maston, "Southern Baptists and the Negro," *Home Life*, September 1966, 38.

157. Chafe, "Paradox of Progress," 567.

158. Juliette Mather, "Women, Convention Privileges of," in *Encyclopedia of Southern Baptists* (Nashville: Broadman Press, 1958), 544.

159. Charles Wells, "The Mothers Men Remember," *RS*, May 1956, 36.

160. Billie Pate, "Girls in Gray Flannel," *RS*, February 1965, 14–15; Annie Averett, "Business Women's Circles, the Challenge of W.M.S.," *YB 1946*, 46.

161. Mrs. Edgar Godbold, "Why Not a Community Missions Day?" Community Missions, *RS*, November 1946, 12.

162. Margaret Bruce, "Who Is She?" *RS*, January 1959, inside front cover, 2.

163. Alma Hunt, "In Step with the Times," *RS*, September 1958, 1. See, for example, BWC Exchange, *RS*, November 1953, 21.

164. Ethalee Hamric, "What Am I?" *RS*, September 1962, 9.

165. Helen Fling, "Maximum Christian Service," *RS*, April 1963, inside front cover.

166. Margaret Bruce, "The Challenge of Changing Times," *RS*, April 1963, 41.

167. Fling, "Maximum Christian Service."

168. George L. Bark, "God Needs Women," *RS*, August 1965, 5.

169. Marie Mathis, "President's 75th Anniversary Message," *WMUAR 1963*, 43.

## Chapter 5

1. Kathryn Bullard, "Women on the Go," *RS*, June 1970, 38.

2. Ethalee Hamric, "Day by Day—Living, an Editorial," *RS*, January 1968, 1.

3. Rosalyn Baxandall and Linda Gordon, "Second-Wave Feminism," in *A Companion to American Women's History*, ed. Nancy A. Hewitt (Malden, MA: Blackwell, 2002), 415.

4. John D. Mandle, *Women and Social Change in America* (Princeton, NJ: Princeton Book, 1979), 174.

5. Rochelle Gatlin, *American Women since 1945* (Jackson: University Press of Mississippi, 1987), 47.

6. Sarah Frances Anders, "Baptist Women Walking Together in America, 1950–2000," *BHH* 40, no. 3 (Summer/Fall 2005): 12.

7. H. Leon McBeth, *Women in Baptist Life* (Nashville: Broadman Press, 1979), 71; Marguerite Woodruff, *Critical Issues: Women in Church and Society* (Nashville: CLC, 1982), 13.

8. Elaine Magalis, "Celebration of Women in Ministry," *Response*, July/August 1978, 26–39; Letty Russell, "Adam's Rib or the Singer of the Magnificat? What Is Woman in the Biblical Tradition?" *Concern*, September 1976, 9–12.

9. Carole Maines, "Missionary Wives: Underused Asset," *Evangelical Missions Quarterly* 19, no. 4 (October 1983): 290–95.

10. Joyce M. Bowers, "Roles of Married Women Missionaries: A Case Study," *International Bulletin of Missionary Research* 8, no. 1 (January 1984): 7. Bowers's research focused on a study conducted during 1980 and 1981.

11. Patricia J. Mortenson, "The Role of Women in Missions," *Gospel in Context* 2, no. 2 (April 1979): 29.

12. "Chicago Declaration of Evangelical Social Concern," Evangelicals for Social Action, http://www.evangelicalsforsocialaction.org/chicago-declaration-of-evangelical-social-concern (accessed October 19, 2013).

13. McBeth, *Women in Baptist Life*, 148.

14. C. Anne Davis, "Liberation, Not Separation," *R&E* 72, no. 1 (Winter 1975): 63.

15. Fletcher, *Southern Baptist Convention*, 225–26.

16. H. Leon McBeth, "The Ordination of Women," *R&E* 78, no. 4 (Fall 1981): 515–30.

17. McBeth, *Women in Baptist Life*, 135.

18. Christine Gregory, interview by Catherine Allen, November 19, 1984, transcript, tape 32, page 32, WMUA.

19. Pamela R. Durso, "American Baptist Polity and the Inclusion-Exclusion of Women, 1639–2004," in *Walking Together: The Struggle of Baptists with Polity in the 21st Century* (Richmond, VA: Center for Baptist Heritage and Studies, 2005), 71.

20. McBeth, "Role of Women," 25.

21. Rogers, "God's Chief Assignment," 3, 9.

22. Clay Price, "A Survey of Southern Baptist Attitudes toward Women in Church and Society" (master's thesis, West Georgia College, 1978).

23. Indy Whitten, "Unused Potential," *Commission*, November 1974, 12–13; Edna Frances Dawkins, "Some Remarkable Achievers," *Commission*, November 1974, 34–35.

24. George Sheridan, "Tremors of Change," *HM*, May 1972, 26–31; Jim Newton, "Beyond the Barriers," *HM*, May 1972, 32.

25. See Susan M. Shaw, "Of Words and Women: Southern Baptist Publications and the Progress of Women in the 1970s," *BHH* 42, no. 2 (Spring 2007): 69–84.

26. "Resolution on the Place of Women in Christian Service," *SBCA 1973*, 87.

27. *SBCA 1974*, 209–10.

28. Johnni Johnson, ed., *Findings of the Consultation on Women in Church-Related Vocations* (Birmingham: Southern Baptist Convention Inter-Agency Council, 1978), 3.

29. Sarah O. Maddox, interview by Elizabeth Flowers, May 25, 2006, cited in Elizabeth Flowers, *Into the Pulpit: Southern Baptist Women and Power since World War II* (Chapel Hill: University of North Carolina Press, 2012), 77.

30. "Resolution on the Role of Women," *SBCA 1980*, 54; "Resolution No. 13—On the Role of Women," *SBCA 1981*, 53.

31. "Resolution on Women," *SBCA 1983*, 71.

32. Libby Bellinger, "More Hidden than Revealed: The History of Southern Baptist Women in Ministry," in *Struggle for the Soul of the SBC: Moderate Responses to the Fundamentalist Movement*, ed. Walter B. Shurden (Macon, GA: Mercer University Press, 1993), 129–50.

33. "Chicago Statement on Biblical Inerrancy," Internet Christian Library, http://www.iclnet.org/pub/resources/text/history/chicago.stm.txt (accessed October 19, 2013).

34. Jerry Falwell, *Listen, America!* (Garden City, NY: Doubleday, 1980), 221–23.

35. Elisabeth Elliot, *Let Me Be a Woman: Notes on Womanhood for Valerie* (Wheaton, IL: Tyndale House Publishers, 1976); Marabel Morgan, *The Total Woman* (Old Tappan, NJ: F. H. Revell, 1973).

36. Robert C. Liebman, Robert Wuthnow, and James L. Guth, *The New Christian Right: Mobilization and Legitimation* (Hawthorne, NY: Aldine, 1983), 119; Grady C. Cothen, *What Happened to the Southern Baptist Convention? A Memoir of the Controversy* (Macon, GA: Smyth & Helwys, 1993), 40.

37. This book uses the term "conservatives" to describe Southern Baptists aligned with this contingent and "moderates" to describe their opponents in the SBC controversy. This reflects the language each group most frequently used to describe itself.

38. Toby Druin, "Groups Meet in 15 States to Push SBC President," *BP*, May 9, 1979.

39. Pressler, quoted in Tom Miller, "Committee Appointments the Key," *RH*, September 18, 1980.

40. Cecil Sherman, "An Overview of the Moderate Movement," in Shurden, *Struggle for the Soul*, 21.

41. Dan Martin, "Doctrinal Unity, Program Unity Rise, Fall Together, Rogers Says," *BP*, May 14, 1982. See Exodus 32:1–4.

42. See Flowers, *Into the Pulpit*.

43. Carolyn Weatherford, "Executive Director's Message," *WMUAR 1979*, 4.

44. Allen, *Laborers Together with God*, 215.

45. Gregory interview transcript, tape 32, page 25, WMUA.

46. Allen, *Century to Celebrate*, 340.

47. Gregory interview transcript, tape 32, page 26, WMUA.

48. Ibid., page 35.

49. Gertrude Tharpe, "From the Editor's Pen," *RS*, May 1983, inside front cover.

50. Marty Bibbee, "A Day in the Life of the *Royal Service* Artist," *RS*, June 1977, 9; Catherine Allen, "The *Royal Service* Girls," *RS*, October 1973, 14.

51. Hunt interview transcript, tape 14, page 144, WMUA; Laurella Owens, interview by James Jay Kieve, November 13, 1995, cited in James Jay Kieve, "The Formation of a Moderate Identity: Efforts of the 1970s Woman's Missionary Union" (master's thesis, Duke University, 1995), 21.

52. Catherine Allen, interview by James Jay Kieve, November 15, 1995, cited in Kieve, "Moderate Identity," 21.

53. Carolyn Weatherford Crumpler, "'Yes, Lord, I'll Go,'" in *Courage and Hope: The Stories of Ten Baptist Women Ministers*, ed. Pamela R. Durso and Keith E. Durso (Macon, GA: Mercer University Press, 2005), 47.

54. Aline Fuselier, "Who, Me?" *C*, April 1973, inside back cover.

55. B. Joyce Clayton, "Woman's Psalm," *RS*, March 1974, 31; "The Woman's Hymn," *C*, June 1978, 35.

56. Irma Cruse, "The Woman in West Africa: Dowries to Motorbikes," *RS*, April 1978, 7; Jeanie Tharpe, "*Contempo* Interview: Christian Women of Other Countries," *C*, January 1981, 9.

57. Lawrence Webb, "People Called Women," *C*, October 1975, 7.

58. "Preface to Study and Action," *RS*, May 1970, 15; Katharine Bryan, "The 'Unordinary' Woman," *RS*, November 1975, 23; "I Am Free," *RS*, February 1977, front cover; Mera C. Hall, "How Women Cope with Crises," Round Table Group, *RS*, May 1983, 27.

59. Rebecca Thompson, "Bright Light," *C*, June 1981, 33.

60. Fern Neiger, "Woman Aware: Response," *RS*, November 1970, 23.

61. Webb, "People Called Women," 7.

62. "Woman's Missionary Union Auxiliary to Southern Baptist Convention Response to Consultation on Women in Church-Related Vocations," Consultation on Women in Church-Related Vocations, vertical file, WMUA.

63. William M. Pinson Jr., "The Impact of Missions," Bible Study Group, *C*, March 1974, 33; Jennifer Anderson, "Women Who Walk Boldly," *C*, February 1981, 16.

64. Lawrence Webb, "Women of Faith and Action: Jochebed," Bible Study Group, *C*, October 1974, 34; Fayly H. Cothern, "Shaping My Personal Mission: Marriage and God's Call," *C*, July 1978, 18; Lawrence Webb, "Women of Faith and Action: The Woman at the Well," Bible Study Group, *C*, May 1975, 36.

65. Margaret Lawrence Crawley, "Priscilla and Aquila: Spiritual Guides, Helpers," Life-Changers in the Bible, *RS*, August 1983, 14; Lawrence Webb, "Women of Faith and Action: Priscilla," Bible Study Group, *C*, August 1975, 32.

66. Hubert L. Drumwright Jr., "Women, Women, and More Women!" Bible Study Group, *RS*, October 1970, 37–39.

67. Velma Darbo Brown, "Growing in Self-Worth and Integrity," Bible Study Group, *RS*, November 1977, 35; Ruth McRoberts Ward, "Uniquely Yours," *C*, November 1981, 21.

68. Baptist Young Women of Lawson Baptist Church, "More about Women," Mailbox, *C*, March 1976, inside back cover.

69. Ethalee Hamric, "How It All Began," *C*, August 1980, 7; Lynette Guy Williamson, "Missionary Women," *C*, October 1976, 8.

70. Williamson, "Missionary Women," 6.

71. Carolyn Weatherford, "To Today's Annie: Go Forward!" *RS*, March 1981, 3; Lynn Madison Barrett, A Cool Drink of Water, *RS*, December 1974, 16.

72. "*Contempo* Interview: Carolyn Weatherford," *C*, October 1978, 23; Carolyn Weatherford, "A Past to Remember . . . A Future to Mold," *RS*, July 1976, inside front cover.

73. Mary Harrison, "Because Someone Walked There First," *C*, May 1982, 30.

74. Martha Nelson, "American Women in Missions History," Baptist Women Meeting, *RS*, February 1976, 21.

75. "New, Missioning Women," *C*, October 1972, front cover.

76. Nancy Carter, "As a Woman and an Asian," Woman of the Baptist World, *RS*, October 1976, 9.

77. Bede Jeffords, quoted in Jacqueline Durham, "Barbara 'Bede' Bedenbaugh Jeffords," She's a Baptist Woman Too, *RS*, June 1980, 28–30.

78. Jacqueline Durham, "Sarah Frances Anders," She's a Baptist Woman Too, *RS*, January 1980, 18–19; Jacqueline Durham, "Martha Layne Collins," She's a Baptist Woman Too, *RS*, November 1980, 22–24; Jacqueline Durham, "Barbara Maxey," She's a Baptist Woman Too, *RS*, March 1981, 42–44; Jacqueline Durham, "Deen Day," She's a Baptist Woman Too, *RS*, May 1981, 36–38; Jacqueline Durham, "Natalie Simmons Roumain," She's a Baptist Woman Too, *RS*, November 1981, 38–40.

79. Jacqueline Durham, "Carmen Dorta," She's a Baptist Woman Too, *RS*, September 1980, 25; Jacqueline Durham, "Mary Odell Littlejohn," She's a Baptist Woman Too, *RS*, July 1980, 26; Jacqueline Durham, "Pearl Holmes Duvall," She's a Baptist Woman Too, *RS*, September 1981, 32.

80. Minette Drumwright, "A Baptist Woman—and Proud of It," *RS*, October 1975, inside front cover.

81. Ann Granberry, "The New, Missioning Woman," *C*, May 1973, 1.

82. Joanne Jackson Lisk, "Women at the Crossroads," A Lead on Something to Read, *C*, November 1983, 35.

83. Pansy Webb, "Nice to Know," *C*, March 1977, 50.

84. Ashley White McCaleb, "Women and Their Peers," Round Table Group, *RS*, September 1980, 34; Beth Cole, "Equality and Submission in Marriage," The Book Stops Here, *C*, October 1980, 34; "The Woman I Am," *RS*, July 1976, back cover.

85. Ruth Wagner Miller, "Mother, Daughter, Sister," Reborn Free, *RS*, July 1977, 8.

86. Mary Ann Ward, "A New Women's Issue for Christian Women," *C*, August 1978, 11.

87. Beth Hayworth, Mrs. Henry M. Mims, and Val Harvey, "Woman Aware: Proposed Rights Amendment May Affect Churches and Agencies," Expression, *RS*, September 1971, 21–22.

88. Dorothy Sample, *RS*, September 1981, 2; Linda Lawson, "Free to Be Responsible," On Womanhood, *C*, November 1975, 6.

89. Margie Kirkland, "Are You Worth Rubies?" *C*, June 1977, 24; Helen Fling, "Are You Ready for Tomorrow?" *RS*, October 1968, 12.

90. Marv Knox, "Equal Rights—to Hear the Gospel," *C*, March 1981, 6–10.

91. Aline Fuselier, "Woman Power," *C*, June 1973, back cover; Mary Ann Ward, "A New Women's Issue for Christian Women," *C*, August 1978, 11.

92. Charlie Warren, "Confessions of a Rabble-Rouser: How to Be an Activist," *C*, April 1979, 20–22.

93. Barbara Burkett, "Are You a Successful Woman?" On Womanhood, *C*, March 1976, 10–13.

94. Ibid., 13.

95. Christine Gregory, quoted in Catherine Allen, "WMU Has a New President. Do You Know Her?" *RS*, January 1976, 1.

96. "The World of Church Vocations," *C*, April 1971, inside back cover.

97. Mary Frances Bailey, "You as God's Agent: Don't Be Undercover," Mission Action Group, *C*, April 1982, 31.

98. A. Carl Hart, "Women in the Chaplaincy?" *RS*, April 1980, 25.

99. Linda Lawson, "God Speaks to Women," *C*, May 1980, 3–5.

100. Mary Ann Ward, "You've Got a Lot to Give," *C*, December 1975, 13.

101. M. Wendell Belew, "God's Bold Plan for Women in Home Missions," *RS*, September 1977, 1.

102. Judy Touchton, "Blossoming in Business," *C*, March 1978, 4–5; Nancy Carter McGough, "We Cannot Keep from Telling When People Need Help," Week of Prayer for Home Missions, *C*, March 1980, 30; Phyllis Thompson, "Joanne's Journey into Missions," *RS*, January 1983, 14–15.

103. Belew, "God's Bold Plan for Women in Home Missions," 3.

104. J. Eldon Jones, "Church Extension Associate—a Home Missions Job with 'WOMAN' Written on It," *RS*, March 1976, 41.

105. Elaine Selcraig Furlow, "Women in Missions: Diminishing Opportunities in a Time of Increasing Need," *C*, February 1977, 14.

106. Mrs. G. R. Ferrell, Letters, *RS*, September 1976, 6.

107. Amanda Thompson, Mailbox, *C*, November 1977, inside back cover.

108. Deena Williams Newman, "What Every Woman Needs to Know about Women in Home Missions," *C*, June 1982, 20.

109. Tim Nicholas, "Under the Bell Jar," *C*, April 1975, 7–9.

110. Mrs. Ed Keys, "Ordination of Women," Mailbox, *C*, October 1975, 48.

111. Mary Jane Welch, "Wives Examine Their Assignments," *Commission*, February 1980, 17.

112. As You Pray, *C*, December 1972, 42; Indy Whitten, "I Direct an Echo," Woman of the Baptist World, *RS*, January 1976, 16–17; Sarah Martin Scanlon, "Women in Foreign Missions," What's around the Corner, *C*, May 1982, 11; Ruth Fowler, "Look for That Woman," *C*, January 1977, 22.

113. Richard M. Styles, "A Unique Role: Women on the Board," *C*, December 1976, 42–43.

114. Ruth Fowler, "Case in Point: Take Foreign Missions," *C*, August 1977, 15.

115. Ruth Fowler, "Is It Worth It—for Her?" *RS*, October 1980, 19–20; Alston A. Morgan, "Single Life versus Marriage? There Is No Blueprint for Life," *RS*, October 1971, 7.

116. Elizabeth Swadley, "Redeemed—Rejoice . . . Proclaim in Malaysia," Week of Prayer for Foreign Missions, *RS*, December 1975, 27; June Ridens, Letters, *RS*, September 1976, 6.

117. Theo Sommerkamp, "Just an Ordinary Pastor," *RS*, September 1970, 6–7.

118. Mary Lane Powell, "Response to Mass Communication," *RS*, April 1970, 14–15.

119. William Clemmons, "Occupation Forecast: Working Women in the 70's," *C*, April 1972, 18.

120. Dixie M. Meyer, "Should a Woman with Small Children Work outside the Home?" Readers Speak Out, *RS*, October 1972, 14.

121. Catherine Allen, "Working Married Mothering," *C*, May 1976, 5–7.

122. Teena Andrews, "Womanhood—Opportunities in Careers and Education," On Womanhood, *C*, February 1976, 8–11.

123. Mary D. Bowman, "Have Job, Will Keep It," Tempo, *C*, April 1973, 8.

124. Kay Wheeler Moore, "Can Your Career Lead You Down the Wrong Road?" Directions, *C*, July 1981, 17.

125. Jerilynn Armstrong, "Woman in Sales," Career Connection, *C*, February 1982, 26–27; Phyllis Thompson, "Not Everyone's a Woman Engineer," Career Connection, *C*, July 1982, 28–29.

126. Gertrude A. Tharpe, "First in a Series on Witnessing on Location through Your Vocation," Career Connection, *C*, October 1981, 32–33.

127. Barbara Burkett, "Shaping My Personal Mission: God's Specific Call for My Specific Shape," *C*, June 1978, 10; "A Word about the Energy Crisis (Mine)," *C*, June 1980, 27.

128. Jerilynn Armstrong, "Getting in Gear: How to Serve the Lord through Your Vocation," *C*, December 1980, 12.

129. Kay Wheeler Moore, "Getting in Gear: How to Serve the Lord through Your Vocation—Communications," *C*, March 1981, 16–17.

130. Ibid., 17.

131. Dear Pastor, *RS*, April 1968, inside back cover.

132. Allen, *Century to Celebrate*, 476–77.

133. "Report of WMU Executive Board," *WMUAR 1970*, 24.

134. "*Contempo* Memo," *C*, September 1980, 29.

135. "Should a Woman with Small Children Work outside the Home?" Readers Speak Out, *RS*, May 1968, 14–15.

136. Mrs. Jim Ritter, Mailbox, *C*, August 1976, inside back cover.

137. Baptist Young Women of Memorial Baptist Church, Mailbox, *C*, January 1977, inside back cover; Mrs. Gene Meador, Mailbox, *C*, November 1976, inside back cover.

138. Veteria Billingsley, "To Be Free," Readers React, *C*, October 1971, 19.

139. Vickie Palmer Schull, "Liberation at Home," *C*, October 1976, 3.

140. Sharon Vanskike, Readers React, *C*, February 1972, 15.

141. Catherine Allen, Mailbox, *C*, December 1976, inside back cover.

142. Judy Hix Abercrombie, "Choosing to Stay Home," Career Connection, *C*, January 1982, 20.

143. Deana Blackburn, "The Decision to Marry," *C*, September 1979, 21–22, 32; Deana Blackburn, "Parenthood: To Be or Not to Be," *C*, October 1981, 20–23.

144. Mrs. John T. Rogers, "Environment for Missions," For Study in Society, May 1968, *RS*, 19; Carolyn Weatherford, "Love's Gifts," *C*, May 1975, 7.

145. Ted Lindwall, "Tribute to a Missionary Wife," *RS*, February 1968, 33.

146. Jann Aldredge Clanton, "Mission Possible Now: Dirty Dishes and a Rabbit," Mission Action Group, *RS*, October 1983, 20.

147. Mozelle Fuller, "A Home That Became a Mission," *RS*, July 1970, 10–11.

148. Terry Cutrer, "Use Me, Lord—a Bible Ceremony for the Engaged," *C*, May 1979, 37.

149. Arlene Grove, "'People Called Women' Opinions Differ," Mailbox, *C*, February 1976, inside back cover; Mailbox, *C*, January 1979, inside back cover.

150. Phyllis Merritt, "A Celebration: A Gift Bible Presentation for an Engaged Couple," *C*, May 1978, 35.

151. C. W. Brister, "When Two Become One," *RS*, January 1969, 10.

152. Jim Cox, "Help! I'm a WMU Daddy!" *RS*, May 1978, 31–32.

153. Virginia Pounds Brown, "Single and Human," *RS*, January 1978, 33.

154. Mary Ann Ward, "Am I Boarding a Sinking Ship?" *C*, September 1979, 1.

155. Frances Greenway, quoted in Alston A. Morgan, "Single Life versus Marriage? There Is No Blueprint for Life," *RS*, October 1971, 6.

156. Barbara Burkett, "Discrimination and the Single Woman," *C*, July 1976, 6.

157. Jacqueline Durham, "Barbara Pellici," She's a Baptist Woman Too, *RS*, October 1979, 22.

158. Andrew D. Lester, "Christians and Divorce," Mission Action Group, *RS*, July 1977, 30.

159. Judy Holley, "Persons in Crisis," Mission Action, *RS*, July 1970, 29.

160. Falwell, *Listen, America!* 223.

161. Anne Leavell Mann Collingsworth, "What's a Nice Girl Like You Doing in a World Like This?" *C*, September 1983, 13.

162. Nelda Gann, "Concern about Divorce," Mailbox, *C*, November 1975, inside back cover; Barbara Burkett, "Divorce: Regardless of the Reason," *C*, July 1977, 24.

163. John H. McClanahan, "They're Getting a Divorce," Help Me Meet My Neighbor's Needs, *C*, November 1974, 14.

164. Anne Leavell Mann, "BYW and the Single Girl," *C*, October 1980, 36.

165. "*Contempo* Interview: Christine Gregory," *C*, February 1979, 2.

166. Marie Mathis and Elaine Dickson, *The Woman's Missionary Union Program of a Church* (Nashville: Convention Press, 1966), 50.

167. Alma Hunt, Minutes, Executive Board, WMU, January 24, 1966, 41, WMUA.

168. Elaine Furlow, "Beverly Hammack," Woman of the Baptist World, *RS*, March 1976, 9–11.

169. Helen Fling, "No Time to Be Afraid," *RS*, October 1969, 3.

170. Ann Granberry, "The New, Missioning Woman," *C*, May 1973, 1–3, emphasis in the original.

171. Charles H. Morris, "She Sets the Captives Free," *RS*, August 1974, 10.

172. Barbara Joiner, "Everybody Ought to Know in Honduras," Current Missions Group, *RS*, April 1974, 29.

173. Mrs. Judson LeCroy, "Pros and Cons Have It," *RS*, September 1969, 35.

174. Mildred Blankenship, We Hear from Readers, *RS*, September 1983, 28.

175. Gay Nichols, "A Big A Story," *RS*, August 1980, 28–29; Gerry Aderhold, "I Was a Stranger and You Invited Me In," *RS*, February 1981, 7–9; Sue Bryan, "The State of BYW in Louisiana," *C*, May 1972, 23.

176. Beth Simonton Cole, "Monkeys and Missions," *C*, July 1977, 7.

177. Mary Gene Allison, "Mission Action Possible," *RS*, January 1982, 20.

178. Katharine Bryan, "Working in a Mission Action Group," Train, *C*, February 1975, 22.

179. Gregory interview transcript, tape 32, pages 53–54, WMUA.

180. Fling interview transcript, tape 105, page 27, WMUA.

181. Lane Powell, "Confessions of a Mad Woman," *RS*, February 1973, 14.

182. Baptist Young Women of Main Street Baptist Church, It's Your Turn, *C*, October 1983, 25.

183. Pat Thompson, "My Opportunity . . . Hope for a Nonreader," Current Missions Group, *RS*, March 1971, 51.

184. Nicy Murphy, "So Send I You—to Care," Baptist Women Meeting, *RS*, July 1977, 15.

185. Stuart Calvert, "Involved with One Another," Mission Action Group, *RS*, October 1977, 35.

186. Helen S. Wood, "Strangers in our Midst," *RS*, April 1974, 10; L. William Crews, "Helping the Prisoner and His Family," *RS*, January 1969, 12–14; Ruth Wagner Miller, "Weighed in the Balance: Will Our Garbage Cans Testify against Us at the Day of Judgment?" Baptist Women Meeting, *RS*, July 1978, 5.

187. Fling interview transcript, tape 105, page 18, WMUA.

188. Ruth C. Clark, "Who, Me, Lord?" *RS*, August 1983, 2–3; Lawrence Webb, "Women of Faith and Action: The Shunammite Woman," Bible Study Group, *C*, January 1975, 36–39; Lawrence Webb, "Women of Faith and Action: Dorcas," Bible Study Group, *C*, June 1975, 36–39. See also Matthew 25:34–35.

189. Ann Oliver, "Where Cities Cry," *C*, January 1972, 29–32; Christine Gregory, "Doers of the Word—with Internationals," Life-Changers Today, *RS*, January 1983, 22–24; Joanne L. Legette, "What Can I Do for You Today?" *C*, January 1977, 6–7; Monte Clendinning, "Jesus Gives Guidelines for Ministry," Bible Study, *RS*, June 1974, 33–35.

190. See Judy Touchton, "Born Again—What?" *C*, April 1977, 5; "Born Again! The Year of the Evangelical," *Newsweek*, October 25, 1976, 76; and John 3:1–8.

191. Carolyn Weatherford, "Women and Missions and Woman's Missionary Union," *WMUAR 1975*, 28.

192. Connie Davis, "Square Blocks in Round Holes?" *C*, February 1979, 7.

193. Dale Helmbold, "How to Give Away a Bible," *C*, October 1976, 36.

194. Margaret Bruce, "The Member Shares Her Faith," *RS*, April 1972, 24; Jane Hix, "WMU Has New Tasks," Laser, *C*, July 1975, 47.

195. Amelia Bishop, "Building Relationships," Mission Action Group, *RS*, October 1979, 35.

196. Marjean Patterson, "Evaluating Mission Action," *RS*, July 1973, 17; June Whitlow, "Needed: A Mission Action Group Guide for Your Mission Action Group," *RS*, January 1969, 38.

197. Elaine Dickson, "Test Your Sensitivity-Awareness," *C*, January 1971, 31; Dorothy K. Thompson, "Helps on Helping the Poor," Mission Action, *C*, August 1973, 29.

198. Ellen Dossett, "Helps on Helping Alienated Youth," Mission Action, *C*, December 1972, 38.

199. "Demonstrating Understanding and Acceptance," Mission Action Group, *RS*, March 1973, 54.

200. Peggy J. Wilson, "What It Means to Be in Baptist Young Women," Ripples, *C*, September 1977, 27.

201. Carolyn Weatherford to Catherine Allen, August 29, 1984, WMU History Research, Biographical Files, WMUA.

202. "*Contempo*," *RS*, September 1970, 14.

203. Ruth Wagner Miller, "Bridging the Gap: Christians Reach out to Other Races," Baptist Women Meeting, *RS*, August 1979, 5.

204. John H. McClanahan, "My New Neighbors Are Black," Help Me Meet My Neighbor's Needs, *C*, August 1975, 20; Nell Tyner Bowen, "Together with National Baptists," *C*, February 1971, 25.

205. "In Expressing Christian Convictions: Growing in Race Relations," *C*, June 1975, 2–7.

206. Gladys Bryant, "The Word Is 'With,'" Current Missions Group, *C*, June 1975, 28.

207. David C. George, "You Are All One in Christ Jesus," *RS*, February 1982, 15; Larry Connelly, "Missions—All around You," *C*, June 1975, 8–9; Monte Clendinning, "Racial Understanding through Cooperative Relationships," Baptist Women Meeting, *RS*, February 1971, 31.

208. Joe Pipkin, "I Feel I Must Offer My Life," *C*, September 1971, 12–16.

209. "A Place for You," *RS*, November 1976, 47; Mary Love, "Help Wanted: Baptists Abroad," Baptist Women Meeting, *RS*, September 1979, 15.

210. Karon Owen, "Is Summer Missions for You?" *C*, January 1979, 22.

211. Beth Sayers Wildes, "Clara Pahl: On Mission with Hammer, Nails, and Saw," Sparks, *C*, November 1979, 24; Erich Bridges, "Tani Jill Murrah: On the Snow Chi Minh Trail," Faith Expressed, *C*, January 1980, 24; Anna M. Ackerman Adams, "Anna and the Children of Saigon," *RS*, June 1975, 17.

212. Jack U. Harwell, "Opal Smith," She's a Baptist Woman Too, *RS*, October 1980, 36.

213. Jennie White, "Victory in Marysville," *RS*, April 1981, 14.

214. Gladys Bryan, "Any Family Can," *RS*, April 1981, 13.

215. Lee Greer, "Make a Missions Summer: South Dakota," *RS*, May 1975, 14.

216. Phyllis Ragan, "Take a Family Missions Vacation," Baptist Women Meeting, *RS*, April 1981, 7–8; June P. Carter, "Missionaries for a Summer," Continuations, *RS*, July 1972, 22–23; Phyllis Merritt, "Your Family and Missions," *C*, May 1983, 9.

217. Dear Pastor, *RS*, July 1974, back cover.

218. June H. McEwen, "Home: Time and Place for Missions," Baptist Women Meeting, *RS*, May 1982, 3; Lynn Madison Barrett, A Cool Drink of Water, *RS*, March 1975, 9.

## Chapter 6

1. "Resolution on Ordination and the Role of Women in Ministry," *SBCA 1984*, 65, emphasis added.

2. Interview with former WMU editor, May 28, 2009. This interviewee and two other former editors of WMU women's magazines asked to remain anonymous.

3. Winona Cobb, "Claiming a Personal Ministry," *C*, July 1984, 16.

4. Vicki Knasel Brown, "Evangelizing the World's Women," *C*, June 1987, 13.

5. Harrell, *Unto a Good Land*, 1202.

6. Tom Strode, "Men Confess Sin, Seek Reconciliation at Promise Keepers' 'Sacred Assembly,'" *BP*, October 6, 1997.

7. Ibid.

8. Carol Porter and Mike Hamel, *Women's Ministry Handbook* (Wheaton, IL: Victor Books, 1992).

9. Vickie Kraft, *Women Mentoring Women: Ways to Start, Maintain, and Expand a Biblical Women's Ministry* (Chicago: Moody Press, 1992), 12.

10. Mary Frances Bowley from First Baptist Church of Peachtree City, Georgia, quoted in Terri Lackey, "Relevance, Not Chitchat, Key to Successful Women's Ministry," *BP*, July 21, 1995.

11. Terri Lackey, "Sunday School Board Announces Women's Enrichment Ministry," *BP*, November 5, 1993; "BSSB Women's Consultant to Become Full-Time Role," *BP*, May 6, 1994.

In 1997 the Sunday School Board (SSB) changed its name to LifeWay Christian Resources; the Foreign Mission Board (FMB) changed its name to the International Mission Board (IMB); and the Home Mission Board (HMB) changed its name to the North American Mission Board (NAMB), at the same time gaining a few new assignments. To avoid confusion, this chapter will use the pre-1997 names for these entities.

12. Trudy Johnson, "Women's Ministries: An Overview for WMU," October 1993, 1, WMUA.

13. Jerry Sutton, *The Baptist Reformation: The Conservative Resurgence in the Southern Baptist Convention* (Nashville: Broadman & Holman, 2000), 118.

14. "Report of the Baptist Faith and Message Study Committee," *SBCA 1998*, 77–82.

15. "The Baptist Faith and Message." SBC, http://www.sbc.net/bfm/bfm2000.asp (accessed October 19, 2013).

16. James L. Guth, "Southern Baptist Clergy, the Christian Right, and Political Activism in the South," in *Politics and Religion in the White South*, ed. Glenn Feldman (Lexington: University Press of Kentucky, 2005), 205.

17. Daniel L. Akin, "The Role of Men and Women in the Church," *The Tie* 71, no. 4 (Winter 2003): 8.

18. James C. Hefley, *The Conservative Resurgence in the Southern Baptist Convention* (Hannibal, MO: Hannibal Books, 1991), 321.

19. Pat Cole, "Patterson Suggests Change for WMU," *BP*, March 8, 1988.

20. Carolyn Weatherford to WMU Executive Board members, state executive directors, and staff, March 9, 1988, Carolyn Weatherford Executive Board Letters 1986–89, WMUA.

21. Susan Todd and Karen Benson, "WMU Executive Director Welcomes 'Monitoring,'" *BP*, February 28, 1990.

22. Minutes, General Session of Executive Board, WMU, September 22, 1990, 934–36, WMUA.

23. Dorothy Patterson to Dellanna O'Brien, October 2, 1990, Dellanna O'Brien SBC Convention Controversy, WMUA. Patterson was responding to Weatherford's earlier accusation of "hostage holding" of Cooperative Program funds by some SBC churches.

24. Bee Garris King to Dellanna O'Brien, August 27, 1992, Dellanna O'Brien SBC Convention Controversy, WMUA.

25. Dellanna O'Brien to Cecil Sherman, June 26, 1992, O'Brien Baptist Entities Miscellaneous 1991–1996, WMUA; "Report of the Work of the Committee," Minutes, Executive Board, WMU, June 6, 1992, 975, WMUA.

26. Larry Lewis, "Statement," Minutes, Executive Board, WMU, January 11, 1993, 65, WMUA.

27. "Motion," Executive Committee, SBC, February 17–19, 1992, Dellanna O'Brien SBC Convention Controversy, WMUA.

28. Recording of FMB/WMU Meeting, July 27, 1992, WMUA; Susan Doyle, "FMB, WMU Board Members Meet to Discuss Future," *BP*, July 28, 1992.

29. Dellanna O'Brien to Nat Kellum, December 9, 1992, Dellanna O'Brien SBC Convention Controversy, WMUA.

30. Minutes, Executive Board, WMU, January 9–13, 1993, 51–53, WMUA. While present-day CBF leaders do not consider the organization part of the SBC, in 1993 CBF was still deemed a Southern Baptist group.

31. "Board Report, Woman's Missionary Union," January 13, 1993, WMUA.

32. Recording of FMB/WMU Meeting, February 8, 1993, WMUA; Robert Dilday, "Rogers Says SBC Should Control WMU," *WR*, March 9, 1993; "WMU Called Adulteress, O'Brien Canceled," *WR*, February 2, 1993; "A Resolution of Concern and Commitment on the Woman's Missionary Union and the Southern Baptist Convention," February 23, 1993, Dellanna O'Brien SBC Convention Controversy, WMUA.

33. "Woman's Missionary Union Report," Spring 1993, 1, 3, WMUA.

34. "WMU Taking Vote on Receipt of $100,000 Gift from CBF," *BP*, March 18, 1994.

35. R. Keith Parks to Dellanna O'Brien, March 3, 1994, O'Brien Baptist Entities Miscellaneous 1991–1996, WMUA.

36. Jerry Rankin to Freddie Tatum, May 5, 1994, Dellanna O'Brien SBC Convention Controversy, WMUA.

37. Minutes, Executive Session of Executive Board, WMU, January 11, 1997, 6, WMUA; Teresa Dickens, "Trademarks, National Training Top WMU Executive Board Meeting," *BP*, January 20, 1997; "WMU to Trademark AAEO, License NAMB to Use It," *BP*, February 17, 1998.

38. Catherine Allen, "Unshackle the Servants of God," in *Stand with Christ: Why Missionaries Can't Sign the 2000 Baptist Faith and Message*, ed. Robert O'Brien (Macon, GA: Smyth & Helwys, 2002), 114.

39. Teresa Dickens, "WMU Expands Product Line with CBF-Related Pieces," July 12, 1995, WMUA.

40. Art Toalston, "WMU Expands Product Line with CBF-Related Pieces," *BP*, July 12, 1995; Larry Lewis to Dellanna O'Brien, August 21, 1995, O'Brien Baptist Entities Miscellaneous 1991–1996, WMUA.

41. Jerry Rankin to SBC leaders, August 25, 1995, WMUA.

42. Dellanna O'Brien, "Statement Regarding the Aug. 25 Letter of Dr. Jerry Rankin," O'Brien Baptist Entities—Foreign Mission Board 1989–1996, WMUA.

43. "WMU Special Report," September 13, 1995, WMUA.

44. Minutes, Executive Board, WMU, January 16, 1996, 70, WMUA.

45. Interview with former WMU editor, May 27, 2009.

46. Dorothy Patterson, interview by Barry Hankins, June 8, 1999, transcript, page 34, Baylor University Institute for Oral History, Waco, TX.

47. Sheryl Churchill Lewis, "Some Important People in BYW's Background," *C*, May 1988, 25.

48. Dellanna O'Brien, interview by Elizabeth Flowers, April 25, 2006, cited in Flowers, *Into the Pulpit*, 138.

49. Wilma Reed, "Unique: What Makes WMU Special?" *C*, May 1988, 26.

50. Carolyn Weatherford, "You, Me, and WMU," *C*, March 1986, 33.

51. Louise Barbour, "How to Attend a Southern Baptist Convention," *C*, June 1986, 10–11; Louise Barbour, *Missions and the SBC* (Birmingham: WMU, 1986).

52. "Pray for the Southern Baptist Convention," Ask of Me, *C*, June 1985, 32.

53. Carolyn Weatherford, "See You in Dallas," *RS*, April 1985, 37; Carolyn Weatherford, Atop New Hope Mountain, *RS*, January 1986, 24.

54. Carolyn Weatherford, "Have You Heard about WMU?" *RS*, February 1985, 34; Carolyn Weatherford, "Who Are Women in Ministry?" The Inside Scoop, *C*, April 1985, 26.

55. Dellanna O'Brien, "Auxiliary: A 104-Year-Old Relationship That Has Worked," *RS*, July 1992, 14; Dellanna O'Brien, "Auxiliary: A 104-Year-Old Relationship That Has Worked," *C*, July 1992, 24–25.

56. "Is There a Place for WMU in the 21st Century?" *C*, July 1995, insert; "Is There a Place for WMU in the 21st Century?" *RS*, July 1995, insert.

57. Wanda S. Lee, "A Call to Prayer for Our Baptist Family," From Missionary Ridge, *MM*, April 2004, 48; Wanda S. Lee, "Women around the World Pray Together for Southern Baptists," From Missionary Ridge, *MM*, June 2004, 48.

58. Dellanna O'Brien, "Making a World of Difference," *RS*, June 1993, 26; Dellanna O'Brien, "Making a World of Difference," *C*, June 1993, 41.

59. Dellanna O'Brien to Wayne White, June 26, 1992, Dellanna O'Brien SBC Convention Controversy, WMUA.

60. Joyce Mitchell, "Serving with Grace," *C*, January 1994, 7.

61. "Now What?" *C*, June 1988, 48.

62. Delane Tew, "A Place for You to Serve," WMU Ministry, *MM*, June 2000, 8.

63. Cathy Butler, "Going beyond the Comfort Zone: WMU's International Initiatives," WMU Ministry, *MM*, December 2002, 28.

64. Sammie Jo Barstow, "I Can Help You," Cover Story, *MM*, February 2001, 10–11.

65. Dellanna O'Brien, From Missionary Ridge, *MM*, March 1999, 64.

66. Catherine Allen, "Shifting Sands for Southern Baptist Women in Missions," in *Gospel Bearers, Gender Barriers: Missionary Women in the Twentieth Century*, ed. Dana L. Robert (Maryknoll, NY: Orbis Books, 2002), 125.

67. June Whitlow, "Do You Know This Woman?" *RS*, February 1984, 2.

68. Susan Stinnett, "My First BYW Meeting Was a Life-Changing Experience," *C*, January 1988, 26; Theda Crawford, "Let's Get More Women Involved," Letters, *MM*, September 2004, 4.

69. "Get 18- to 25-Year-Olds Involved in Missions," *MM*, December 1996, E4. For a few years the magazines used letters to designate executive pages.

70. Cindy Lewis Dake, "A Time to Grow," *C*, June 1995, inside front cover.

71. Sue Sprenkle, "Meetings: Let's Grow!" Help for Leaders, *MM*, September 2006, 47.

72. Debra Berry, "Missions Is for All Women!" Insight, *MM*, October 2005, 5.

73. Betty Shoe, "Mighty Women on Mission," Women on Mission, *MM*, December 2000, 6.

74. Edna Ellison, "Ask Edna," *MM*, February 1999, E7.

75. "Celebration Experience: A Place for You," *MM*, October 1995, E7.

76. Arnette E. Smith, "How Important Is the Local Church?" *RS*, September 1989, 3; April M. Heddleston, "Disks, Diapers, and Discipline," *C*, August 1995, 6.

77. Arnette Smith, "What's a Working Woman to Do?" *RS*, October 1986, 36.

78. Vickey Young Brasington, "All in a Day's Work: Missionary Women and

Their Vocations," *C*, July 1984, 18–21; Cindy Lewis Dake, "The Missionary Woman: Competent in Vocation," *C*, May 1990, 14–17.

79. Linda M. Clark, "More than a *Paycheck*," *MM*, August 1996, 48–49.

80. Dorothy Patterson, interview, 31; interview with former WMU editor, May 16, 2009.

81. B. J. Burch Funderburg, "Have Call, Will Travel," Missions and the Single Woman, *C*, September 1984, 20.

82. Joyce Mitchell, "Who Are You Today?" *MM*, November 1995, 16.

83. Dana Ketchum, "Home vs. Work," *MM*, February 2001, 18.

84. Interview with former WMU editor, May 28, 2009.

85. Ibid.

86. "Welcome to Women on Mission!" *MM*, October 1995, 4, emphasis in the original; Linda M. Clark, "Growing to Know You: Growing in Godliness," *RS*, March 1995, H.

87. Minutes, Executive Board, WMU, January 12, 1993, 70, 111–16, WMUA.

88. Pat Lemonds Sullivan, "Bible Study Group Procedures," *RS*, December 1994, K.

89. Andrea Mullins, "Helps for Officers," Planning, *RS*, April 1992, 40.

90. Pat Lemonds Sullivan, "An Unlikely Place for Spiritual Renewal," Panorama of Service, *MM*, October 1997, 31.

91. Amelia Bishop, "One Woman's Library," *RS*, August 1994, 18; "Seeking Sabbath," *MM*, November 1997, E6; Teri Easterling, Books for Your Journey, *MM*, August 1996, 26–27; Jean McLean, "A Heart Like His," Round Table Book Club, *MM*, July 2000, 9.

92. Linda Hood Hicks, "Childless Is Not Less," Bookshelf, *C*, September 1986, 30; "Love Is in the Air," *MM*, November 2006, inside front cover; Laura Williams, "Books for Your Journey," Recommended Reading, *MM*, January 1996, 48.

93. *Magazette*, June 1989, 1.

94. "Helping All Women Find Their Place in Missions," Women's Ministry, *MM*, February 2000, 46.

95. Susan Todd, "'Renewed Commitment to One Purpose' Sets Tone for WMU Board Meeting," *BP*, January 13, 1989.

96. Dellanna O'Brien to Dolores Davis, August 18, 1992, Dellanna O'Brien SBC Convention Controversy, WMUA.

97. "Shirley and the Celebration Experience," *MM*, February 1996, E6.

98. "Why Have Retreats Just for Women?" *MM*, January 2006, 5.

99. "Do You Hunger for the Deep Things of God?" *MM*, July 1997, E27.

100. Caroline Clamp Ward, "Why Pray for Missions?" *C*, October 1987, 10; Randy A. McCollum, "The Touch of the Master's Hand," Bible Study, *MM*, July 2006, 22; "Introduction," *C*, October 1986, 1; Deborah Brunt, "At Home with Bea," Risk Takers, *MM*, December 1995, 28.

101. Frances J. Riley, "What Do You Mean: Lost," Personal Witnessing Group, *RS*, February 1991, 18.

102. Jane Lippy, "Journey of a Lifetime," Round Table Book Club, *MM*, April 2000, 9; Dianne Swaim, "Listening for God's Gentle Whisper," Prayer Patterns, *MM*, November 2006, 31.

103. Jennifer Kennedy Dean, "Heart's Cry Retreat," *RS*, October 1992, 47.

104. Helen Begaye, "My Place among the Stars," Response Willing, *C*, June 1992, 3.

105. Ginny Bridges Ireland, "Role Models Who Reflect God," Bible Study, *C*, November 1992, 21.

106. Debra Berry, "Esther: Woman of Wisdom," Bible Study, *MM*, February 2001, 25–27.

107. Jo Ellen Duke, "Sacrificial Doing—or Not Doing?" *C*, April 1990, 5.

108. Laura Williams, "New Hope, New Future," *MM*, June 1997, 7; Allison Swain Becker, "What Does Your Family Value?" Stewardship, *C*, May 1994, 23.

109. "Christian Women of Excellence," *RS*, July 1992, 24.

110. "Meet the Heartfelt Needs of Women," Women's Ministry, *MM*, November 2000, 46.

111. "A Garden Path to Mentoring," *MM*, April 1997, 33; "Are You Ready for Her to Look Up to You?" *MM*, April 2000, back cover.

112. Cindy Lewis Dake, "More than Pieces in a Puzzle," Biblical Mentoring, *MM*, June 1999, 37; Cindy Lewis Dake, "A Natural Mix: Witnessing and Mentoring," *MM*, July 1999, 37.

113. Porter and Hamel, *Women's Ministry Handbook*, 145; Susan E. Field, "All We Need Is Love: Mentoring by Christ's Example," *MM*, June 1998, 44.

114. Betty Patton Lawson, "The Power and the Presence," Bible Study, *C*, February 1987, 22.

115. Mary Langford, "The Well the Spirit Indwells: Convicted," Bible Study, *C*, January 1991, 17; Cindy Ketron, "The Line That Divides," *C*, November 1993, 6.

116. Mary Langford, "The Well the Spirit Indwells: Consumed," Bible Study, *C*, February 1991, 21.

117. Julia Sims Harris, "Skilled, Willing, and Able," Finding My Place in Ministry, *MM*, May 1996, 17.

118. "The Accountability Factor," *C*, December 1991, back cover.

119. Frances Lee Street, "Gifts Given with Love," BYW Meeting, *C*, September 1993, 9; Dorothy D. Godsoe, "Your Gifts for Service: What Is in Your Hand?" Devotional, *RS*, October 1986, 9; "Life Skills Quiz," *MM*, October 1997, E17.

120. Leslie Peacock, "A Time to Grow through Daily Time with God," *RS*, May 1995, 26.

121. Interview with former WMU editor, May 16, 2009.

122. Warren Myers and Ruth Myers, *How to Have a Quiet Time* (Colorado Springs: NavPress, 1989); Kraft, *Women Mentoring Women*, 55.

123. Kathy Affolter, Seek Him, Meet Him, *C*, February 1986, 34.

124. Deborah Price Brunt, "Commitment: Counting the Cost," *C*, July 1989, 9.

125. Edna Martin Ellison, "Thy Word Have I Hid in My Heart," *RS*, January 1994, D.

126. Randy A McCollum, "Living in Holy Relationship," Bible Study, *MM*, November 2001, 25.

127. Jan Kirkland, "Helps Me Grow," Letters, *MM*, February 2003, 4.

128. Anne Leavell Collingsworth, "Direct Access," Baptist Women Meeting, *RS*, July 1989, 4.

129. Kraft, *Women Mentoring Women*, 46.

130. Cleota Lenert, "Visionary," *RS*, August 1987, 39.

131. Debbie Sanders, "Habitually Praying," *C*, June 1990, 5.

132. "How Prayer Can Be Incorporated into Your Everyday Lifestyle," *MM*, January 1998, 14; Sylvia Gunter, "And I Will Pray: How to Get Started," *C*, December 1985, 2.

133. Karen Simons, "Exercise: ACTS toward Good Health," *MM*, April 1999, 22–23; Karla Worley, "What's the Magic Word?" Prayer, *MM*, September 2005, 16–18; Tricia Scribner, "No More Umbrella Prayers," Prayer, *MM*, October 2005, 16–18.

134. Laura L. Savage, "Prayer Retreat Procedures," *RS*, December 1994, E; Juanita S. Tew, "Walking, Driving, and Praying," *MM*, July 1999, 5.

135. Jean M. McLean, "Praise: The Music of Prayer," Prayer, *C*, December 1990, 43.

136. Dave Keith, "Prayer and the Status Quo," Prayer, *C*, October 1990, 28.

137. Kathryn Grant, "Claiming the Assurance of Answered Prayer," Intercessory Prayer, *C*, January 1992, 28; Don L. Madaris, "Relate to God Like Jesus Did," Bible Study, *MM*, December 2004, 22.

138. Jill Branyon, "A Denomination Praying," *RS*, April 1988, 39; Betty Lawson, "The Image of the Praying Woman," Prayer, *C*, July 1990, 28.

139. Phyllis Godwin, "The Roar at the Starting Line," Prayer, *MM*, November 2003, 21; Yvonne Lewis, "Lead Others through Prayer: Baptist Women as Prayer Warriors," *RS*, December 1992, 63; Esther Livengood, "Proclaim It Boldly," Patchwork, *RS*, May 1992, 23.

140. Teresa Mapp Cavitt, "Recognizing the Lost," Missions Im.p.ulse, *C*, January 1991, 15–16; Karen Estes Lowry, "The Link between Philippi and Detroit," *MM*, February 1997, 23.

141. "Prayer Is the Key," *MM*, October 2005, 18.

142. Joanne Parker, "Put on the Gloves," From the Editor, *MM*, June 2004, 1.

143. "Prayer Is the Key," *MM*, September 2005, 18.

144. Betsy Criminger Lowery, "You Are Invited to a Concert," *C*, December 1987, 3.

145. Sanan Brazzeal, "The Image of the Praying Woman," Prayer, *C*, October 1989, 28.

146. Nancy Carter McGough, "To Pray or Not to Pray," Life Decisions, *C*, December 1988, 29; Caroline Ward, "Prayers with Your Name on Them," *C*, October 1986, 5.

147. Barbara Tetlow Beevers, "Baptist Women Pray for Missions," Baptist Women Meeting, *RS*, October 1987, 6.

148. *RS*, July 1989, 1.

149. Edwina Davis, "Missions and You: The Practice of Prayer," *C*, June 1990, 10; "Report Card Time," Women's Ministry, *MM*, August 2000, 46.

150. Deirdre LaNoue, "Declare His Glory," Prayer, *C*, October 1986, 28; Mary Royals Driskill, "What Prayer and Grocery Shopping Have in Common," Missions Focus, *C*, April 1992, 28.

151. Cathy Butler, "A Heart to Heart Talk," Prayer, *MM*, August 2003, 21.

152. "Adopt a Missionary," *C*, June 1994, 41.

153. Kay Rice, "The Intercession Connection," *C*, November 1984, 3; "Missionary Links Her Survival to Your Prayers," Panorama of Service, *MM*, January 1997, 29.

154. Ron Johnson, "Pray for Our Nation and Our Christian Leaders," *C*, March 1989, 2.

155. Randy Sprinkle, quoted in Jane Lippy, "Virtual Prayerwalking," Prayer, *MM*, October 2002, 20–21.

156. Margaret Goodroe, "Pray . . . That They May Believe," Week of Prayer for Home Missions, *RS*, March 1989, 2.

157. Judy Hix Abercrombie, "Prayer Leads to Ministry," Prayer Profile, *C*, July 1984, 27.

158. Sharon Reece Neff, "Learning the Power of Prayer," *C*, February 1984, 12.

159. Judi Page, "Alone No More," *MM*, November 2003, 23.

160. Kathryn W. Kizer, "Prayer Project," Potpourri, *C*, October 1994, 21.

161. Ethel Robinson, "In His Name . . . Pray," Prayer Group, *RS*, January 1990, 26.

162. Ginny Bridges Ireland, "Prayer: A Strategy for Reaching the Lost," *C*, October 1994, 25; Ginny Bridges Ireland, "Prayer: Jesus' First Step in Evangelism," *C*, November 1994, 25–28.

163. Jennifer Kennedy Dean, "Prayer and Witnessing: Parts of the Same Whole," Prayer, *RS*, December 1993, 35.

164. Edna Ellison, "Forever Friends," Ministry/Witness, *MM*, October 2002, 19.

165. Ella Robinson, "Sharing the Greatest Gift," *C*, September 1993, 5.

166. Darrell Robinson, quoted in Mark Wingfield, "HMB Introduces New Evangelism Emphasis," *BP*, September 25, 1990.

167. Barbara Jean Davis, "Uniquely Yours," *C*, May 1984, 27.

168. Laura Fite Edwards, "Overflow Is Not a Performance," *C*, February 1987, 3; Linda Eason Berry, "Shrewd as Snakes and Innocent as Doves," Close Encounters, *C*, January 1990, 8.

169. Barbara Donaldson, "Between 'Pleased-to-Meet-You' and 'Good-Bye': Witnessing in One-Time Encounters," *MM*, July 1998, 15.

170. Frances Lee Street, "Love Never Gives Up," Missions Im.p.ulse, *C*, July 1991, 15.

171. Ibid.

172. "Report Card Time," Women's Ministry, *MM*, August 2000, 46.

173. Laura Savage, "Let's Party," Women's Ministry, *MM*, July 2002, 46; Laura Savage, "Need Fresh Ideas?" Women's Ministry, *MM*, June 2002, 46.

174. "LIVINGtouch," *C*, January 1992, back cover.

175. Jo Ann Walton Parham, "Called to Evangelism: Who Authorized This?" *RS*, December 1986, 27.

176. Terri Staines, "Sharing Christ beyond Telling Your Salvation Experience?" Ministry/Witness, *MM*, June 2005, 20; Betty Baggot, "Using Our Opportunities," Baptist Women Meeting, *RS*, April 1984, 4.

177. Mildred Patterson, "My Gift, My Call," *RS*, June 1987, inside front cover.

178. Sharon Reece Neff, "Who Will Win Your Family and Friends?" Week of Prayer for Home Missions, *C*, March 1987, 14.

179. "Now What?" *C*, July 1988, 48.

180. Deirdre LaNoue, "Witnessing Models in the Bible," Bible Study, *C*, January 1990, 17.

181. Jo Ann Walton Parham, "Called to Evangelism in the Beginning," *RS*, October 1986, 15.

182. Mindi Long Chancellor, "You Are My Witnesses," Personal Witnessing Group, *RS*, February 1989, 26; Melba Tiller, "She Kept Her Divine Appointment," Letters, *MM*, September 2001, 4; Edna Ellison, "Instant Encounters," Lifestyle, *MM*, August 2002, 16–17.

183. "Missionary Glossary," *C*, January 1993, 39.

184. Anita Bowden, "The Way We Want to Be Tomorrow," Challenge to Tomorrow, *RS*, September 1986, 14.

185. June Holland McEwen, "Empowered! for Missions by the Holy Spirit: Missions through Service," Bible Study Group, *RS*, March 1991, 25. See Matthew 25:34–40.

186. Breena Paine, "Empowered to Meet Needs," BYW Meeting, *C*, February 1991, 10.

187. Mary Ann Anderson, "I Will Tell the Good News," *RS*, March 1992, 28.

188. "Witnessing Encouragement Card," *MM*, July 1997, E23; Deirdre LaNoue, "You Will Be My Witnesses," Bible Study, *C*, February 1990, 18–21.

189. Martha Minardi, "Evangelism with No Pulpit," Baptist Women Meeting, *RS*, February 1987, 2–6.

190. "Witness Training Tips," *MM*, November 1996, E23.

191. "Dayspring," *RS*, July 1994, back cover; Cathy Butler, "What's a LIVINGtouch?" *RS*, October 1991, 26.

192. Mary Ann Ward Appling, "Sharing Your Faith in Your Own Backyard," *RS*, June 1994, 33.

193. Sammie Jo Barstow, "Teaching God's Word through Literacy Missions," In the Spotlight, *MM*, May 2005, 11.

194. "My World: I'm Involved in It," *C*, September 1984, 31.

195. Ruth Ward, "Attitude Checkup," Potpourri, *C*, December 1984, 38.

196. Holly Bowers Welborn, "Following Christ's Servant Example," *MM*, October 1997, 23.

197. Dorothy D. Godsoe, "Your Gifts for Service: The Greatest Ministry," Devotional, *RS*, August 1987, 7.

198. "The Way We Ministered," *RS*, May 1988, 16.

199. Laura Fry Allen, "How Far Does Your Love Really Reach?" *C*, March 1986, 4.

200. Laura L. Savage, Letter from the Consultant, *MM*, October 1997, 4.

## Chapter 7

1. Margaret L. Bendroth, *Fundamentalism and Gender, 1875 to the Present* (New Haven: Yale University Press, 1993), 2.

2. Linda Clark, Prayer Patterns, *MM*, August 1998, 54.

3. Mrs. Nathan Maynard, "Modern Japan," Program for April, *OMF*, April 1908, 4.

4. Union Notes, *OMF*, January 1910, 6.

5. "The Spirit of *Royal Service*," *RS*, July 1915, 28.

6. Myrtle Creasman, "Woman's Contribution to the Kingdom," Program, *RS*, March 1936, 22.

7. Mrs. C. D. Creasman, "Measuring the Home Task," Program for February, *RS*, February 1931, 26.

8. Walter Gilmore, "Every Member Canvass," *RS*, November 1934, 12.

9. Mrs. A. L. Aulick, "On the Rock or on the Rocks?" Your Program, *RS*, June 1950, 29.

10. Kate Ellen Gruver, Call to Prayer, *RS*, October 1957, 36.

11. Velma Darbo Brown, "Numbers, Names, Values," Study Material for Current Missions Group, *C*, April 1972, 33.

12. Jacqueline Durham, "The New, Missioning Woman: Helen Neiger," *C*, October 1972, 2.

13. Teresa Shields Parker, "Dare to Ask. Go Ahead, Dare!" Week of Prayer for Home Missions, *C*, March 1979, 40.

14. "Why Have Retreats Just for Women?" *MM*, January 2006, 5.

15. Anna Kathryn Hardin, "Perfect Timing," Ministry/Witness, *MM*, April 2004, 23.

16. Linda M. Clark, "Growing to Know You: Growing in Godliness," *RS*, March 1995, H.

17. Mrs. H. M. Wharton, "Report of Personal Service Department," *WMUAR 1912*, 51.

18. Mrs. C. D. Creasman, "The Christian Home, Our Immediate Task," Program, *RS*, March 1948, 23.

19. "Talk Back," *C*, April 1971, 25.

20. Edith Robbins, "Lack of Depth," Letters, *MM*, January 2002, 4.

21. Alma Hunt, quoted in Frances R. King, "Explore the Possibilities," Round Table Group, *RS*, April 1988, 19.

22. Dellanna O'Brien, interview, cited in Flowers, *Into the Pulpit*, 138; Cecil Sherman, "On the Other Hand: Don't Vote with the Extremists," *C*, November 1970, 16–18.

23. Mrs. F. W. Armstrong, "Centennial Commitments," Editorial, *RS*, January 1945, 3.

24. Charles Thompson, quoted in Mrs. George Hillman Whitfield, "Home Mission Survey," Program for September, *RS*, September 1915, 8.

25. Willie Jean Stewart, "'Of One': A Study of Christian Principles and Race Relations," Book Reviews and Study Suggestions, *RS*, March 1946, 6.

26. Carolyn Weatherford, "A Past to Remember . . . A Future to Mold," *RS*, July 1976, inside front cover.

27. Mrs. John Love Jr., Mailbox, *C*, October 1976, inside back cover.

28. Paul Harvey, "Saints but Not Subordinates: The Woman's Missionary Union of the Southern Baptist Convention," in *Women and Twentieth-Century Protestantism*, ed. Margaret Bendroth and Virginia Brereton (Urbana: University of Illinois Press, 2002), 5.

# Bibliography

## Archival Records


Biographical Sketches. WMUA.

"Board Report, Woman's Missionary Union." January 13, 1993. WMUA.

Consultation on Women in Church-Related Vocations. SBHLA.

Consultation on Women in Church-Related Vocations. Vertical file. WMUA.

Dickens, Teresa. "WMU Expands Product Line with CBF-Related Pieces." July 12, 1995. WMUA.

Fling, Helen. Interview by Catherine Allen. February 14, 1985. Transcript. WMUA.

Former WMU editor. Interview by Melody Maxwell. May 16, 2009. Interviewer's personal files.

Former WMU editor. Interview by Melody Maxwell. May 27, 2009. Interviewer's personal files.

Former WMU editor. Interview by Melody Maxwell. May 28, 2009. Interviewer's personal files.

Gregory, Christine. Interview by Catherine Allen. November 19, 1984. Transcript. WMUA.

Hunt, Alma. Interview by Catherine Allen. August 28, 1984. Transcript. WMUA.

Johnson, Trudy. "Women's Ministries: An Overview for WMU." October 1993. WMUA.

O'Brien, Dellanna. Baptist Entities—Foreign Mission Board, 1989–1996. WMUA.

O'Brien, Dellanna. Baptist Entities Miscellaneous, 1991–1996. WMUA.

O'Brien, Dellanna. Dellanna O'Brien SBC Convention Controversy, 1990–1994. WMUA.

Patterson, Dorothy. Interview by Barry Hankins. June 8, 1999. Transcript. Baylor University Institute for Oral History, Waco, TX.

Rankin, Jerry. Letter to SBC leaders. August 25, 1995. WMUA.

Southern Baptist Women in Ministry. Vertical file. WMUA.

The Woman's Meeting in Richmond, Virginia. Minutes, May 11, 1888. WMUA.

Woman's Missionary Union Executive Board. Minutes, 1906–2006. WMUA.

"Woman's Missionary Union Report." Spring 1993. WMUA.

Woman's Mission to Woman. Minutes, 1872–1880. SBHLA.

Women. Vertical file. WMUA.
Women—Christianity. Vertical file. WMUA.
Women's Role in Church, Ordination—SBC. Vertical file. WMUA.

## Magazines and Newspapers

*Alabama Baptist*. Alabama. Selected issues, 1878 to 1896.
*Associated Baptist Press*. Nationwide. Selected issues, 1990 to 2006.
*Baltimore Baptist*. Maryland. 1883 to 1888.
*Baptist Basket*. Nationwide. 1888.
*Baptist Press*. Nationwide. Selected issues, 1948 to 2010.
*Baptist Standard*. Texas. Selected issues.
*Biblical Recorder*. North Carolina. 1868, 1886 to 1888.
*Commission*. FMB. Selected issues.
*Concern*. United Presbyterian Women. 1976.
*Contempo*. WMU. 1970 to 1995.
*Foreign Mission Journal*. FMB. Selected issues.
*Heathen Helper*. Nationwide. 1882 to 1888.
*Home Missions*. HMB. Selected issues.
*Light and Life for Women*. Woman's Board of Missions, Congregationalist Church. 1900, 1903 to 1907.
*Magazette*. WMU. 1989 to 1996.
*Missions Mosaic*. WMU. 1995 to 2006.
*Our Mission Fields*. WMU. 1906 to 1914.
*Religious Herald*. Virginia. 1874 to 1888.
*Response*. United Methodist Women. 1978.
*Royal Service*. WMU. 1914 to 1995.
*Western Recorder*. Kentucky. 1872, 1887 to 1888.
*Woman's Work for Woman*. Woman's Board of Foreign Missions of the Presbyterian Church USA. 1904.

## Articles and Chapters

Akin, Daniel L. "The Role of Men and Women in the Church." *Tie* 71, no. 4 (Winter 2003): 8.
Allen, Catherine. "Shifting Sands for Southern Baptist Women in Missions." In *Gospel Bearers, Gender Barriers: Missionary Women in the Twentieth Century*, ed. Dana L. Robert, 113–26. Maryknoll, NY: Orbis Books, 2002.
Anders, Sarah Frances. "Baptist Women Walking Together in America, 1950–2000." *Baptist History & Heritage* 40, no. 3 (Summer/Fall 2005): 8–16.
Anderson, Gerald H. "American Protestants in Pursuit of Mission: 1886–1986." In *Missiology: An Ecumenical Introduction: Texts and Contexts of Global Christianity*, ed. Frans J. Verstraelen et al., 374–420. Grand Rapids: Eerdmans, 1995.
Bendroth, Margaret L. "Fundamentalism and Femininity: Points of Encounter between Religious Conservatives and Women, 1919–1935." *Church History* 61, no. 2 (June 1992): 221–33.

Blevins, Carolyn DeArmond. "Patterns of Ministry among Southern Baptist Women." *Baptist History & Heritage* 22, no. 3 (July 1987): 41–50.

Bowers, Joyce M. "Roles of Married Women Missionaries: A Case Study." *International Bulletin of Missionary Research* 8, no. 1 (January 1984): 4–7.

Braude, Ann. "Women's History *Is* American Religious History." In *Retelling U.S. Religious History*, ed. Thomas A. Tweed, 87–107. Berkeley: University of California Press, 1997.

Brumberg, Joan Jacobs. "Zenanas and Girlless Villages: The Ethnology of American Evangelical Women, 1870–1910." *Journal of American History* 69, no. 2 (September 1982): 347–71.

Carver, W. O. "Baptists and the Problem of World Missions." *Review & Expositor* 17 (July 1920): 317–29.

Chafe, William H. "The Paradox of Progress." In *Our American Sisters: Women in American Thought and Life*, ed. Jean E. Friedman and William G. Shade, 563–78. Boston: Allyn and Bacon, 1982.

Davis, C. Anne. "Liberation, Not Separation." *Review & Expositor* 72, no. 1 (Winter 1975): 63–69.

Deweese, Charles. "Baptist Women Deacons and Deaconesses: Key Developments and Trends, 1609–2005." *Baptist History & Heritage* 40, no. 3 (Summer/Fall 2005): 65–79.

Flowers, Elizabeth. "The Contested Legacy of Lottie Moon: Southern Baptists, Women, and Partisan Protestantism." In *Through a Glass Darkly: Contested Notions of Baptist Identity*, ed. Keith Harper, 112–44. Tuscaloosa: University of Alabama Press, 2012.

———. "Southern Baptist Evangelicals or Social Gospel Liberals? The Woman's Missionary Union and Social Reform, 1888 to 1928." *American Baptist Quarterly* 19, no. 2 (June 2000): 106–28.

Guth, James L. "Southern Baptist Clergy, the Christian Right, and Political Activism in the South." In *Politics and Religion in the White South*, ed. Glenn Feldman, 187–213. Lexington: University Press of Kentucky, 2005.

Hogg, W. Richie. "The Role of American Protestantism in World Mission." In *American Missions in Bicentennial Perspective*, ed. R. Pierce Beaver, 354–402. South Pasadena, CA: William Carey Library, 1977.

Holcomb, Carol. "Building a Publishing Empire: The Annie Armstrong Era of WMU, SBC." *Baptist History & Heritage* 47, no. 1 (Spring 2012): 18–38.

Leonard, Bill. "Southern Baptists and Southern Culture." *American Baptist Quarterly* 4, no. 2 (June 1985): 200–212.

Maines, Carole. "Missionary Wives: Underused Asset." *Evangelical Missions Quarterly* 19, no. 4 (October 1983): 290–95.

Mather, Juliette. "Women, Convention Privileges Of." In *Encyclopedia of Southern Baptists*, 544. Nashville: Broadman Press, 1958.

Mathews, Shailer. "Social Gospel." In *A Dictionary of Religion and Ethics*, ed. Shailer Mathews and G. B. Smith, 416. New York: Macmillan, 1921.

McBeth, H. Leon. "The Ordination of Women." *Review & Expositor* 78, no. 4 (Fall 1981): 515–30.

———. "Perspectives on Women in Baptist Life." *Baptist History & Heritage* 22, no. 3 (July 1987): 4–11.

———. "Role of Women in Southern Baptist History." *Baptist History & Heritage* 12, no. 1 (January 1977): 3–25.

Mortenson, Patricia J. "The Role of Women in Missions." *Gospel in Context* 2, no. 2 (April 1979): 28–31.

Robert, Dana L. "What Happened to the Christian Home? The Missing Component of Mission Theory." *Missiology* 33, no. 3 (July 2005): 325–40.

Rogers, Joyce. "God's Chief Assignment to Women." *Southern Baptist Journal* 2, no. 1 (January 1974): 3, 9.

Shaw, Susan M. "I Am Woman: Southern Baptist Women and Feminism." *Baptist History & Heritage* 45, no. 2 (Spring 2010): 6–19.

———. "Of Words and Women: Southern Baptist Publications and the Progress of Women in the 1970s." *Baptist History & Heritage* 42, no. 2 (Spring 2007): 69–84.

———. "The Paradox of Submission: Southern Baptist Women and Male Headship." *Perspectives in Religious Studies* 38, no. 4 (Winter 2011): 383–401.

Tew, C. Delane. "On the Conservative Side: Woman's Missionary Union in the Progressive Era." *Baptist History & Heritage* 47, no. 1 (Spring 2012): 52–59.

Tucker, Ruth A. "Women in Mission." In *Toward the Twenty-First Century in Christian Mission*, ed. Gerald H. Anderson, James M. Phillips, and Robert T. Coote, 284–94. Grand Rapids: Eerdmans, 1993.

Vickers, Gregory. "Models of Womanhood and the Early Woman's Missionary Union." *Baptist History & Heritage* 24, no. 1 (January 1989): 41–53.

———. "Southern Baptist Women and Social Concerns, 1910–1929." *Baptist History & Heritage* 23, no. 4 (October 1988): 3–13.

Weatherford, Carolyn. "The Role of Women in Baptist Missions." *Baptist History & Heritage* 27, no. 3 (July 1992): 25–33.

## Books and Dissertations

Allen, Catherine. *A Century to Celebrate: History of Woman's Missionary Union*. Birmingham: WMU, 1987.

———. *Laborers Together with God: 22 Great Women in Baptist Life*. Birmingham: WMU, 1987.

Ammerman, Nancy. *Baptist Battles: Social Change and Religious Conflict in the Southern Baptist Convention*. New Brunswick, NJ: Rutgers University Press, 1990.

Armstrong, Annie, and Keith Harper. *Rescue the Perishing: Selected Correspondence of Annie Armstrong*. Macon, GA: Mercer University Press, 2004.

Barbour, Louise. *Missions and the SBC*. Birmingham: WMU, 1986.

Bays, Daniel H., and Grant Wacker, eds. *The Foreign Missionary Enterprise at Home: Explorations in North American Cultural History*. Tuscaloosa: University of Alabama Press, 2003.

Beaver, R. Pierce. *American Protestant Women in World Mission: A History of the First Feminist Movement in North America*. Grand Rapids: Eerdmans, 1980.

Bebbington, David W. *Evangelicalism in Modern Britain: A History from the 1730s to the 1980s*. London: Unwin Hyman, 1989.

Bendroth, Margaret L. *Fundamentalism and Gender, 1875 to the Present*. New Haven: Yale University Press, 1993.

Bendroth, Margaret, and Virginia Brereton, eds. *Women and Twentieth-Century Protestantism*. Urbana: University of Illinois Press, 2002.

Bliss, Edwin Munsell. *Organization and Methods of Mission Work*. Chicago: Student Volunteer Movement for Foreign Missions, 1897.

Broadus, John Albert. *Should Women Speak in Mixed Public Assemblies?* Louisville: Baptist Book Concern, 1880.

Carpenter, Joel A., and Wilbert R. Shenk, eds. *Earthen Vessels: American Evangelicals and Foreign Missions, 1880–1980*. Grand Rapids: Eerdmans, 1990.

Carrothers, Julia D. *The Sunrise Kingdom, or Life and Scenes in Japan: And Woman's Work for Woman There*. Philadelphia: Presbyterian Board of Publication, 1879.

Center for Baptist Heritage and Studies. *Walking Together: The Struggle of Baptists with Polity in the 21st Century*. Richmond, VA: Center for Baptist Heritage and Studies, 2005.

Cothen, Grady C. *What Happened to the Southern Baptist Convention? A Memoir of the Controversy*. Macon, GA: Smyth & Helwys, 1993.

Daggett, L. H. *Historical Sketches of Woman's Missionary Societies in America and England*. Boston: L. H. Daggett, 1879.

Durso, Pamela R., and Keith E. Durso, eds. *Courage and Hope: The Stories of Ten Baptist Women Ministers*. Macon, GA: Mercer University Press, 2005.

Eaton, T. T. *The Bible on Women's Public Speaking*. Louisville: Baptist Book Concern, 1895.

Ecumenical Conference on Foreign Missions. *Ecumenical Missionary Conference, New York, 1900*. Vol. 1. New York: American Tract Society, 1900.

Edwards, Wendy J. Deichmann, and Carolyn De Swarte Gifford, eds. *Gender and the Social Gospel*. Chicago: University of Illinois Press, 2003.

Eighmy, John Lee. *Churches in Cultural Captivity: A History of the Social Attitudes of Southern Baptists*. Rev. ed. Knoxville: University of Tennessee Press, 1987.

Elliot, Elisabeth. *Let Me Be a Woman: Notes on Womanhood for Valerie*. Wheaton, IL: Tyndale House, 1976.

Estep, William R. *Whole Gospel—Whole World: The Foreign Mission Board of the Southern Baptist Convention, 1845–1995*. Nashville: Broadman & Holman, 1994.

Falwell, Jerry. *Listen, America!* Garden City, NY: Doubleday, 1980.

Fletcher, Jesse C. *The Southern Baptist Convention: A Sesquicentennial History*. Nashville: Broadman & Holman, 1994.

Flowers, Elizabeth. *Into the Pulpit: Southern Baptist Women and Power since World War II*. Chapel Hill: University of North Carolina Press, 2012.

Friedan, Betty. *The Feminine Mystique*. New York: W. W. Norton, 1963.

Gardner, W. W. *The Heathen Lost without the Gospel*. Louisville: Baptist Book Concern, 1892.

Gatlin, Rochelle. *American Women since 1945*. Jackson: University Press of Mississippi, 1987.

Greene, Kathryn A. *Royal Service Seventy-Fifth Anniversary Album*. Birmingham: WMU, 1981.

*A Handbook of Personal Service*. United States: WMU, undated.

Hankins, Barry. *Uneasy in Babylon: Southern Baptist Conservatives and American Culture*. Tuscaloosa: University of Alabama Press, 2002.

Harper, Keith. *The Quality of Mercy: Southern Baptists and Social Christianity, 1890–1920*. Tuscaloosa: University of Alabama Press, 1996.

Harrell, David Edwin. *Unto a Good Land: A History of the American People*. Grand Rapids: Eerdmans, 2005.

Harvey, Paul. *Redeeming the South: Religious Cultures and Racial Identities among Southern Baptists, 1865–1925*. Chapel Hill: University of North Carolina Press, 1997.

Heck, Fannie E. S. *In Royal Service: The Mission Work of Southern Baptist Women*. Nashville: Broadman Press, 1948.

Hefley, James C. *The Conservative Resurgence in the Southern Baptist Convention*. Hannibal, MO: Hannibal Books, 1991.

Hewitt, Nancy A., ed. *A Companion to American Women's History*. Malden, MA: Blackwell, 2002.

Hill, Patricia Ruth. *The World Their Household: The American Woman's Foreign Mission Movement and Cultural Transformation, 1870–1920*. Ann Arbor: University of Michigan Press, 1985.

Hill, Samuel S. *Southern Churches in Crisis*. New York: Holt, Rinehart, and Winston, 1967.

———. *Southern Churches in Crisis Revisited*. Tuscaloosa: University of Alabama Press, 1999.

Holcomb, Carol Crawford. "Mothering the South: The Influence of Gender and the Social Gospel on the Social Views of the Leadership of Woman's Missionary Union, Auxiliary to Southern Baptist Convention, 1888–1930." PhD diss., Baylor University, 1999.

Hunt, Alma. *History of Woman's Missionary Union*. Nashville: Convention Press, 1964.

Hunt, Rosalie Hall. *The Story of WMU*. Birmingham: WMU, 2006.

Hunter, Jane. *The Gospel of Gentility: American Women Missionaries in Turn-of-the-Century China*. New Haven: Yale University Press, 1984.

James, Janet Wilson, ed. *Women in American Religion*. Philadelphia: University of Pennsylvania Press, 1980.

Johnson, Johnni, ed. *Findings of the Consultation on Women in Church-Related Vocations*. Birmingham: Southern Baptist Convention Inter-Agency Council, 1978.

Kieve, James Jay. "The Formation of a Moderate Identity: Efforts of the 1970s Woman's Missionary Union." Master's thesis, Duke University, 1995.

Kraft, Vickie. *Women Mentoring Women: Ways to Start, Maintain, and Expand a Biblical Women's Ministry*. Chicago: Moody Press, 1992.

LaFarge, John. *The Race Question and the Negro*. New York: Longmans, Green, and Co., 1943.

Latourette, Kenneth Scott. *A History of Christianity*. New York: Harper, 1953.

Laymen's Foreign Missions Inquiry and William Ernest Hocking. *Re-Thinking Missions: A Laymen's Inquiry after One Hundred Years*. New York: Harper & Bros., 1932.

Leonard, Bill. *Baptist Ways: A History*. Valley Forge, PA: Judson Press, 2003.

———. *God's Last and Only Hope: The Fragmentation of the Southern Baptist Convention*. Grand Rapids: Eerdmans, 1990.

Liebman, Robert C., Robert Wuthnow, and James L. Guth. *The New Christian Right: Mobilization and Legitimation*. Hawthorne, NY: Aldine, 1983.

Mandle, John D. *Women and Social Change in America*. Princeton, NJ: Princeton Book, 1979.

*Manual of W.M.U. Method*. Nashville: Sunday School Board, 1917.
Marsden, George M. *Fundamentalism and American Culture: The Shaping of Twentieth Century Evangelicalism, 1870–1925*. New York: Oxford University Press, 1980.
Masters, Victor I. *Baptist Missions in the South*. Atlanta: Home Mission Board, 1915.
Mathis, Marie, and Elaine Dickson. *The Woman's Missionary Union Program of a Church*. Nashville: Convention Press, 1966.
McBeth, H. Leon. *The Baptist Heritage*. Nashville: Broadman Press, 1987.
———. *Women in Baptist Life*. Nashville: Broadman Press, 1979.
Montgomery, Helen Barrett. *The Bible and Missions*. West Medford, MA: Central Committee on the United Study of Foreign Missions, 1920.
———. *Prayer and Missions*. West Medford, MA: Central Committee on the United Study of Foreign Missions, 1924.
———. *Western Women in Eastern Lands*. New York: Macmillan, 1910.
Moon, Lottie, and Keith Harper. *Send the Light: Lottie Moon's Letters and Other Writings*. Macon, GA: Mercer University Press, 2002.
Morgan, Marabel. *The Total Woman*. Old Tappan, NJ: F. H. Revell, 1973.
Newman, Mark. *Getting Right with God: Southern Baptists and Desegregation, 1945–1995*. Tuscaloosa: University of Alabama Press, 2001.
Noll, Mark, et al., eds. *Eerdmans' Handbook to Christianity in America*. Grand Rapids: Eerdmans, 1983.
O'Brien, Robert, ed. *Stand with Christ: Why Missionaries Can't Sign the 2000 Baptist Faith and Message*. Macon, GA: Smyth & Helwys, 2002.
Pitman, Emma Raymond. *Missionary Heroines in Eastern Lands: Woman's Work in Mission Fields*. London: S. W. Partridge, 1884.
Porter, Carol, and Mike Hamel. *Women's Ministry Handbook*. Wheaton, IL: Victor Books, 1992.
Price, Clay. "A Survey of Southern Baptist Attitudes toward Women in Church and Society." Master's thesis, West Georgia College, 1978.
Queen, Edward L. *In the South the Baptists Are the Center of Gravity: Southern Baptists and Social Change, 1930–1980*. New York: Carlson, 1991.
Raymond, Maud Wotring. *The King's Business: A Study of Increased Efficiency for Women's Missionary Societies*. West Medford, MA: Central Committee on the United Study of Foreign Missions, 1913.
Robert, Dana L. *American Women in Mission: A Social History of Their Thought and Practice*, ed. Wilbert R. Shenk. Macon, GA: Mercer University Press, 1996.
———, ed. *Gospel Bearers, Gender Barriers: Missionary Women in the Twentieth Century*. Maryknoll, NY: Orbis Books, 2002.
Scales, T. Laine. *All That Fits a Woman: Training Southern Baptist Women for Charity and Mission, 1907–1926*. Macon, GA: Mercer University Press, 2000.
Scanzoni, Letha, and Nancy Hardesty. *All We're Meant to Be: A Biblical Approach to Women's Liberation*. Waco, TX: Word Books, 1974.
Scudder, John. *An Appeal to Christian Mothers in Behalf of the Heathen*. New York: American Tract Society, 1840.
Shaw, Susan M. *God Speaks to Us, Too: Southern Baptist Women on Church, Home, and Society*. Lexington: University Press of Kentucky, 2008.
Shurden, Walter B. *The Struggle for the Soul of the SBC: Moderate Responses to the Fundamentalist Movement*. Macon, GA: Mercer University Press, 1993.

Smith, Page. *Daughters of the Promised Land: Women in American History*. Boston: Little, Brown, 1970.

Southern Baptist Convention. *Annual of the Southern Baptist Convention*. Various cities: SBC, various years.

Spain, Rufus. *At Ease in Zion: A Social History of Southern Baptists, 1865–1900*. Nashville: Vanderbilt University Press, 1967.

Sullivan, Regina. *Lottie Moon: A Southern Baptist Missionary to China in History and Legend*. Baton Rouge: Louisiana State University Press, 2011.

Sutton, Jerry. *The Baptist Reformation: The Conservative Resurgence in the Southern Baptist Convention*. Nashville: Broadman & Holman, 2000.

Sweeney, Douglas A. *The American Evangelical Story: A History of the Movement*. Grand Rapids: Baker, 2005.

Tew, C. Delane. "From Local Society to Para-Denomination: Woman's Missionary Union, 1890–1930." PhD diss., Auburn University, 2003.

Walker, Nancy A. *Women's Magazines, 1940–1960: Gender Roles and the Popular Press*. Boston: Bedford/St. Martin's, 1998.

Williams, Daniel. *God's Own Party: The Making of the Christian Right*. New York: Oxford University Press, 2010.

Willis, Alan Scot. *All According to God's Plan: Southern Baptist Missions and Race, 1945–1970*. Lexington: University Press of Kentucky, 2004.

Woman's Missionary Union. *Annual Report*. Various cities: WMU, various years.

Woman's Missionary Union. *Year Book*. Various cities: WMU, various years.

Woodruff, Marguerite. *Critical Issues: Women in Church and Society*. Nashville: Christian Life Commission, 1982.

Woodward, C. Vann. *The Burden of Southern History*. Baton Rouge: Louisiana State University Press, 1968.

Zuckerman, Mary Ellen. *A History of Popular Women's Magazines in the United States, 1792–1995*. Westport, CT: Greenwood Press, 1998.

# Index